DRAWING AND PAINTING FUNGI

An artist's guide to finding and illustrating mushrooms and lichens

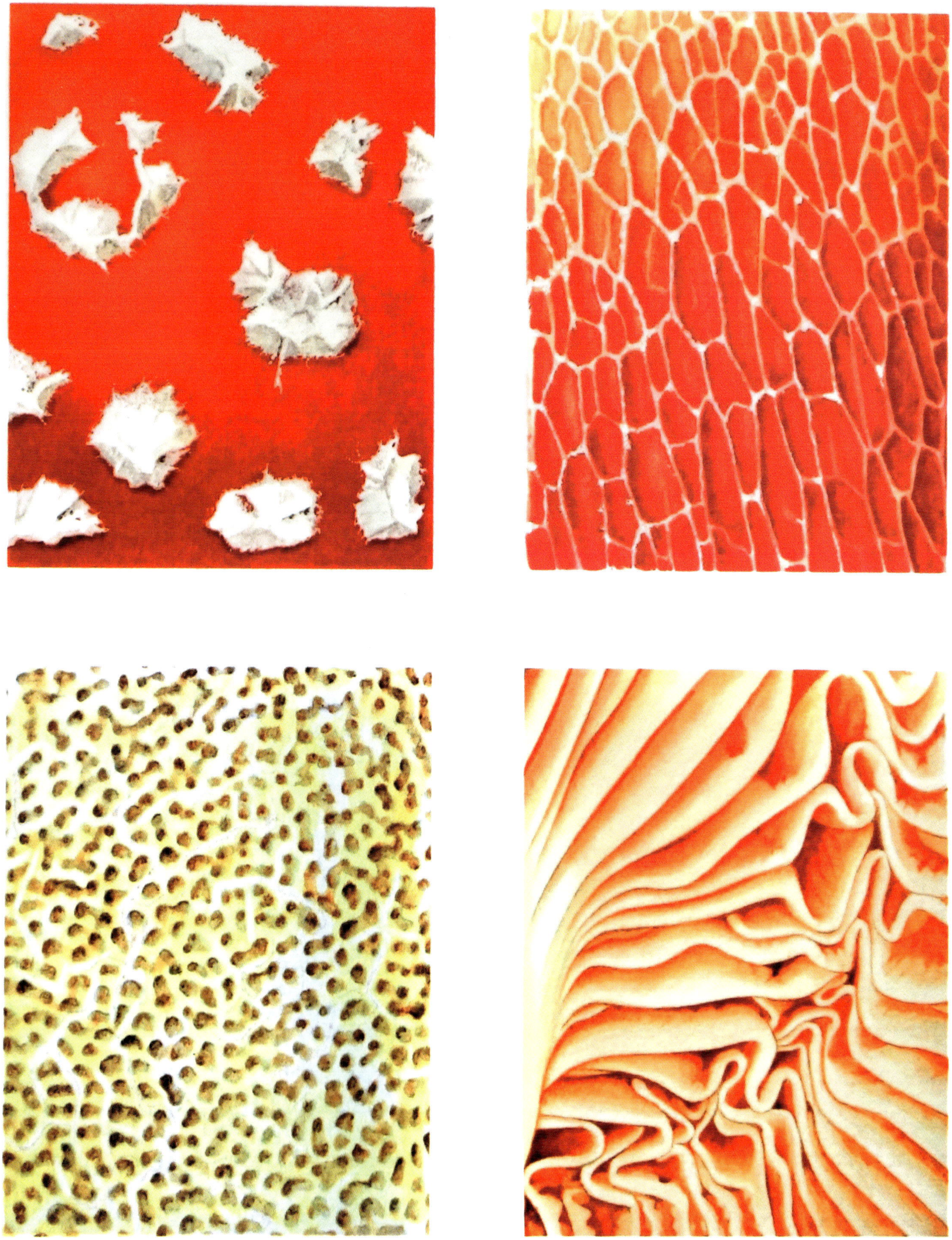

Mushroom mosaics. Close ups in watercolour, clockwise: fly agaric cap, stipe textures on the bitter beech bolete, a view looking into the gills of the meadow waxcap and the pores of the bitter beech bolete.

Claire Kathleen Ward

DRAWING AND PAINTING FUNGI

An artist's guide to finding and illustrating mushrooms and lichens

THE CROWOOD PRESS

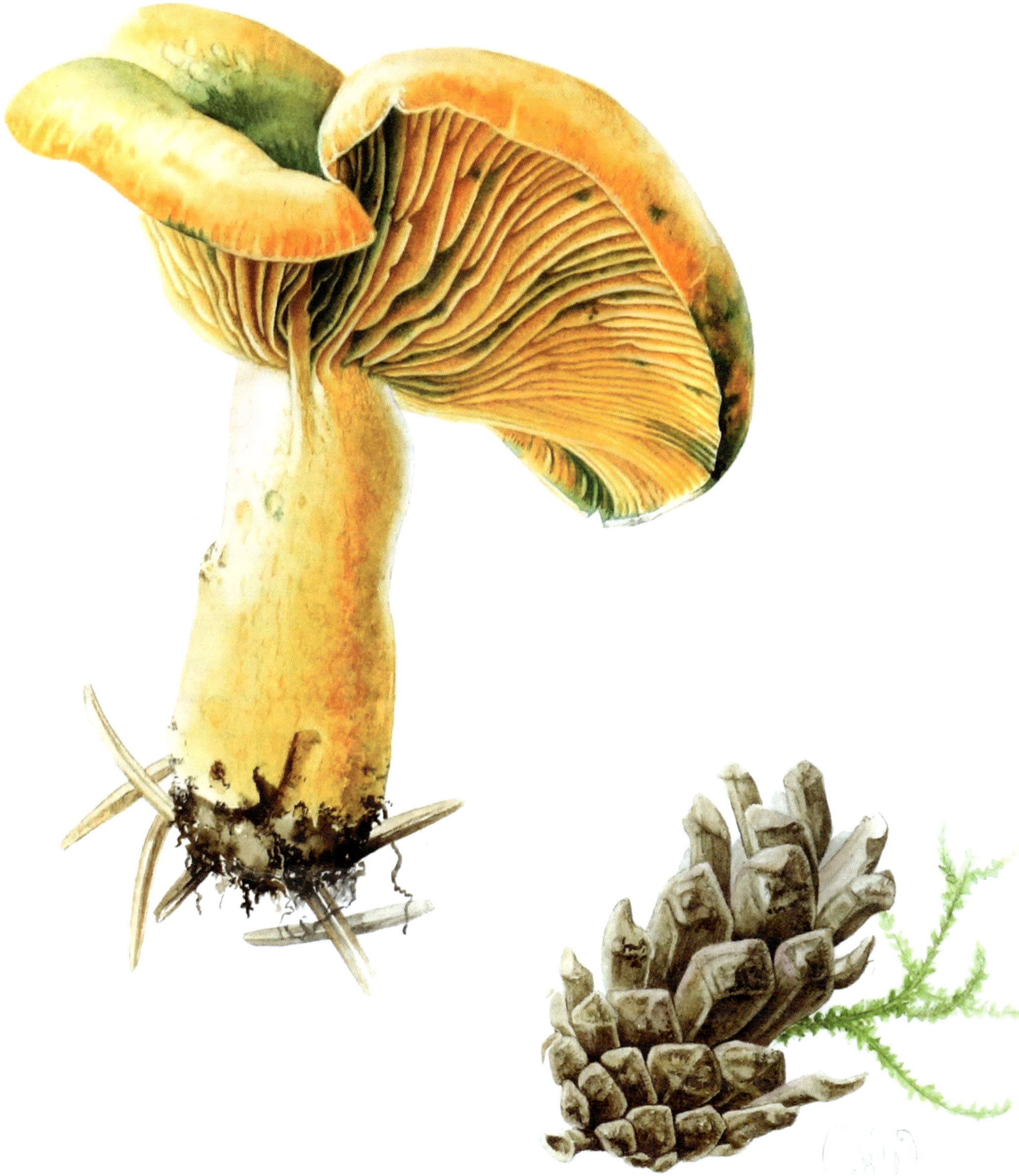

CONTENTS

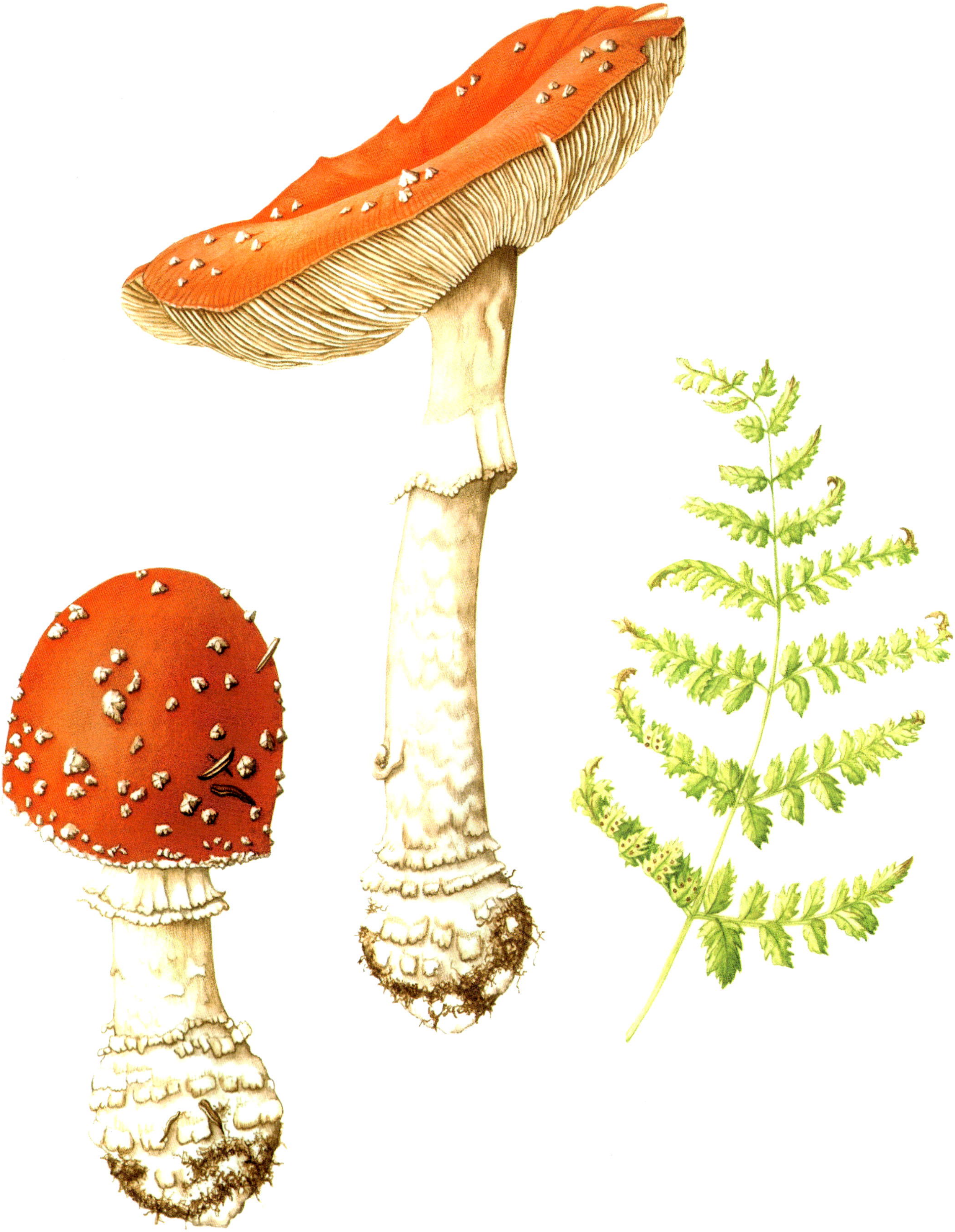

Fly Agaric and Fern painted in 2006. This is poignant as it is one of my first fungi paintings. *Amanita muscaria* is a beautiful and very well-known mushroom that is also a common find, adding colour to an autumn woodland – a must for the artist.

PREFACE: WHY PAINT FUNGI?

'Nature alone is antique, and the oldest art a mushroom.'

THOMAS CARLYLE

Fungi are fascinating and I've been hooked on drawing them for many years. In fact, they were one of the first natural history subjects that I began illustrating. I had enrolled on a botanical illustration course with Moya Davern, an RHS award-winning Welsh artist, and it being autumn, the subject matter was fungi. It's safe to say that I've been obsessed from that moment.

Fungi come in so many different shapes, sizes, and colours with an array of amazing textures to depict, some are strangely beautiful. But capturing their myriad forms by painting them is not the whole story. First there's the thrill of hunting for them, as if on a quest for hidden treasures and you just never know what you're going to find. Then comes the research and the challenge of identification; it's all part of the adventure and the uncovering of their fascinating lives. Time is of the essence, as they are ephemeral and can rot down and vanish quickly, disappearing back into the earth and leaf litter as if they were never there at all. Sometimes, they are frustratingly erratic in their appearance, which makes it even more special when they do spring up. Some years are better than others, as they are for most tree fruit and nuts, probably to do with weather conditions throughout the year.

Searching for fungi is also a great focus for getting outdoors in the fresh air and into nature with all the positive health and well-being benefits that it brings, physically and mentally. The foray forces you to slow down and take note of your surroundings, to engage the senses. As you slow down you begin to notice more – the glistening of dew on a spider's web, the smell of the earthy woodland floor, or the rasping call of a jay hunting for acorns. The peace and beauty of a misty autumn woodland can work wonders for the weary soul, re-establishing a connection with nature.

An important reason why I paint fungi is that I want to highlight how fascinating they are, as well as to encourage others to engage and to also become fascinated with these amazing organisms and their ecology. Ultimately, I would love to inspire, encourage, and maybe even spark an interest in people to want to study mycology and conservation for the future health of our natural world and the ecosystems within it; to raise the profile of fungi, as organisms that underpin the health of our natural habitats and the realisation that many of these would fail or become diseased without them.

This book will largely concentrate upon the species found within the larger fungi groups, the mushrooms, brackets, jellies and other fascinating forms, including lichens. As I am based in the UK, the majority of species were found here, but you will find most of them in the US and Europe, although some may have different species and varieties within that genus. I have specified US- or European-only species.

It is a privilege to be able to write this book on the wonderful world of fungi and lichens; to share the fascinating lives and stories of fungi that I've encountered.

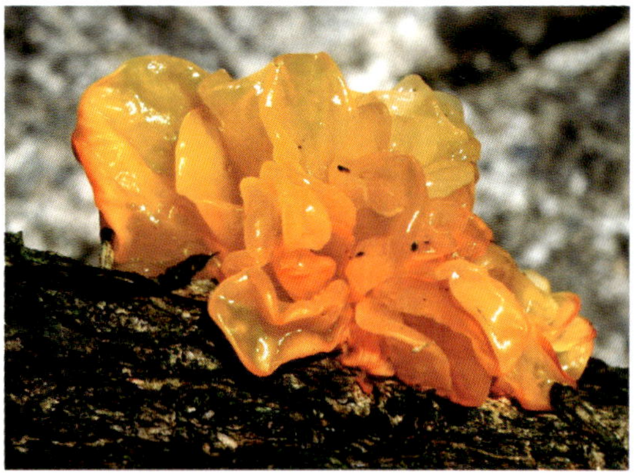
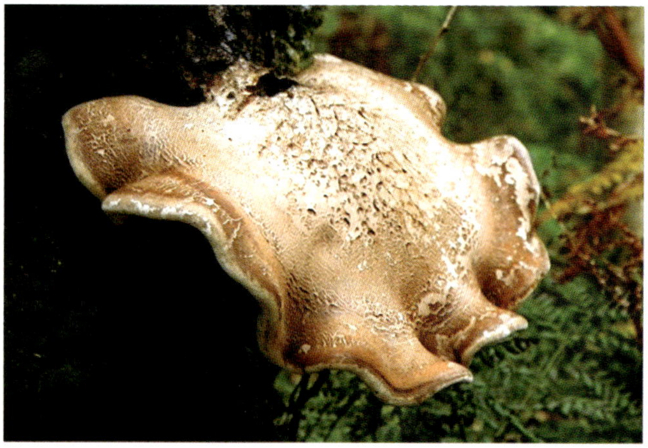
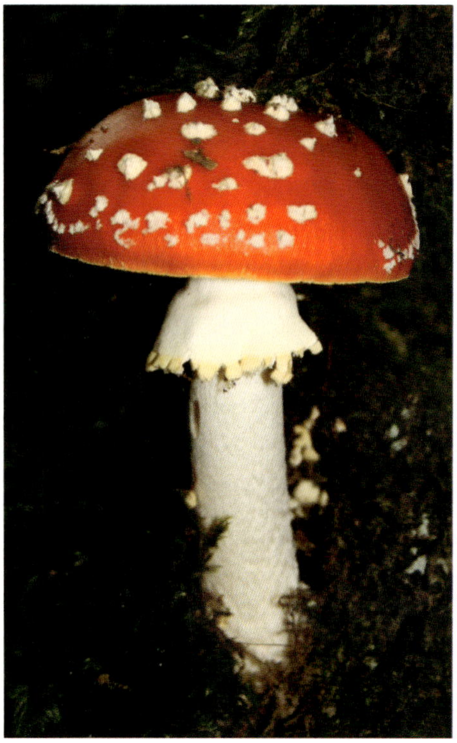
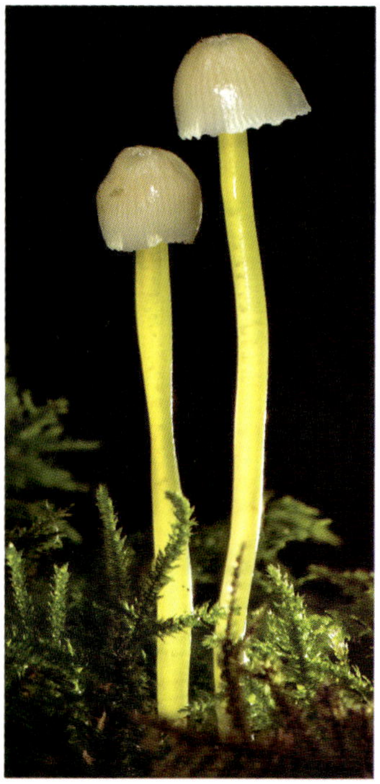
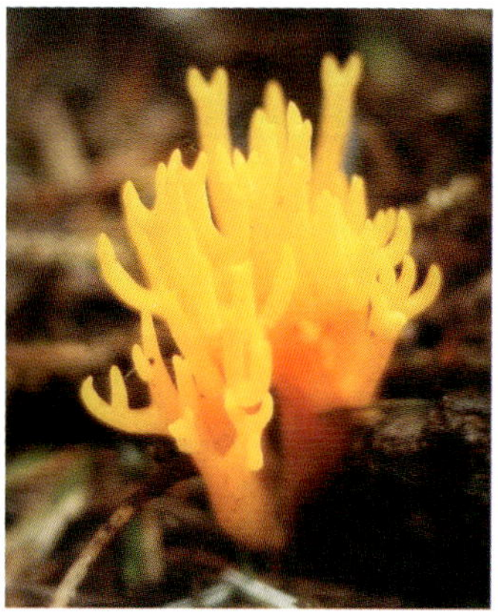
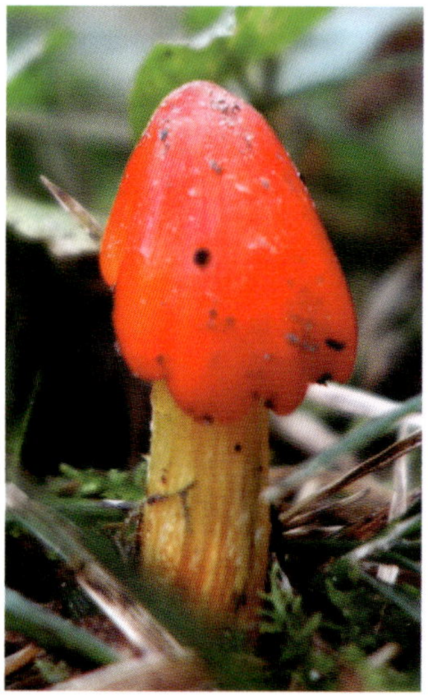
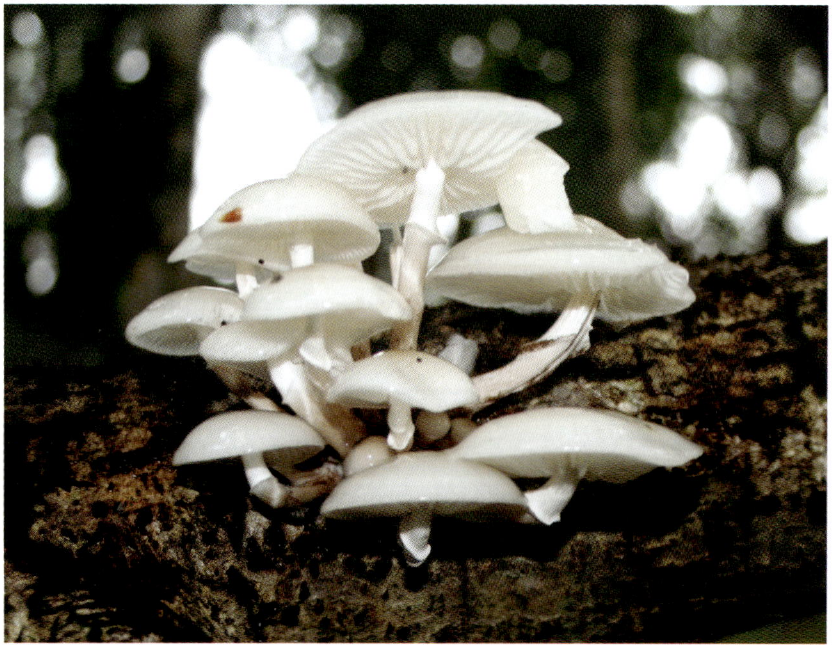
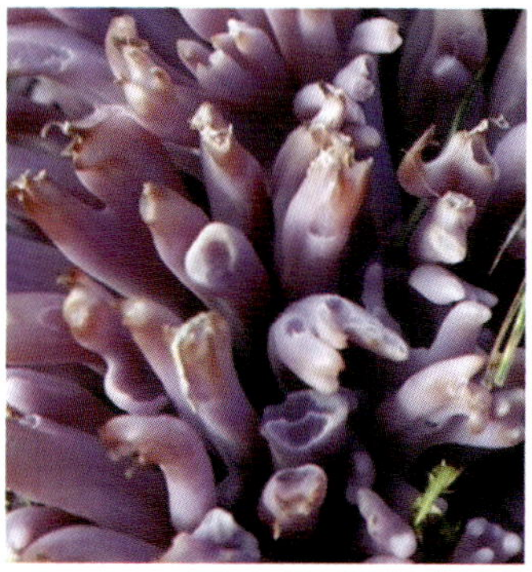

INTRODUCTION

Most people only think of mushrooms in relation to food, with questions such as: is it edible or poisonous? Will that be tasty with garlic butter? How do you cook those? Indeed, when I tell people that I'm going to paint a mushroom, they look at me strangely and say, 'You mean you're not going to eat it?'

But fungi carry so much more significance than this, even within culinary terms, being crucial for baking breads, brewing beer and wine, the blue in your blue cheese and Marmite (love it or hate it), among many other things. Mushrooms are often termed as being 'meaty' and indeed have been a meat alternative for many years; this is especially important in current times, as eating less meat is considered more eco-friendly. We have products including Quorn and tempeh, and edible wild mushrooms such as the so-called 'chicken of the woods' or the apricot-hued chanterelles.

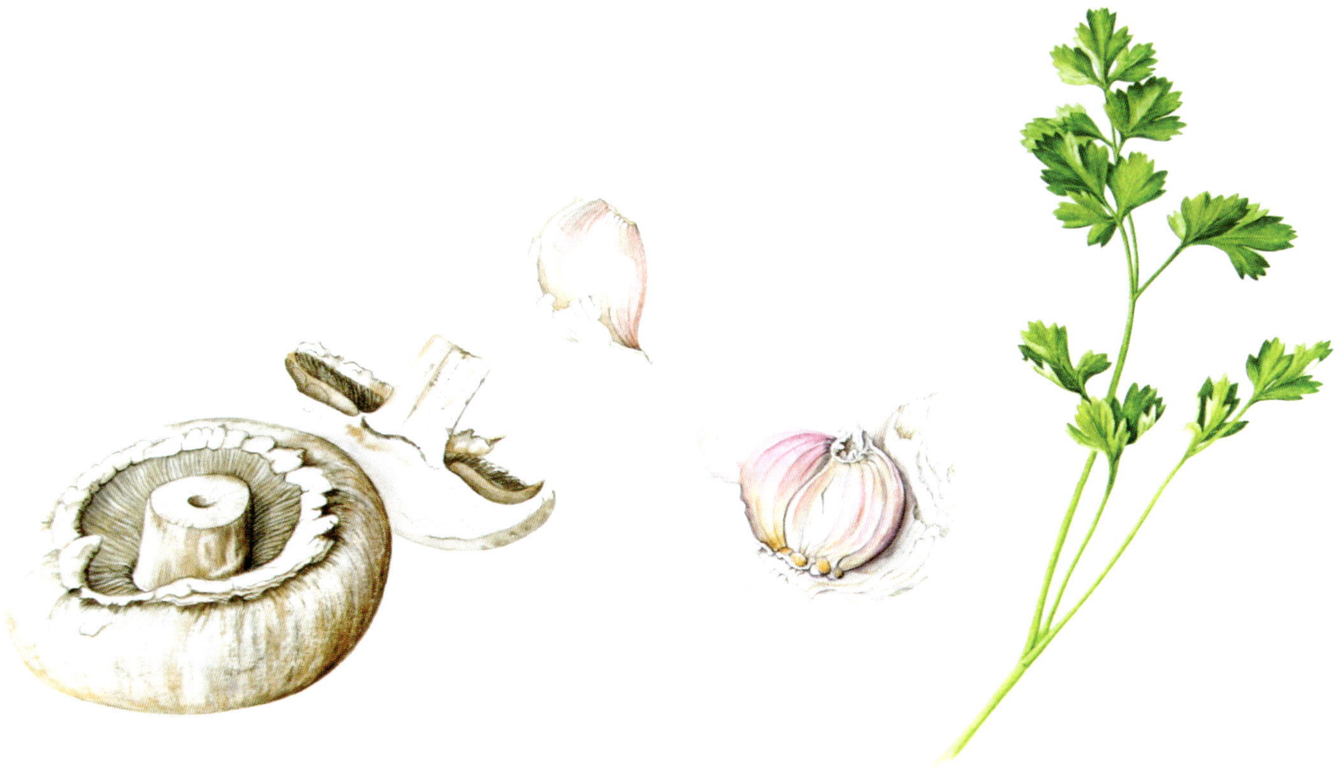

Garlic Mushrooms, a painting I did when I was a chef many years ago. I have cooked a lot of these over the years, with lashings of cream and lots of parsley sprinkled over the top!

A colourful collage showing the fantastic range of fungal diversity, an array of hues, textures and forms, all with the potential to become painting subjects.

THE IMPORTANCE OF FUNGI

Fungi are important as decomposers and natural recyclers and without them the planet would be drowning in dead trees, leaves, plant detritus and matter that would not be able to rot down. Considering how important these organisms are to the fundamental processes of our planet, they are often still much maligned and misunderstood. In the UK, the name toadstool is usually given to poisonous mushrooms and in the past, they were once seen as evil or magical as they mysteriously appeared overnight from mud and dung. This fear of fungi or mycophobia was commonplace in Western countries, but not so much in southern Europe and further east, where fungi were relished. They have always been a favourite food of the Greeks and Romans, with delicacies such as the Caesar's mushroom – *Amanita caesarea* – most definitely on the menu. In China and Japan, shitake mushrooms have been in cultivation for many centuries.

The name 'toadstool' may have come from the German word '*tode*' meaning death and in some tales, toads were sometimes pictured sitting on mushrooms catching flies with their tongues. Interestingly, toads do secrete poisonous alkaloids from their skin that are similar to some mycotoxins. It is also said that the Celts regarded eating fungi as a religious taboo and only members of the priesthood could consume them. The Welsh name of *caws llyffant*, literally meaning 'toad's cheese' gives a similar regard to fungi as the rest of the country.

In many cultures around the globe, certain mushrooms were used in religious ceremonies in order to speak with the ancestors, connect with the gods or for spiritual enlightenment. The mushroom stones of the Maya are relics from this time. It is also believed that some mushrooms were used to enhance performance, with examples of Viking warriors to athletes in the ancient Olympics.

The ancient Egyptians thought of mushrooms as 'the plants of immortality' and they were also described as 'the food of the gods' in the Egyptian Book of the Dead; they were sacred, and only the pharaohs and members of royalty were allowed to consume them. Many species are seen depicted in hieroglyphs that are 4,500 years old.

Of course, there is a darker side to fungi; a few are deadly poisonous, and some are parasitic on plants, animals and even other fungi. Others can cause serious problems for agriculture and forestry. A water mould called *Phytophthora ramorum* has caused extensive damage to forests, infecting many tree species, and large swathes of larch have had to be felled to keep it in control.

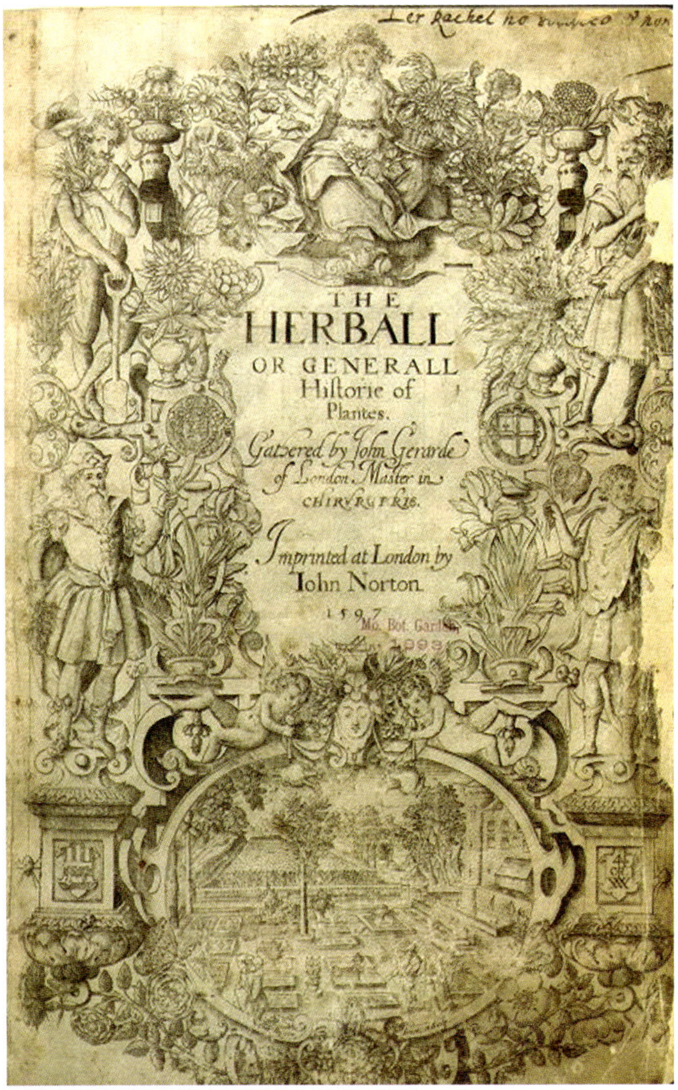

'Poisonous mushrooms as Dioscorides saith, groweth where old rusty iron lieth, or rotten clouts or neere to serpents dens, or roots of trees that bring forth venomous fruit.' Quote from *The Herball or Generall Historie of Plantes* by John Gerard, which was first published in 1597. With quotes such as these, one can see how the British at this time feared all things fungal. Image from the Biodiversity Heritage Library.

Recently, ash dieback has also caused havoc with our native woodlands here in the UK, and also honey fungus with its pernicious black bootlaces.

On the flip side, they can also protect plants from being eaten by pests by allowing them to create chemical defences to counter any attacks. So, although there are some fungal parasites that damage their hosts, the majority of fungi are saprophytic, acting as nutrient recyclers of dead plant and animal matter, and even tough material such as lignin in dead wood.

Fungi are hugely important to us as many medicines are derived from them, including *penicillin* (and other antibiotics), *cyclosporin*, an immunosuppressant drug used in organ transplants, many anticancer drugs, cholesterol lowering statins, and *psilocybin*, the psychedelic substance recently found to help with depression. But as well as curing, fungi are capable of causing serious diseases in us too.

Fungi are present underfoot in soils all year round, and not just in autumn with their strange and ephemeral fruiting bodies. The cells of most fungi grow underground as thread-like structures called 'hyphae' and they form networks of mycelium. These fungal root-like filaments connect and envelop the roots of trees and plants to form symbiotic relationships. In fact, over 90 per cent of all plant species have mycorrhizal relationships with fungi and would struggle to survive without them. The fungi can help the plants grow by increasing the uptake of water and essential compounds, such as nitrate and phosphate, and the fungi receive sugars in return. These vast networks that spread beneath our woodlands have become known as the 'wood wide web' and they connect trees to one another, allowing them to transmit signals and balance out nutrients between them, effectively communicating underneath the ground; they even look like a neural network. Some plants that contain no chlorophyll such as bird's-nest orchids (*Neottia nidus-avis*) gain their nutrients via this mycelial network.

There is now evidence that these associations were essential in the first land plants millions of years ago; the actual age of the Fungi Kingdom is estimated to be over a billion years old, when life on Earth was still confined to the oceans. Fossilised fungi called *Prototaxites* have been found that date back to around 450 million years ago. These fungi were the largest organisms around at that time and may have resembled tree trunks.

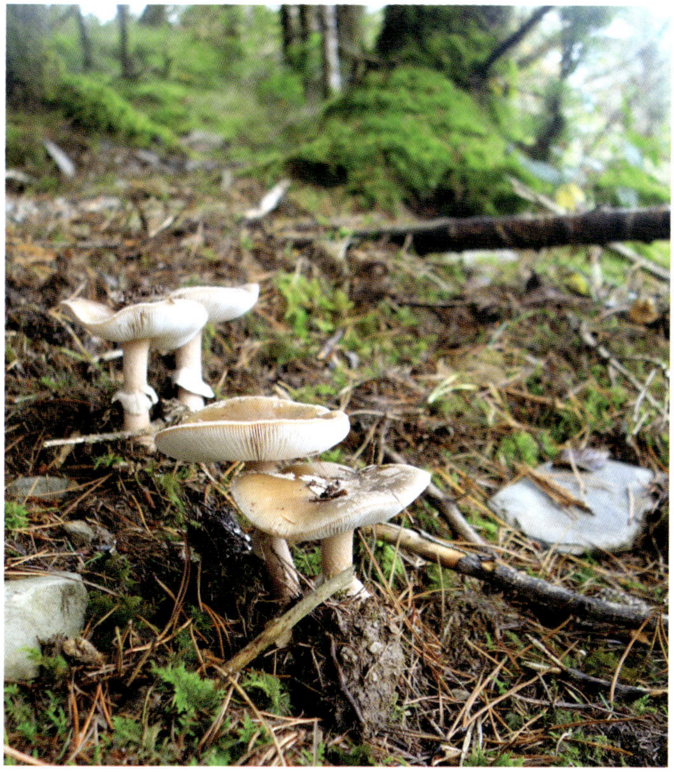

These interactions between fungi and forest are unseen above ground and we do not see how interconnected everything is; a quiet and secret mycorrhizal world runs beneath our feet.

Many insects also have symbiotic relationships with fungi, including leafcutter ants and some termites, primarily farming the fungi as a food source. Fungi can help the insect kingdom too. As a defence against predators the Marbled White butterfly contains toxins. These are derived from its caterpillars targeting grasses that have fungi within them that produce alkaloids. Great news for our honeybees too, fungi species have been discovered that can attack and kill the *Varroa* mite that is responsible for devastating bee populations around the world.

> 'If you go off into a far, far forest and get very quiet, you'll come to understand that you're connected with everything.'
>
> ALAN WATTS

THE CLASSIFICATION OF FUNGI

Fungi were once thought of as lower plants and so classified within Plantae, the Plant Kingdom, but in 1969, were at last given their own kingdom. They are very distinct from plants in that they do not photosynthesise, and they have cell walls made from the protein 'chitin' and not cellulose. Fungi are genetically more closely related to animals than to plants; insects and crustaceans have exoskeletons also composed of chitin.

They cannot ingest their food but instead their hyphae secrete digestive enzymes that break down their substrates to simpler components that they can then absorb as nutrients. You could think of them as inside-out organisms.

Kingdom Fungi is incredibly large and diverse including microorganisms such as moulds, rusts and yeasts, as well as the more familiar mushrooms. There are roughly 100,000 species worldwide but there could be many, many more still unrecorded.

The study of fungi is known as mycology, and the word comes from the ancient Greek *mykes*, meaning mushroom. The word mushroom may have come from the old French term *mousseron* meaning moss, possibly suggesting its preference for damp, mossy habitats, or a likeness to lower plants.

Here the Kingdom Fungi is split into five branches making up the True Fungi: with the *Basidiomycota* being the most advanced and *Chytridiomycota* being the most primitive and possibly the ancestors of all fungi.

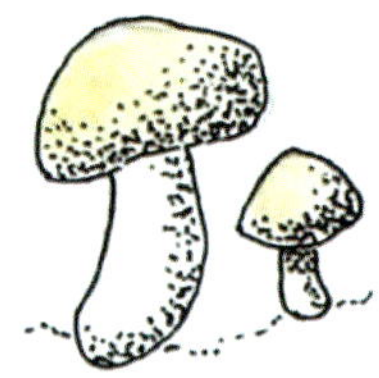

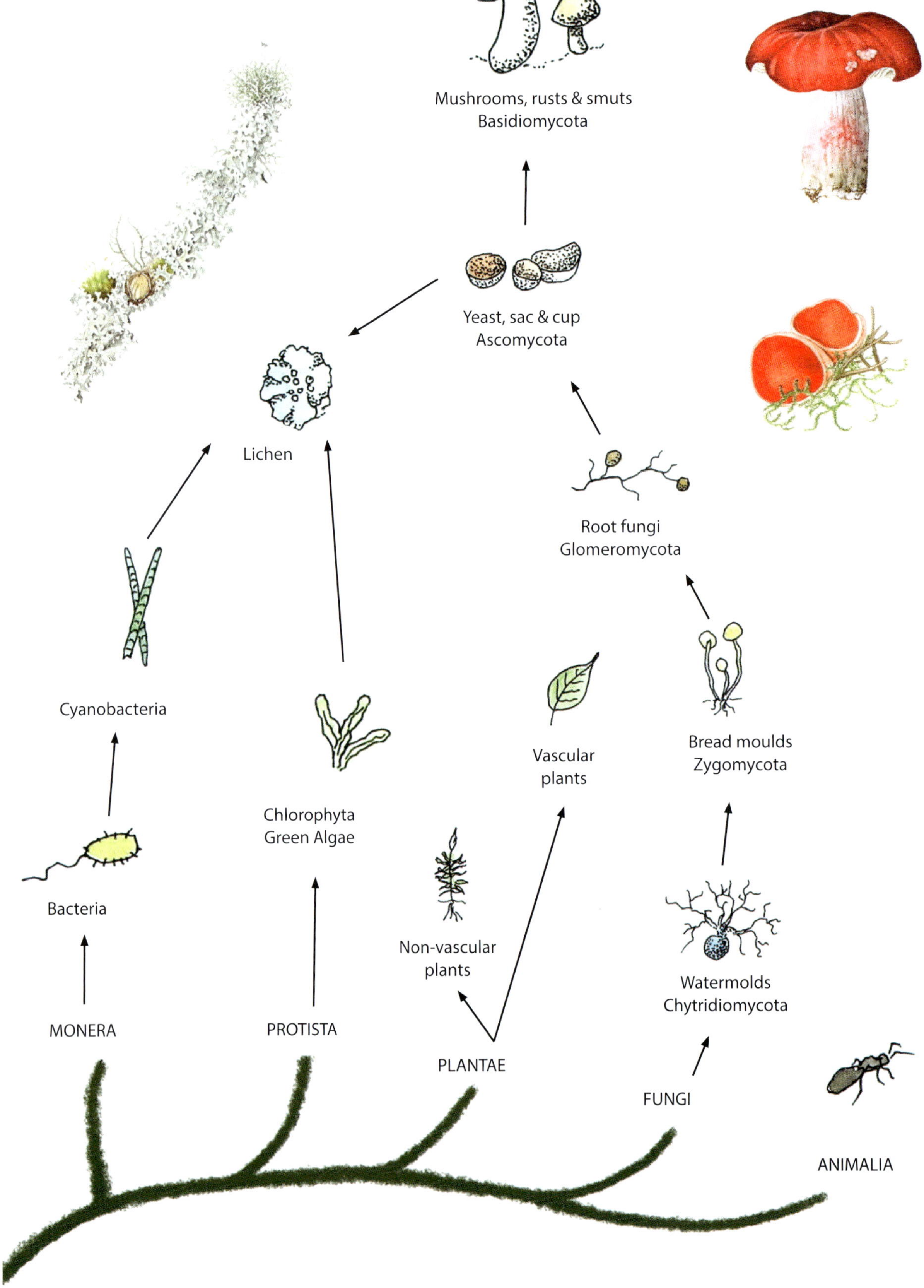

The Kingdoms of Life

NAMING OF SPECIES

The British Mycological Society is now over 100 years old and has done much to bring Kingdom Fungi to the attention of the general public. They recently published a list of English common names for fungi on their website, to hopefully engage people with this somewhat unknown world more on a personal level. The list can be downloaded from there and you'll find some wonderful and charming names such as woollyfoot webcap, yellow mascara disco and the Camembert brittlegill.

In the past, not all mushrooms acquired common names; some species actually have more than one and they are different in other parts of the world, so for that reason I prefer to use the scientific names for certainty of identification. In this book, I have included those familiar names of the commoner species that I'm aware of, and the scientific names are written in *italics.*

The naming of species can be a little frustrating as over the years, fungi have been and still are being reviewed using DNA sequencing to confirm correct lineage. While this evolution is no bad thing, it has led to lots of name-changing, making identification much harder. Over the years, fungi such as inkcaps and boletes have been subdivided into new genera as mycologists unravel the secrets of their identities. So, there are lots of synonyms and incorrect name-calling, making it a bit harder to keep track of – the nightmare of nomenclature!

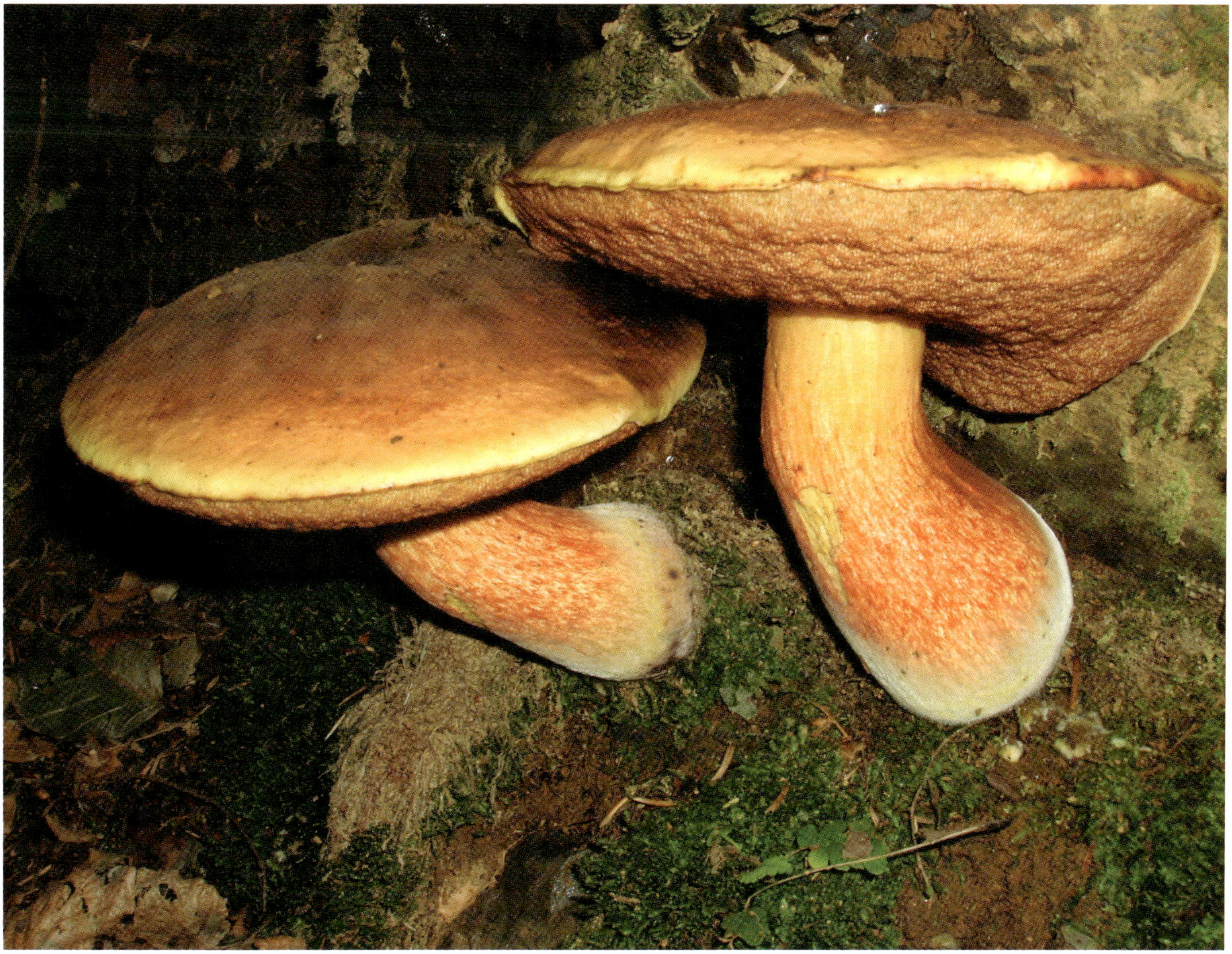

The frustration of name changes! Annoying but necessary. I've always known this mushroom as *Boletus erythropus* – the scarletina bolete – but it's now known as *Neoboletus luridiformis.*

AMAZING MUSHROOM FACTS

- A species of Honey fungus, *Armillaria ostoyae*, is reputed to be the largest organism in the world and in 2021, holds the Guinness World Record for this. It grows in a vast network underneath the Malheur National Forest in Oregon, USA, and occupies an impressive total area of at least 965 hectares (2,385 acres), which is around 3.5 square miles. Its age is thought to be at least 2,400 years old, but it may well be a lot older. I've heard it being called the 'Humongous Fungus'!
- There are some fungi out there, around seventy species in the world, which display bioluminescence, causing them to glow eerily with a faint greenish light. The honey mushroom – *Armillaria* spp. – is well known for this phenomenon, although not the fruit bodies themselves but the underground mycelium. Some fruit bodies are known to glow faintly, including species within the genera of *Mycena* but to see it you may need an SLR camera where you are able to manually lengthen the time exposure. The gills of the jack-o'-lantern – *Omphalotus illudens* and *O. olearius* – may be seen when eyes are accustomed to the dark. The bitter oyster – *Panellus stipticus* – supposedly has the brightest bioluminescent glow, but this is mainly seen in the North American specimens.
- Some species of fungi are known to be able to consume plastic, including oyster mushrooms. The first found was in 2011 from the Amazon rain forest, called *Pestalotiopsis microspora*. It can eat a specific polymer of polyurethane, converting it into organic matter. It can survive without air so could be very useful in cleaning up landfill waste sites.
- Mushroom mycelium is now being grown to be used as an eco-friendly building and packaging material such as polystyrene, but it is biodegradable and non-toxic.
- Many mushrooms such as the oyster mushrooms (*Pleurotus* spp.) produce vitamin D when exposed to the sun as they contain the pigment melanin. This is also contained in our skin, and it gives us UV protection from the sun.
- Oyster mushrooms and a few other species too, are actually carnivorous, and they are able to catch tiny nematodes with loops in their hyphae and then ingest them.
- If you should come across a species of woodland mushroom like a *Russula* or a *Boletus*, perched in a tree and wonder how it got there, it could just be a squirrel's dinner! Squirrels are now well known for storing and drying mushrooms for a tasty meal later on.

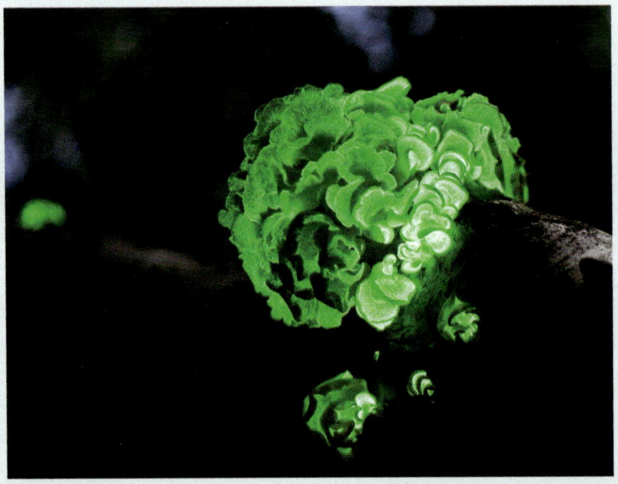

The bitter oyster – *Panellus stipticus* – glowing eerily with bioluminescence: the camera was exposed for 8.5 minutes to capture this much light in this image by Ylem.

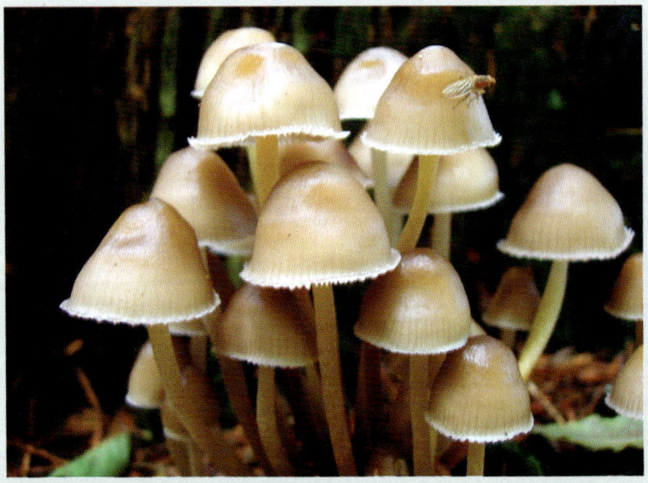

The yellowleg bonnet – *Mycena epipterygia*, is one species of this very large genus that displays bioluminescence. Some have glowing fruit bodies but with this species, it's just the mycelium.

PAINTING FUNGI: ARTISTS FROM THE PAST

Beatrix Potter (1866–1943) One cannot write a book about painting fungi without the mention of Beatrix Potter, whose wonderful paintings are held in the Armitt museum in Cumbria, UK. She captured her subjects with intricate detail and well-balanced compositions, producing around 350 illustrations. Approaching her fungi studies from a very scientific method, she used microscopes to study spores, as she was fascinated by the reproduction of fungi. She also cultivated spores from different species herself and wrote a scientific paper called 'On the Germination of the Spores of the *Agaricineae*'. In those times, women were not permitted to join the Linnean Society, but in 1897, her scientific paper was reviewed and debated by the Society. It was decided that it needed more work before publication, so she withdrew the paper and later decided not to resubmit it.

R. Baker painted a variety of fungi between 1883 and 1906. There is a collection of around nineteen paintings by this unknown artist held in the Wellcome Library in Euston Road, London.

Henrietta Page was an avid fungi sketcher from North America who kept wonderful sketchbooks dated from between 1899 and 1903. Henrietta was a member of the Boston Mycological Club and the Boston Society of Natural History.

Anna Maria Hussey (1805–1853) British mycologist, writer, and illustrator who contributed to many publications and in 1847 also wrote *Illustrations of British Mycology*. In the introduction to *Illustrations*, she notes that: 'A basket is in the first place needful, and if the student should leave home without one, a profusion of lovely and rare objects will be certain to strew his path; in which case there are but two alternatives, to dissect on the spot, always an imperfect operation, or to carry away the spoil in hat or handkerchief, when on arrival at home, a heterogeneous mass of caps, stems, etc., presents itself – *disjecta membra!*'

Mary Emily Eaton (1873–1961) was a talented British botanical artist who also spent many years in the US. She was more known for her illustrations of cacti, but she illustrated *The Field Book of Common Gilled Mushrooms*, from 1928.

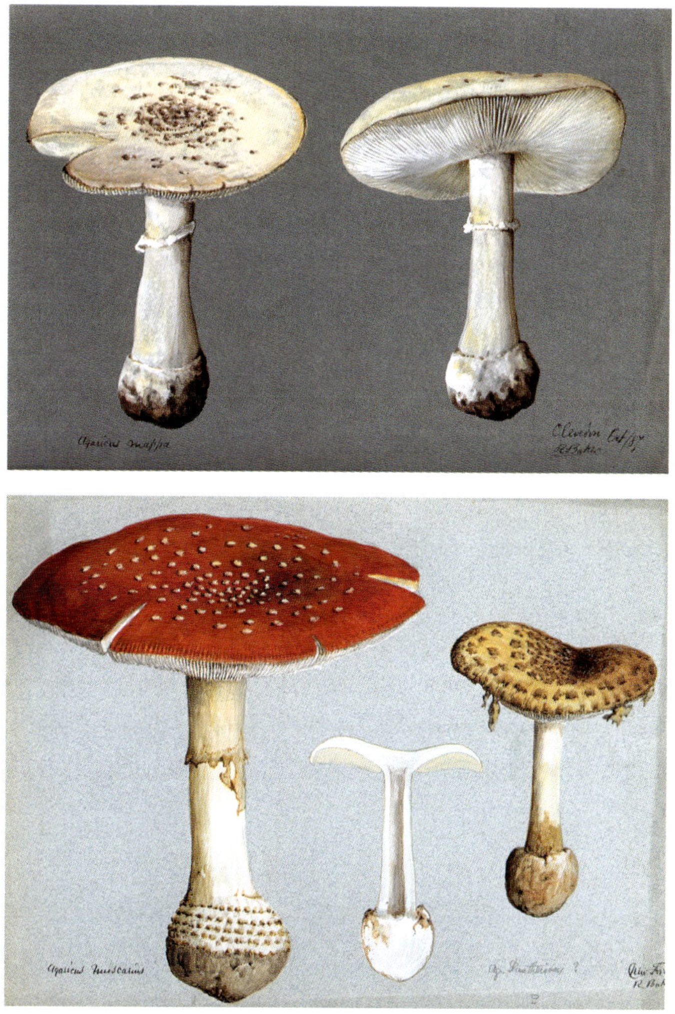

Two studies by R. Baker. Top image: False Death Cap, *Amanita citrina*; bottom image: Fly Agaric – *Amanita muscaria* from 1890–93. The Wellcome Collection states that they were possibly painted at an art class in the Severn region, Avon. They were beautifully observed and painted on toned paper using opaque pigments.

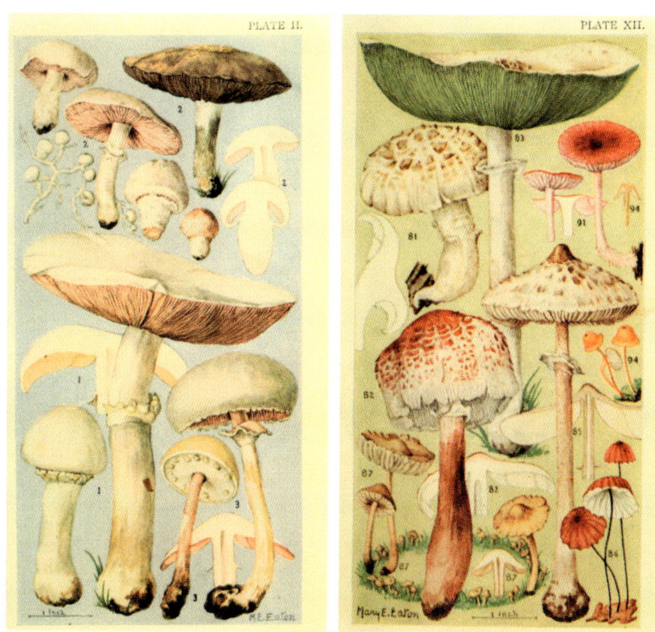

Mary Emily Eaton was a British artist more well known for painting cacti. These colourful images are from *The Field Book of Common Gilled Mushrooms*, New York: G.P. Putnam's Sons, from 1928 and sourced from the Biodiversity Heritage Library, contributed by the Harvard Botany Libraries.

Suzanne Lucas MBE (1915–2008) was the founder of the Society of Botanical Artists that was formed in 1985. She had a deep fondness for Kingdom Fungi – or the 'Third Kingdom', as she called it, and was one of the most prolific fungi artists, with hundreds of paintings under her belt. She was awarded a total of thirteen RHS gold medals for her whimsical fungi illustrations.

CONTEMPORARY ARTISTS

Fungi illustration has become much more popular in modern times and is seen by some as a branch of botanical art owing to its mycorrhizal connections to plant life, although it probably should be labelled as natural history illustration. Not many artists purely focus on Kingdom Fungi, most painting a variety of subjects within the natural world.

Alexander Sasha Viazmensky is one artist whose main focus is painting mushrooms. He has painted a wealth of stunning artworks of many fungi families and has fungi paintings in the prestigious Shirley Sherwood Collection of botanical art.

STEP BY STEPS

These are the step-by-step sequences given in this book, together with the type of media and techniques used.

- Chapter 4 – Drawing Shitake mushrooms with graphite pencils
- Chapter 4 – Drawing on white paper with charcoal
- Chapter 4 – Drawing on toned paper with charcoal
- Chapter 5 – Layering watercolour – Painting the cap of a Blusher
- Chapter 5 – Using masking fluid – Fly Agaric
- Chapter 5 – Painting Chanterelles in gouache on black paper
- Chapter 6 – Creating a Loose Background with ferns
- Chapter 7 – Enlarging a subject and using a limited palette – Plums and Custard
- Chapter 9 – Using water-soluble graphite – Drawing a Morel
- Chapter 10 – Mixed media – Lichen Mosaics on Stones

FOCUS STUDIES AND EXPERIMENTS

- **Chapter 5:** Capturing Translucence – Parrot Waxcap
- **Chapter 6:** An approach to adding a background – Birch Polypore
- **Chapter 6:** Using pen and wash – Velvet Shanks
- **Chapter 9:** Different shading methods – Scarlet Elf cup

These images by Henrietta Page are from the Biodiversity Heritage Library and contributed by the University of Connecticut Libraries, which has digitised the entire collection. Henrietta's sketchbooks include detailed sketches with comprehensive notes, including spore prints and even some dried-out specimens.

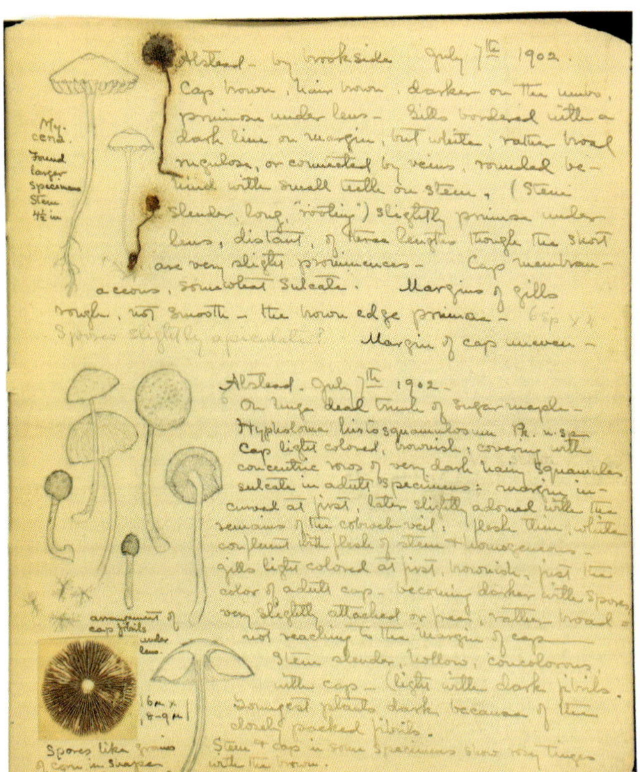

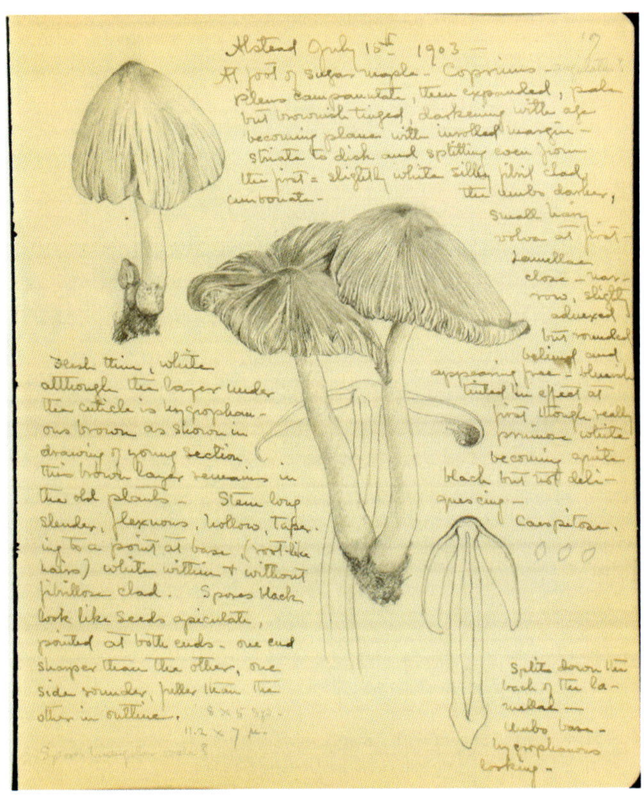

Forest Bouquet 1 by Alexander Sasha Viazmensky, watercolour 16 x 12in (40.5 x 30.5cm). A wonderful collection of mushrooms including *Boletus edulis*, *Leccinum* sp, *Russula* spp. and *Cortinarius* sp. (© Alexander Viazmensky)

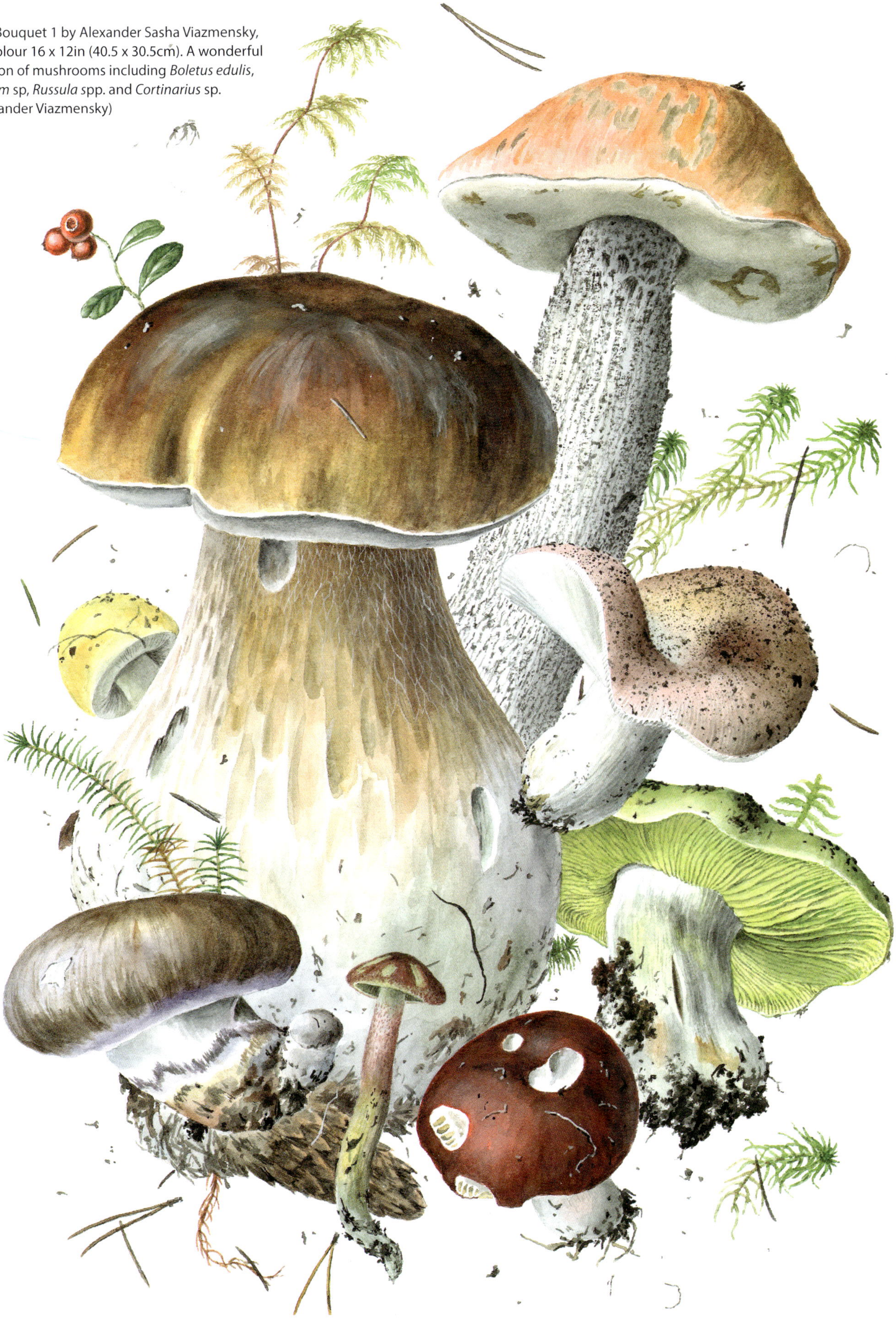

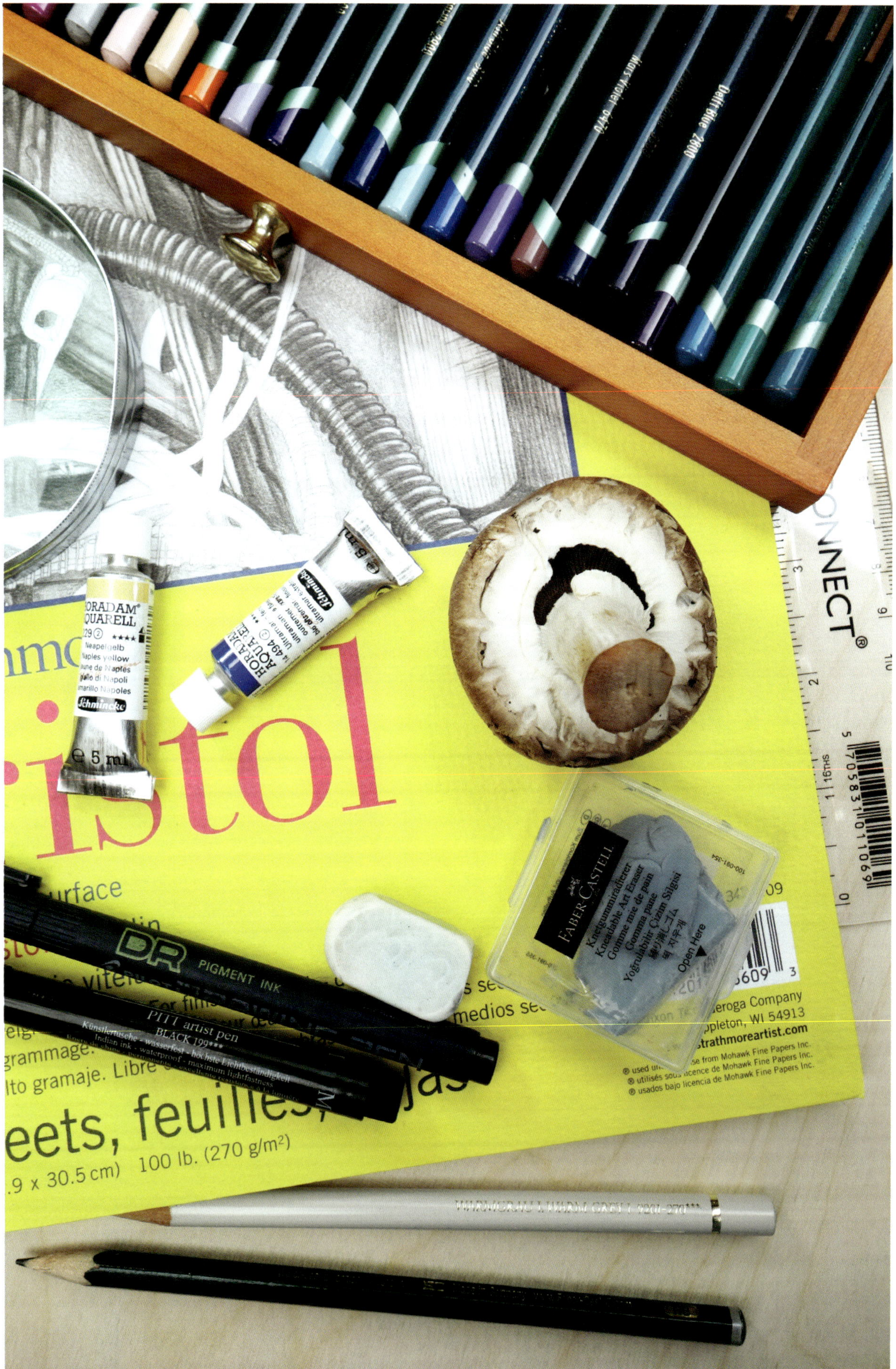

HORADAM®
AQUARELL
Neapelgelb
Naples yellow
Jaune de Naples
Giallo di Napoli
Amarillo Napoles
Schmincke
e 5 ml
ristol
urface
medios se
strathmoreartist.com
ppleton, WI 54913
eets, feuilles,
.9 x 30.5 cm) 100 lb. (270 g/m²)
DR PIGMENT INK
PITT artist pen
BLACK 199***
Indian ink · waterproof · maximum lightfastness
FABER-CASTELL
Knetgummiradierer
Kneadable Art Eraser
Gomme mie de pain
Gomma pane
Yoğrulabilir Çizim Silgisi
Open Here
ONNECT®
16THS

CHAPTER 1

MATERIALS AND EQUIPMENT

Fungi can be depicted successfully in any medium, whether it's in watercolour, in pen or plain graphite alone. It is completely up to you, your preferred medium of choice and how you'd like to portray them.

There is a staggering array of materials to purchase these days and the amount of choice can feel a little overwhelming, not to mention expensive. I have found over the years that I've bought and collected so many materials that I could open my own shop! Some I have hardly used and many of my students say the same. I like to push them out of their comfort zones by making them try mediums that they don't use often; to get out those unused materials and start using them. Many a student is pleasantly surprised and appreciates the push!

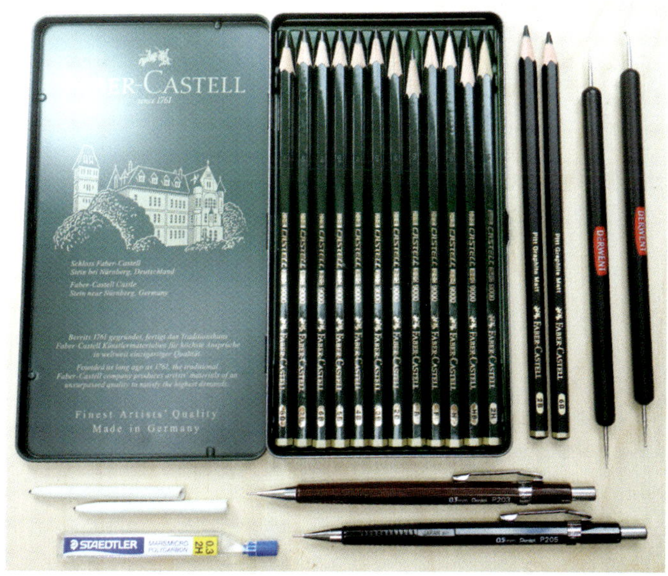

My personal favourites are the Faber-Castell 9000 series seen here in this set of twelve. The matt graphite pencils are seen to the right of the tin, along with the useful Derwent indenting tools. Below are two Pentel mechanical pencils that I load with size 0.3mm lead.

GRAPHITE

The word graphite comes from the Greek word *graphein* meaning 'to write'. A large deposit was discovered in Borrowdale in the Lake District, UK, in 1564. It was found to be of a very high quality and so extremely valuable. At first, people thought it was black lead and this is why we still call pencils lead today. In 1795, the French chemist Nicolas Conté developed a process combining clay and graphite that is seen in modern-day pencils.

Graphite is a perfect way to learn about and understand tone before heading into colour. It is mainly used for sketching and the under-drawing before beginning a painting, but it is also a beautiful medium in its own right. It is cost-effective and very forgiving, being very easy to erase. You don't need lots of supplies, just a small range of pencils to start off with. A full range would be from 9H to 9B but I find a range from 2H to 6B is enough for me to achieve good tones.

The H pencils are harder as they have a higher proportion of clay to graphite in them. The B ranges are softer as they contain more graphite and this makes them great for loose sketching but more prone to smudging.

Graphite is a lubricant, and you can get a hint of this with its slick and sometimes polished look. Some people may not like the 'shiny' look that you can get from certain angles when viewing a graphite drawing. This is due to the flat, plate-like structure of graphite that reflects the light, making it appear shiny. You can now purchase matt graphite pencils that reduce this graphite shine somewhat. If you prefer a denser, blacker finish, then you can opt for charcoal, carbons and the many other matt black pencils on the market now, such as Pierre Noir and Staedtler Mars Lumograph. Using a black coloured pencil in the finishing

A collection of various art materials.

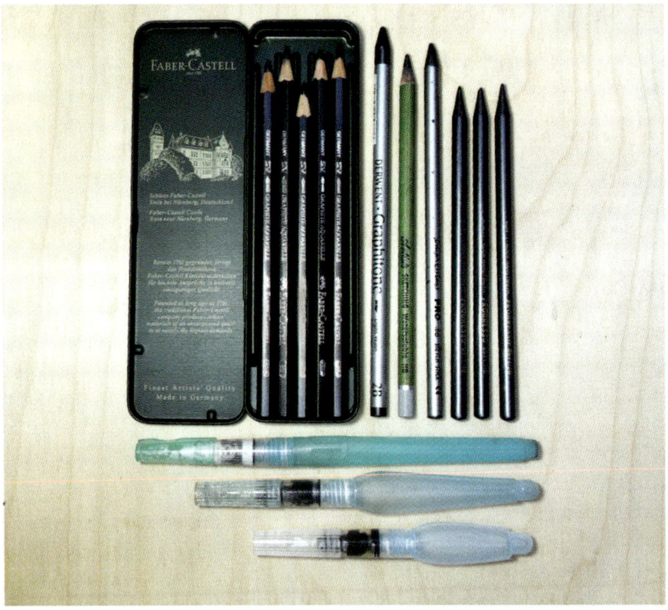

Other graphite media include Koh-I-Noor pure graphite sticks, water-soluble graphite pencils by Faber-Castell and Daler-Rowney, Graphitone by Derwent – a water-soluble graphite stick. Water brushes are useful for outdoor sketching.

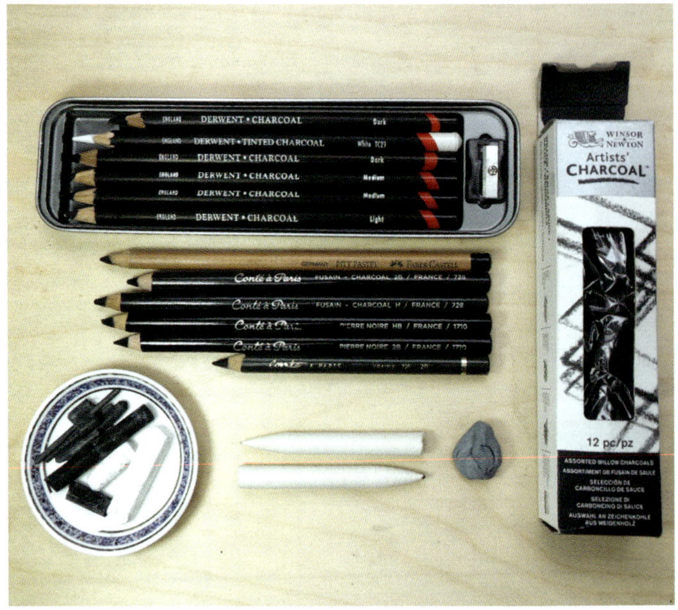

Assorted charcoal pencils by Conté, and Derwent; they can give more precision to work but the points wear down very quickly. Pierre Noir by Conté – these pencils will give denser, darker tones and more precision but are more difficult to erase. Assorted pastel and willow charcoal sticks by Winsor & Newton that you can snap to size and use to sweep in tone on their sides. Messy to use but wonderful to blend and erase and if you want to loosen up.

stages can also get those darkest darks into a graphite drawing, increasing the tonal range. Graphite, though, does have the upper hand when it comes to control and attaining realism and detail. There are many quality brands of graphite pencil on the market. Faber-Castell is the world's oldest pencil manufacturer and was founded in 1761. Other quality brands include Derwent, Staedtler, Conté, Lyra, Koh-I-Noor and Caran d'Ache.

CHARCOAL AND CARBON

Charcoal has to be the oldest drawing material; one can imagine early paleolithic man using charcoal from the fire to mix to a paste in order to adorn the walls of caves with animal drawings. Unlike graphite, it has coarse granules that do not reflect the light. This helps it achieve a much denser, very dark and matt finish. It also has some excellent blending qualities. The downside is that it may be gritty and messy to work with and not allow for the fine detailing that is wanted in a realistic drawing.

Vine or willow charcoal comes in stick form of varying widths. The pieces can be snapped to create smaller pieces to work with. It is perfect for loose, gestural sketching, with expressive and energetic line and experiments with tone and contrast. Drawing with charcoal can allow you to stop fussing over small details in order to see the bigger shapes and values, and concentrate on tonal contrasts. For this reason, it can be the perfect medium for roughing out and designing a starting composition. It also allows for the creation of atmospheric effects due to its capacity for soft blending.

Charcoal pencils are usually made with a form of charcoal that has been mixed with gum and then compressed. They are a better bet for achieving a little more control and precision in drawing. You can get similar grades to graphite, although not as many are needed. Some manufacturers just have hard, medium and soft grades while others have some of the H to B ranges. Cheaper brands and H grades can be very scratchy to use and so can be off-putting.

Carbon pencils are a mix of graphite and charcoal. They display qualities of both mediums, having a deeper, denser black than graphite and being smoother than charcoal. They may not be as easy to lift or erase as ordinary graphite.

Pierre Noir pencils by Conté are made of filtered paste pigment. They are very silky, smooth, dense and black and feel a little bit like a crayon to use. These pencils are less messy and may be easier to control than charcoals for a beginner.

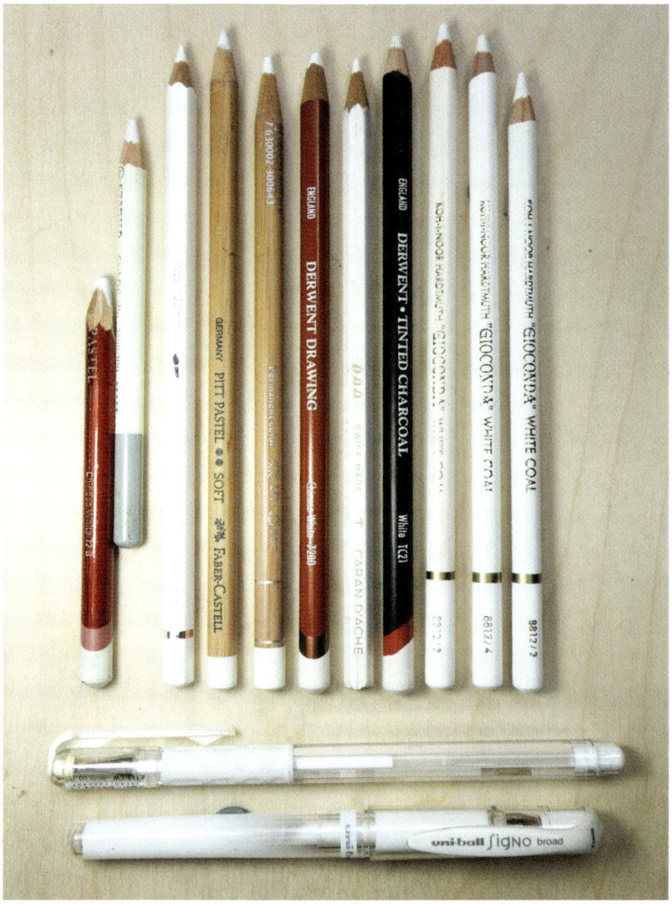

An assortment of white drawing media, ranging from white coloured pencils, and pastels, to Uni-ball gel pens and white charcoals (so-called, but likely to be pastel). I have only tried Koh-I-Noor and Derwent and they are very similar.

White charcoal pencils are usually made with calcium carbonate and a binder, although some may have a titanium white pigment in them, similar to white pastel pencils. Good brands will include Generals, Koh-I-Noor and Derwent.

COLOURED PENCILS

The ancient Greeks and the Romans used wax-based coloured crayons as documented by Pliny the Elder (23–79AD), the great Roman naturalist and writer of some of the first natural history encyclopaedias. Incidentally, Pliny wrote about fungi noting that they were just the 'dirt' of trees and other decomposing matter, and not organisms in their own right.

The first artist's coloured pencils were invented in 1908 by German manufacturer, Faber-Castell and then followed by Caran d'Ache in 1924. Many other brands followed soon after, including Derwent. Now there is a plethora of brands to choose from, all of varying quality and price, as they become more popular with fine artists.

Coloured pencils can be oil based, wax based or a blend of the two and can be soft and easy to blend on the paper. They can be used on toned or black papers as well for extra versatility. The artist's quality pencils are obviously superior to student brands, using higher concentrations of quality pigments and taking permanency into consideration. You can check the manufacturers' websites for information on lightfastness ratings.

PEN AND INK

The oldest pens were used by the Egyptians, who made pens out of reeds. Then for many centuries dip pens made from feathers were used. Today there are many varieties of pen to choose from, each with differing characteristics.

- **Ball point pens/biros**: can be good to sketch with and very inexpensive, but many do not have archival/lightfast ink, so not to be used if you want your drawings to last. However, they may be fine in a sketchbook, kept out of the light.
- **Fibre-tip artist pens**: these have archival ink, are waterproof, many are good value and come with many different nib sizes and colours. They are not refillable.
- **Fountain pens:** refillable and give an expressive variety of line but are more expensive to buy. Nibs may clog or scratch the paper surface.
- **Dip pens:** versatile with an expressive variety of line, nib sizes and used with separate ink pots so an array of colours is available. Nibs may clog or scratch.

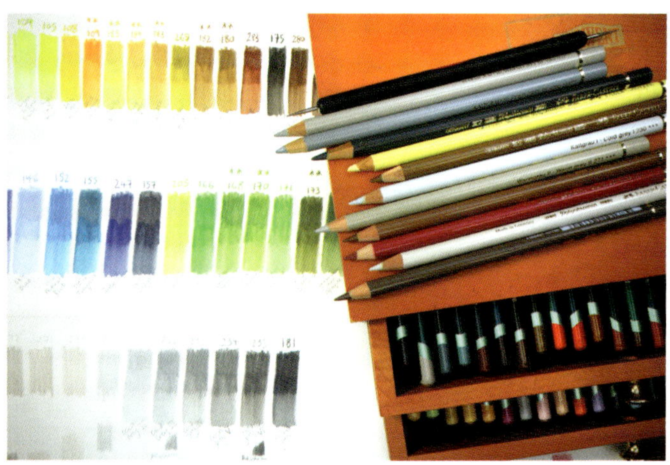

Faber-Castell Polychromos are high-quality, oil-based coloured pencils and in the box are Derwent Artists pencils that are wax based. A swatch chart is helpful to see all the colours laid out.

Inks

Ink is one of the oldest mediums used for drawing. The earliest inks would have been made from carbon or lampblack, which comes from the soot left over from fire remains. India ink was actually first seen in China, but is so called due to it being traded from India. This ink can have particles suspended within it that can cause interesting textures, but that can clog ink pens. Shellac medium is used in many inks to prolong their life.

Another ink from the past is iron gall or gallnut ink, which is made by mixing ferrous sulphate (iron and sulphuric acid) and the tannins from galls. These are growths that are formed upon plants by the actions of tiny insects called gall wasps, to house their larvae. Iron gall ink is very acidic and many documents and manuscripts from the past were in danger due to its corrosive nature.

With inks there is lots of choice in colours, and levels of permanency. You can purchase dye-based inks, pigment-based inks and acrylic inks. You can even make your own inks using tea, foraged fruits, acorns and oak galls (as previously mentioned).

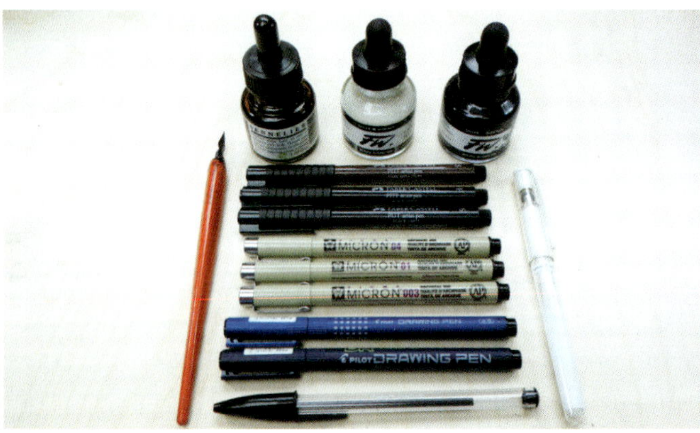

Assorted pens and inks of all different shapes and sizes; there is a lot of choice available.

Fungi Ink

Ink can be made from members of the Inkcap family, such as the shaggy inkcap – *Coprinus comatus* – and the common inkcap – *Coprinopsis atramentaria* – in a process called deliquescence. This is when the cap of a mushroom liquifies after a few days of sprouting, in order to help spread the spores. It forms a black ink-like liquid that was once used as ink in the past.

To make ink:

- Collect a few fully matured inkcaps. They are commonly found on lawns, in fields and parklands. Remove the stipes (stems) and store the caps in an enclosed container in the fridge for three or four days.

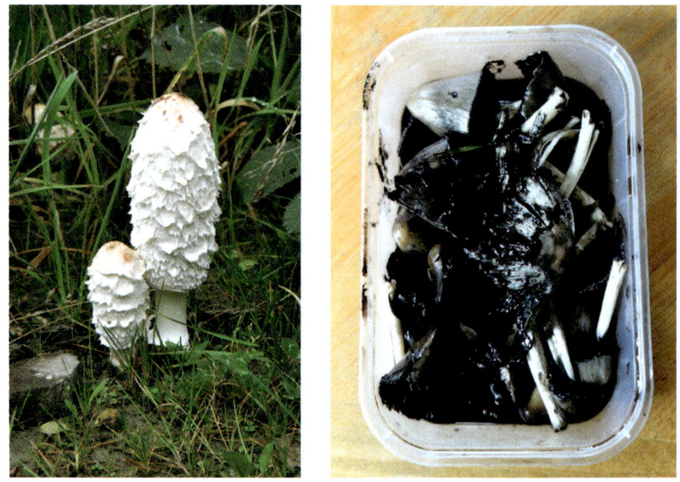

Shaggy inkcaps – *Coprinus comatus* – a lovely looking mushroom when young and supposed to be quite tasty as well, but they deliquesce very quickly. On the right are the liquefying inkcaps after a couple of days.

- They will have formed a mushy grey 'soup' that can now be blended with a hand blender.
- This can then be boiled to sterilise it and help prevent mould growth, along with a couple of added cloves. I saw this in Roger Phillips' excellent book, 'Mushrooms and other fungi of Great Britain and Europe'. You don't need to boil it if you just want to use it fresh and do not need to save it – just use it straight away.
- Cool down, then strain the liquid through a sieve, into a glass jar that has also been sterilised.
- The ink can now be used from the jar and stored in the fridge to prolong its shelf life. As it is a natural product it may not last too long, so it's best to make only a little at a time and a lightfastness test is needed.

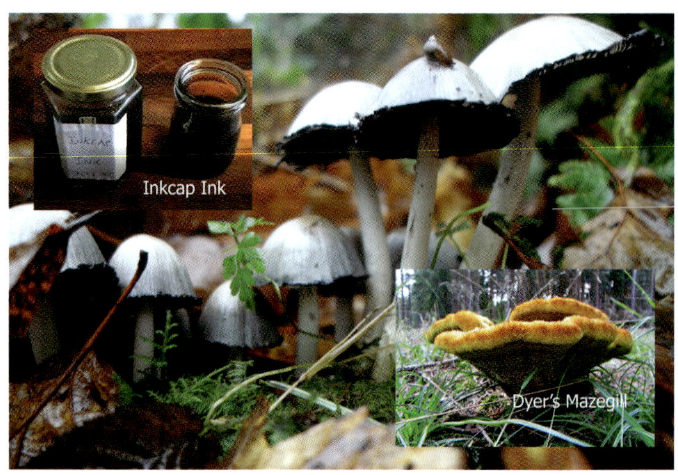

Common inkcaps – *Coprinopsis atramentaria* – can make ink too but are a bit smaller than the shaggy inkcaps. The Dyer's Mazegill is quite a common, large bracket fungus traditionally used for dyeing yarn.

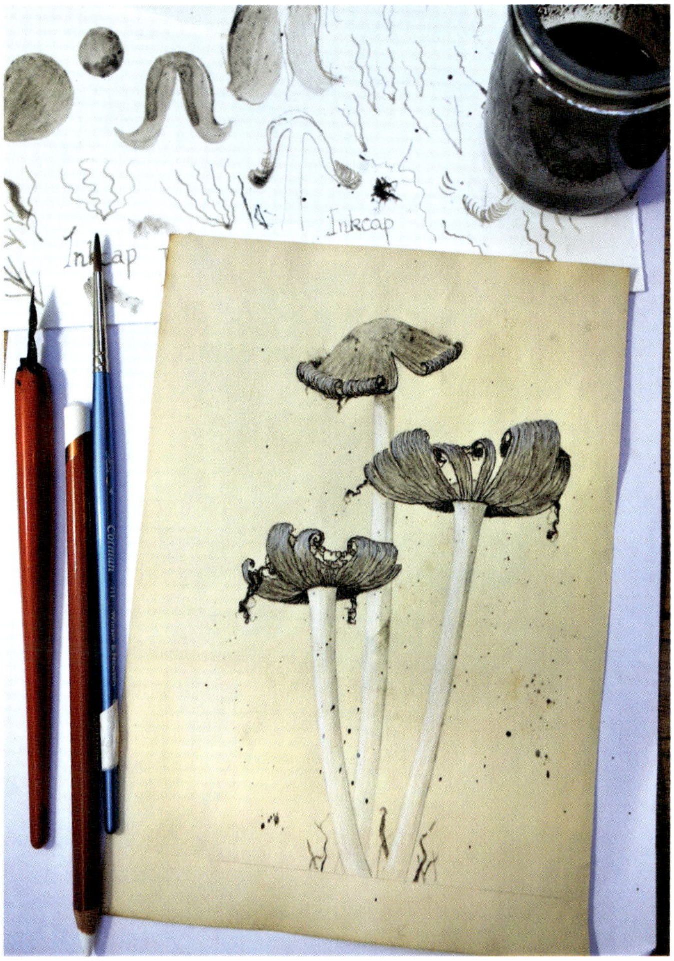

Painting common inkcaps with inkcap ink on the Dyer's Mazegill toned paper. The fungi ink is quite pale toned, so I complimented the drawing with black acrylic ink to boost the dark tones. The highlights were added with the Derwent Chinese white pencil, and it's finished with some splatter!

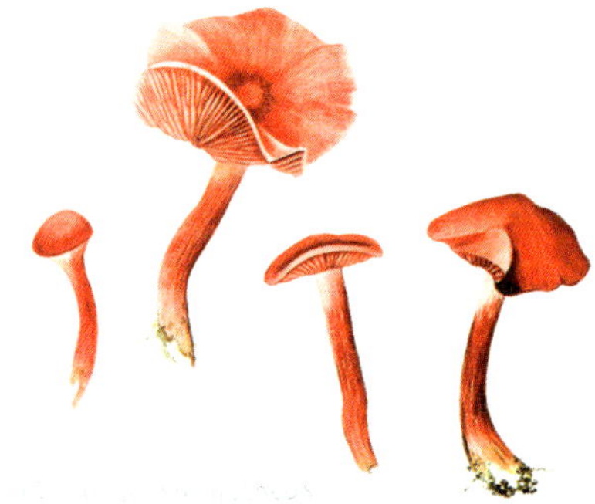

Cortinarius sanguineus in the journal. I found a patch of these mushrooms while on a walk through a dark conifer plantation; the sun was streaming through tiny gaps in the branches and these little mushrooms were suddenly lit up with a dusky red glow. The conifers have since been felled for timber, so I've not seen them again.

Dyer's Fungi

There are some mushrooms that have been used for making fabric and yarn dyes and they may have this attribute in their common name, for instance the dyer's mazegill – *Phaeolus schweinitzii*. This parasitic/saprobic bracket is found in conifer forests at the base of trees and can make various shades of yellow through orange to brown. I found a specimen and experimented with paper dyeing. Breaking up the bracket easily into pieces, I simmered it in water in a big stock pot for a while until it had released its amber colours. Then I dunked some paper in it, just a thicker weight cartridge paper. I let it dry and the result was a stained paper very similar to tea dyeing (only tea staining is a lot easier and quicker, so I won't be doing it again!).

The blood red webcap – *Cortinarius sanguineus* – is a species of mushroom that has colourful fruiting bodies, from which dyes can be made. It is mainly used to dye fabrics by boiling them in water with a handful of the dried mushrooms for a couple of hours to achieve beautiful and natural pink to red shades.

WATERCOLOURS

The first watercolours were probably used in the paleolithic caves of Europe. Clays, ochres, chalk and charcoal were mixed up with saliva or animal fats, which were used as a binder.

In the Middle Ages, pigments consisting of earth ochres or plants were ground to a powder and bound with gum or egg. They were used to adorn vellum manuscripts, mainly for religious purposes.

Albrecht Dürer, the German artist of the Renaissance period, mainly worked with engravings but he also used watercolours and helped to popularise them. He painted many natural history subjects among other things, including one of his most famous nature studies *The Great Piece of Turf*, painted in 1503. It was purely painted as a practice piece – natural history art was certainly not the order of the day in those times.

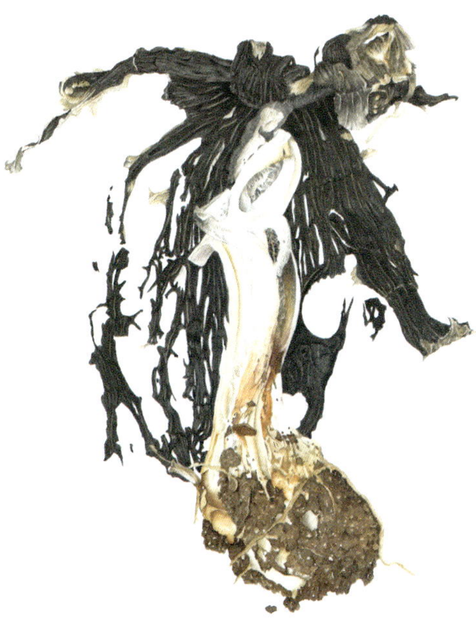

Exploding Inkcaps, a watercolour by my friend and botanical artist Jackie Isard. This inkcap mushroom has been captured deliquescing and releasing its inky spores back to the earth. (© Jackie Isard)

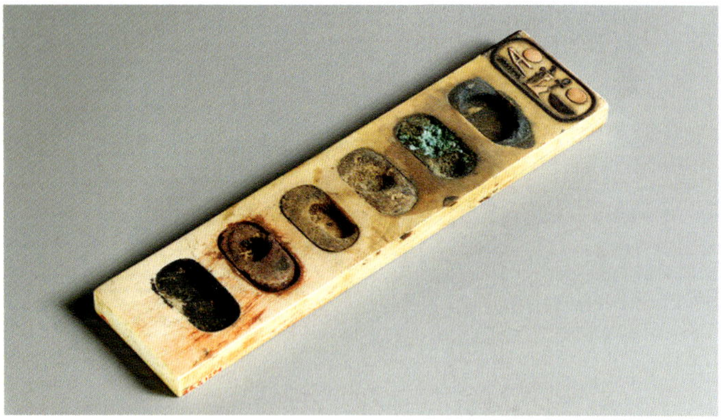

This Ancient Egyptian paint palette was found, carved from a single piece of ivory, with six oval wells that contained cakes of pigments including blue, green, brown, yellow, red, and black. The oval cartouche at one end encircles the throne name of Amenhotep III, Nebmaatre, and the epithet 'beloved of Re'. (Met Museum collection)

Watercolour Characteristics

Watercolour paint is made from a mix of finely ground pigment and a binder such as gum arabic that is made from the sap of the acacia tree. Other additions such as glycerine, glucose and stabilisers are added to the mix in varying proportions. Some paints, such as M. Graham and Sennelier, have honey in them. The best paints to use are artist's quality as they have more pigment and fewer additives.

All watercolour is transparent when mixed with water, but its character varies with every pigment. Transparent pigments are very finely ground by the manufacturer and so have small particle sizes. This attribute makes them excellent for working in layered washes and glazes where their transparency allows the white paper to shine past them. This creates clean, jewel-like tones and optical mixing of the underlying layers. Some colours are labelled as semi-transparent.

Opaque and semi-opaque pigments have larger particles, which can stop the shine of the white paper passing through them, depending on their level of dilution, and so can appear dull and sometimes chalky. Taking care while mixing can avoid muddy colours, but it really depends upon the subject matter and what you wish to achieve. They can be perfect for surface details, autumnal and fungi subjects.

Some pigments, such as ultramarines and umbers, have heavier particles than other pigments and so cause the washes to settle out into the grain of the paper, creating texture and granulations. They have a courser grind mainly due to being made from clays and stones from the earth. They also tend to sit upon the surface of the paper and so can be easier to lift, but in being so, that can make them difficult to layer. Flocculation is when the particles are attracted to one another, forming clumps in the wash; this is seen in cerulean.

Generally, modern, synthetic, dye-based pigments such as quinacridones and perylenes tend not to granulate. They have smaller particles that dissolve and sink into the paper, staining the surface and making it harder to lift and reveal the white paper underneath. Mineral-based and natural earth pigments tend to have less staining power.

I would recommend checking the paint labelling on the tubes or packaging for pigment properties such as transparency, granulation and the pigment's number. This is a code given to each pigment; for example, PR122 is Pigment Red #122, which is quinacridone magenta in most brands. Different manufacturers like to give their paints different and interesting names, so checking this pigment number can help you avoid buying duplicate paints and save you money.

There are many types of watercolour pencils and sticks, again of varying qualities and expense, many of which I've never tried. Watercolour pencils are an interesting medium that can be used dry as a normal pencil, or by brushing on water to blend out into a watercolour wash. You can also dissolve pigment from the tip with a damp brush and then paint on as if painting from a watercolour pan, perhaps for versatility out in the field.

Watercolour sticks are whole blocks of pigment that can be drawn on using the sides for larger expanses of colour in one sweep, or using the tips to create different dry textures that can be dissolved into washes or left.

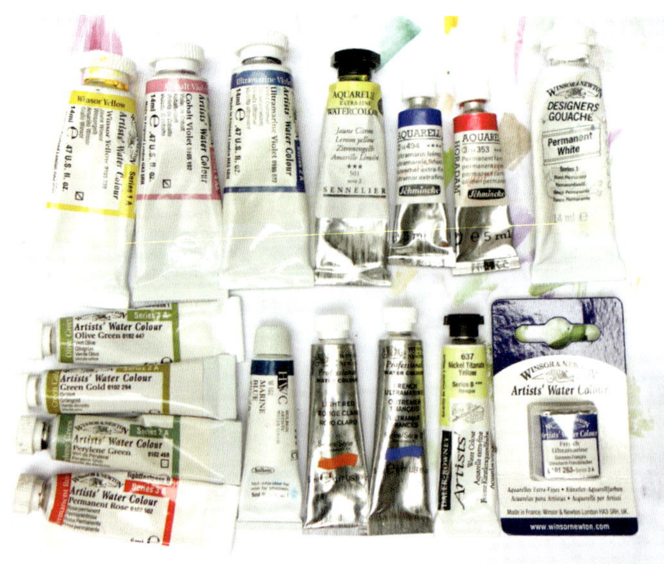

A selection of paints from different manufacturers including Winsor & Newton, Schmincke, Daler-Rowney, Sennelier and Holbein.

GOUACHE

Gouache is an opaque watercolour with a thicker consistency and is often used by illustrators of all kinds and it falls somewhere between watercolour and acrylics. It produces matt, flat and very vibrant colour that is quick drying and very useful for reproduction purposes. Unlike acrylics, which are permanent, gouache is liftable and so care must be taken when layering colour on top to avoid lifting previous layers of paint.

Forms of gouache have been used since the time of the ancient Egyptians, some with a honey-based binder. The name is derived from the Italian word for mud – *guazzo* – which was used to describe an opaque painting technique. In the eighteenth century in France, opaque watercolour became known as gouache, and was now made by mixing an opaque white pigment with traditional watercolours. You can mix transparent watercolours with white to create opaque watercolour instead of buying lots of gouache paints, with variable amounts of success. If you do purchase gouache paints, make sure they are artist's quality such as Schmincke Horadam if you are going to paint finished artworks to hang or sell. These paints have a higher pigment ratio and better lightfastness. I check the pigment numbers on the tubes or the manufacturer's website information and go for the same pigments that I'd use in ordinary watercolours.

Acrylic gouache is also available, which is a permanent gouache that is much like acrylic. It cannot be reactivated when dry, but it has the matt look of traditional gouache. I use synthetic round watercolour paintbrushes when using gouache, and I keep older sable paintbrushes that were bought for transparent watercolours that have become worn or damaged.

Lightfastness

I would recommend buying artist's quality when purchasing any paints, pigments or coloured pencils as the student grades often have a low pigment load and extra fillers, and some colours have an inferior lightfastness. If your paintings are destined for exhibitions or to sell, then look for information regarding durability on the side of the tubes or on the manufacturer's website. Most artist's quality paints are classified as being extremely permanent, permanent, moderately durable or fugitive, or similar classifications, depending on which country you are in.

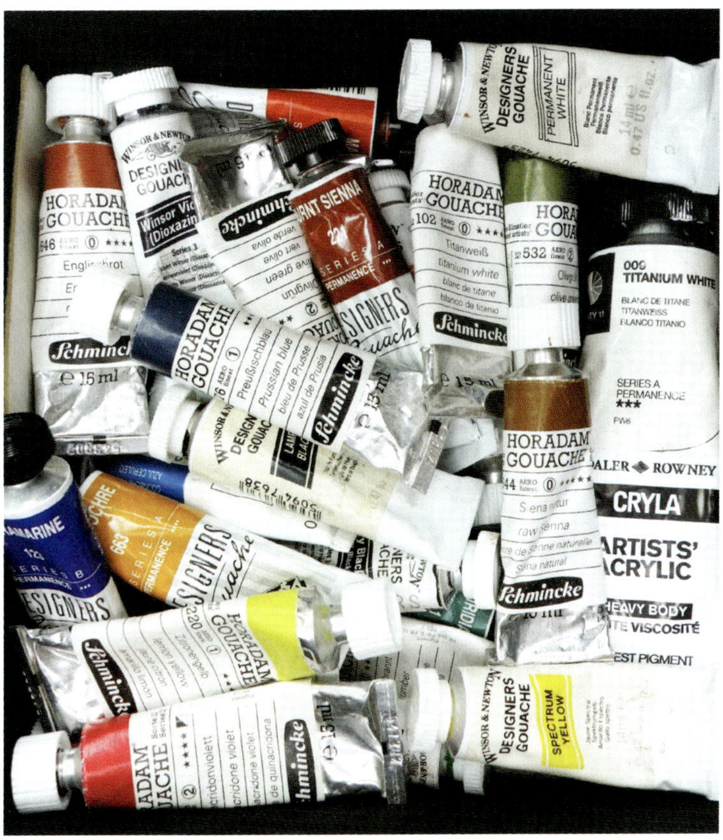

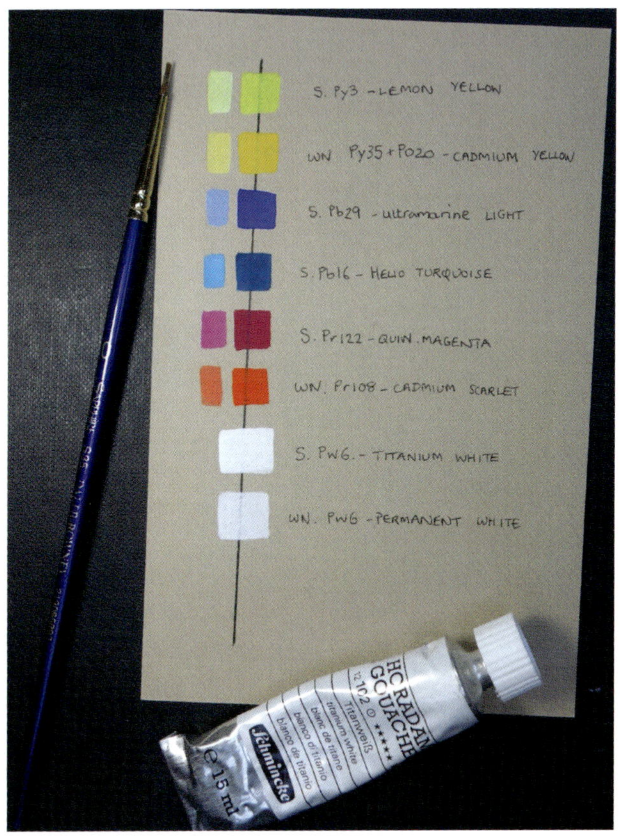

A selection of my gouache paints from Schmincke Horadam, Winsor & Newton and Daler-Rowney. It's very useful to make a swatch chart to see the colours on their own and with white added and painted over a black line to show the opacity of the paints.

There aren't many fugitive paints to avoid these days; modern pigments tend to be very durable. A few that stand out are alizarin crimson, opera rose, of which the fugitive component is a fluorescent dye, and aureolin, which can change colour over time. Of course, if you are only going to paint in a sketchbook or journal where paintings will be stored out of the light, then lightfastness isn't such an issue.

PAINTBRUSHES

For fungi illustration I recommend round watercolour brushes of different sizes from 0 up to 8, higher if you want to lay large washes. I like the brushes from Raphael and Rosemary & Co. Flat brushes are good for landscape and if you wanted to paint fungi with background habitats then they may be useful but not essential. However, a small flat size 2 would be useful for lifting techniques; they're sometimes called an eradicator.

There are many value brushes, but I do recommend buying a few good-quality ones that will tend to (hopefully) keep their points for longer, as long as they are stored correctly and looked after. There are good-quality synthetics as well as sables or other types such as squirrel. The animal hair brushes do hold more water and they are softer. Synthetics tend to be stiffer and also hog or ox bristle brushes are useful for thicker and heavier media such as acrylic or oils. I have a mixture of both synthetic and natural haired and I always keep old brushes, no matter how ruined they are; they are useful for mixing paints up in the palette or applying masking fluid with.

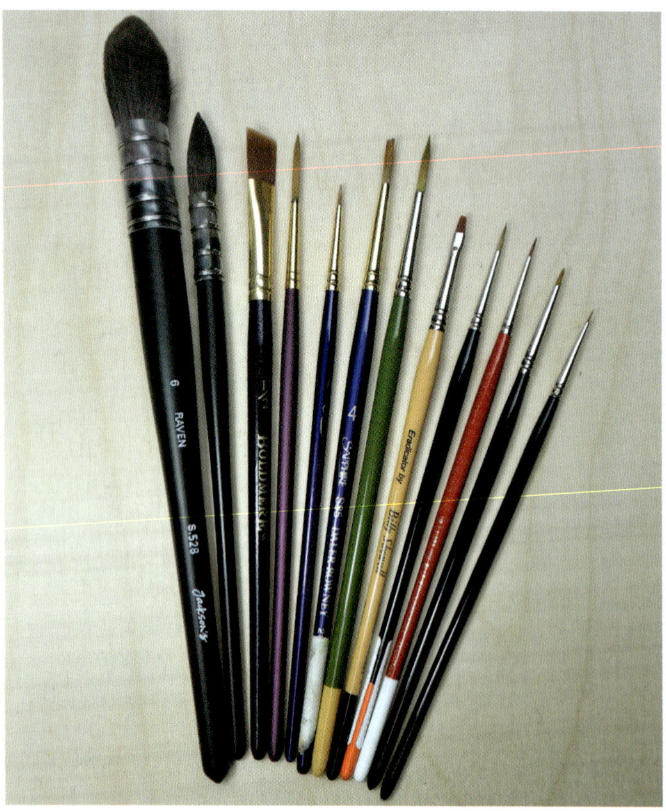

A selection of paintbrushes: from left, large mops and flats for looser work, then the blue ones are for gouache and the rest are for watercolours.

PALETTES

There is an assortment of palettes to suit everyone, and I find that white ceramic is best for mixing on as some plastics can make the paint bead up annoyingly. You can choose to buy a palette that has mixing areas and wells for squeezing paint from tubes into, to form a chosen palette of colours. I like to use small ceramic saucers bought from kitchen shops for mixing paint on.

PAPER AND GROUNDS

There is much to consider when it comes to paper, from its weight to its surface texture and of course, your budget. There is a lot of choice out there, but it really comes down to the medium that you want to use. There's a paper for every art practice, from laying out preliminary sketches to finished artworks, in every genre.

Papers come in all sorts of qualities but it's important to opt for acid-free paper which is pH neutral to help protect it against aging and yellowing over the years. I recommend buying several sample packs and testing them out to find what will work for your techniques and chosen media.

Drawing Papers

- Cartridge paper is a smooth, cellulose paper, typically around 125gsm.
- Bristol paper is heavier in weight than a cartridge paper with a choice of surface. Smooth surface is suited for more precision drawing, markers, and pen and ink, and vellum surface has a slight texture that is suited for graphite, charcoal, coloured pencils and mixed media.
- Textured papers such as Ingres can come in many colours and have a deep lined texture able to grip looser media such as pastel and charcoal.

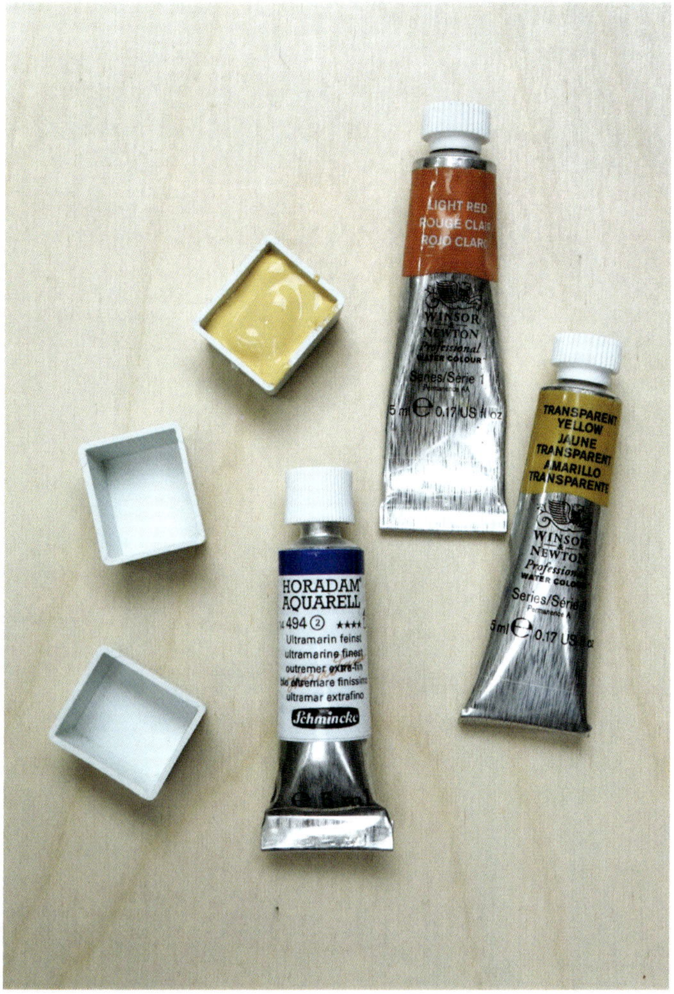

I tend to squeeze paint from tubes into empty pans so that I have the choice between using fresh tube paint for larger washes and pans for everything else.

Watercolour Papers

These papers come in different weights and thicknesses, most commonly from 190gsm (90lb), 300gsm (140lb), and 638gsm (300lb). 'Gsm' stands for grams per square metre and 'lb' stands for pounds per ream. The heavier papers will take more water with less buckling or warping than the lighter weights of paper. Thinner papers less than 140lb can be stretched first, but this is not essential if you tend to work in smaller washes and areas.

The papers also have a choice of different surface textures: hot press, cold press and rough. **Hot press** is a very smooth paper that is perfect for fine detail. It is pressed between hot metal rollers when produced, hence the name. **Cold pressed** or NOT paper is pressed through cold metal rollers and gives a more textured surface. **Rough** paper is pressed with felt while drying, which gives a very textured surface suitable for looser painting techniques.

During the manufacturing process of paper, sizing, which is usually made of an organic compound, is added to the pulp. This internal sizing coats the fibres and helps to control the absorbency, otherwise it would be like painting on blotting paper. A surface sizing is also added to give the paper surface strength and helps the paint sit more on the surface and so achieve brighter colours. This can be a type of starch or gelatine, and egg whites have been used traditionally.

Some of the whitest papers usually have some sort of optical brightener added, so a creamier, off white colour seems more natural.

DIFFERENT PAPERS, SURFACES AND SUPPORTS

- 100 per cent cotton makes the best quality and most robust papers that are made from old fabric and textile scraps. These papers are also naturally acid-free to promote longevity, but will be a little more expensive than a cellulose paper.
- Wood-pulp paper that has been neutralised to make it acid-free. This is usually done with calcium carbonate to raise the pH and that acts to counter the acidic lignins present in the wood pulp.
- 50 per cent cotton papers are a mixture of the two.
- Watercolour board is watercolour paper that is mounted onto board to give rigidity and makes it less prone to buckling when adding washes.
- YUPO is a plastic-like paper made of polypropylene. It is very robust, waterproof and wipes clean so a complete alternative to absorbent cellulose or cotton papers. Paint or ink may need varnishing for protection of final artworks on this surface.
- Coloured papers give a variety of toned grounds to work on, from black to cool greys through to warm tans and creams. Stonehenge Aqua, Strathmore and Stillman & Birn *Nova* series are all good brands for toned papers.
- Pastelmat and Uart are also toned papers, but with a gritty surface that grabs hold of pastel or coloured pencils. It feels like sandpaper to the touch.
- Vellum parchment is prepared animal hide that has been used for many centuries for manuscripts. The term comes from the old French for calf, but many different skins can be processed, including goat and sheep. It is gaining popularity as a ground for watercolour and produces a translucent and vibrant finish. You can get different types of vellum – Kelmscott, manuscript and natural.
- Paper vellum is made from processed cotton and plant fibres or synthetic ones and creates an often translucent paper useful for tracing.

I use a variety of hot press and cold press papers for wet media, such as Stonehenge Aqua, Arches and Fabriano and many different Strathmore Bristol papers from their range for dry media. I would recommend 100 per cent cotton paper when wanting to use lots of glazes and layering in watercolour. The cheaper, cellulose papers will be fine for pen and wash, or paintings completed in a single layer as the paint tends to sit on the surface more. Each brand of paper will have different levels of sizing and so react in their own way to each technique from glazing to lifting and will also affect the brightness of paint colours.

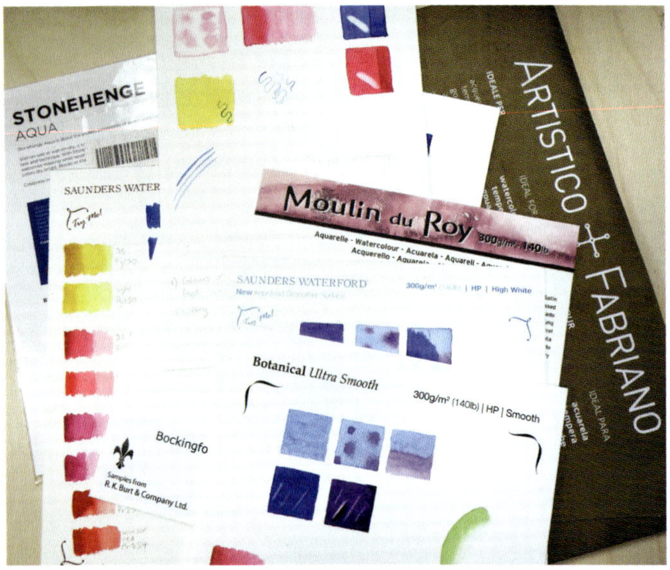

Testing out a variety of different sample papers to see how they perform with tests such as lifting out, glazing, masking fluid and colour intensity.

Sketchbooks

As with artist papers, there is a vast array of sketchbooks to choose from depending on the size and type of surface that you like to work on. Books to choose from or to consider:

- Cartridge paper sketchbooks with a lighter weight paper that are best for dry media. These books are obviously the best value but may not take watercolour well. Always choose acid-free to avoid yellowing of the pages over time. I regret not doing this in some of my first sketchbooks as many pages have now discoloured.
- Watercolour sketchbooks for wet media. I like the Stillman & Birn range of books that have a range of sizes, paper surfaces and toned papers. The *Zeta* series is hot press paper for detailed work, *Beta* series is their cold press. There are many sketchbooks now that have a cotton paper, including brands such as Kilimanjaro, Etchr Everyday and Strathmore 500, but these will command a higher price.
- Coloured paper sketchbooks will give you tones of grey, tan or black to work on for mixed media studies or for using opaque mediums. You can get recycled toned paper which has an interesting texture, really suited to autumnal studies. The Stillman & Birn Nova trio has the mix of three tones – grey, beige, and black in one book.
- The type of cover – spiral-bound, hardback or softcover. If working out in the field a softcover book will be of a lighter weight to carry around.

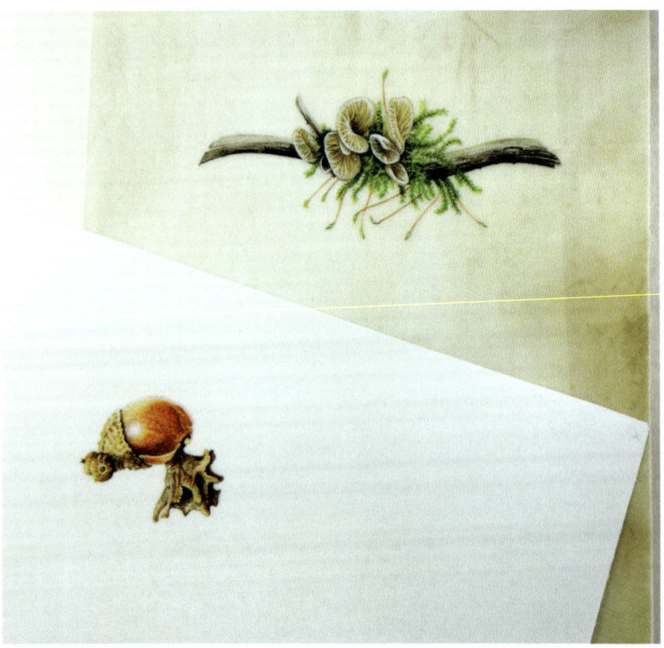

Here is the paler coloured Kelmscott vellum on the left and the warmer toned natural vellum with its subtle textures.

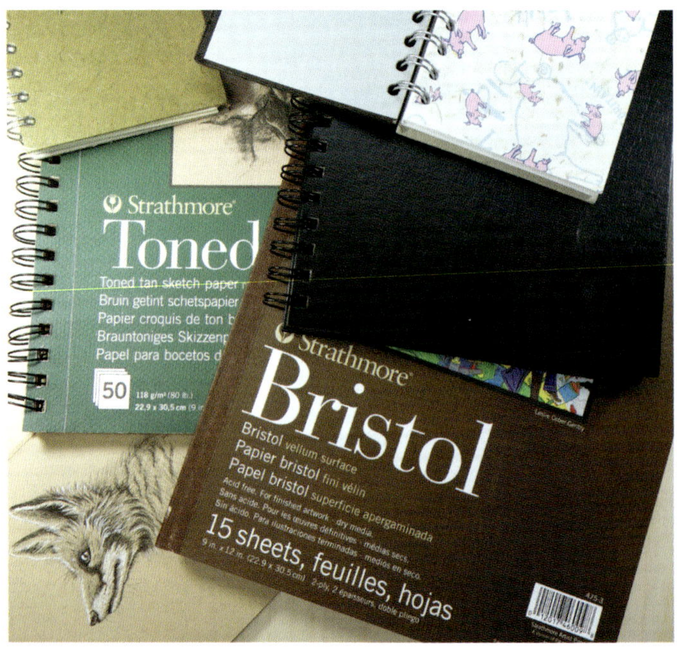

There is a bewildering array of different papers and sketchbooks on the market for different techniques.

Making Polypore Paper

For a long time I had wanted to make some paper at home and I own a mould and deckle kit that has been long unused. But instead of making normal paper, I decided to see if I could make paper from a mushroom. I know that one of the best fungi for this is the birch polypore, *Fomitopsis betulina.* Winter is a good time of year for finding this large bracket fungus on birch trees and it is common in my area.

I found a young, quite large specimen, and I carefully cut it from the tree. Then at home the bracket was peeled, cut up and blended in a blender into a gloopy pulp with some additional water. Then it was sloshed into a tray and ready for me to dip the deckle and mould frame into it.

This job was becoming messier by the minute (and smellier – it has a very strong, medicinal smell), and it would have possibly been best done outside or in the shed! But I got the first layer draining on the mesh in the mould and then tried to drop the formed layer of pulp out onto some j-cloths and towels. This was the hardest bit as it didn't come away from the mesh easily and took some fiddling about. Eventually it came free, and I dabbed it with a sponge to soak up the excess water. It then needed compressing with something flat and heavy; I used a piece of slate. I sponged it a bit more and then left it to dry flat. I managed to make three pieces of paper roughly about A4 size.

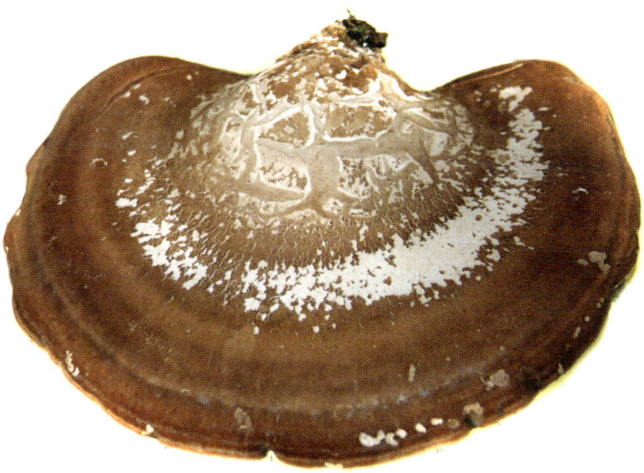

The birch polypore can grow to quite a large bracket. It is also known as the razor strop bracket as barbers were known to use strips of this fungus to sharpen their razors. *See* Chapters 6 and 8 for more on this bracket.

The dried-out fungi paper has turned out quite well; it has a little bit of texture and natural creamy colour and turned out reasonably flat.

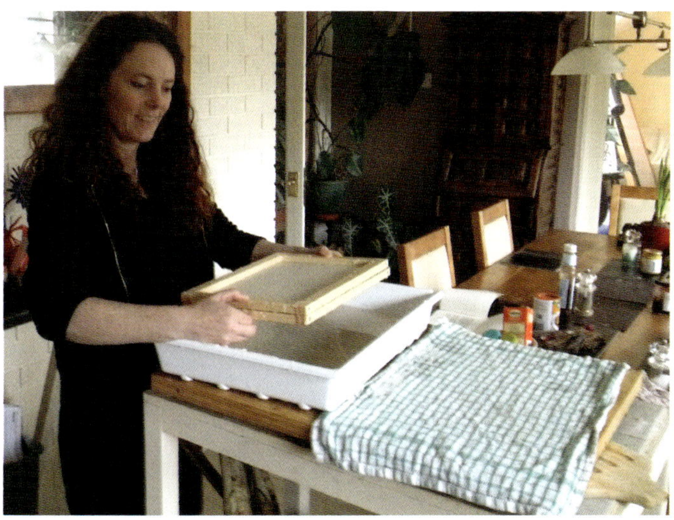

Here I am levelling a layer of the mushroom slush that I'd just blended onto the mesh, ready to place onto the towels in front.

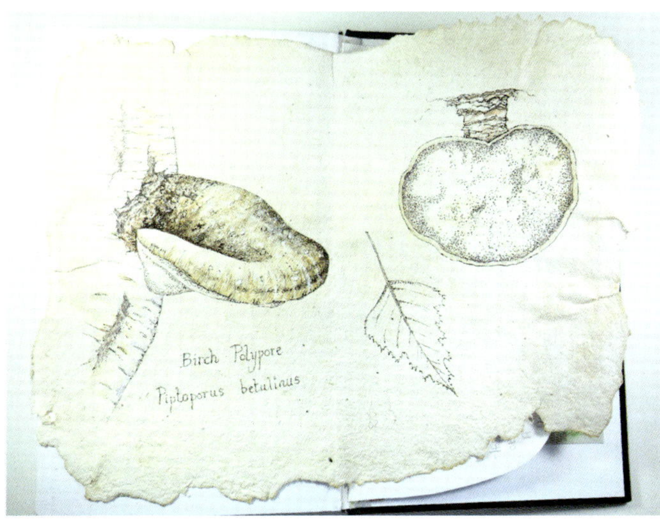

The finished drawing on the mushroom paper. It took the pen really well and even a little bit of watercolour. I note that this bracket has now had a name change from *Piptoporus* to *Fomitopsis*.

MISCELLANEOUS MATERIALS

The following equipment is useful for any art kit.

Erasers

This very handy tool for the pencil artist was discovered in 1770 by the English scientist Joseph Priestly, who also discovered oxygen. He observed that India rubber, a tree resin, could erase pencil marks on paper very well indeed. Before that, breadcrumbs were used to erase!

It's useful to have a few erasers for different purposes. Plastic/vinyl erasers are good for general erasing. Putty or kneadable erasers are good for lifting graphite before painting or creating highlights. Eraser pens are excellent for use in detailed graphite work, such as lifting thin lines of highlight or cleaning up edges.

Pencil Sharpeners

There are lots of different sorts of sharpeners and it really depends on your media; if you're getting into coloured pencils then a sharpener with a hand crank such as the Rapesco 64, or a battery-operated one could be a good idea but for graphite pencils you can get by with a small quality sharpener such as a KUM, or even just a sharp craft knife.

Tortillions and Blending Sticks

These are useful for blending dry media, especially graphite and charcoals. Tortillions are just tightly rolled up lengths of paper. Also available to buy are blending tools that have different shaped silicone tips – either rounded, flat or chisel shaped that are really useful for blending

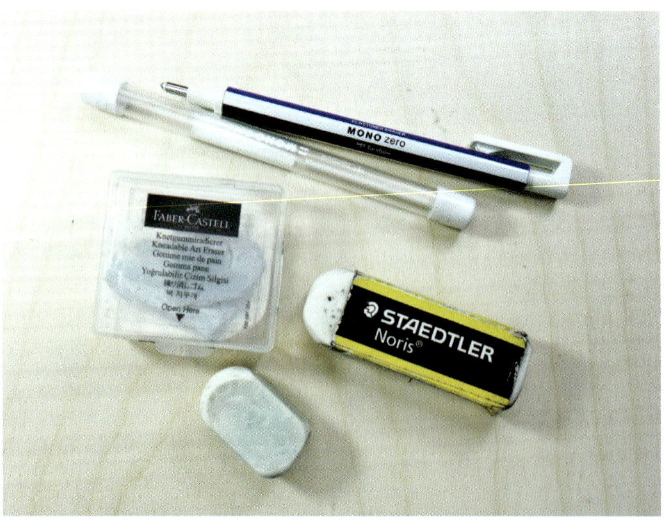

Erasers including the larger vinyl erasers, kneadable or putty eraser and the very useful Tombow Mono zero eraser pen that I wouldn't be without.

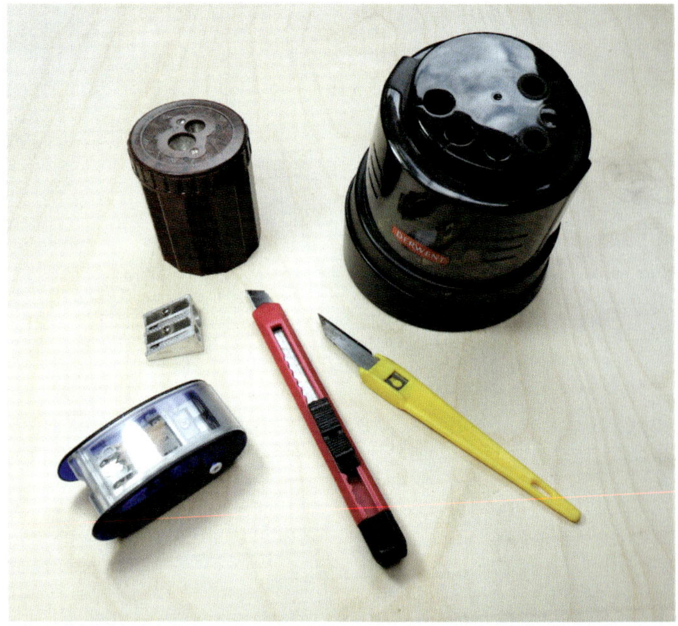

Various sharpening tools, including the KUM automatic long point sharpener at bottom left, an old trusty barrel sharpener, the large Derwent battery-operated sharpener and ordinary craft knives.

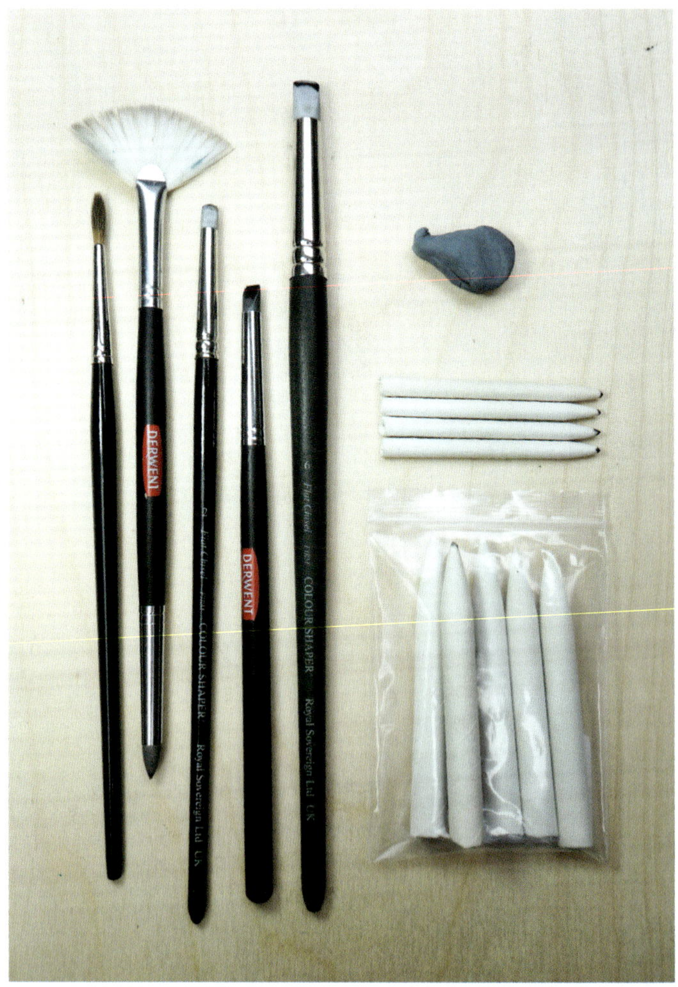

Blending tools including flat chisel silicone colour shapers, Derwent blenders with fan brush, assorted tortillion paper stumps and some kneadable eraser used for blending purposes only.

pastel or charcoals. But you don't have to buy anything to be able to blend; you can use a tissue wound up to a point, a kneadable eraser or a cotton wool bud (preferably a biodegradable one!).

Masking Fluid

This rubbery fluid is useful for watercolour techniques to preserve the white paper and give interesting effects. It is painted or drawn on with a suitable tool, from a cocktail stick or ruling pen to an old paintbrush dipped in washing up liquid to protect the hairs. When it has thoroughly dried, the painting can be worked on with whites fully protected. Then after the paint is dry it is carefully rubbed off to reveal the whites. It's great for experimenting with but test your papers before using, especially hot press papers, as some cannot take it, ripping up the paper surface on removal.

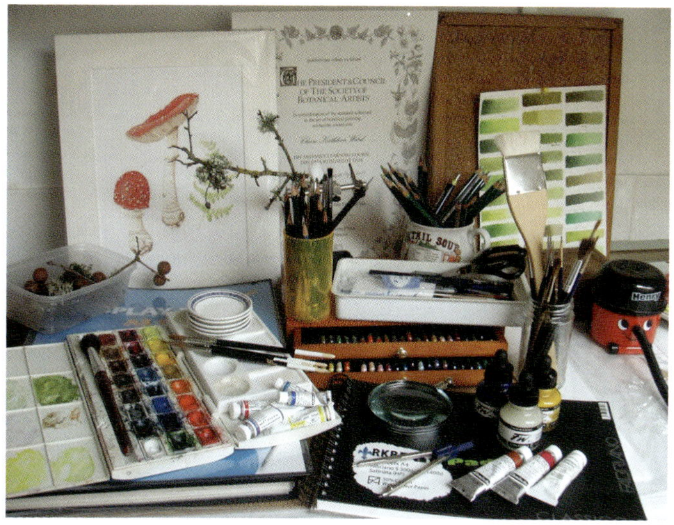

A little selection of items from the studio. It's amazing how much equipment is collected over time and hoarded.

STUDIO SETUP

Setting up a quiet and suitable workspace at home is a good idea. If you have somewhere that you can call a studio and be able to leave out your paints and work all the better, a spare bedroom or office or a quiet corner of the dining room. A comfortable chair is important and to be aware of your posture. Good lighting is vital and rooms with a north-facing window are the best, as they have a constant light all day with no full sun flooding in. It will be easier to colour match your subjects in this natural light as well. It can help to use extra illumination on your subject to accentuate contrasts. Lighting up subjects from the left is a convention in natural history illustration if you are right-handed. Swap it over if you're left-handed so that you don't shade your work while drawing. I use an ordinary movable Anglepoise lamp with a daylight simulation bulb in it to light up my subjects. These bulbs can be purchased in all good art stores and will always be superior to ordinary incandescent bulbs that give a warm yellow light and other lights may give a cooler bluer light.

It is very important to look after your eyes; this seems obvious, but using the best optics and glasses are essential, as are taking regular breaks when focusing on tight detail for too long as it can cause eyestrain.

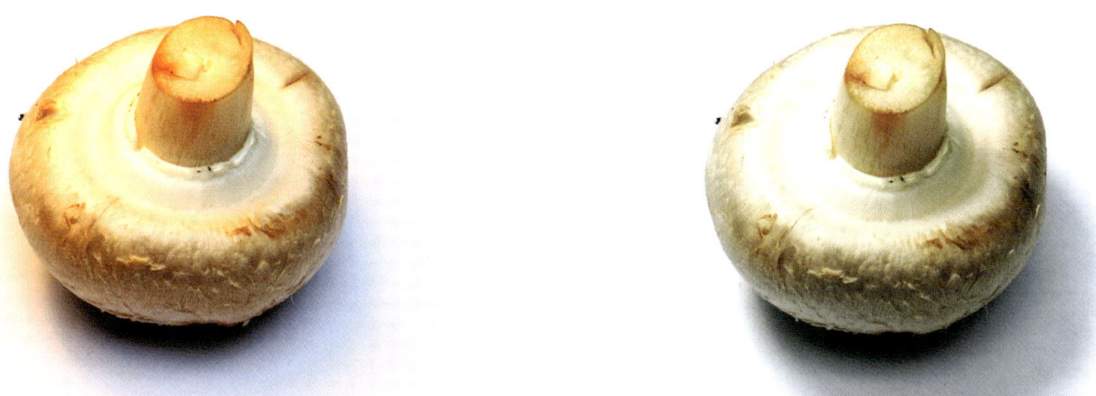

You can see the influence of artificial lighting on a white subject here. The first mushroom has a distinctly warm golden glow from an incandescent light bulb, whereas the second mushroom is lit up with a daylight simulation bulb.

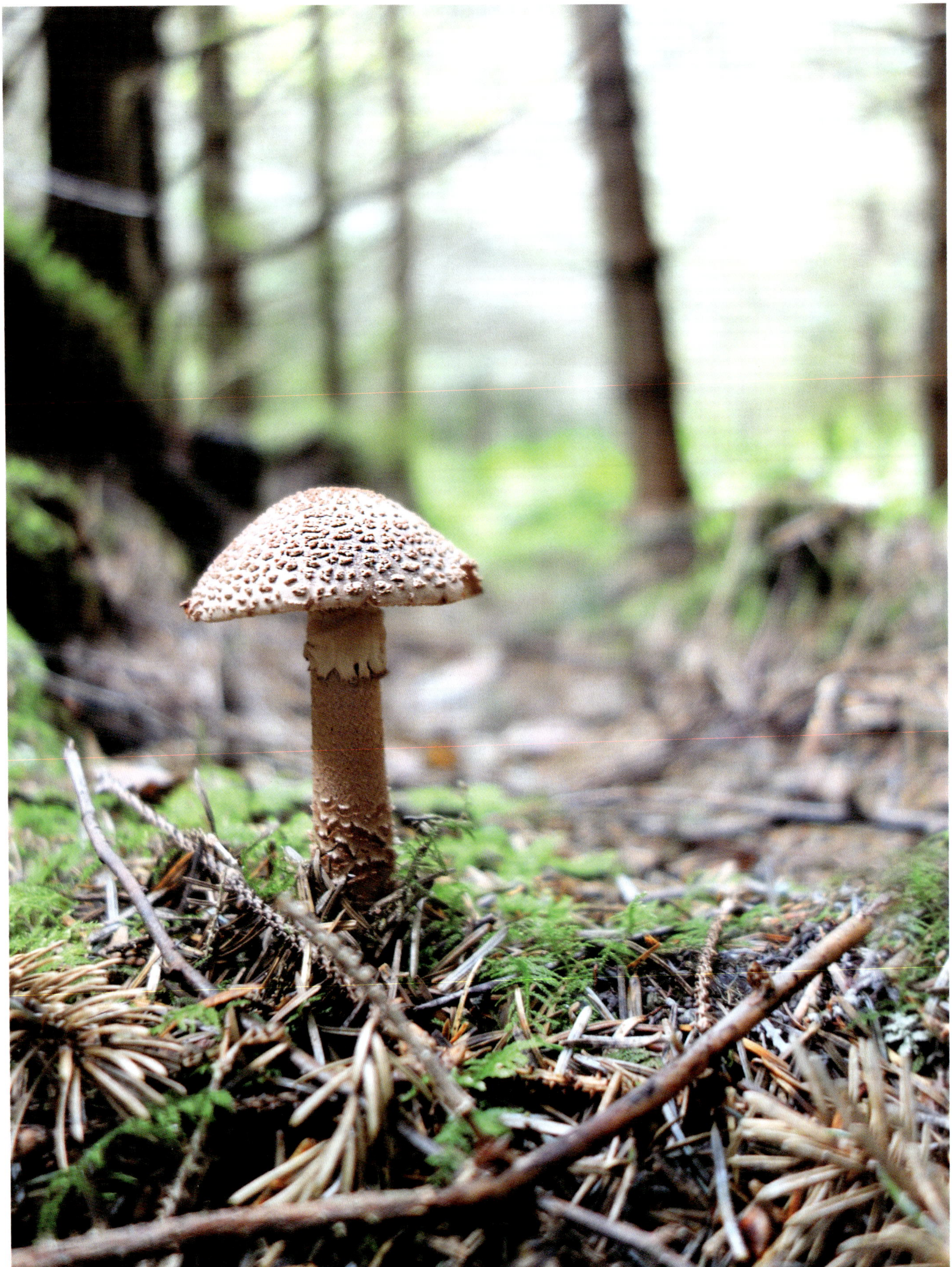

CHAPTER 2

FINDING SPECIMENS AND IDENTIFYING THEM

So now on to the hunt for interesting specimens to study and paint. You can head out alone or join a foray led by an expert. The fungal foray is the hunt for mushrooms in an organised group, perhaps with a local nature reserve, mycological society or wildlife centre. They have become popular now in many regions so look out for these events in your local area if it's something you'd be interested in. You can learn a lot about mushroom identification from a foray.

WHEN AND WHERE?

Mushrooms are synonymous with the summer's end and mostly appear in the autumn. This main fruiting season is quite brief, usually finishing at the first frosts. But there are some species that persist into winter, such as the velvet shank (*Flammulina velutipes*), winter chanterelle (*Craterellus tubaeformis*), blewits (*Lepista* spp.) and the herald of winter (*Hygrophorus hypothejus*).

Many bracket fungi can be found, some lasting all year as they are composed of tougher material. They sprout from rotting stumps, logs, and are found hidden in old hedging as well as higher up on tree trunks, so it's worth looking up as well as down.

There are a few species that can be found in spring, such as morels, St George's mushroom (*Calocybe gambosa*), spring fieldcap (*Agrocybe praecox*), some cup fungi such as elf cups and the strange little forms of bog beacons (*Mitrula paludosa*). Then in summer, some *Amanita* spp., *Russulas* spp., puffballs, chanterelles and boletes among others, may appear especially after damp, cool spells, so it's well worth keeping an eye out for them all year round.

It pays to revisit a great woodland for fungi a few times over late summer – sometimes I have missed the best crops and when I get there the mushrooms are slug-eaten and maggot-infested or bleached beyond recognition from the sun!

An issue of our times is litter. A few times I've gone after a crumpled takeaway coffee cup or bright bit of plastic thinking it was an interesting fungus to be found, and I end up going home with litter to dispose of instead of a mushroom to draw!

The Blusher – *Amanita rubescens* showing off its textured scales in my local conifer woodland.

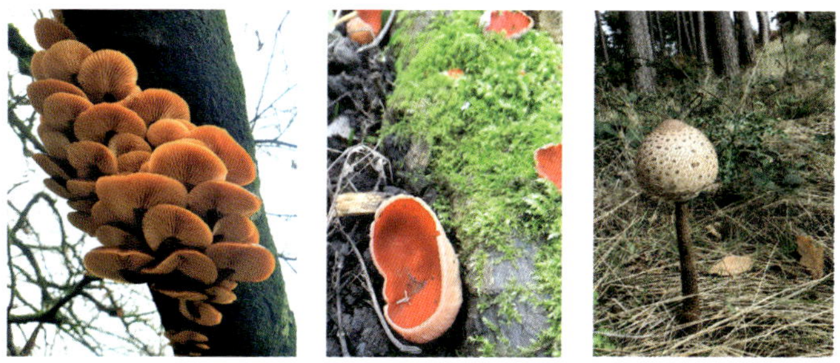

From left: Velvet shanks are found growing gregariously on tree trunks in the winter months. The vibrant scarlet elf cup can be seen in spring and sometimes as early as January. The elegant parasol can be seen in late summer gracing woodland edges, roadside verges and meadows.

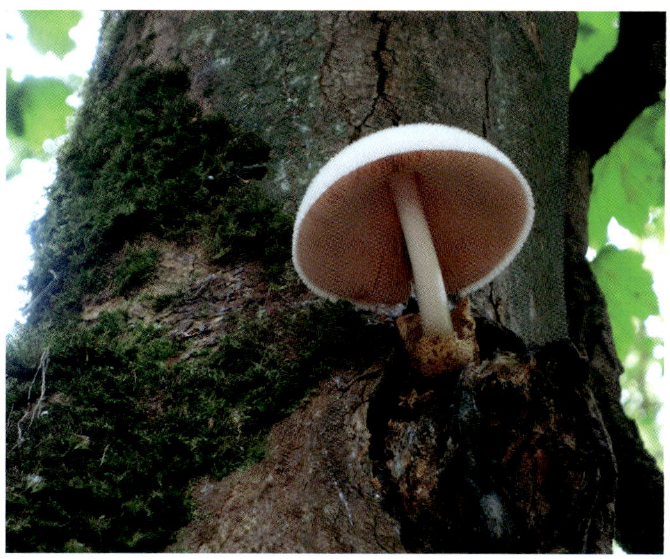

Silky rosegill – *Volvariella bombycina* – is a beautiful and quite uncommon mushroom that can be found sprouting higher up in trees from knots or decay. So it pays to look up as well as down.

It can help to know your trees when hunting down a specific woodland species. Many fungi grow in a symbiotic relationship with certain trees, such as the brown birch bolete (*Leccinum scabrum*) whose common name helpfully states its tree partner. So, knowing what fungi grow with which trees can be a help. Some fungi don't seem as fussy, such as the chanterelles, which grow with a variety of tree species. Others are found in just conifer or broad-leaved forests. The trees that seem to have the most mycorrhizal relationships in the UK are oak, beech, birch, Scot's pine and spruce. There are many more tree species on other continents and in other places some fungi may associate with different tree species. Mycorrhiza actually means 'fungus root', and different species work in different ways with the trees' roots; they can reside within the root cells – endomycorrhizas – or surround the outside of the roots – ectomycorrhizas. They cause no harm to the trees but make them grow stronger by increasing their uptake of water and nutrients.

A few species may prefer a particular soil type, such as morels and the panther cap (*Amanita pantherina*), both preferring a more base-rich or calcareous soil while others, such as the bay bolete, favour more acidic soils. Others are species of grasslands, such as the waxcaps (*Hygrocybe* spp.) and in some countries such as the US, waxcaps can be found growing in woodlands too, so fungi may favour different habitats according to your region. In the UK, productive waxcap meadows tend to have a good covering of moss and are free of intensive farming practices such as fertilising or ploughing.

While out in meadowland or similar habitats, you may come across a 'fairy ring', which is a roughly circular group of mushrooms sprouting from the edge of their underground mycelium. The grass may be growing better or greener with the additional help of the mycelium in the line of the ring also.

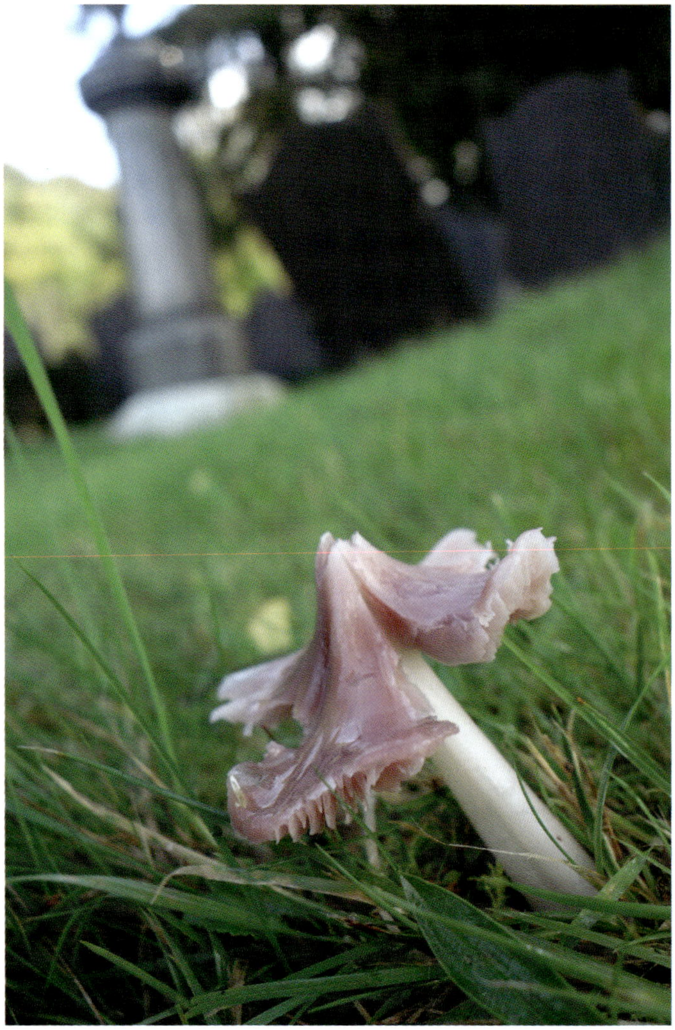

Beautiful ballerina waxcaps are very often found in graveyards and cemeteries as long as they are sensitively mown and it's best that the grass trimmings are moved aside so as to not raise the soil fertility.

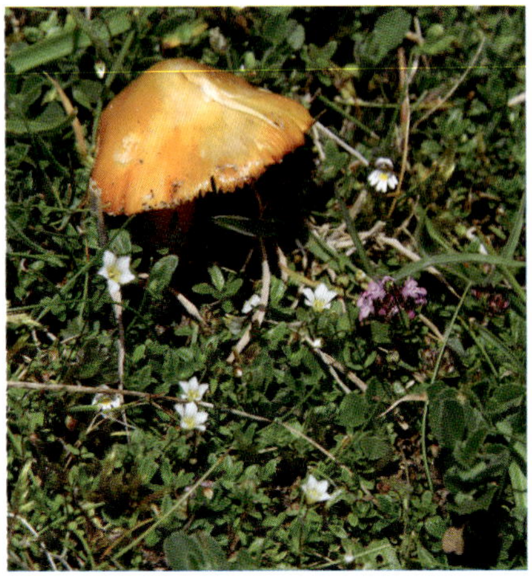

A colourful waxcap species in a summer meadow with flowers. Some waxcap species can emerge early in summer if weather conditions are suitable; they can add colour to meadows as early as June.

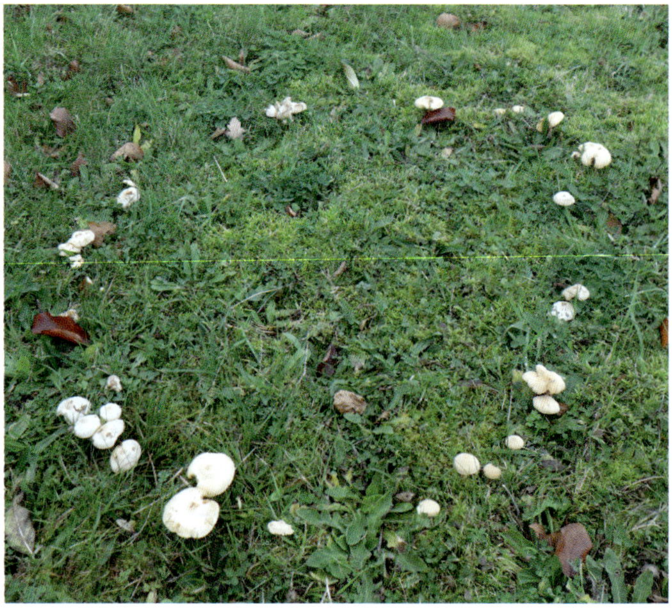

A fairy ring. Here are some common field mushrooms – *Agaricus* sp. – that I came across growing in a ring formation on a local football field.

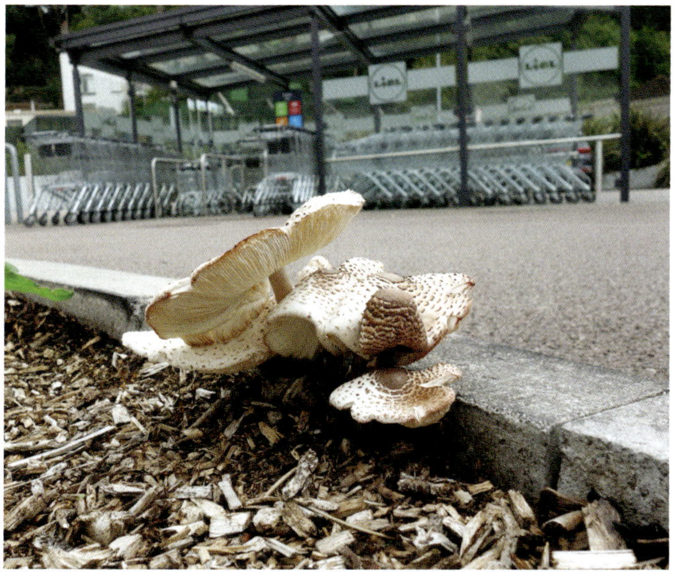

I found this beautiful species of *Lepiota* growing at the road's edge on woodchip in a supermarket car park, so you never know where they might pop up!

The forest and the meadow are the two main and obvious places to look, but it may be worth scouting local sand dunes and their dune slacks, heathland and bogs, lawns, parkland, gardens where woodchip has been spread and old graveyards. This last place may be unusual, but these quiet and peaceful places are like an oasis and can be a treasure trove of waxcaps and other delights, especially if the site has been sensitively mown.

Coal spoil heaps and contaminated land can be cleaned up by fungi, as they are able to break down toxic pollutants within the soil into more basic compounds and render them harmless. But because of this, it's worth noting that fungi growing on contaminated sites take these poisons into their fruiting bodies and so must never be eaten. There has also been research to show that wild fungi take up radioactive compounds into their tissues. Certain species of ectomycorrhizal fungi had the highest concentrations of radiocaesium within them, thought to be left over from the Chernobyl disaster.

IS IT POISONOUS?

> 'All mushrooms are edible, but some are edible only once.'
>
> EASTERN EUROPEAN QUOTE

As there are many species of poisonous plants around the world, so there are also many poisonous species within the fungi kingdom, some of which are deadly, so it is wise to be careful when handling unknown fungi. Always try to identify them correctly at least to the genus. If you are sure that you have a deadly mushroom, then you can choose to leave well alone or wear gloves to hold them for any length of time, just to be cautious; you would need to eat them to cause any reactions, but I have known of psychosomatic symptoms after handling poisonous fungi and so wearing gloves will remove this fear. It is wise to treat fungi with the utmost care and respect.

I wouldn't recommend it, but if you decide that you want to eat any fungi after you paint, it is wise to study and completely familiarise yourself with all the listed deadly mushrooms or get the advice of an experienced forayer or mycologist. There are many lookalike mushrooms or poisonous mushrooms that look similar to edible ones, so only ever eat fungi that you are 100 per cent sure of. Personally, I'm not keen on them to eat so any I've picked, I just paint and then leave them in my garden for any hungry creatures to snack on.

A few years ago, I found a saffron grisette (*Amanita crocea*) on a road verge that I was able to take home to paint. Afterwards, I placed it under the birch trees in my garden to allow the spores to disperse and for it to return to the earth. Two years later, in late summer, two saffron grisettes popped up under the birches – a fantastic surprise!

BEAUTIFUL – BUT DEADLY!

The deadliest mushrooms have fascinating and fearful names such as these:

Death cap – *Amanita phalloides*
Destroying angel – *Amanita virosa*
Western North American destroying angel – *Amanita ocreata* (US)
Eastern destroying angel – *Amanita bisporigera* (US)
Panther cap – *Amanita pantherina*
Fool's conecap – *Conocybe filaris*
Deadly webcap – *Cortinarius rubellus*
Fool's webcap – *Cortinarius orellanus*
Funeral bell – *Galerina marginata*
Deadly galerina – *Galerina autumnalis* (US)
Fool's funnel – *Clitocybe rivulosa*
Ivory funnel – *Clitocybe dealbata*
Angel's wings – *Pleurocybella porrigens*
False morel – *Gyromitra esculenta*
Deadly fibrecap – *Inocybe erubescens*
Deadly dapperling – *Lepiota brunneoincarnata*
Fatal dapperling – *Lepiota subincarnata*
Brown roll-rim – *Paxillus involutus*

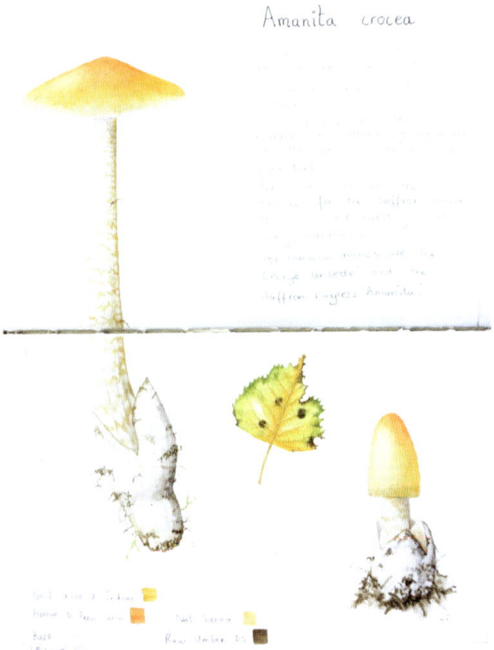

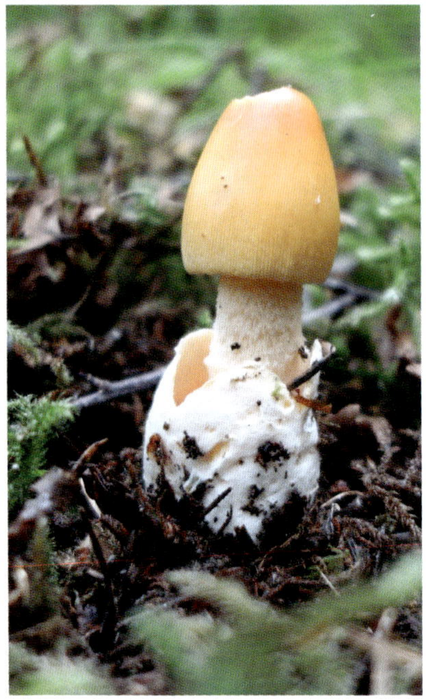

Sketchbook study of the saffron grisette seen sprouting from its large volva, a characteristic of the *Amanitas,* found growing underneath the birch trees in my garden.

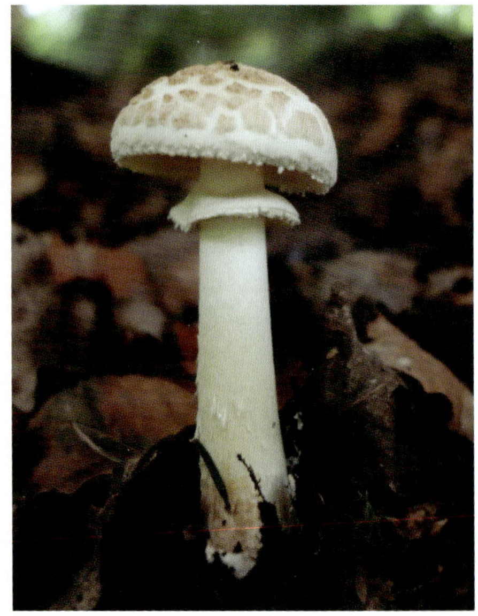

False death cap – *Amanita citrina.* This mushroom grows commonly in broad-leaved woodlands. It has a lemony yellow colouration to the cap, often with scales, and smells of raw potatoes unlike the death cap, with its smooth cap and sweet scent.

The poisonous lookalikes include:

Yellow stainer – *Agaricus xanthodermus* – that looks like the field mushroom, *Agaricus campestris.*

The false chanterelle – *Hygrophoropsis aurantiaca*, the jack-o'-lantern – *Omphalotus olearius* and the Eastern jack-o'-lantern – *Omphalotus illudens* (US) – all of these species can look like the common chanterelle – *Cantharellus cibarius.*

False morel – *Gyromitra esculenta* – can look like the true morels – *Morchella* spp.

Angel's wings – *Pleurocybella porrigens* – can look like oyster mushrooms – *Pleurotus ostreatus.*

Death cap – *Amanita phalloides* – the young emerging mushrooms of this can look like puffballs from the genera of *Lycoperdon, Calvatia* and *Calbovista* spp. So extra caution is needed here. This *Amanita* and many others contain the lethal mycotoxin *Amanitin*, which causes terrible sickness symptoms for a few days. Then a false sense of wellness comes over the sufferer before the liver fails and they finally succumb to death.

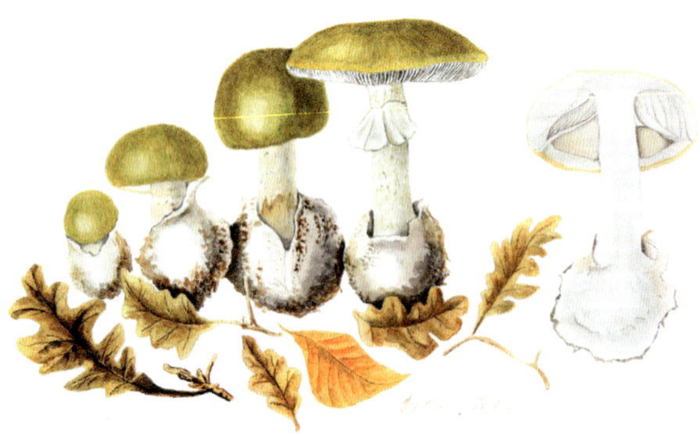

Death Caps – *Amanita phalloides* by Kathleen Baker. These mushrooms have a greenish colour to their caps and the very characteristic pronounced volva of this species. You can see their progression well here from button to full grown. (© Kathleen Baker)

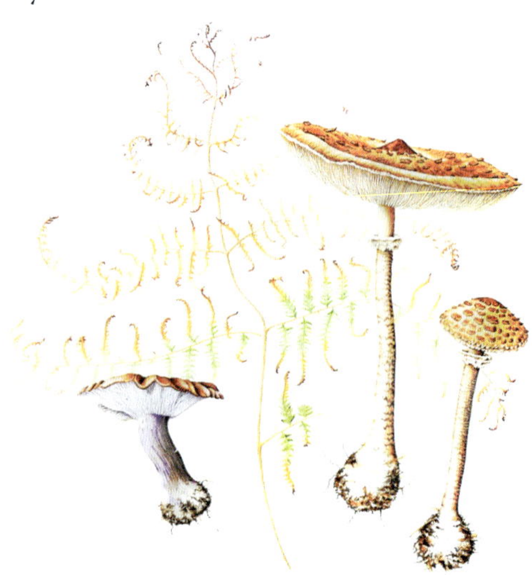

Parasols and wood blewit in watercolour, both apparently very tasty edible species that I found growing together on a road verge with lots of bracken, but there is no mycorrhizal link here.

FUNGI CHARACTERISTICS TO IDENTIFY

The part of the fungus that we actually see, the mushroom, is really only the fruiting body which produces masses of spores. One way that fungi are classified is by the structure of the parts that produce these spores. The Kingdom of Fungi is split into groups: the *basidiomycetes*, or 'club' fungi, which comprises the typical agaric type mushrooms, among others, and the *ascomycetes*, which includes the stranger looking cup and sac fungi. We will look at these individual groups in more detail in later chapters.

The Structure of the Agarics

Agarics are the typical, gilled mushrooms of species such as the *Amanitas*, and the usual edible mushrooms that we find in a supermarket. It is an ancient word from the Greek *agarikon*, which means 'of the countryside'.

Looking at the *Amanita* spp; when these mushrooms first appear, some of them sprout from an egg-like form,

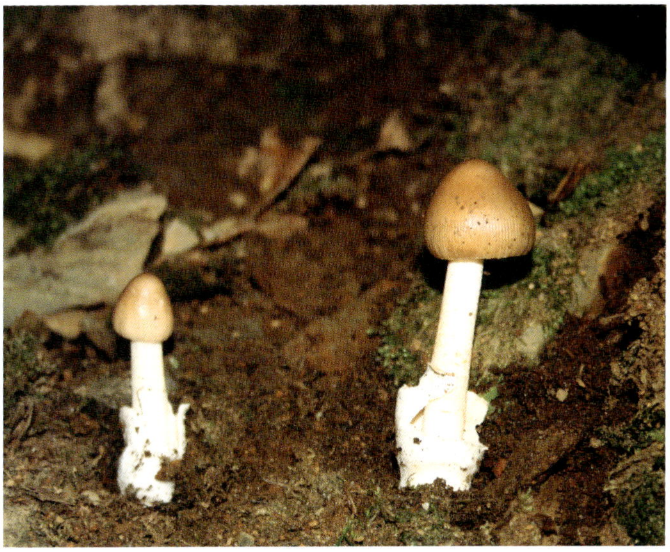

Two Tawny Grisettes – *Amanita fulva* with the distinct cup-like structure called the volva at base. These *Amanitas*, however, do not have a ring on their stipes.

referred to as a button, which is covered by a membranous tissue called the universal veil. The mushroom expands quickly by taking on water and as it grows, it splits open the veil tissue and in some, leaves behind a cup-like structure called a volva. It is remnants of this veil membrane that may create scales or warts on the cap, as in the fly agaric. The volva can be hidden in soil or leaf litter so it's important to check the base for signs of this.

The *Amanitas* also have a partial veil, which is a membrane that extends from the upper stem to protect the forming gills and then eventually splits open to become a ring or *annulus* on the stem. Other agaric-like mushrooms will have some or all of these characteristics to look out for. Species from the *Cortinarius* genera have a partial veil that gives the young specimens a fuzzy, cobweb-like coating called a *cortina* and it is this characteristic that gives the genera its name. This feature also gives them their common name of webcaps.

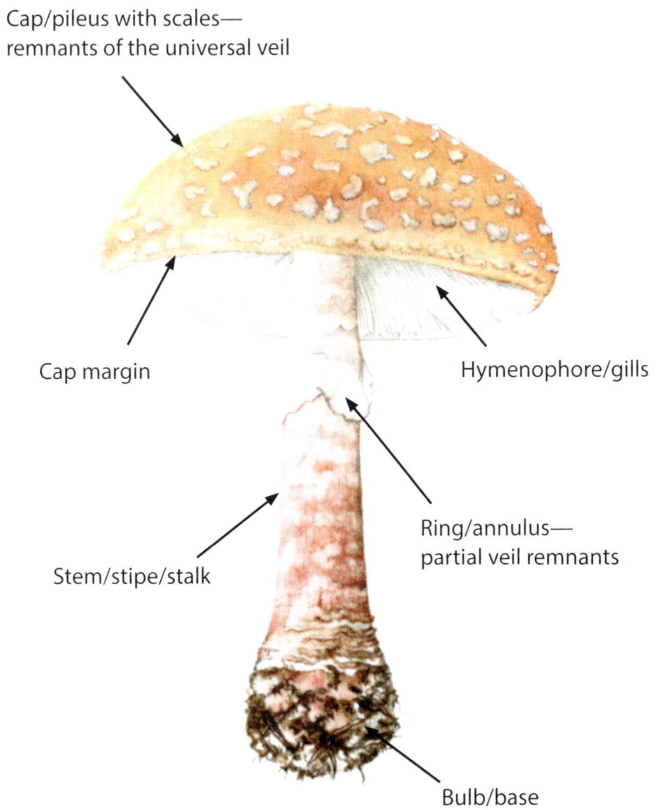

Amanita rubescens - The Blusher

The structure of a typical mushroom form. This is *Amanita rubescens* – The Blusher, one of the 'friendly' *Amanitas* that has a blushed red stem.

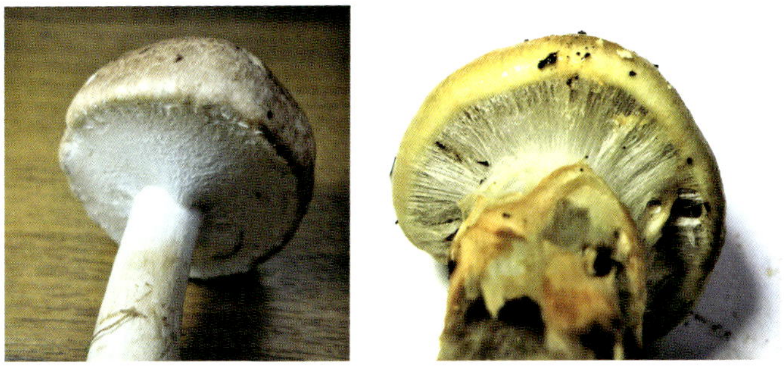

On the left is a young *Agaricus* sp. that has a cottony partial veil covering the gills and when the cap swells with growth, it will tear away to form a ring around the stem. On the right is a species of *Cortinarius* that is showing the fuzzy protective webbing covering the gills, called a *cortina* and characteristic of this genera.

ON THE FORAY

When out on the fungal foray it is important not to stray onto private land and to gain any landowner's permission. It's best practice not to pick from nature reserves and Sites of Special Scientific Interest (or SSSIs) or if you think you have discovered a rare species. This is when working in the field will be the best option and I will give more information on this in the next chapter.

Also, if you're out foraying alone and afar, let people know where you've gone and when you're likely to be back home.

THINGS THAT MAY BE USEFUL TO TAKE OUT WITH YOU ARE

- A bag or basket which can hold containers in to protect them while in transit (a fishing tackle box can hold smaller specimens in for a short while)
- A pocket knife, handy but not essential
- A small mushroom guidebook (if not too heavy)
- Some tissues or wet wipes, to keep clean
- A camera or phone for photographic reference – make sure the battery is fully charged!
- Notebook and pen
- Sketching kit (we'll look at this in more detail in Chapter 3)
- Walking boots and depending on weather conditions – waterproofs, sun cream, sun hat or gloves and warm hat
- A stick can be useful, to move foliage away or to carefully move debris in order to check the bases of specimens. It could be a stick or twig that you find while out
- Insect repellent to ward off mosquitos, horseflies or ticks. To deter ticks, wear long-sleeved shirts and long trousers; wear pale clothes so that ticks can show up on them and be easily seen, and tuck your trousers into socks or boots. Some essential oils can be a beneficial, non-toxic alternative here, especially lemon, lemon grass and lavender but I've also found that horseflies hate Vicks VapoRub (or similar), which is useful as long as you like eucalyptus!

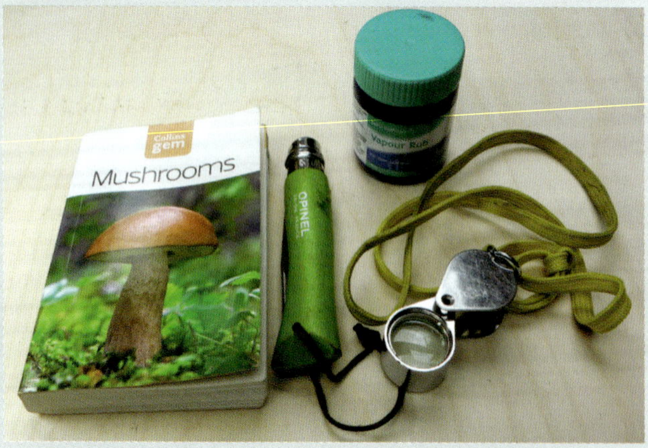

On the hunt for fungi with small ID book, pocket knife, hand lens and not forgetting the VapoRub!

Collecting and Recording

When you've found an interesting specimen, make notes describing the habitat (*see* the first notes on habitat coming next). You can make a life-size field sketch if the weather allows and take photographs. If you'd like to take it home to study further, first look for any volva at the base that may be hidden under the soil or leaf litter that could aid identification. Then gently twist the mushroom out of the ground. Don't dig the mushroom up too deeply, as that could damage the mycelium. It's worth saying that the most damage to mycelium comes from trampling while harvesting, so tread lightly. Brush off any dirt and store it in a paper bag, or other container and place in your basket or bag, protecting it from being crushed. I sometimes collect a few small brown paper bags from the veg section in the supermarket to use, or just store in an old Tupperware container. When collecting, there's no need to over-pick them; just take one or two if they are different sizes and take photographs for reference if needed. Don't pick them if you think they are a rare species or there is just one. A lot of people who gather mushrooms for the pot use slatted baskets or netted bags to allow the spores to disperse through the holes while still walking around the habitat.

Look for all of the characteristics listed here, either in the field or as soon as you get back home. It's worth mentioning that if you are studying your fungal finds back in the studio, then open a window for some ventilation, as some people may be allergic to certain spores just as they may be to pollen.

Habit and Habitat

- Is the specimen growing on its own (singular), scattered apart – perhaps in a ring, or in a group (gregarious)? If in a group, are they joined at the base?
- Make a note of where the fungus is growing and what it's growing on; for example, broad-leaf woodland, open grasslands, in a plantation on needles, or on a dead conifer stump.
- Record the date and location name.
- Is it growing under a certain tree, maybe pine, oak or birch? This can really help to confirm an identification. Collect some of the leaf litter, leaves or bits of moss found with it.

There are specific names that you can use to describe the growing habitat:

Terrestrial – on soil
Lignicolous – on wood
Coprophilous – on dung

Fly agarics have a mycorrhizal relationship with birch trees; as you see here, many can appear under birches, but they can also be seen with conifers too.

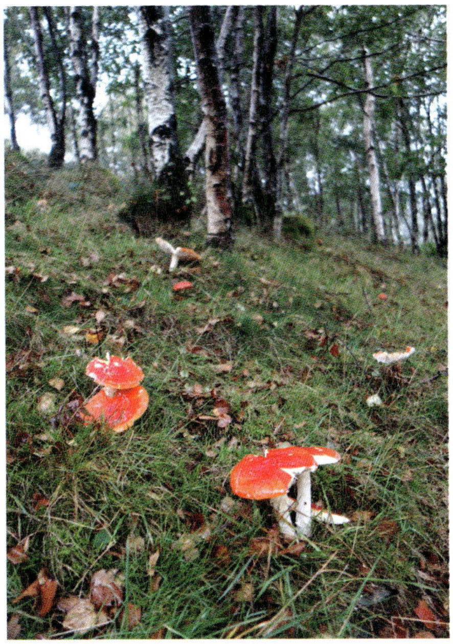

Cap/Pileus

- Note its size, shape, texture and colour; also note any colour change on drying – called *Hygrophanous* (*see* notes on colour on page 42).
- Is there any colouration or bruising on cutting?
- Look for striations (streaks or grooves) and the presence of scales or warts.
- Is it dry, sticky, or slimy – *viscous*?
- What's the texture like – is it velvety, smooth, or shaggy?
- Is the cap margin wavy or in-rolled?

SHAPES OF CAP

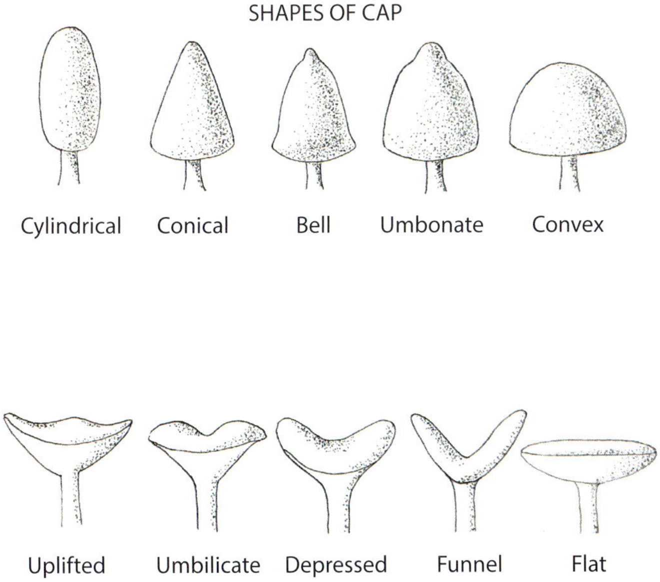

There are so many variations on the shapes of the cap for different species. Here are a few of the important ones to note that could help to visualise their shapes.

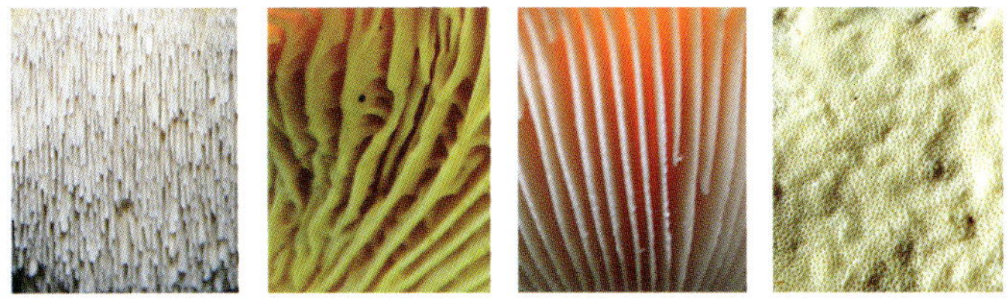

What's under the cap? Mushrooms don't just have gills; here there are spines, false gills, true gills, and pores.

Gills, Pores or Spines?

- Examine where and how they are attached to the cap and stipe. For instance, decurrent gills run down onto the stipe.
- Also notice their colour, shape and whether they are crowded together or widely spaced.
- Do they bruise or change colour when touched or damaged?

GILL ATTACHMENTS

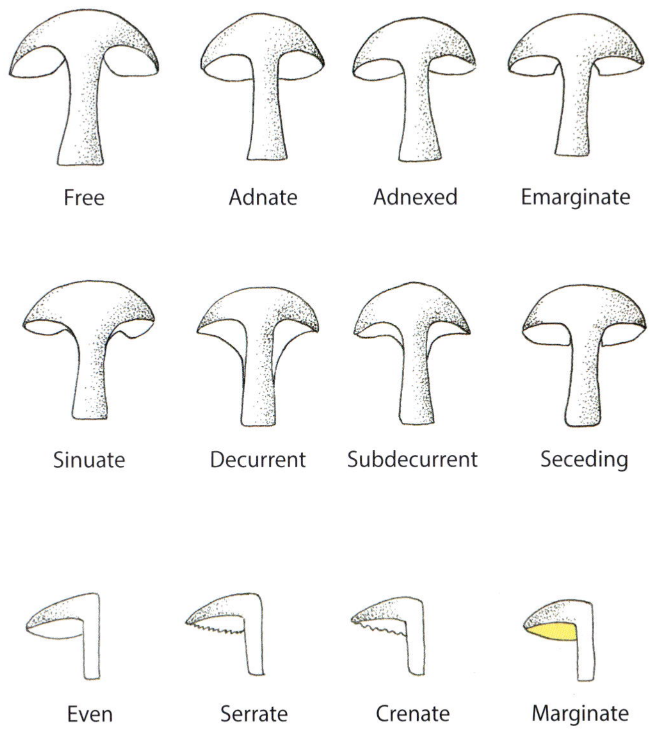

Free – gills not attached to stipe; Adnate – widely attached; Adnexed – narrowly attached; Emarginate – notched before attaching; Sinuate – notched before running a little way down; Decurrent – running down stipe; Subdecurrent – briefly running down; Seceding – attached but starting to break away.

Gills may have differing edges: even or serrated, crenate is scalloped and marginate is of a different colour.

GILL SPACINGS

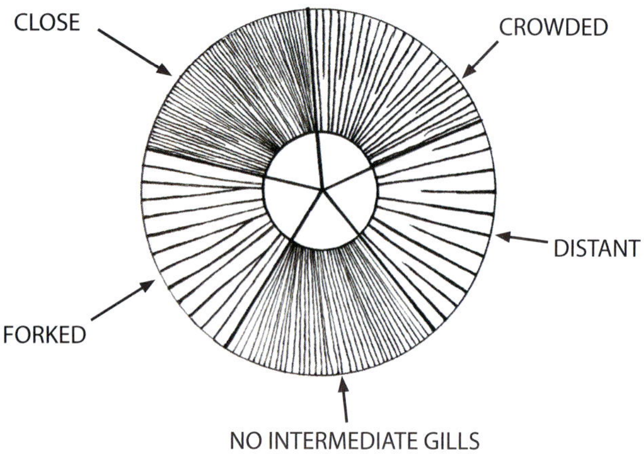

Gills can be spaced out differently, from extremely close together gradually getting further apart in distance. They can be forked, have intermediate gills or not, and also some are anastomosing, which means that the gills form small, ridged connections between each other.

Stalk/Stipe

- Measure its height and width and note its shape, colour and texture; some can be really fibrous, and others can be viscous or slimy.
- Check for the presence of a ring or skirt (this is also called an *annulus* and is a remnant of the partial veil).
- Always remember to check the base; is there a cup-shaped volva, does the stem taper down to it, or is it bulbous or rounded? Are there any textures or concentric rings? Is it a different colour?
- Some stipes can have interesting patterns, including a net-like pattern that is called *reticulation*. Others can be covered in scales (squamose), tiny dots (punctate) or lines (striate).

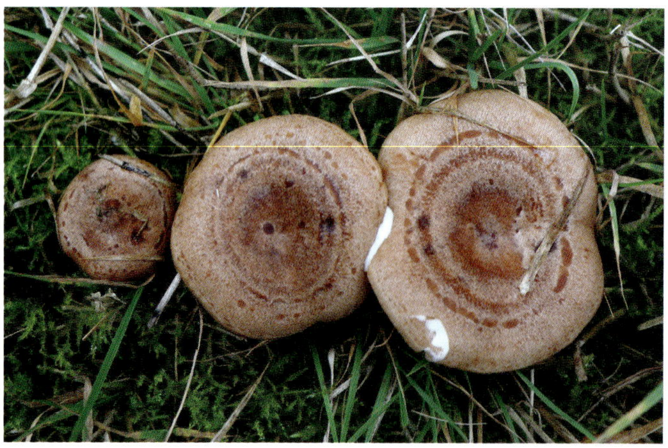

Here you can see a lovely group of Milkcaps – *Lactarius* sp. some releasing milk where they've been damaged – note the concentric ring patterns on the cap.

STIPE BASES, BULBS & VOLVAS

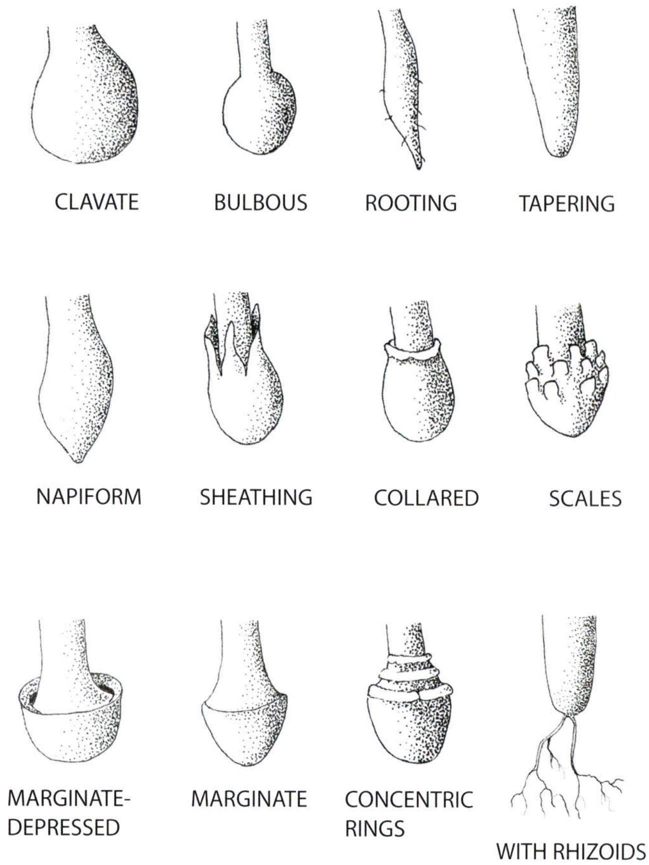

The stipes can feature so much diversity with many different types of base to them. Six different types here are a feature belonging to the *Amanita* family: the sheathing, collared, scaled, both marginate types and the concentrically ringed base.

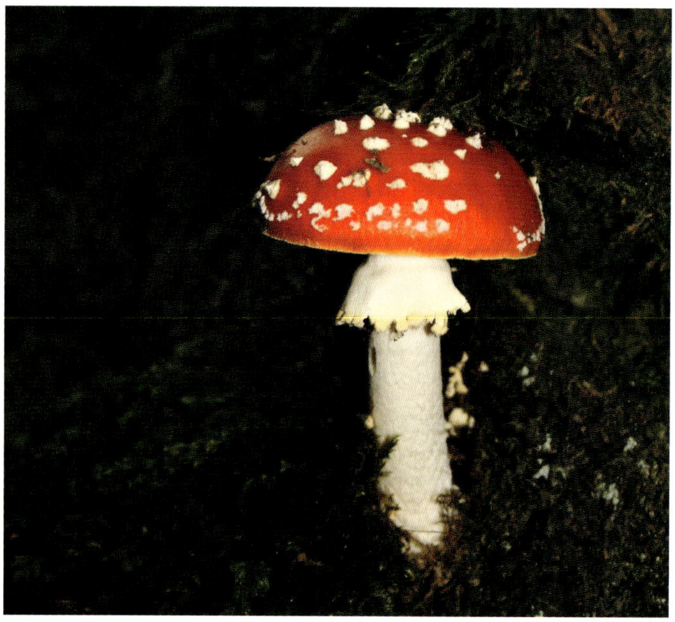

The fly agaric with a showy ring or *annulus* on its stipe; not all *Amanitas* have a ring on their stipes but those that do, note their textures – some rings are smooth, and others are grooved and this can be an important characteristic.

Flesh

- Record its colour, plus any changes in colour when the flesh is broken or bruised.
- What is the consistency? Firm, soft, spongy, delicate, brittle, tough, and so on.
- Examine its texture and check for the presence of latex or 'milk'. If you find any, note its colour and whether it changes colour as it dries.

Smell

- Do the fungi smell of anything? Most will just smell earthy, but you may be surprised by some and this can be an important and interesting characteristic. You may come across such aromas as coal tar, ammonia, stewed apples, burnt rubber and raw potatoes.

Among my favourite mushroom aromas are the fragrant aniseed funnel (*Clitocybe odora*) that smells like a sweet from my childhood, the aniseed ball, and the cedarwood waxcap (*Cuphophyllus russocoriaceus*). This is a small white mushroom with the strong aroma of cedarwood or Russian leather. Another strange smell also belongs to a waxcap (*Neohygrocybe ovina*) which is described as having a chemical or nitrous odour but to me smells just like a carpet shop – the aroma of Carpetright! That's the thing with mushroom aromas; they are very subjective and what can smell delicious to one, can smell awful to another.

Another intriguing little mushroom is the mousepee pinkgill (*Entoloma incanum*) found in alkaline meadows. It can smell of mouse urine as the common name suggests and has a distinctive yellow stipe with bright turquoise green base.

Fungi Aroma Chart

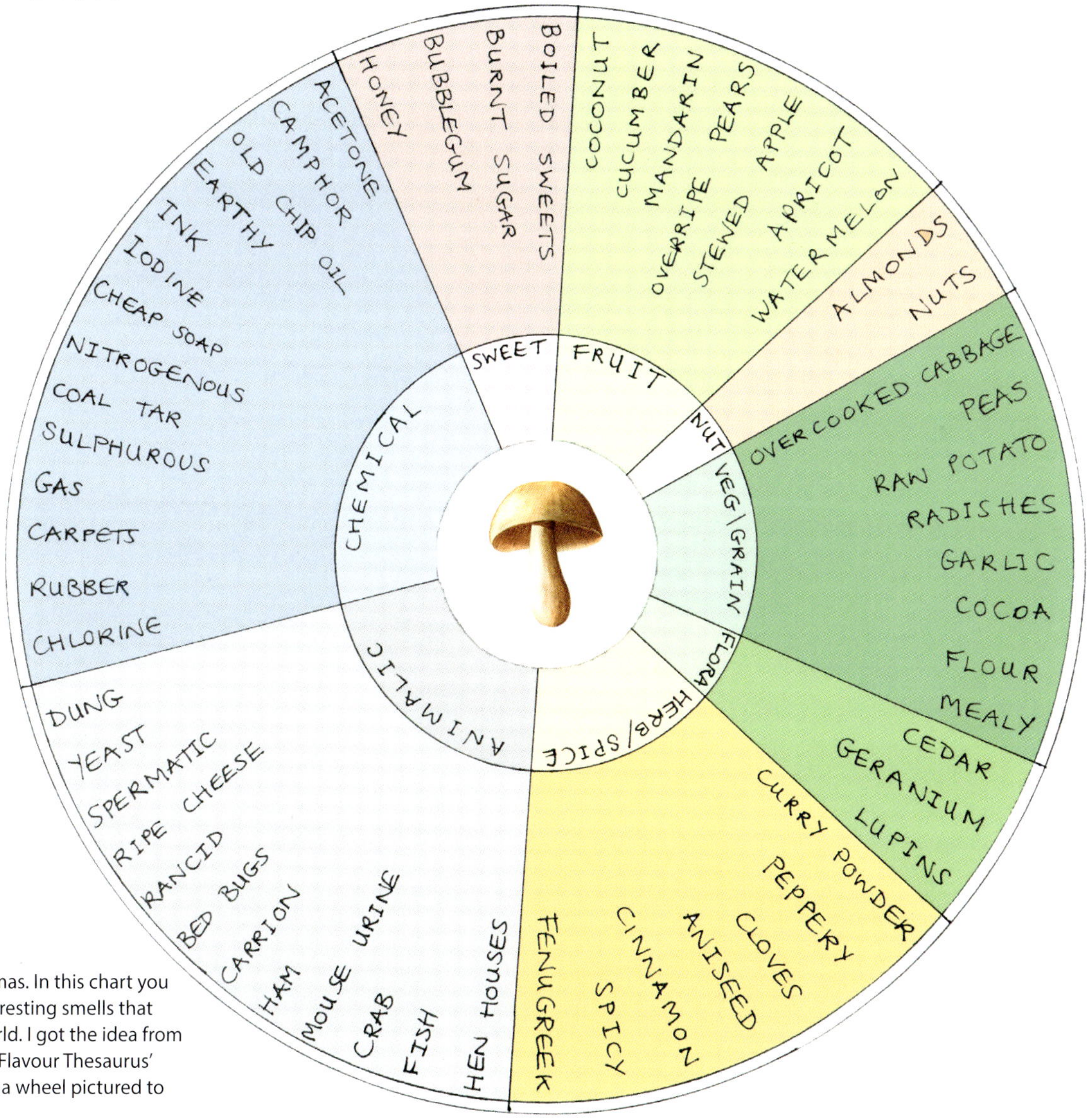

The wheel of mushroom aromas. In this chart you can see the different and interesting smells that can be found in the fungi world. I got the idea from a book that I own called 'The Flavour Thesaurus' by Niki Segnit, where there is a wheel pictured to categorise flavours.

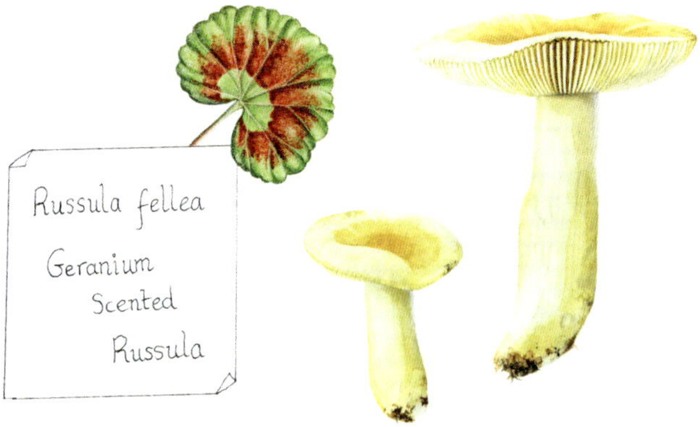

Russulas can be hard to identify but *Russula fellea* is quite easy owing to its aroma. To me some did smell like stewed apples, but a few did really smell like pot geraniums (*Pelargoniums*).

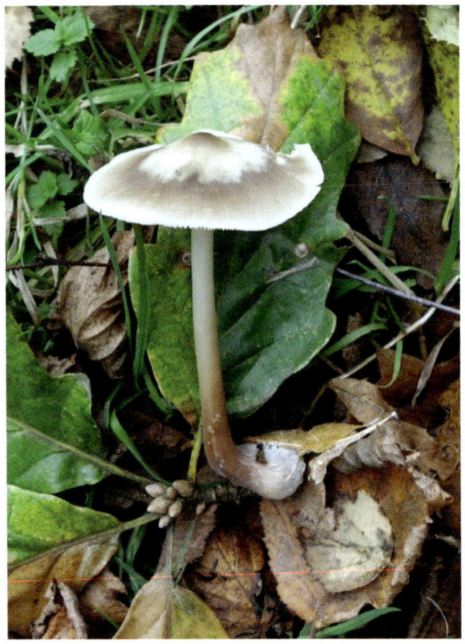

This photo displays the two-tone effect termed as *hygrophanous* on the cap of the butter cap – *Rhodocollybia butyracea.*

Taste

Experienced forayers use taste as a diagnostic, but beginners should avoid this aspect for obvious reasons! So be sure to only use taste when you have learnt all the deadly poisonous species that there are out there.

To taste a mushroom, just a tiny piece is bitten off and then spat out completely afterwards. Some have tastes described as hot, acrid and sweet. Some are more specific, such as garlic.

Colour

Colour is one of the most important characteristics used in the identification of mushrooms and is likely to change drastically as the mushroom dries. This is termed as *hygrophanous* and mostly gives a two-tone effect to the cap.

Bright colours in nature tend to attract animals to eat them and this is one way to spread spores. Others may need to be camouflaged within the soil and leaf litter to enable them to reach maturity and hence sporulation; perhaps this is why there are so many little brown mushrooms. Some colours fade quickly and may change even before the mushroom has got back to the studio. That is why it's important to take colour notes and photographs in the field, or get back home to draw and paint swiftly. The specimens must be drawn straight away as the longer they are left, the more they will start to dry up, shrivel and change. Some may even be a home for hidden insects or larvae that may eat up your drawing subject before you've had a chance to draw it! Indeed, mushrooms don't stay whole for long, being a tasty food for many creatures.

Some mushrooms have a different toned cap when fresh and they change as they mature, either becoming lighter or darker. Environmental conditions such as sunlight or

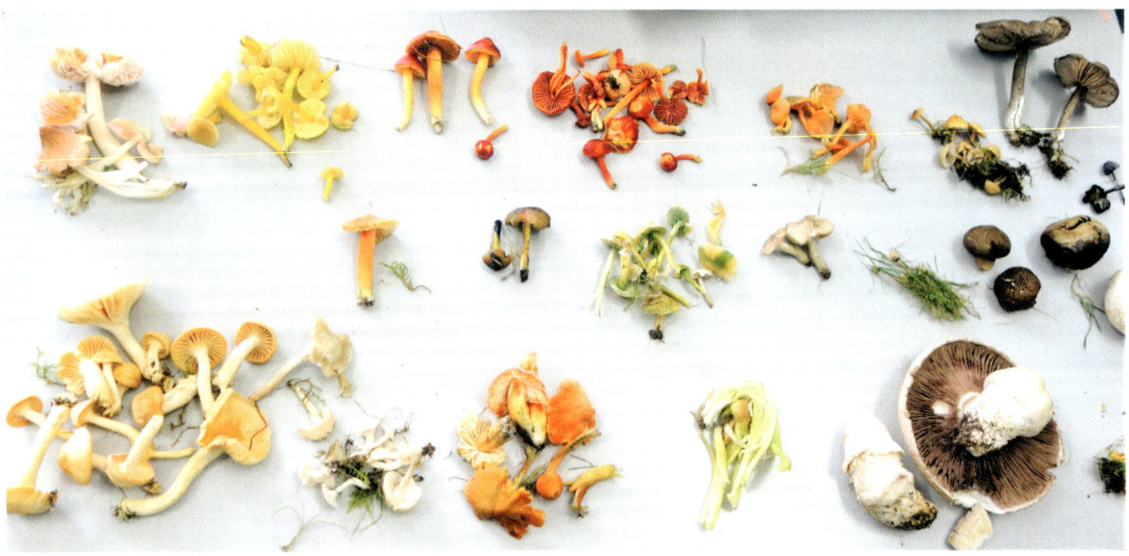

An array of grassland fungi with the most colourful being the jewel-like waxcaps. This table was set up at a waxcap workshop that I attended.

humidity can cause variations in cap colours and tones as well. Colour can be bleached out by sun or washed off with rain.

Some mushrooms do have flesh that can change colour when bruised or cut. This can happen very quickly after the damage to the flesh, but could take longer in some species. Some boletes are called blue boletes and they change to a very vivid bright blue when bruised or cut. This occurs when different acids found in the flesh, such as variegatic acid are being oxidised by the air in the presence of oxidase enzymes.

Fungi are known to produce a wide array of pigments such as the maroons of anthraquinones, the yellows of carotenoids, the reds of naphthoquinone and the browns and blacks of melanin.

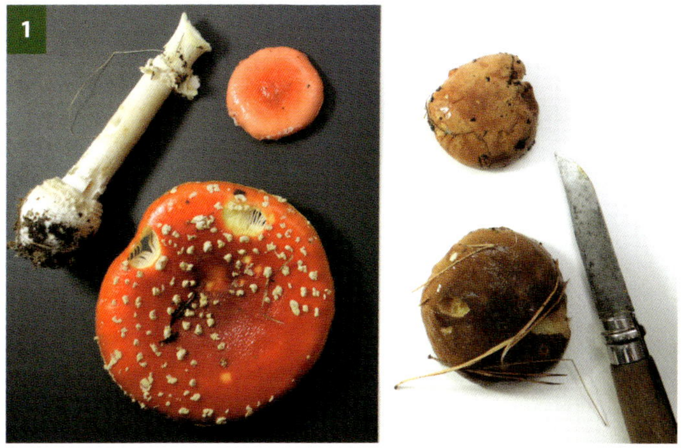

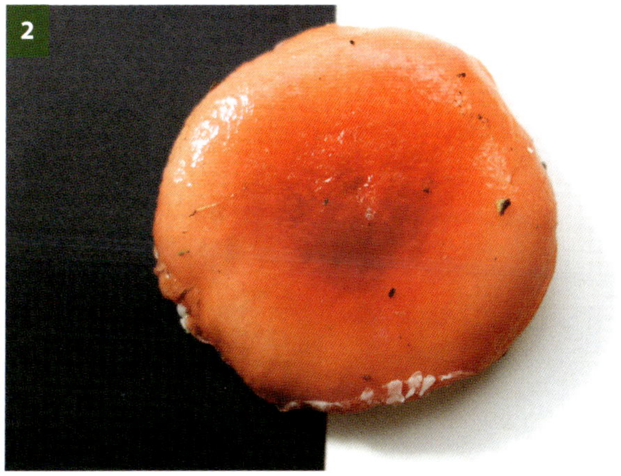

Spore Prints

After drawing your subject, you may want to take a spore print. These are a great help with the identification of your subjects as each genera have a specific colour to their spores. The colours include white, which is the most common, cream, pink, brown, rust, black, purple-brown, lilac-grey and yellow. If you want your spore prints to last, you could try very carefully spraying with a fixative.

Step 1: To make a spore print, get some black and white paper ready. If the paper is very thin it may buckle if the mushroom cap is damp. Cut off the stipes to your mushrooms and place onto the paper colour that you think will show up the spore deposit.

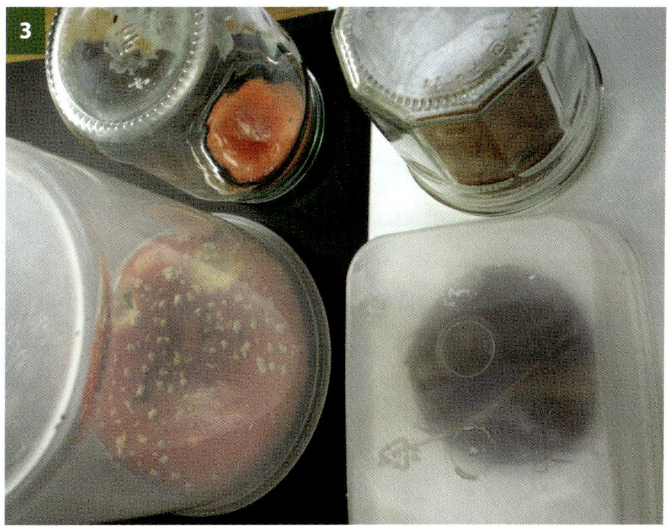

Step 2: If you're undecided whether there will be a light or a dark spore deposit, then just place the mushroom cap halfway over both black and white paper.

Step 3: Cover your fungi caps with a jar, a cup or a lid of some sort with a drop of water on the cap if it's very dry. Then leave for a few hours or overnight to let the spores drop onto the paper, showing the colour and pattern of gill arrangement.

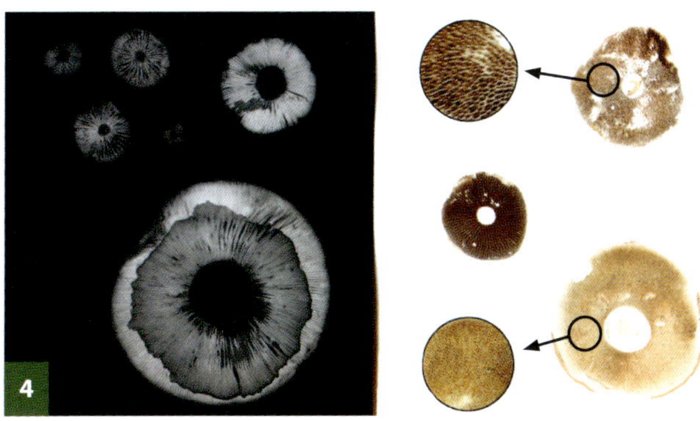

Step 4: After carefully lifting off the lids, you can then use the colour of the spores and the other noted characteristics to find out the genus using a key in any good mushroom guidebook. Here on the black paper you can see the smaller waxcaps, fly agaric and *Russula nobilis* showing their white spore gill patterns. On the white paper at the top is *Chalciporus piperatus*, in the centre a *Cortinarius* species and at the bottom is *Suillus luteus* with much smaller pores. The pores have been enlarged to show the different structures.

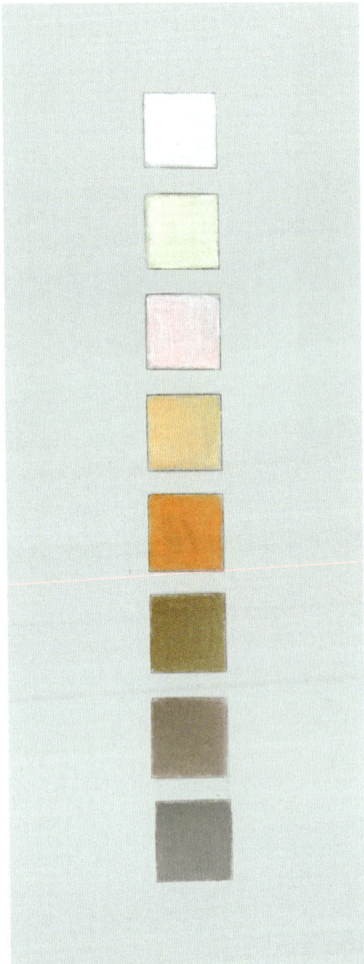

White - *Hygrocybe, Russula, Lactarius, Lepiota, Laccaria, Amanita, Clitocybe, Mycena, Tricholoma, Pleurotus, Collybia*

Cream - *Melanoleuca, Calocybe, Lactarius, Armillaria*

Pink - *Lepista, Volvariella, Clitopilus*

Salmon Pink - *Pluteus, Entoloma*

Rust - *Cortinarius, Conocybe, Galerina*

Light Brown - *Inocybe, Hebeloma, Agrocybe, Suillus,* some *Boletus*

Dark Brown - *Hypholoma, Agaricus, Stropharia, Geastrum, Scleroderma*
Violet brown

Black - *Coprinus, Psathyrella, Panaeolus, Lacrymaria*

A spore colour chart using pastel pencils on grey toned paper. It shows the families that are associated with each spore colour. White is the most common colour for spores.

Which Species is it?

Spore prints will help you get your subjects into their correct families, but some will certainly have you scratching your head and are notoriously hard to identify to species level. There are so many unidentifiable little brown mushrooms (sometimes labelled as LBMs!) so it can be enough to just get the subject to genus level. Ultimately it is up to you how far you want to take the identification and how important it is to you. If you want to be really accurate and look for positive IDs, then the aid of a microscope can help to be able to view the spores and other micro features. You will also need certain chemicals to help show up the details better. Fungi have translucent cells that are very hard to see and so stains and reagents are used to make them stand out and be seen, often giving stunning colours and interesting contrasts.

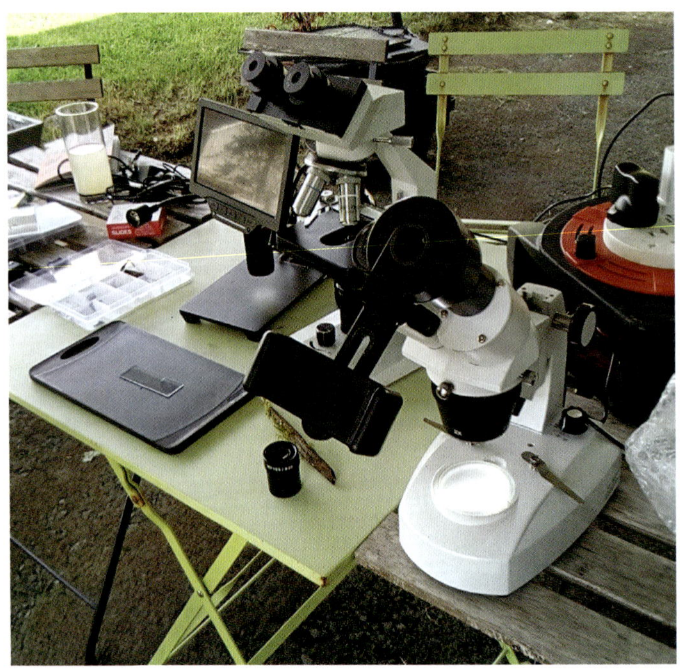

A table set up for some microscope work for studying tiny ascomycetes.

Some species have beautiful spore structures such as the brittlegills – *Russulas* spp. that have interesting knobbly spores. This could be an extra element to research

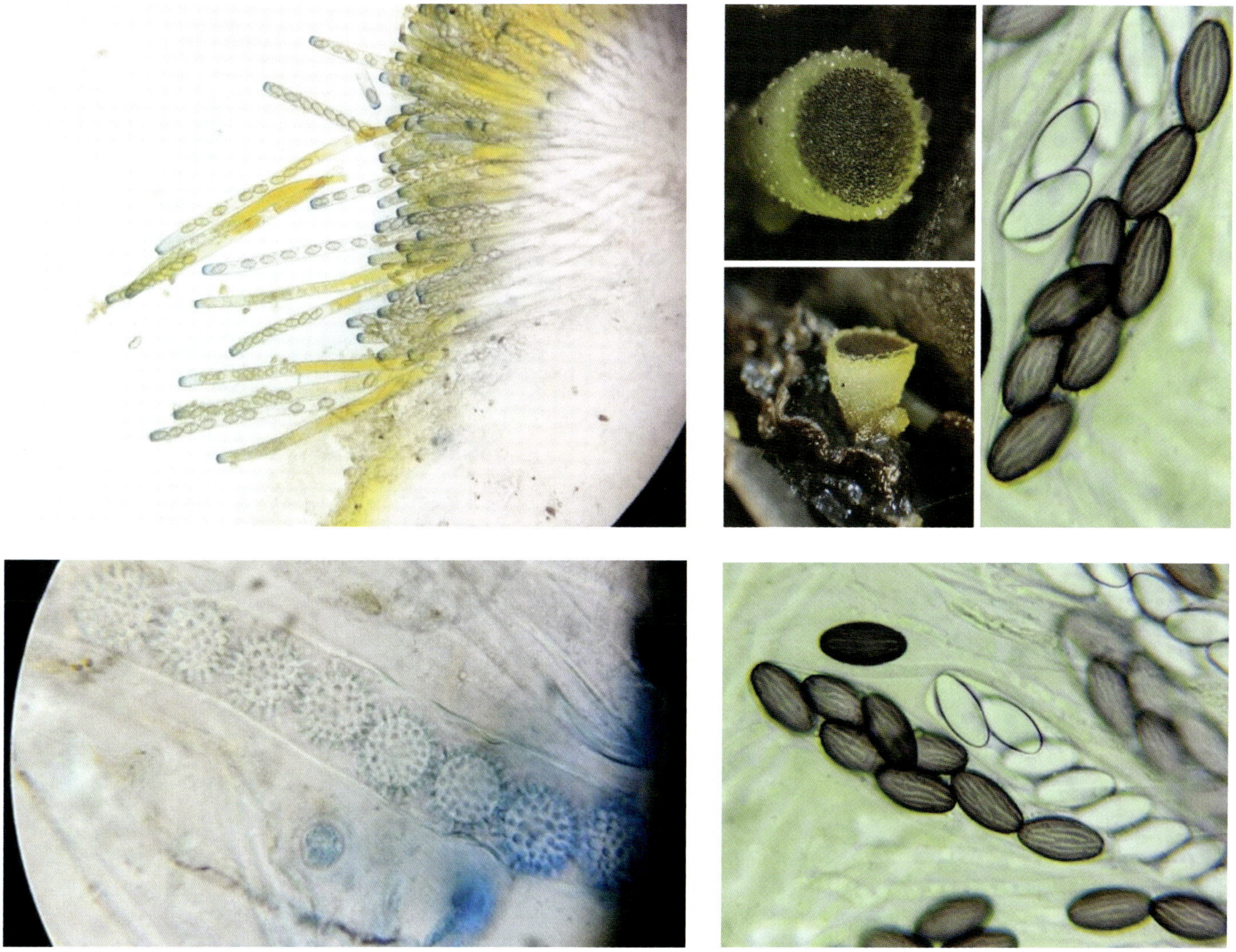

A fantastic collage by mycologist Emma Williams. Top left – *Peziza* sp. with meltzers for staining. Below left – The warted spores of *Scutellinia trechispora* within the asci, using stains to show them up, Right – *Ascobolus* spores.

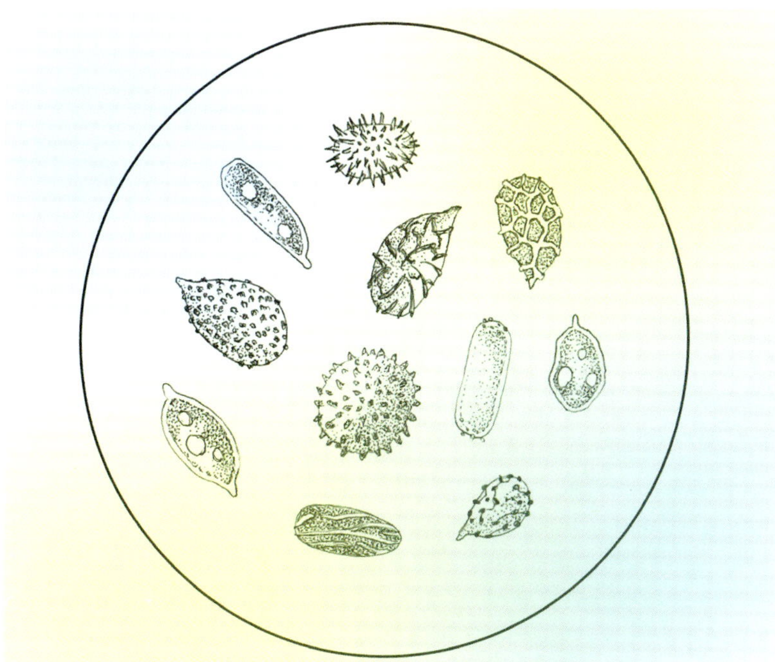

Spores make interesting studies drawn in pen while viewed under the microscope. The round composition gives the feel of the microscope view.

if you are interested in the miniscule and have access to a microscope. It could open up a whole new world of fascinating forms to draw and study. You'd need a microscope with a minimum magnification of 400x, and up to 1000x is ample.

Sp. or Spp.

If you're not sure of the species name, then just write the genus name plus 'sp.' for a single species and genus plus 'spp.' if it's plural and concerning a group of species within that genus.

Another way to help with Identification is to photograph the subject with clear shots of gills, stem and cap, and good notes on habitat and so on, then post to groups on social media such as the British Mycological Society and the North American Mycological Association, among others, for help. There are also Identification apps available on phones too, but I'm not sure how good they are.

THE CONSERVATION OF FUNGI

Fungi have always been under-studied and their study is underfunded, considering how important they are. Loss of forests are devastating to many species, and there could even be species that haven't been discovered yet being lost. This loss of biodiversity is damaging to our ecosystems and to us ultimately.

Fungi are certainly not as protected as mammals and birds, but some things are changing for the better. In my area, the charity Plantlife UK has a waxcap surveying scheme that is attempting to find out the numbers and locations of these beautiful species, which are threatened with industrial farming and agricultural methods such as fertilising and ploughing.

It can sometimes be difficult to judge how rare a species is; it may just be under-recorded for various reasons, such as erratic fruiting, being hidden under leaf litter or just being very small and overlooked! Even mycologists and lichenologists are rarer than some of the species themselves! But generally, some fungi are declining due to pollution, climate change and loss of habitat. It is simple, though – look after the habitat and the fungi will look after themselves.

Foraging has become a common pastime now, thanks to celebrity chefs and health fads but respect is due and it's a shame that forests are being stripped bare of fungi. This pastime can be sustainable as long as some are left to sporulate and feed other creatures in the ecosystem. In the UK, large-scale foraging for restaurants in forests has become more of a threat in recent times. Now all mushroom picking has been banned in the New Forest in the south of England, in order to reverse any damage done to that environment by over-picking or trampling. In the USA too, fines are issued now for anyone caught picking or foraging in certain reserves.

I do see picking a mushroom as quite similar to picking an apple from a tree; it is just the fruit body and so if the mycelium is not damaged it shouldn't cause any issues to the main underground body of the fungus, but that doesn't mean that they can and should all be picked. The most important thing is to leave some mushrooms where they are to be able to spread their spores, for other people to appreciate or for creatures to munch! Dangers come with heavy trampling and raking of sites, which has been shown to have an impact on fruiting numbers in subsequent years. But ultimately, it's not the picking that's the crime, it's the loss of habitats.

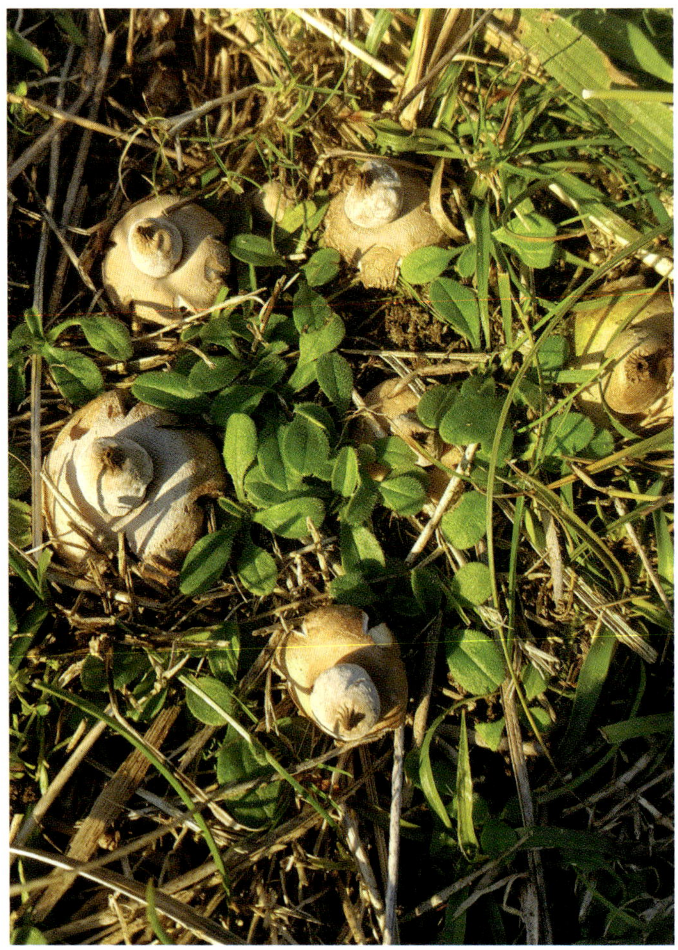

A conservation species, the rare elegant earthstar – *Geastrum elegans* found in my local sand dunes. An example of when to use field sketches and photograph reference only.

There are fungi classed as endangered species and so considered rare and they are listed upon the European 'Red List' covering twenty-three countries. This classification makes it illegal to collect any of those listed under the Wildlife and Countryside Act of 1981. So, any listed rare species found are for studying in the field and taking photos only. If you think you may have found a rare or an interesting species in the UK, you can report it to the LERC in your area (Local Environmental Records Centre). I use the LERC Wales app on my phone to record interesting findings, sending them a photograph of the species with location and date.

The app 'what3words' may be helpful for finding locations that you may wish to revisit.

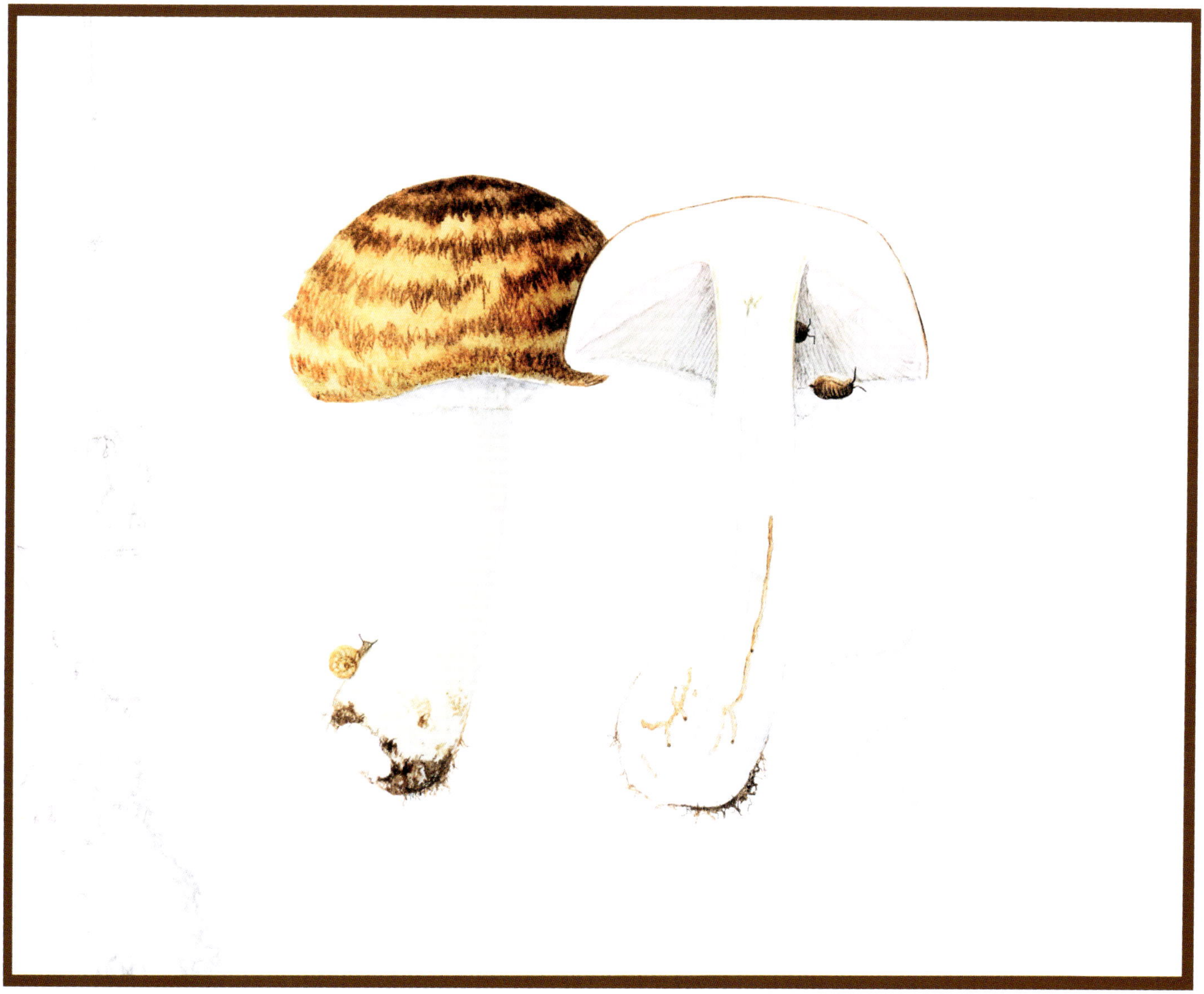

Fungi are such an important food source for many invertebrates. A longitudinal section of this *Agaricus* species reveals its secret occupants: a family of woodlice, maggots and a tiny snail; something to remember when taking fungi back to the studio.

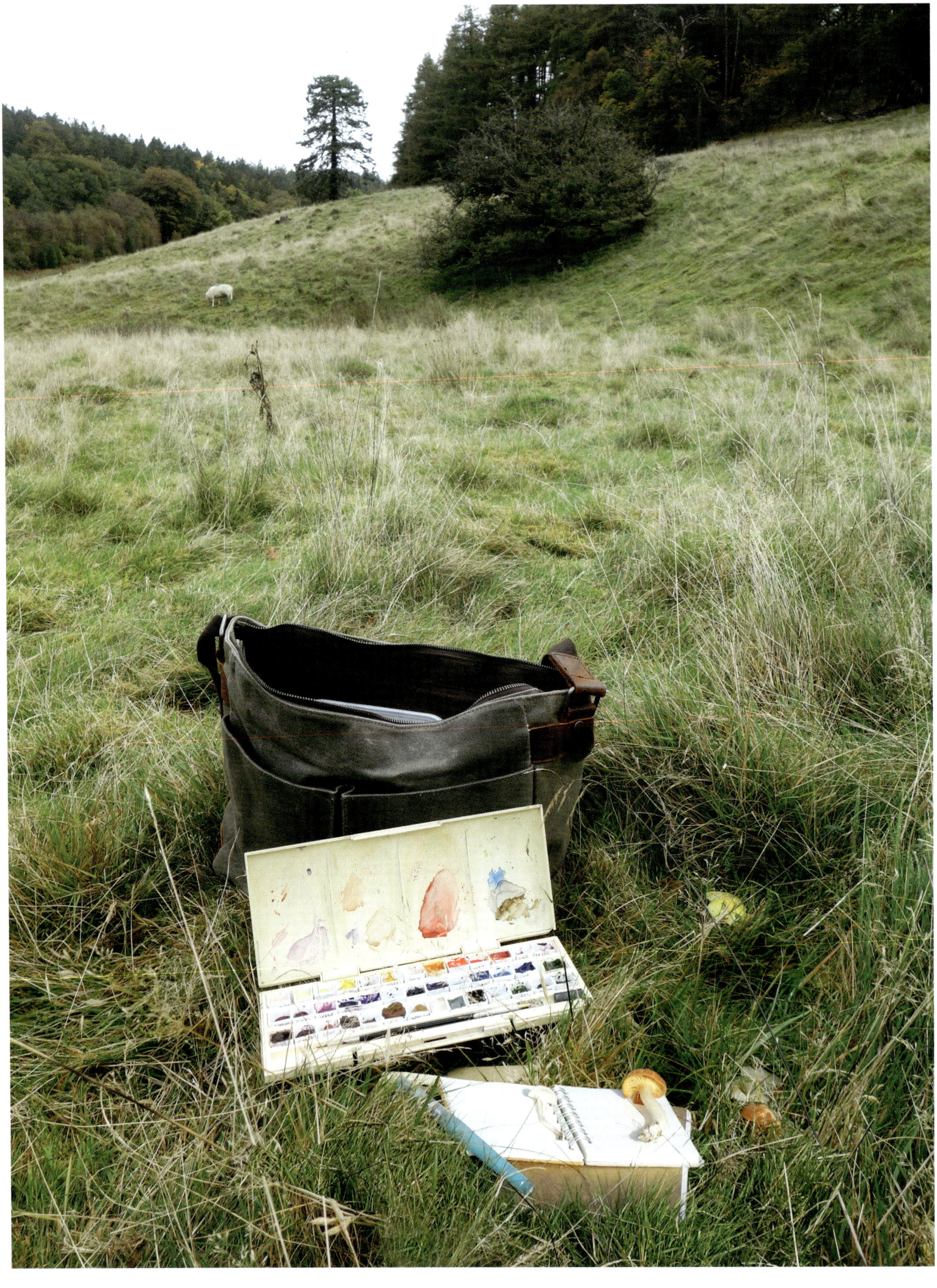

CHAPTER 3

SKETCHING IN FIELD OR STUDIO

'I have learned that what I have not drawn, I have never really seen.'

DUTCH AMERICAN SCULPTOR,
FREDERICK FRANCK (1909–2006)

Having a sketchbook or journal is an invaluable tool for the artist, whatever the genre. It is the place to store knowledge, research your subjects, plan compositions and try out new techniques or materials; the place to experiment. It could be just a nature journal where you document your surroundings year by year just for pleasure, or where you collect ideas to work on for future paintings.

Working in a sketchbook takes away the pressure of perfection that comes with creating a finished artwork; it allows you to draw in a more relaxed way, and so can become more enjoyable. Over the years, filled sketchbooks become treasured possessions and flicking through their pages conjures memories of times and places visited. Many people, I have found, really value being able to look at sketchbooks even more than viewing finished artworks, to see the progress of the pieces and thoughts of the artist: a working insight.

The book itself doesn't have to be perfect or pristine, just a tool to document your discoveries in nature. Some of mine are really quite threadbare and held together with gaffer tape, but they have a certain charm! But of course, you may wish it to be a beautifully bound volume, and to look more aesthetically pleasing. If this is so, you can work in rough sketchbooks wherever you go out in the field, then you can repaint and perfect in the actual book at home in the comfort of your studio.

In my sketchbooks, I like to add even more information than is listed in Chapter 2; any items of interest about the species such as medicinal values and other uses, folklore and even quotes or poems! It all makes for a really interesting book to look back on.

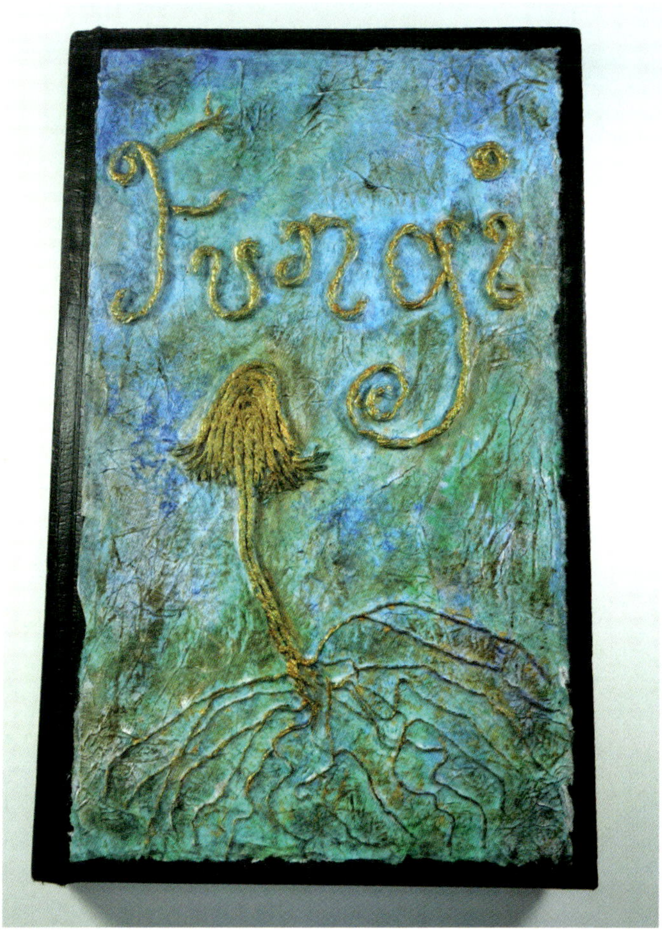

This is one of my fungi journals. I was quite imaginative with the cover using tissue paper, string and gold paint; I just used whatever I had to hand. It's good fun to get carried away, to be free to just create.

Sketching waxcaps outdoors in a late summer meadow; my sketching shoulder bag is comfortable to carry and has plenty of pockets and room for everything.

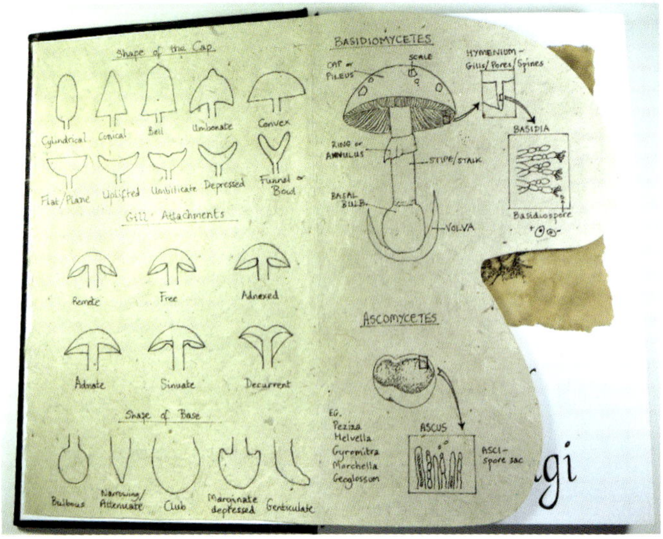

Page two of my fungi journal is drawn out in pen on Lokta handmade paper and glued in. It has fungi characteristic diagrams to help with ID.

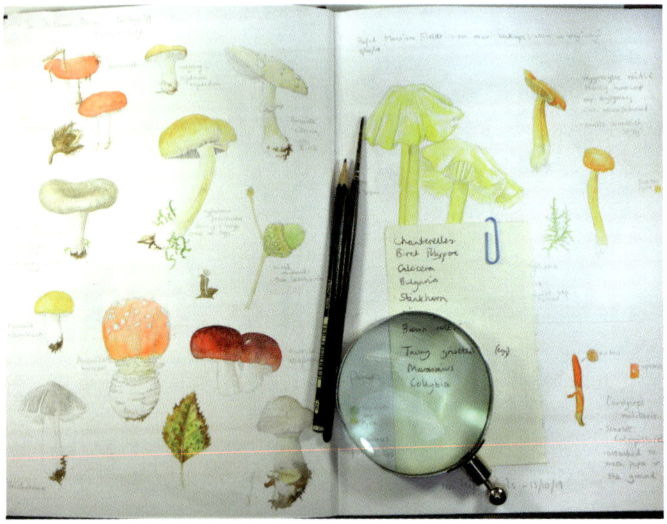

Sketchbook pages with woodland species from Dartmoor and meadow species such as waxcaps in Wales. This sketchbook is a value Seawhite's of Brighton A4 book with ordinary cartridge paper; these cheaper books stop me being worried about perfection!

THE IMPORTANCE OF SKETCHING

Like everything in life, the more you make time for something and practise, the better you get at it, so sketching a little bit every day is the ideal, whatever the subject. However, most people, including me cannot find time to draw every day, but even if it's just a doodle on a lunch break at work or while watching television in the evening, it all helps to develop hand-eye coordination and to create a drawing habit.

It's important to experiment with different techniques that can encourage fluid and spontaneous drawing that becomes second nature and to help boost confidence in drawing by eye.

SKETCHBOOK TYPES AND STORING SKETCHES

There are many types of artist sketchbook in many different sizes to choose from, all depending on what you wish to achieve and the medium that you'd like to use; wet, dry or mixed media. They can be bound books, spiral pads or even loose sheets of paper clipped to a small board or kept

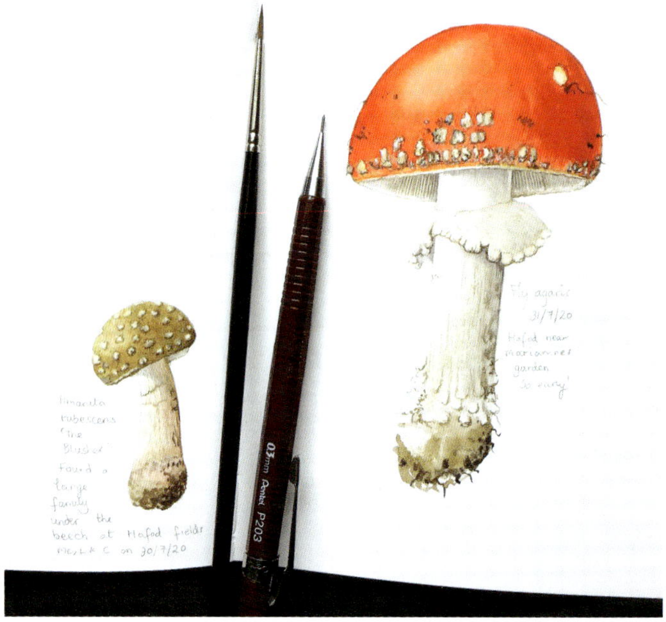

This is an *Amanita* sketchbook page featuring the blusher and the fly agaric. It is a Stillman and Birn, Zeta series sketchbook with a hard cover. Zeta series has hot pressed watercolour paper that takes washes well and is perfect for more detailed studies.

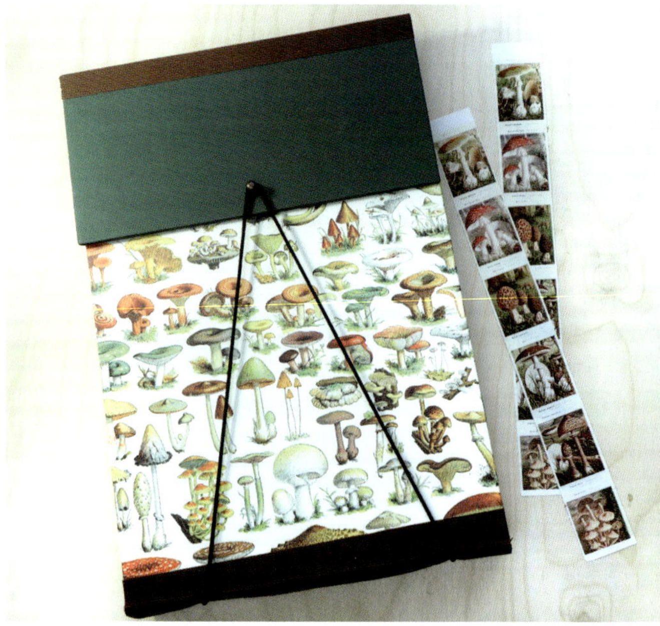

A homemade sketchbook holder made with recycled cardboard that I covered with mushroom papers and tied up with elastic. It's just over size A4 to accommodate that size paper.

in a portfolio. Loose sheets could be bound together to make a book when enough pages are finished.

A good way to store loose sketches is to keep them in a ring binder; they are very cheap to buy. It's also really easy to make your own, just two sheets of card covered with your choice of paper for the front and back covers. You can purchase the rings online or use twine for a rustic look. Punch holes in the front and back covers, clip on the rings, then store your sketches. Ring-bound books have the added bonus of being able to move the pages around.

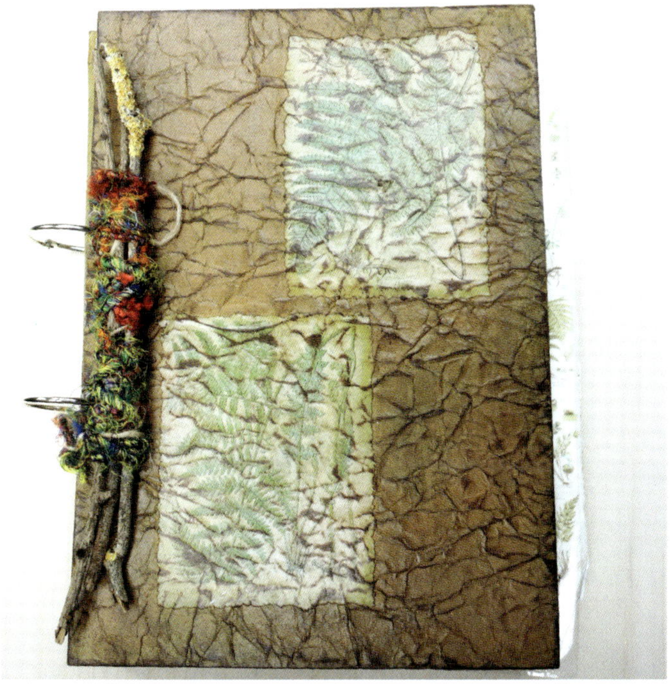

A homemade ring binder for storing loose sketches. It's made from two sheets of A4 recycled greyboard covered with wrapping paper. A3 sketches are folded in half.

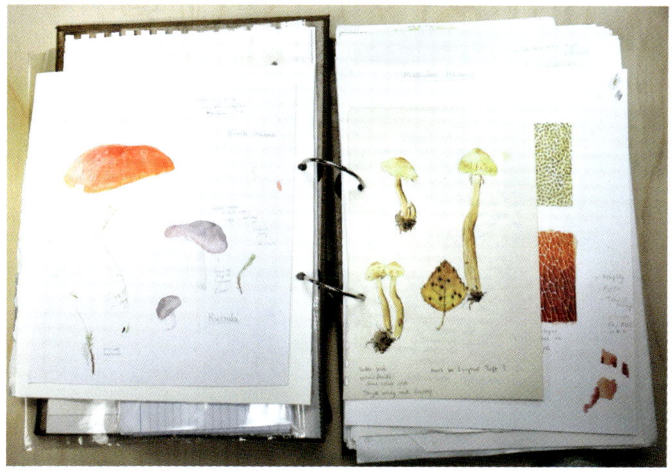

Inside one of my homemade ring binder sketchbooks for loose works. Sketches can be hole punched or stored in poly pockets.

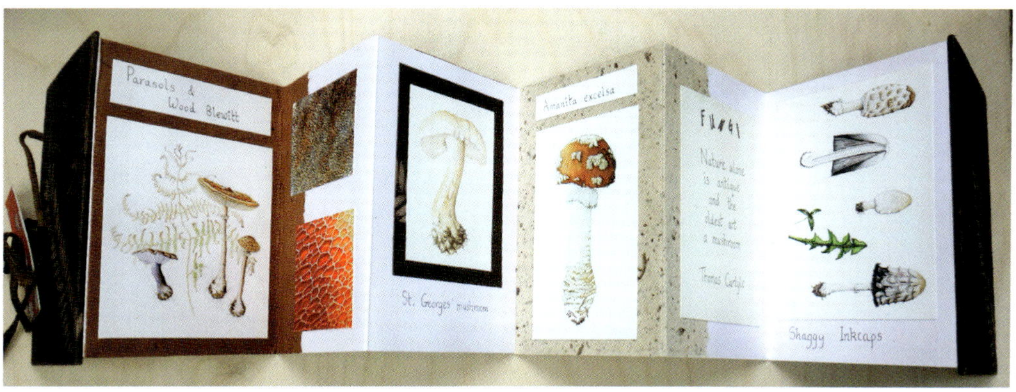

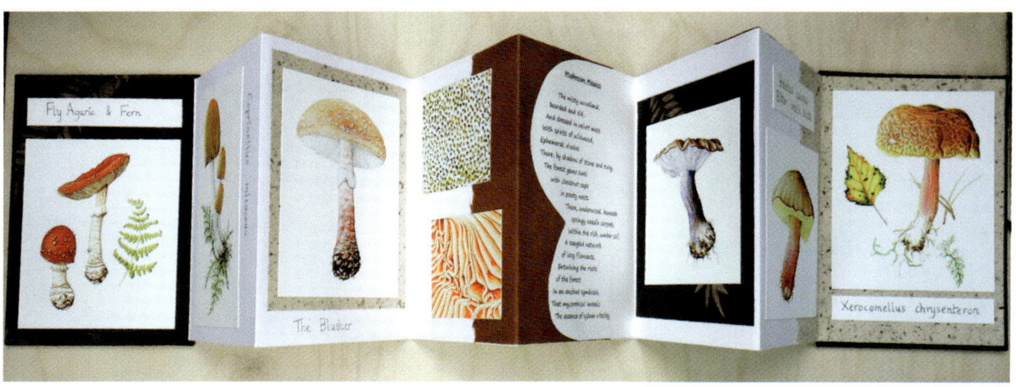

A different sort of sketchbook is the concertina type of book that folds up. This one is a book of prints of my work that are mounted and glued inside and decorated with a variety of handmade papers.

SKETCHING IN THE FIELD

There is no doubt that sketching outdoors can be very challenging, but it can also be a highly rewarding experience and a great day out in nice weather. You may want to work in the field for the entire length of the fungi season or do most of your drawing in the studio with subjects that you find and take home, or indeed a mix of the two. Also as mentioned previously, there will be times when you come across a possible rare species that you don't want to remove, akin to finding a rare orchid or other plant, and so sketching in the field in combination with reference photographs will be called for. They don't have to be complete, finished, and precise paintings, just plenty of notes and observations as seen in Chapter 2, and quick sketches; all depending on how much time you have to devote to the subject and, of course, the weather conditions – this is the number one challenge and off-putting factor. It's not too much fun trying to sketch in the pouring rain, dampening the spirits as well as the paper. So, keep an eye on weather forecasts for apt times to go on sketching forays.

It's all too easy to get carried away and take too much stuff out with you, so whittle it down to the essentials; keep it simple and think portable. If you keep the gear by the door, ready packed in a lightweight bag or backpack, you'll be prepared for impromptu excursions.

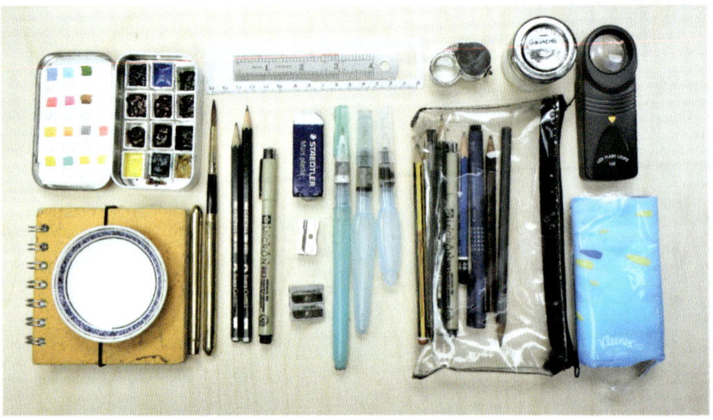

My sketching in the field kit containing everything listed and more. The small watercolour tin is made from an empty Altoids mint tin and the brushes are Winsor & Newton travel brushes that can be unscrewed and taken apart.

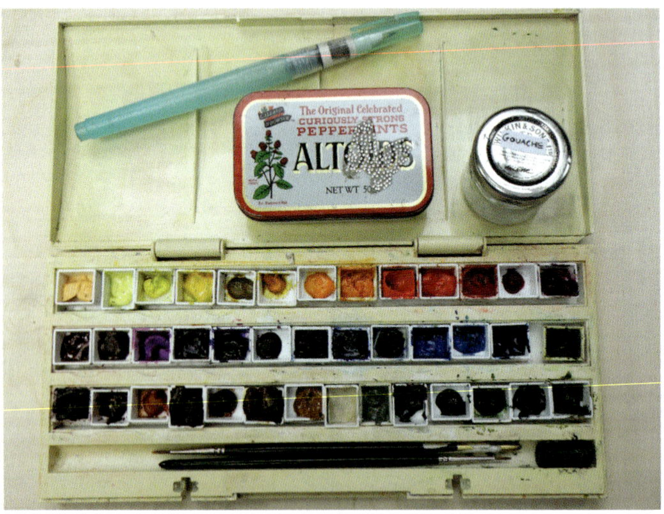

Extra-large watercolour set with palette for fieldwork if I'm not going far. It also contains finer brushes. Water brushes are useful but can be temperamental with their water release, so tissues are needed.

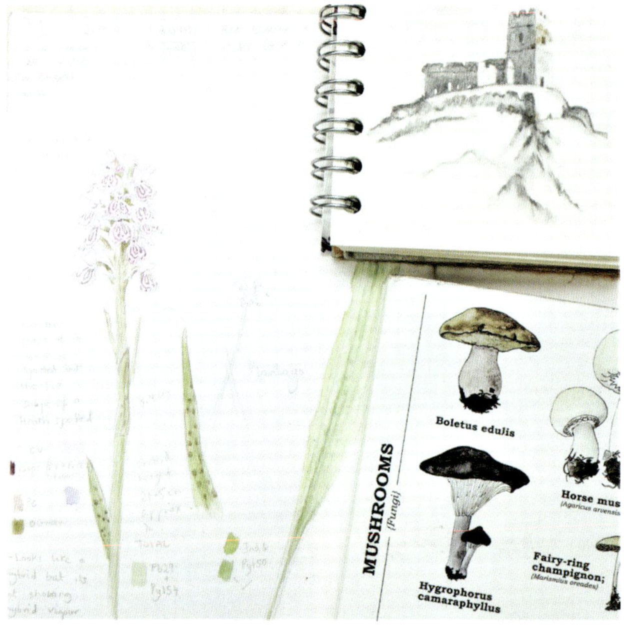

It is a good idea to have lightweight softcover sketchbooks and notebooks; so much easier to carry around on longer excursions.

A GOOD SKETCHING KIT COULD CONTAIN

- Your chosen sketchbook or notepad – as lightweight as possible
- Graphite pencils – a small range. I like 2H, HB and F
- Pens (if you use them)
- An eraser and a sharpener
- A small watercolour kit, maybe with travel brushes
- A water brush or two – I have makes by Kuretake and Pentel, with different-sized nibs
- A small bottle of water – for drinking and refilling the water brushes
- Some paper towel sheets or pack of tissues
- A camera or phone
- A small ruler to take measurements
- A hand lens or loupe – not essential for fungi but essential for lichens, useful for seeing close-up details

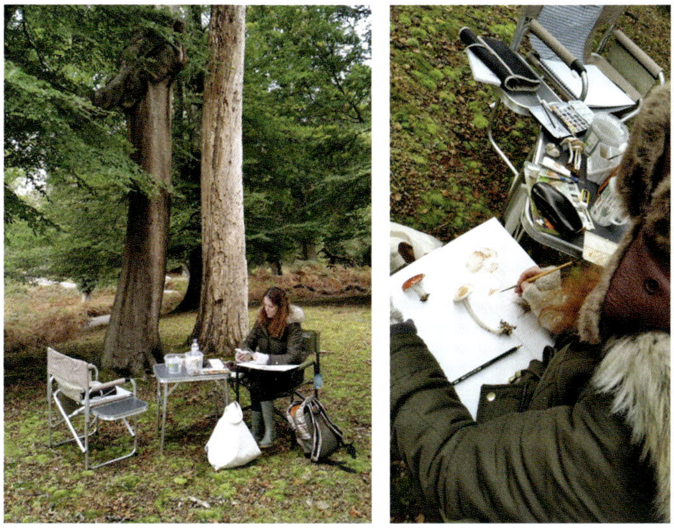

A day in the autumn woodland with my friend and fellow artist Sarah Morrish. We were very organised with a fold-out table and chairs easily set up from the boot of the car. It was a cold October day, but we had a gas stove with a kettle and lots of tea!

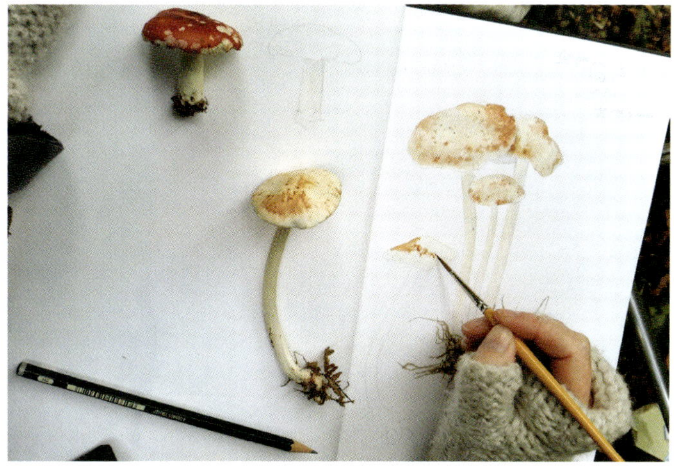

My sketchbook page in full swing from our day out – note the excellent and warm fingerless gloves – much easier to paint and draw in, in cold weather!

Also important is to wear appropriate clothing according to the habitat. Stout but comfortable walking boots are a good idea if going on a long trek. It's worth repeating that light-coloured trousers and clothing can show up ticks and keeping skin covered up can protect against being bitten by these annoying pests.

A plastic carrier bag is useful for sitting on in damp weather or if you drive, you can keep a fold-up chair in the car boot, as long as you don't have to carry it too far! I also have a cushion that I put into a plastic carrier bag to sit on outdoors if I'm not going far, and you can also buy specific seat pads that you fold up. Hopefully, you'll be able to find a place to sketch where you won't be too disturbed by dog walkers and 'interested' people. This can be distracting and dogs off leads can be destructive too!

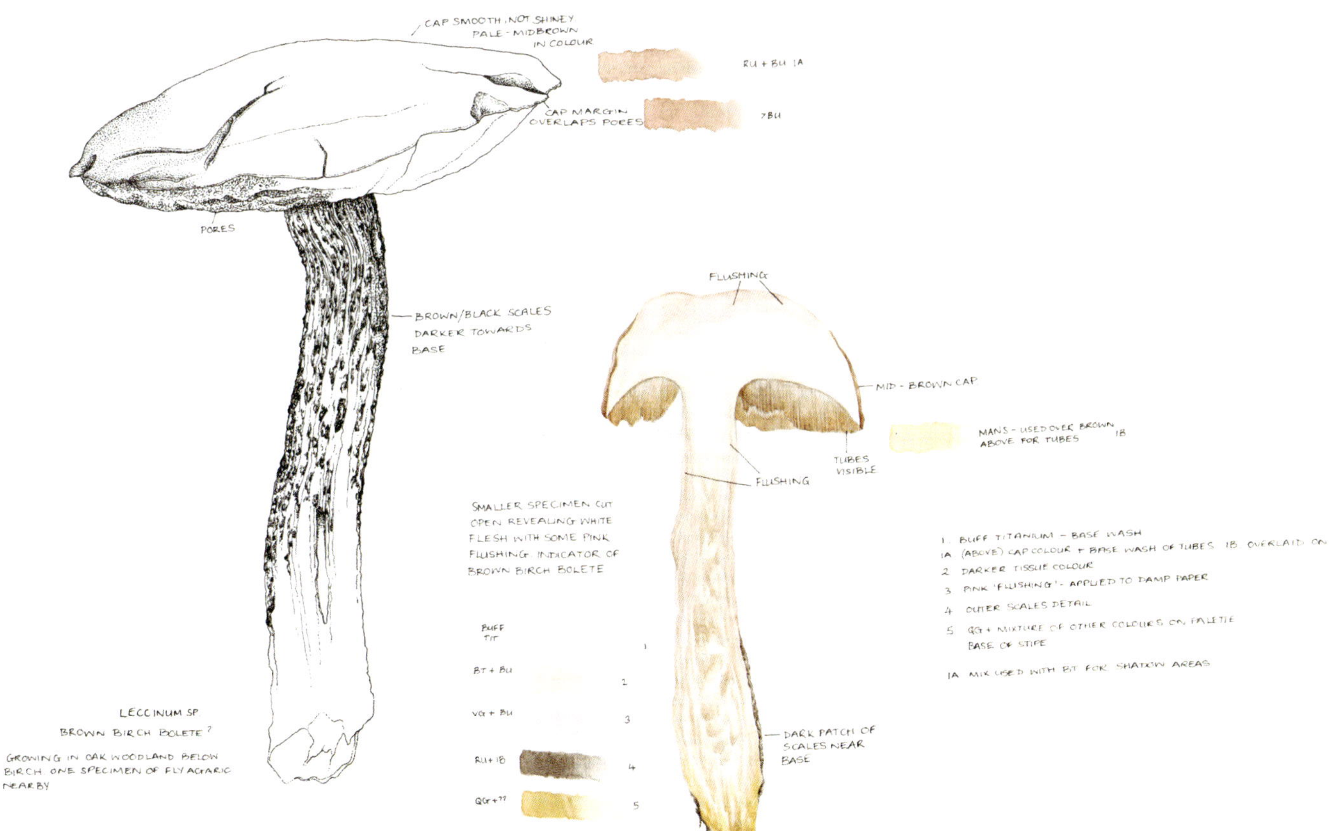

A wonderfully detailed page from Sarah Morrish's sketchbook showing the brown birch bolete – *Leccinum* sp. It's interesting to see a longitudinal section of the mushroom for even more information. (© Sarah Morrish)

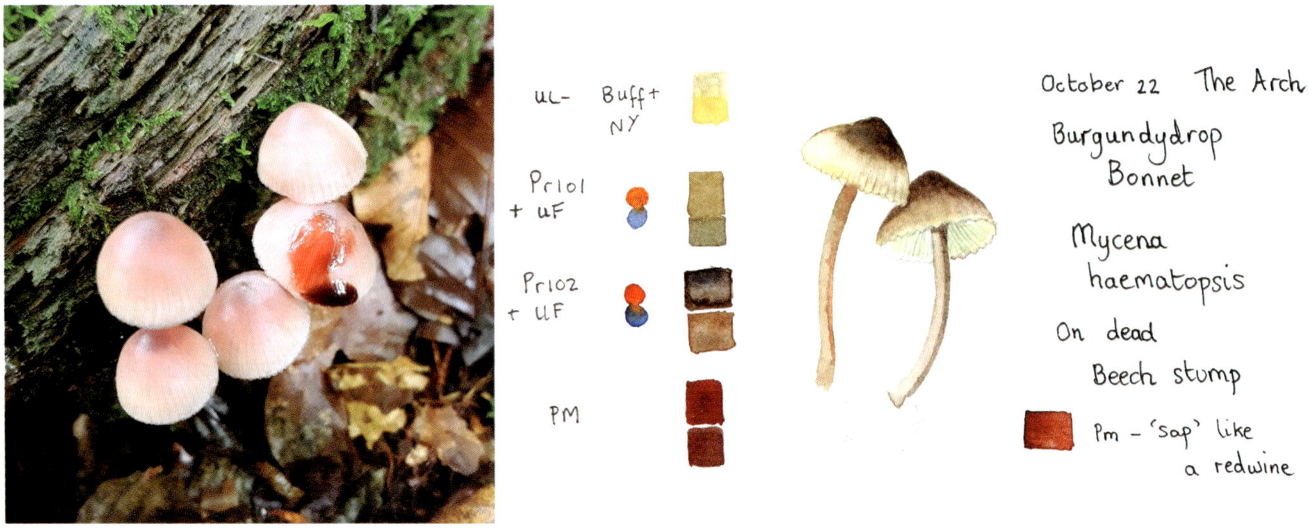

Burgundydrop bonnets – *Mycena haematopsis* – are interesting little mushrooms that grow on dead or diseased tree stumps. When cut they 'bleed' a wine-red liquid. Here's a sketchbook study working out and recording their colours.

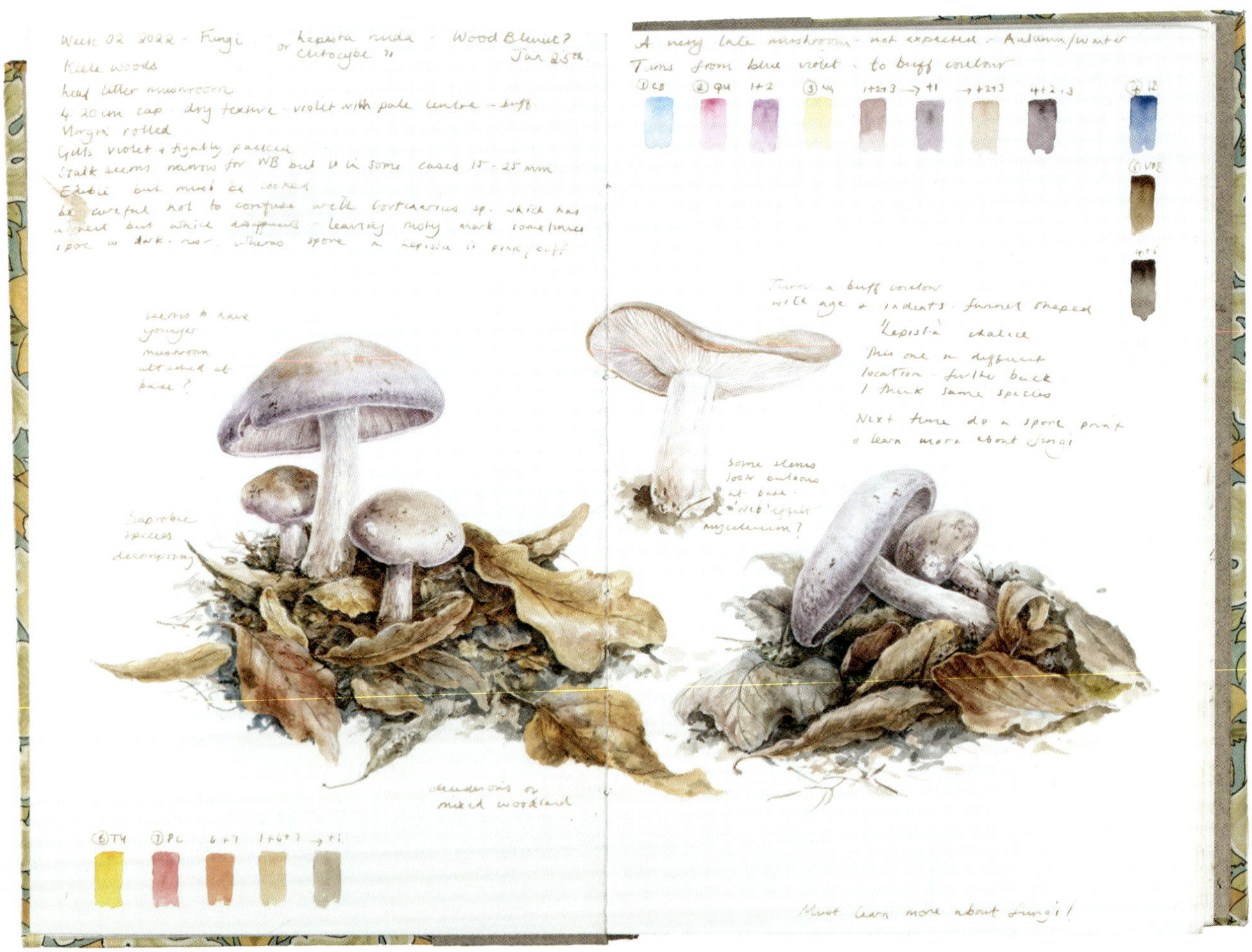

A sketchbook page of wood blewits by Dianne Sutherland. Dianne says "The beautiful lilac colour caught my attention as it pushed through the leaf litter. I had to include it in a project I've been involved with since February 2021 with fellow botanical artist Debbie Crawford. It marked the beginning of my mushroom hunting and several more have been added to the sketchbook since!" (© Dianne Sutherland)

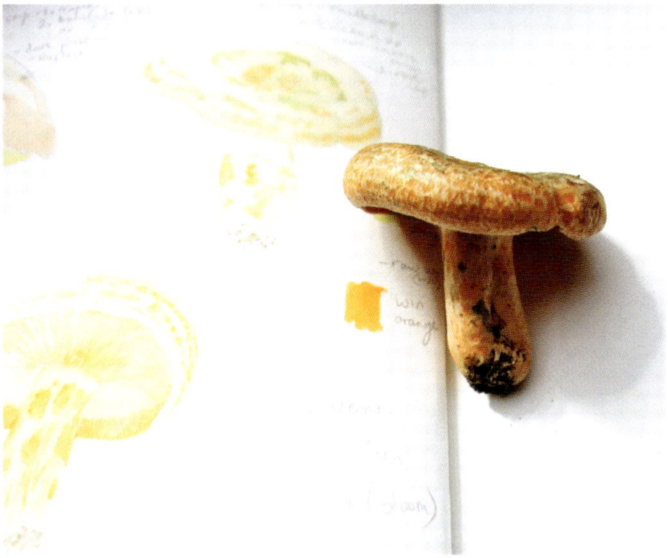

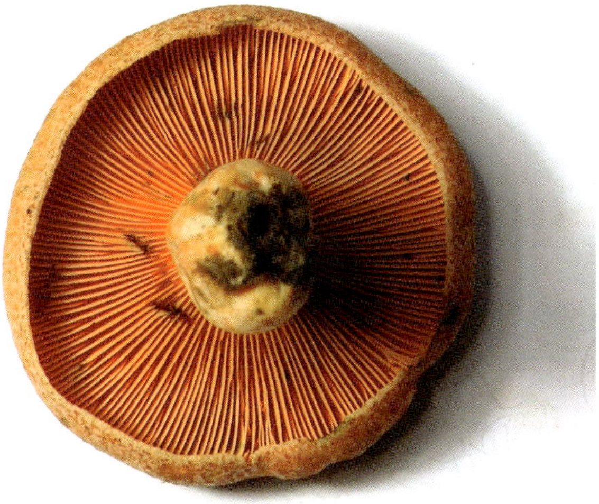

Drawing a sketchbook page of the saffron milkcap – *Lactarius deliciosus*. Nothing can beat being able to study your subject from life; to be able to pick it up and observe it from every angle. It's also good to have reference photos to remind you how vibrant the colours can be, like these gills, but essential to make colour notes when the mushroom is still fresh – not to rely on photographs.

PHOTOGRAPHS

It's always going to be better to work from life whenever possible as you can see the true form of the subject and observe what is hidden around the sides and behind. Nothing will beat picking up your subject and turning it over in your hands, observing its textures and form from all angles. Much information can be gathered from a good photo, but there really is no genuine alternative for drawing from life and the gaining of real drawing skills. However, the use of photographs is an essential asset for the depiction of rarities, for close-ups of important characteristics and details when enlarging, and especially for occasions when time is lacking to finish a study before the mushroom has disintegrated. Obviously, there are subjects that will be difficult to pick or remove to take home, such as brackets or species higher up in trees. So, a few well-snapped shots can be taken as reference for when back in the studio. Be sure you take some from different angles, distances and close-ups too. Fungi can be very photogenic as well as wonderful drawing subjects. They stay perfectly still for you, not swaying about in the breeze like a delicate wildflower!

The camera doesn't have to be a high-end SLR with the latest detachable lens to take decent photographs; cameras on smart phones are such good quality and much more portable and lightweight. One of the difficult aspects of working from photographs is getting the correct scale, so notes on measurements are important and you can prop up a ruler next to the subject before taking a shot to capture its dimensions if time is limited to sketch at life-size.

It's important to think about the direction of the light source and light levels. Sometimes in dim woodlands, photographs can come out disappointingly dark or blurred. To aid with stability, a small tripod or resting the camera on something steady can avoid blurring. To help see the subject and provide a neutral backdrop, it can be helpful to prop up a blank sketchbook page behind it to show it up before snapping.

As fungi mostly grow close to the ground, it may be necessary to get low down, even lie on the ground to take a good photo. A couple of times I've been asked what I am doing by curious passers-by, so perhaps wait to be alone before attempting this to avoid possible embarrassment! Hunting in meadows can also arouse suspicion from others as to the species of mushroom one is hunting for and whether they are magic or not!

Building up a reference library of your own mushroom photographs is not only a fantastic resource but it's wonderful to look through at times when fungi are not about for inspiration, and it always brings about a recollection of the time or place when found.

It's important to know that working exclusively from photographs will have its limitations. Issues such as distortion, flattening of forms, over/under exposures, and inaccurate colours can occur, so I find sketching from life with as much information as possible collected in the field is the best course of action, and then photos can be used as backup if needed. A lot of subjects are quite small and so don't take too long to make a detailed study, so often photographs are not needed at all.

RECORDING IN THE SKETCHBOOK

'To draw' is from Old English – *dragan* – to draw, drag, pull; 'to sketch' from Ancient Greek – *skhédios* – made quickly. I refer to a sketch as a quick, rough study that is usually made for planning a more detailed artwork or for compositional ideas. A drawing refers to a more detailed, finished or refined piece of work.

Mushrooms are a great drawing subject for the beginner. Here are a few techniques to help with drawing

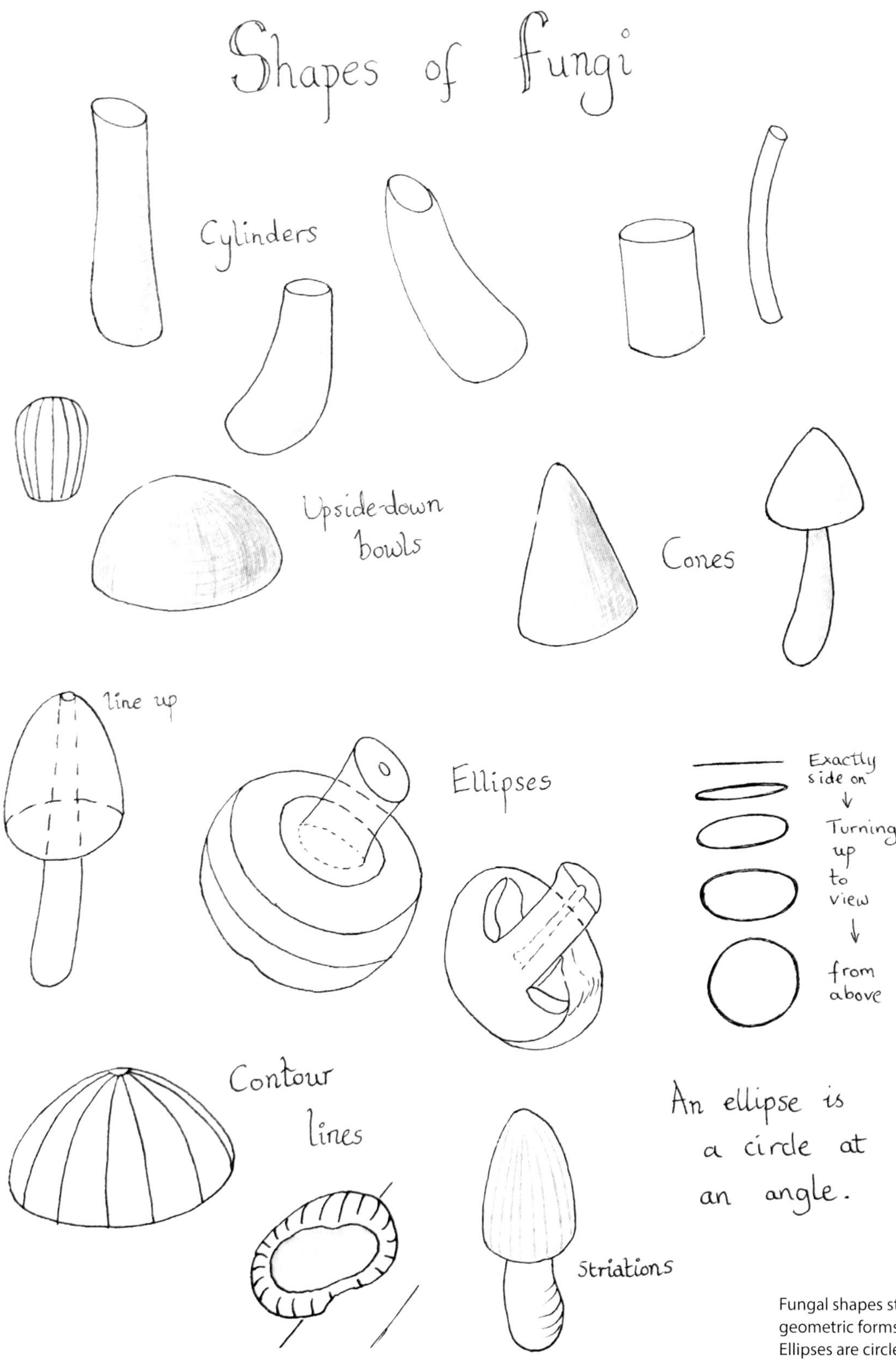

Fungal shapes study page showing geometric forms within the subjects. Ellipses are circles at an angle.

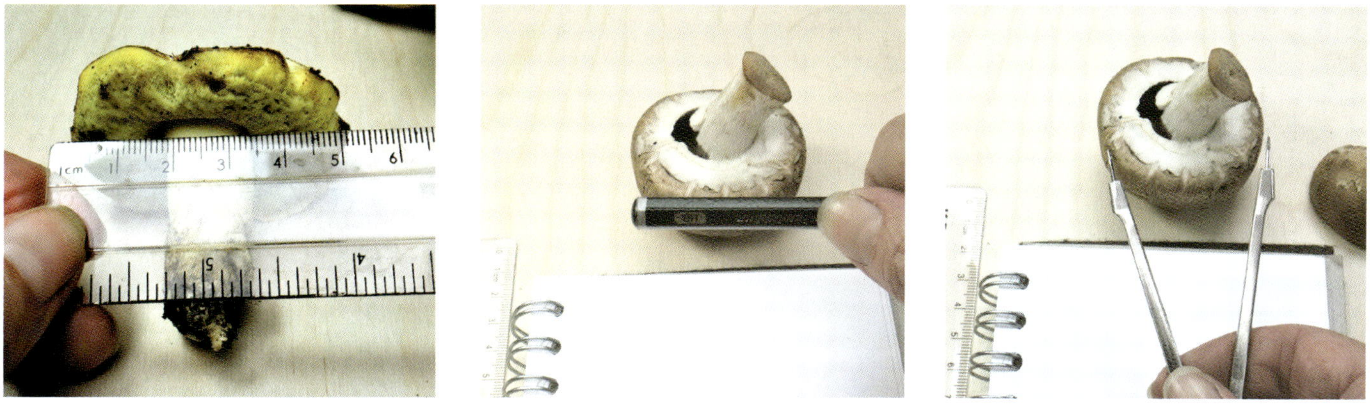

Different ways to measure the subject: simply use a transparent ruler or dividers to measure and plot on paper. These seen here are just inexpensive school maths set dividers. Or you can just use a thumb and pencil measurement.

or sketching your subjects. The first thing to do is to thoroughly observe the subject, study the contours of it and evaluate the techniques that you'll need to render it. Notice how the light is falling on it. Any notes taken previously on the form of the subject will help, such as the shape of the cap. Is it depressed in the centre, conical or perhaps with a distinct central bump, which is called an umbo?

Look for any simpler, geometric shapes within the underlying geometry of the subject. In this respect, fungi are easier to draw than other natural history subjects, tending to be of simpler shapes and so easier to see geometric form within them; think of circles, ellipses and cylinders. Looking for these forms can help to abstract the process of drawing.

Observe the size of your subject, find its centre, and note where this will be on your paper. It can be easy to start drawing too quickly and not give the subject enough room on the page, ending up with a squashed look or having to erase and start again further down the page! If you want to draw at life-size and you are not confident with your drawing skills, then you may want to measure the height and width of the subject and plot this out lightly on the paper. You can use a ruler, a pair of dividers or a pencil and thumb measurement. I always try to draw by eye initially, then if needed I check my proportions using dividers to make sure I'm on the right track. This is favourable as it will increase drawing skills rather than always relying on tools to measure.

Start to sketch in the shapes that you see, drawing lightly with the pencil so as not to indent the paper and not to draw with such a hard line that cannot be erased if a mistake is made. A 2H, F or H pencil will give a paler line. When you've drawn the outline shape, think about the contours of its surface. Fungi are composed of rounded forms, so it's easy to see these curving undulations as contour lines to be able to make them look three-dimensional.

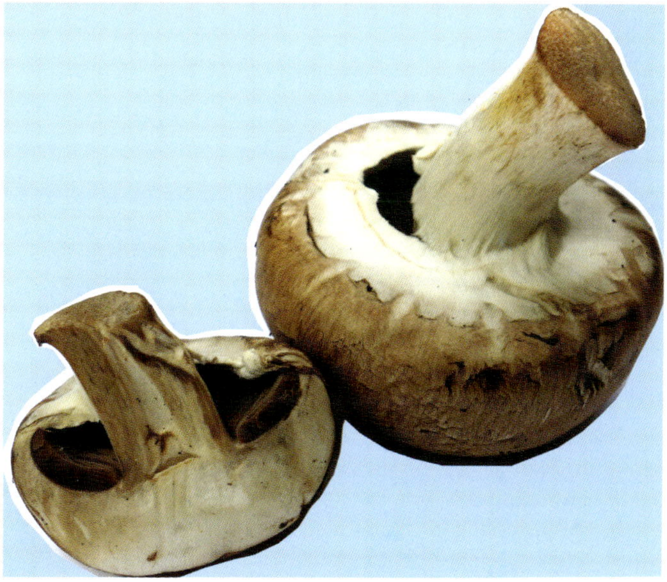

You can see the negative space around the mushrooms highlighted as the blue areas. If you look at these spaces surrounding your subjects and draw them it can help you to draw what you see.

When drawing the gills, mark down or imagine the centre point to the top of the stipe, and make sure that the gills line up to this centre point to draw them accurately. Then when the line drawing is complete, use the softer B grades of pencil to start to add tones using the shading techniques that you prefer. These will be looked at in the next chapter in more detail.

HANDY DRAWING TIPS FOR BEGINNERS

- Observe the negative space or empty space around the object and draw this; the subject is the positive shape. This works because the brain does not recognise those abstract shapes and so there are no preconceptions about how they should look.
- Look at the angles within the subject; how do they line up against each other?
- Do you have the subject's correct proportions? This concerns the height and width. It is so important to get the initial drawing proportions and perspectives right. Keep checking that these ratios are in tune with each other by seeing how many times the width goes into the height (or vice versa), with a pencil, a pair of dividers or a ruler.
- You can establish correct measurements by using dividers. With dividers be very careful to keep them on the same picture plane every time while measuring. You can suppose that there is an imaginary pane of glass between you and the subject and place the dividers on this to help keep it in the same plane. Avoid skewing the dividers or it will cause a distortion in your measurements. However, you don't have to have dividers, you can use your thumb and a pencil to measure or simply a transparent ruler.
- Many mushroom caps have built-in contour lines in the form of striations that will help you to sculpt the shapes and curves of their domes, mapping out the undulations upon their surfaces.
- Remember to self-analyse. Don't say 'that drawing is no good!' Say 'what went wrong with that drawing and how can I make it better next time?'

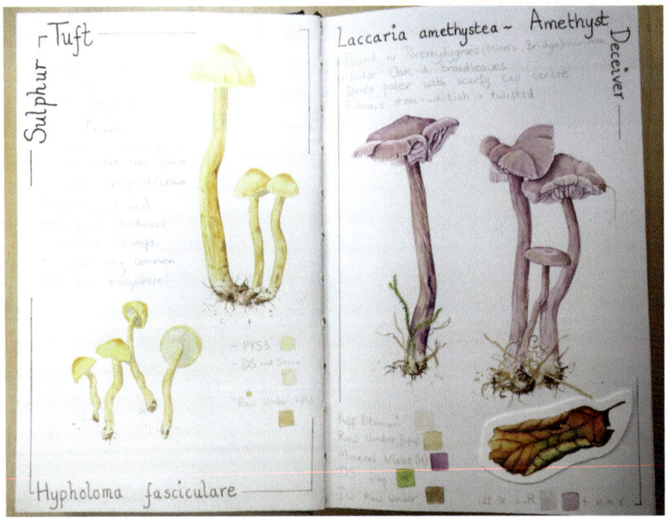

Here's a typical sketchbook page featuring sulphur tufts and amethyst deceivers. Sulphur tuft is probably one of the commonest mushrooms in the UK, being quite a conspicuous yellow mushroom. I like the combination of complimentary colours of violet and yellow on this double page.

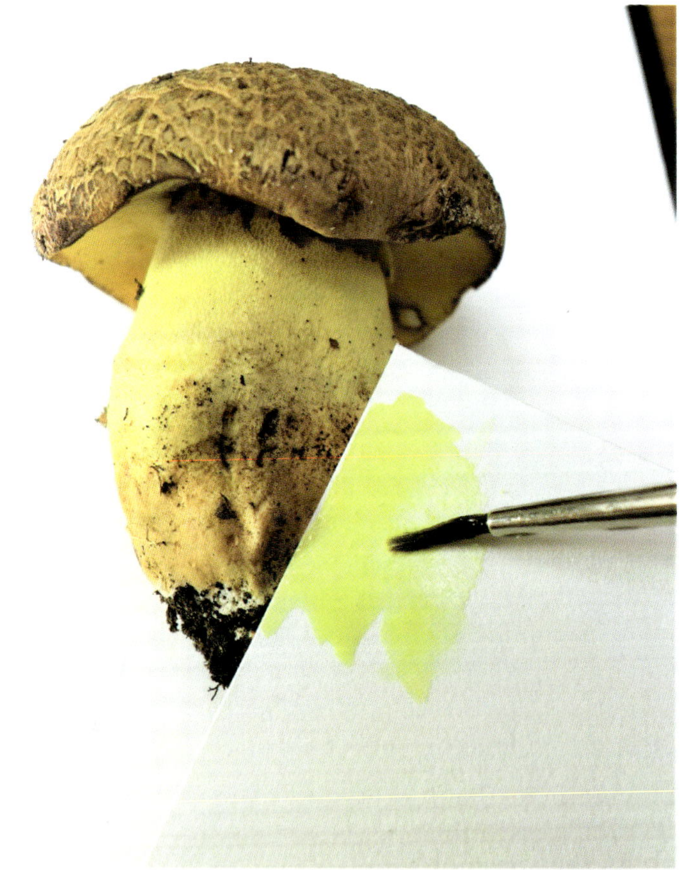

When the subject is drawn out, colour notes can be obtained. As with most subjects that I paint, I try out colour mixes on spare paper and hold up to the subject to get a close colour match, then swatch and record in the sketchbook.

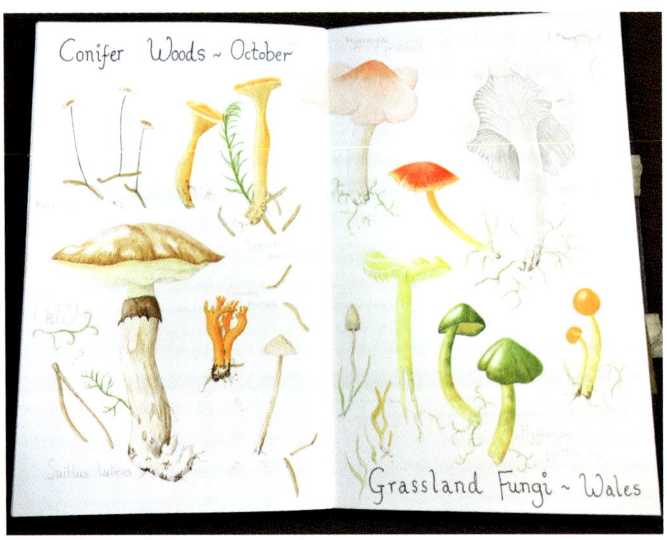

A sketchbook study double page spread of woodland and grassland species. It was completed by me for a friend on the Nature Sketchbook exchange that I was a part of with fifteen other artists around the world that started in 2014.

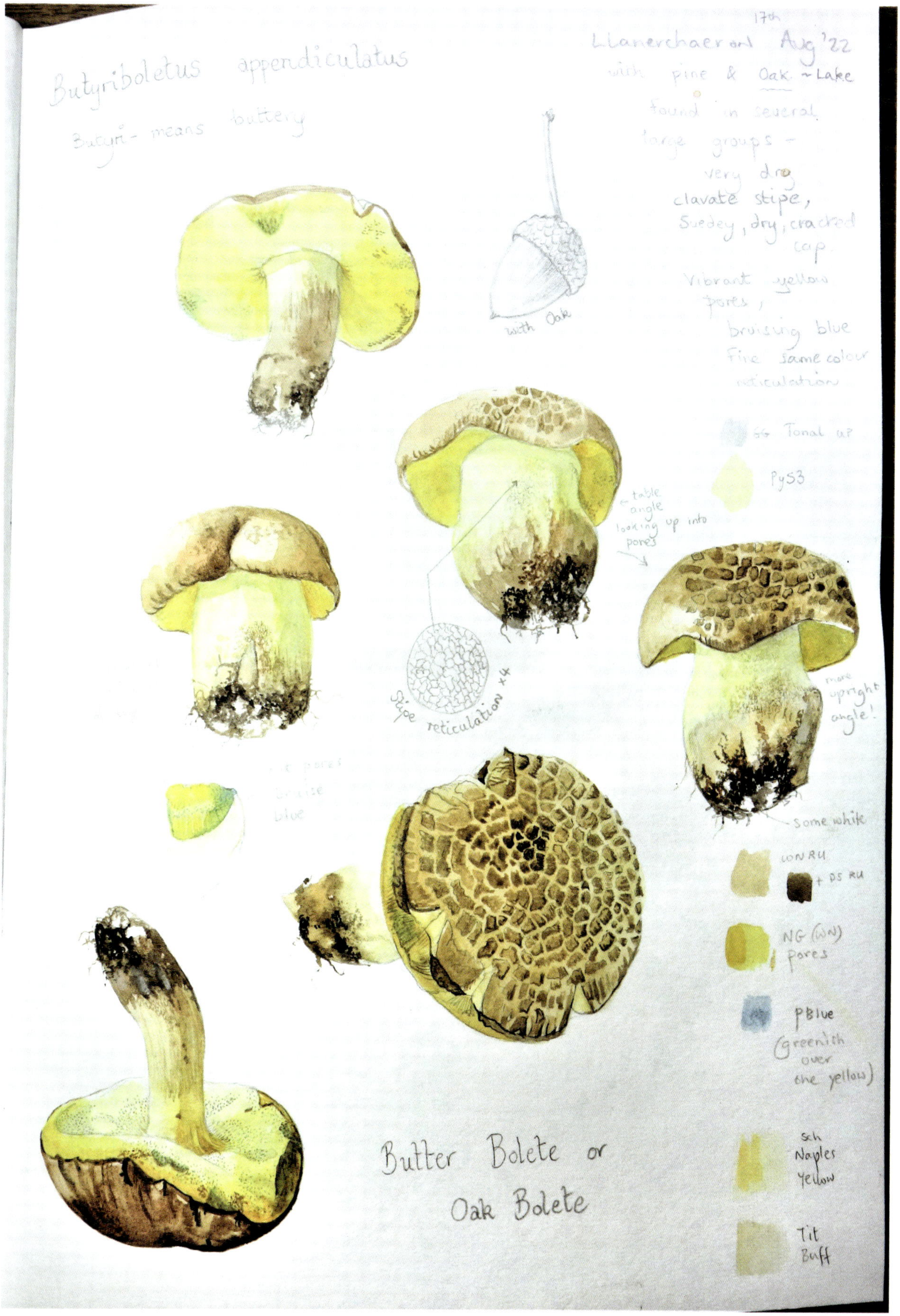

Full page study of oak boletes with plenty of detail and colour notes, including the blue reaction and their wonderfully cracking caps.

Using Reference – The Grid Method

For most fungi subjects, it's best to work from life and a photograph is just used as a side reference when the subject has long ago disintegrated. But if you feel unconfident with your drawing skills, or you're wanting to tackle a very complex composition, then a simple technique to use is the grid method and a photograph. It is also a way to enlarge or reduce your subjects and your sketches also – not just photos.

First print off a copy of the photograph that you wish to draw, then using a ruler and a pen, draw on a grid using inch squares (or other measurement). You then, very lightly in pencil, add the same size grid to your paper or other surface if you want to draw the subject matter at the same size. The photograph can then be translated onto your paper by just duplicating what you see in each little square. Then when the image has been drawn out, gently erase the grid. This should give you an accurate drawing to work with. If you intend to use this method regularly, then a grid drawn onto a transparent acetate sheet with permanent pen could be a time saver.

FROM SKETCH TO PAINTING

I have many sketchbooks for research and initial studies for working on finished paintings, gathering all the information needed to complete an artwork. Then when an artwork is ready to begin and you have the paper laid out to start, you can transfer the sketches using tracing paper. This helps to cut down any damage done to the surface of your watercolour paper by keeping any erasing of graphite down to a minimum.

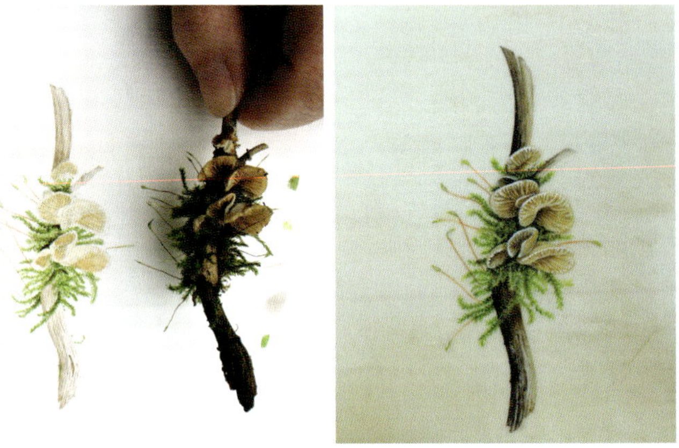

Crepidotus variabilis. From sketch to finished painting – in this case transferred onto natural vellum. As vellum is quite transparent, it can be placed over the original sketch and then traced lightly onto the vellum. The original sketch may need a little darkening for it to be seen through, or you could try the tracing paper method – it's trial and error.

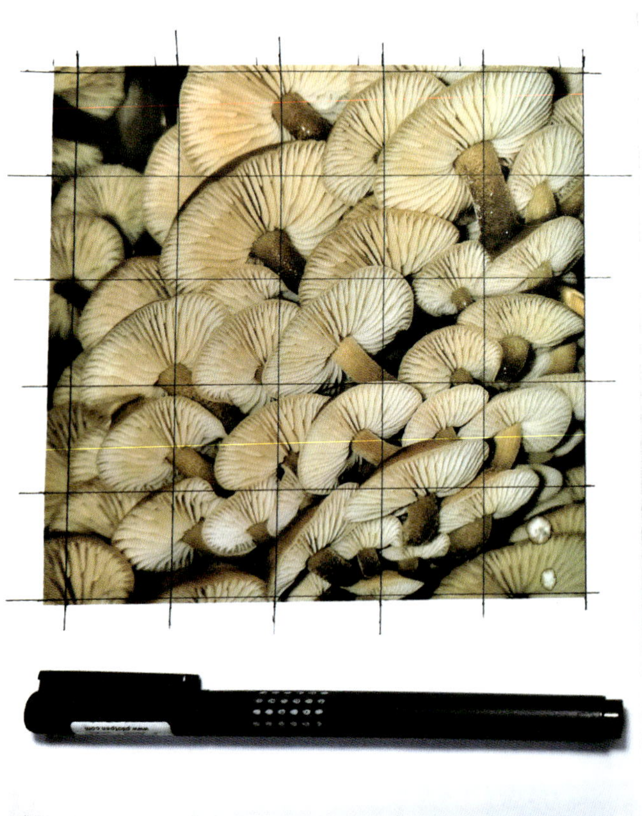

Using the grid method to transfer a complex image from photograph to paper with accuracy. Here the image is copied at the same size, but the beauty of this method is the ease of enlarging. This drawing is finished using pen and wash in Chapter 6.

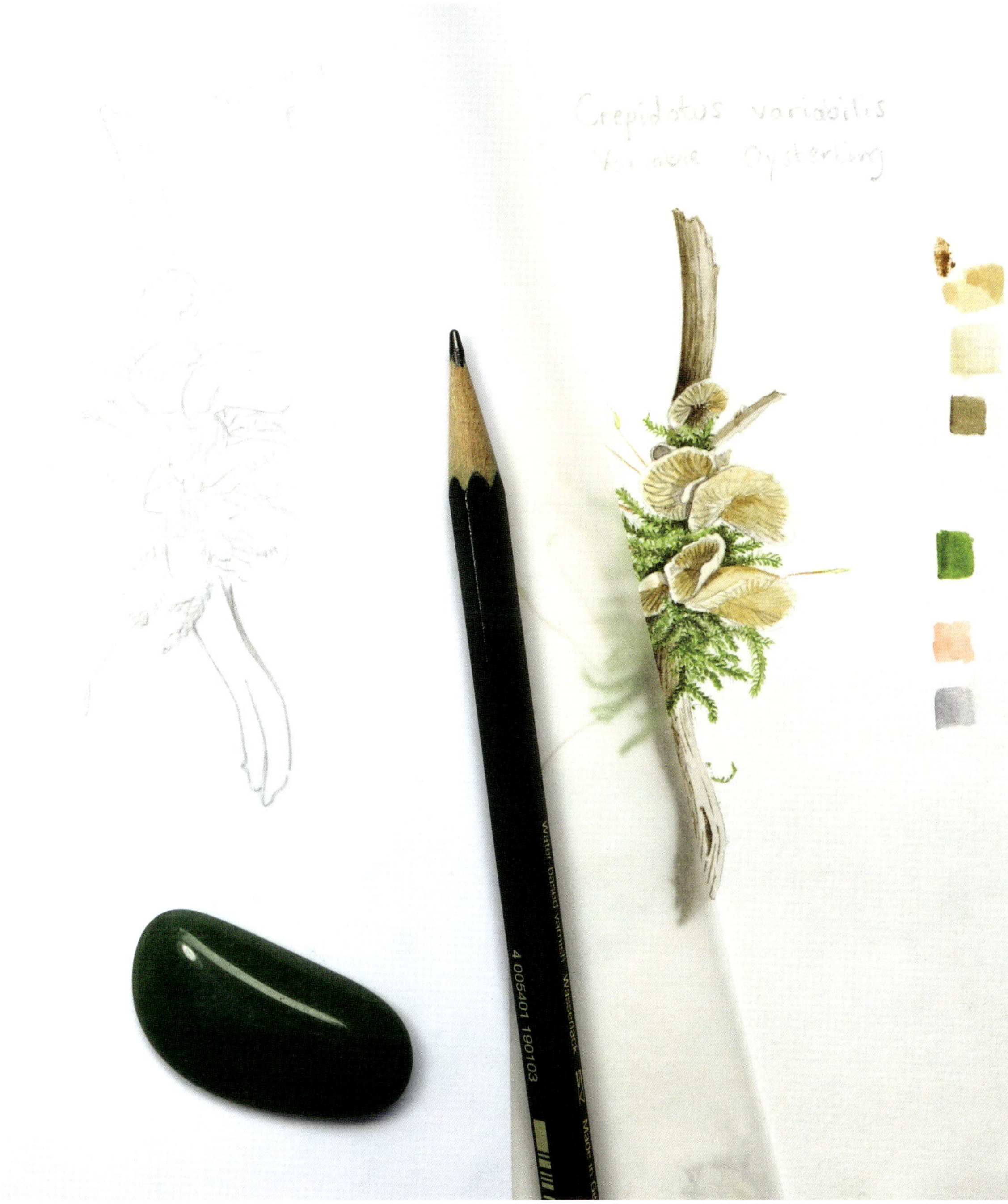

A sheet of tracing paper is placed over the sketch and traced over, using a pencil or pen. Note which side is the top side. Flip over and redraw on the back using an F or HB pencil. Flip it back over to the top side again and tape down to the painting surface with low-tack masking tape. Then rub over with a pencil, smooth gemstone or burnishing tool to transfer the graphite image onto the paper.

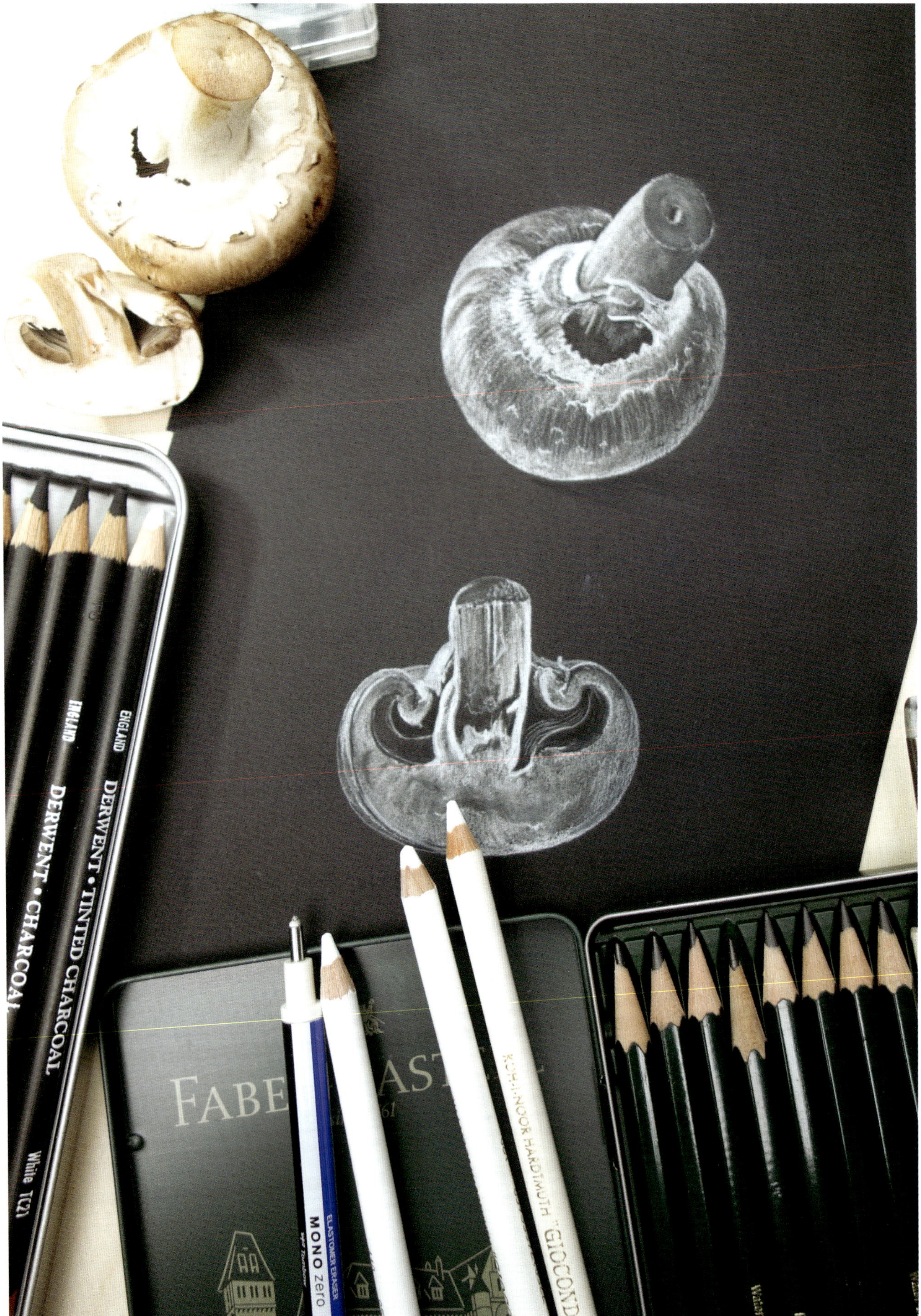
ENGLAND
DERWENT • TINTED CHARCOAL
White
ENGLAND
DERWENT • CHARCOAL
ELASTOMER ERASER
MONO zero
KOH-I-NOOR HARDTMUTH
GIOCONDA

MONOTONE DRAWING WITH DRY MEDIA

'All the visible world is only light on form.'
ANDREW LOOMIS

In this chapter we'll look at the basic fundamentals of art, the elements of line, form, tone, and texture, and the techniques of drawing and mark making that are needed to achieve these using many different dry media. All will be in monotone, so any dry media in colour will come in the following chapter. These step by steps will be the most basic; suitable for beginners to explore tone using shop-bought mushrooms. Fungi subjects can be drawn and studied at any time of year easily after a trip to the market. The commonest mushrooms to buy are mainly portobellos, buttons, and chestnut mushrooms that are all the same species – *Agaricus bisporus* – just at different stages of life. You can also find interesting wild mushrooms in more specialised shops, fungi such as shitake and oysters, among others. All these types are fantastic for studying tone and form.

TONE OR VALUE

This is a really important element that warrants proper study when you are trying to draw and paint realistically. It can sometimes be rushed and overlooked to get to the colouring stage, as if it's not as important but it is fundamental to get it right. Most artists will agree that it is just as, if not more important than, colour. In fact, you can paint a subject using any colours that you like and as long as the tones are correct, it can still look realistic.

Tone is the lightness and darkness of the colours or shades within a subject; from the darkest shadows to the lightest highlights and all the gradations of mid-tones in between. In order to achieve a realistic looking drawing or painting, you need to focus on getting the tonal values correct. Many artworks are let down by a lack of tonal contrast and simply don't get the darks and shadows dark enough. The brightest highlights are the palest areas, which, on certain shiny subjects can be left as the white paper unless using an opaque medium with white pigment.

MODELLING LIGHT

Observing how light interacts with a subject is fundamental to being able to draw it realistically if this is your aim. Then, it is advisable to learn the anatomy of shadows; study a sphere that has been lit up from the top left to see the effects of light upon it. You'll see a highlight to the top left of the sphere and the core shadow in the lower right. Taking this principle to all the subjects that you observe will help you to be able to model them into works with a sense of volume and convincing 3D qualities.

In the studio, you can boost the tones by illuminating the subject properly – best from the top left as previously mentioned. This can be achieved by using a daylight bulb in an Anglepoise lamp or similar purpose-made light. Then study where the light hits the subject; note where this highlight is, and then observe the shadows and the mid-tones that all create the form of the subject. On the rounded form, the tones gradate from light to dark smoothly with no hard edges. You may also see shadows cast by the subject onto itself often called self-shadows, especially under the cap onto the stipe in our fungi subjects.

Cast shadows are shadows cast onto the surface where a subject is sitting, and they are thrown out in the opposite direction of the light source. They can give weight to a painting or anchor a subject to its surroundings. Shadows

A collection of drawing materials including charcoals, graphite pencils and toned papers.

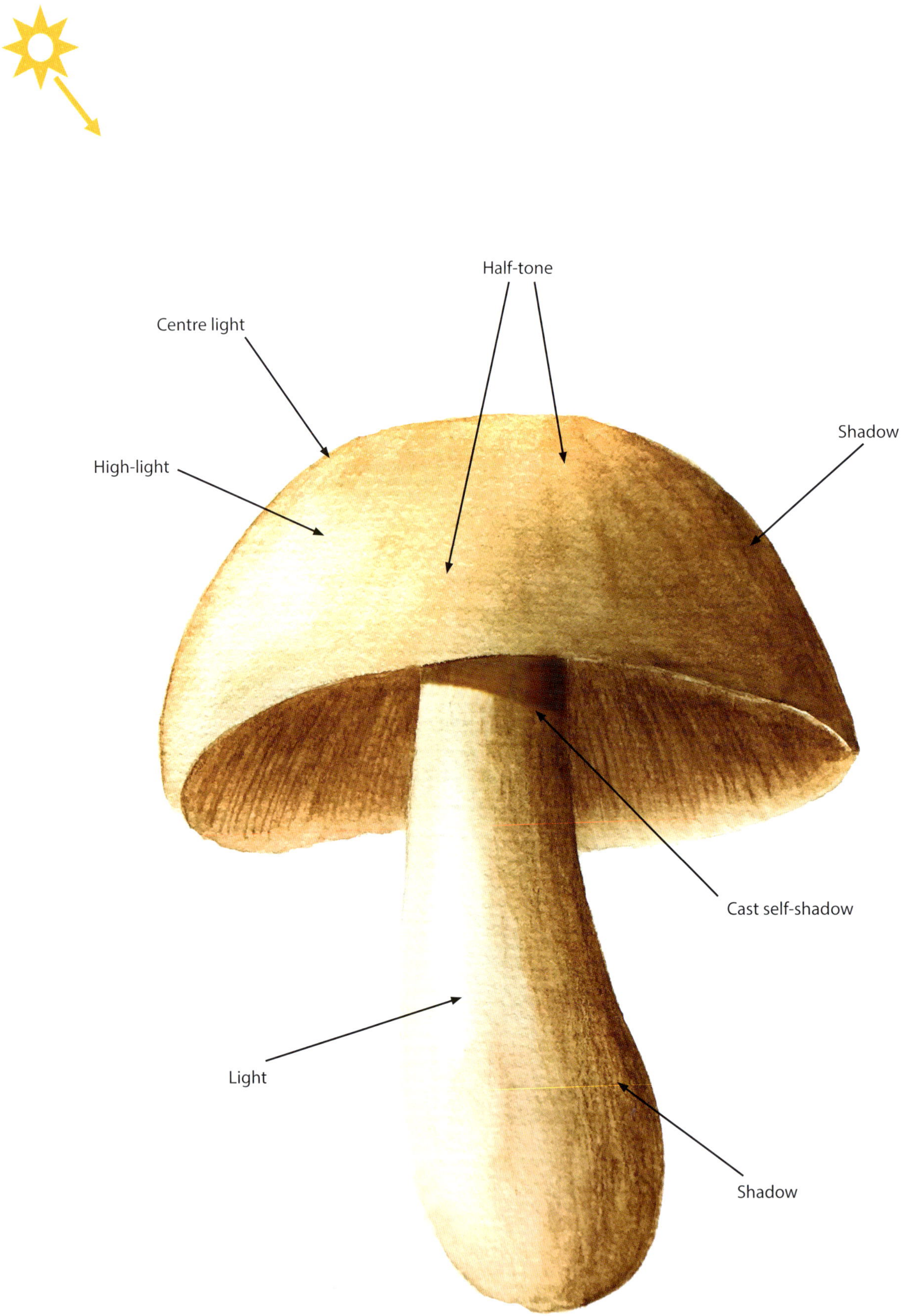

Fungi Form – a tonal mushroom. Here you can see the effects of light and shade sculpting the form of a typical mushroom with highlight, halftones and core shadows.

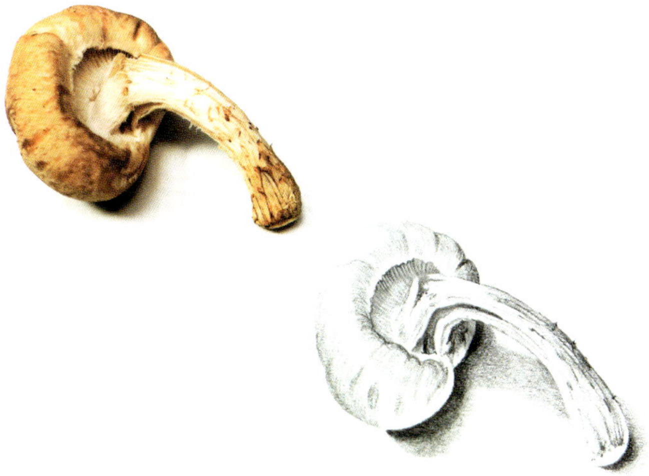

The cast shadow seen just underneath the subject is the darkest area, known as the occlusion shadow. In this drawing, the areas of pale mushroom next to the dark shadows are left very pale – these juxtapositions of tone are important to model the light and shade effectively.

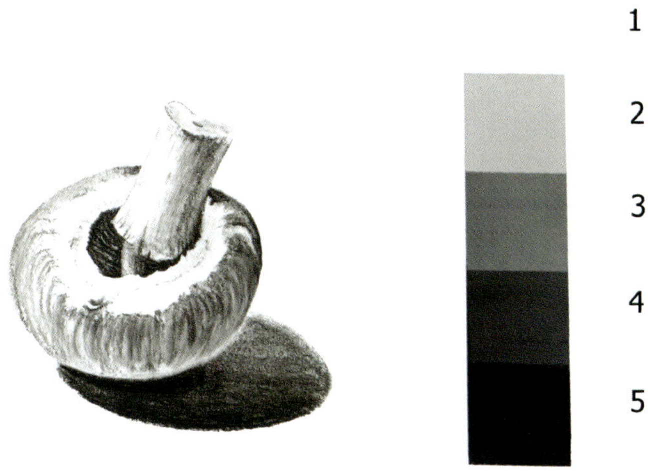

Here you can see a 5-step grey scale that can help with finding and assessing tonal values; one is the brightest value ranging to five that is the darkest. Against a subject you can really assess the tonal range well.

are usually a transparent pale grey or violet colour and can reflect colours from the subject itself as well as the environment. Cast shadows can also give the artist an opportunity to play with negative space and composition to make a painting more interesting and dynamic. They are not normally seen in natural history illustration or botanical art; the subjects float within a white space, with all the attention on their forms, colours and textures. Shadows are more of a feature of the still life genre.

Reflected light will be seen on your subjects if they are shiny or viscid. This is light that is reflected or bounced back from the environment or the surface where the subject is sitting. It usually creates a lighter, cooler area just underneath the core shadow, but observation of the subject is key to create a realistic look. A matt subject will not have as much reflected light to see.

If you're struggling to see tones, try squinting your eyes while viewing the subject and imagine that it is stripped of all colours. This will eliminate details and show the effects of light much more, and you should be able to differentiate the tonal variations better without worrying about colour.

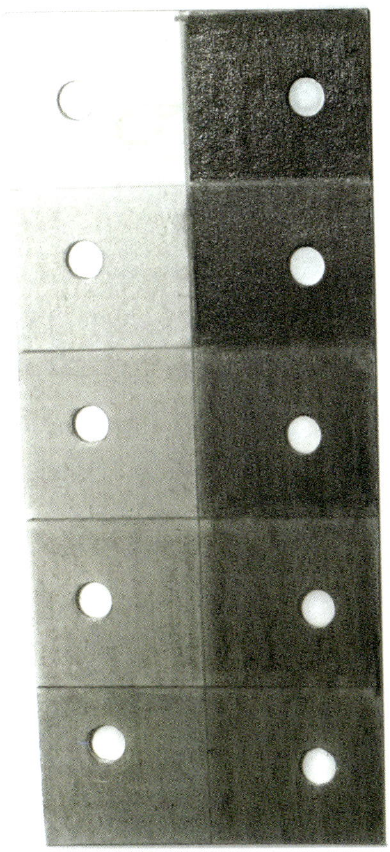

The 5-step grey scale is fine, but you can also add more grey tones as in this 10-step value scale swatched out from graphite. The holes are punched in to help with assessing tones while holding up against a subject.

RUSKIN ON ROUNDNESS

This is an excellent quote from John Ruskin in *The Elements of Drawing, in Three Letters to Beginners* (1857):

> 'All drawing depends, primarily, on your power of representing Roundness. If you can once do that, all the rest is easy and straightforward; if you cannot do that, nothing else that you may be able to do will be of any use. For Nature is all made up of roundnesses; not the roundness of perfect globes, but of variously curved surfaces. Boughs are rounded, leaves are rounded, stones are rounded, clouds are rounded, cheeks are rounded, and curls are rounded: there is no more flatness in the natural world than there is vacancy. The world itself is round, and so is all that is in it, more or less, except human work, which is often very flat indeed.'

DRAWING TECHNIQUES FOR TONE, TEXTURE AND MARK MAKING

Using Graphite

Where you hold your pencil can make a difference. Holding it in the centre can help to loosen up your drawing technique and would be great for gestural sketching. Holding it near the tip in the writing hold is the best for precision and detail work; having a well-sharpened pencil point will help with this, or you can use a mechanical pencil.

These are the main techniques used in graphite drawing.

Continuous tone

This is a method commonly used in natural history illustration, as it gives a smooth, blended gradation of tones from light to dark and so is conducive to realistic-looking drawings. There should be no directional marks seen.

The pencil is used in small, elliptical movements to shade in the area of tone. It's important to not press too hard and I find a pencil that is slightly worn down on one side is preferable to a very sharp point that may indent the paper. When using this method, try to achieve a smooth, even look with no visible pencil marks.

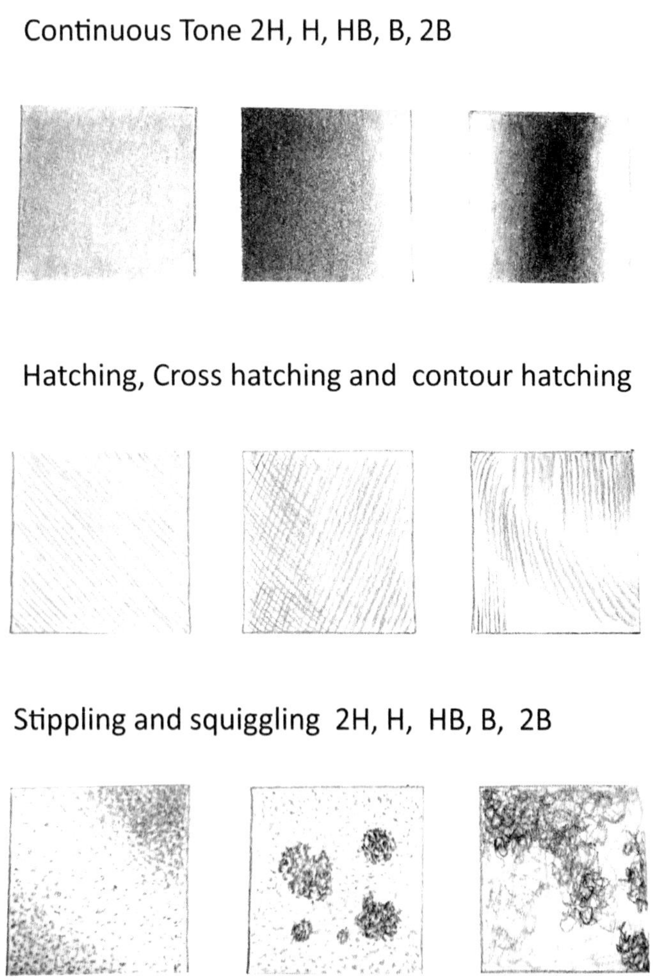

Graphite Shading Techniques. Practise using these shading methods in little squares. For realistic drawing, it's worth practising the continuous tone as in the top right-hand boxes, attaining very smooth gradations of tone from dark to light.

The tone is worked up in layers from the palest areas near any highlights using the H pencils to the darker areas and shadows using the softer grades in the B ranges. To iron out any graininess that you may see, a little blending on top can help either with a tortillion blender, a paper stump or a 2H pencil on top.

Hatching, contour and cross hatching

Hatching came about in the Middle Ages and was used in print making, for creating woodcuts and engraving. This method uses lines to describe the tones and forms of a subject bringing them closer together to depict shadow and darker tones.

Straight hatching is the simplest and uses straight parallel lines which can vary in length. I find contour hatching to be the most useful technique. This hatching uses lines that follow the curves around the contours of a subject. Following the undulations and contours like this will describe the planes and angles of a subject very well and will help to give a three-dimensional and realistic look. Cross hatching is a harder technique to get right and is where the lines criss-cross over themselves. Leonardo Da Vinci used cross hatching techniques in many of his studies.

Stippling

This is also a very old technique that was used for engraving purposes. Today it is used in many precise scientific illustrations. It is the creation of tone using dots with the tip of the pencil. The darker tones are made by placing the dots closer together and in the lighter areas spacing them further apart, leaving more of the white paper.

It is worth being patient when stippling to avoid a messy look, so some mindful deep breaths and meditational thoughts can help when stippling to get into the zone! I love the look of stippling and do find it a therapeutic method of tonal shading, although sometimes I find that I lack the patience.

Scumbling

This can be a great method of mark making to create tone as well as texture. I sometimes just refer to scumbling as squiggling, as I usually just make lots of small, squiggly, haphazard marks with the pencil to give a textured look.

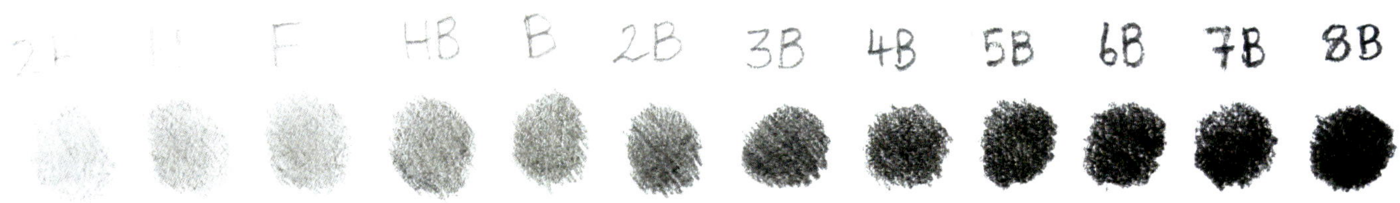

A good exercise is to create a swatch chart of your range of graphite pencils to clearly show their individual depths of tone.

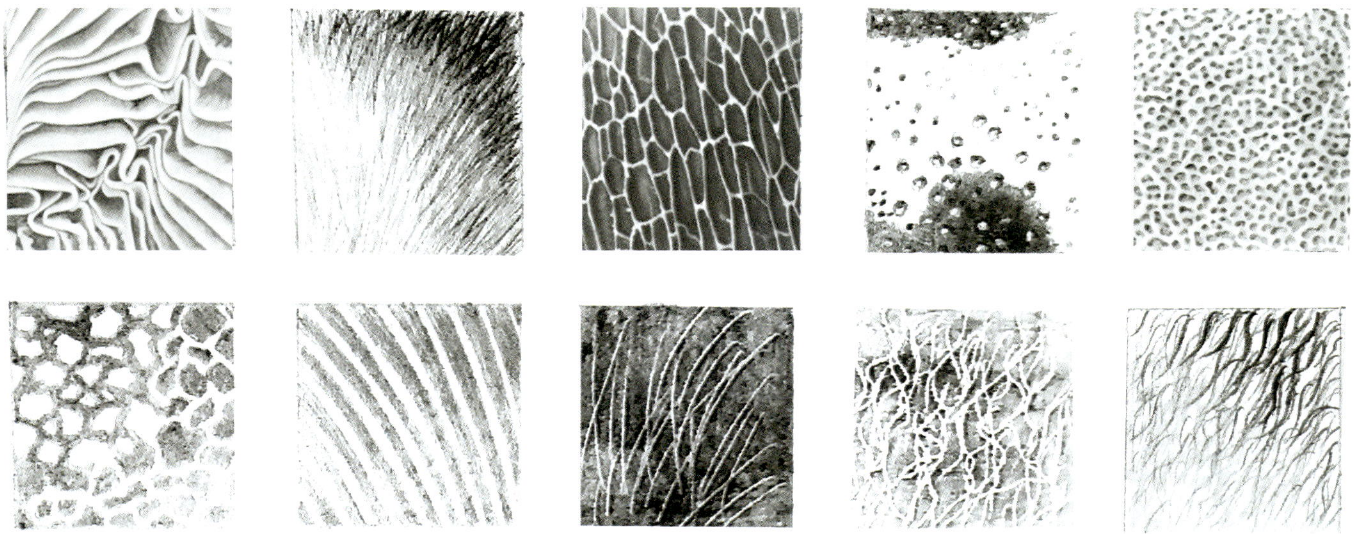

Graphite textures for fungi from top left: 1. Gill textures using continuous shading. 2. Furry textures. 3. Stipe textures. 4. Interesting marks and shading for colour. 5. Pore textures. 6. Positive and negative shading. 7. Gill textures. 8 and 9. Indenting with a sharp point to create highlighted lines. 10. Tonal curving lines.

Using an Eraser

Plastic erasers are best for cleanly removing mistakes from the paper. Kneadable or putty erasers can subtly lift graphite to create high or low lights and be moulded into points to add textures. They are useful for lifting out any excess graphite after transferring from a tracing onto watercolour paper. Don't rub with the putty eraser as you would with a plastic eraser, just roll over or dab the graphite. They can also lift little particles of charcoal rather than sweeping them away with a soft brush as you would with eraser crumbs. To clean it, just stretch it out and knead it a few times and it will become clean. The eraser pens are so useful for more control and refined erasing of smaller areas, cleaning up edges or sweeping out fine lines of highlight.

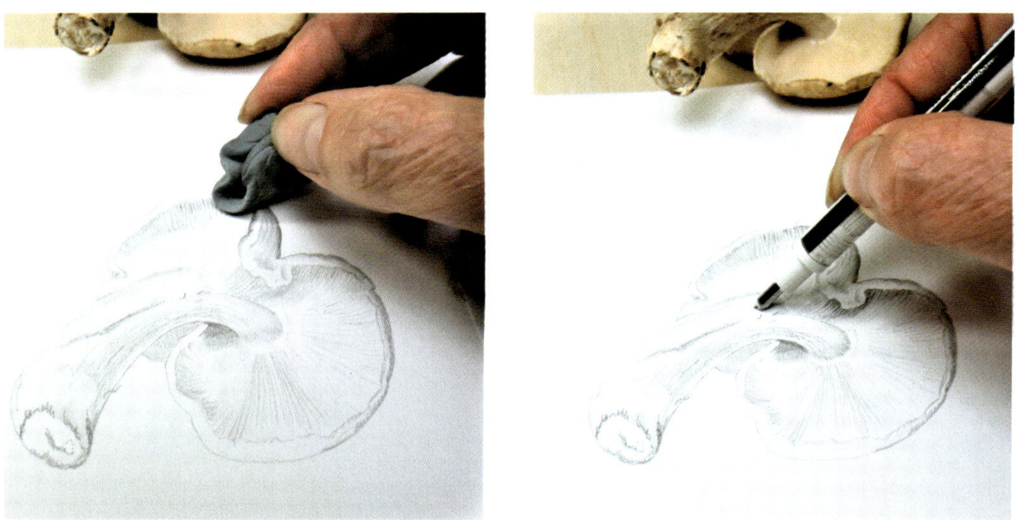

Here the kneadable eraser is dabbed onto an area of graphite to subtly lighten the tone there as I felt it had gone too dark. On the right, the eraser pen is lifting out a small area of highlight.

STEP-BY-STEP: USING THE GRAPHITE SHADING TECHNIQUES

This drawing of shitake mushrooms uses some of the shading techniques described, mainly the continuous tone, contour hatching and squiggly lines, to create their forms and textures on their surfaces. I used a Bristol vellum paper here which has a texture to it and that is fine but if you want to achieve extra fine detail, a Bristol smooth paper could be better.

Shitake mushrooms – *Lentinula edodes* – are the well-known mass cultivated fungi from East Asia. It has been known to be in cultivation in China since the thirteenth century.

MATERIALS USED:

- Strathmore Bristol 400 vellum paper
- HB, B, 2B and 4B graphite pencils
- HB Pentel mechanical pencil
- Eraser pen
- Kneadable eraser
- Derwent indenting tool
- Tortillion blending stump

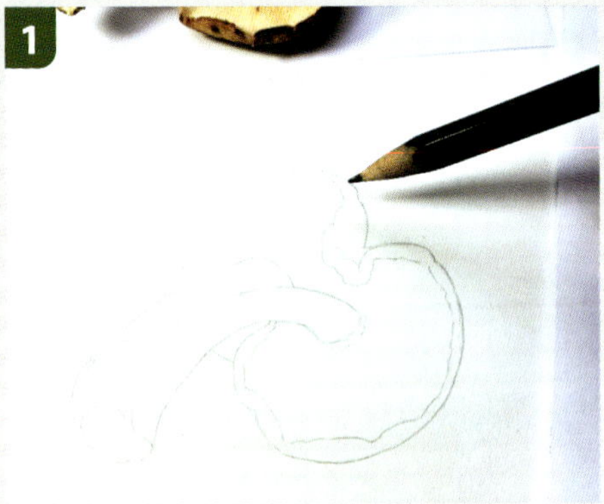

I drew out the main outline lightly using an HB so that the drawing showed up in the picture, but normally I would use a 2H. I didn't hold the pencil close to the tip and it was not too sharp as I didn't want to indent the paper. This mushroom had such an interesting shape, looking like twin mushrooms about to split into two.

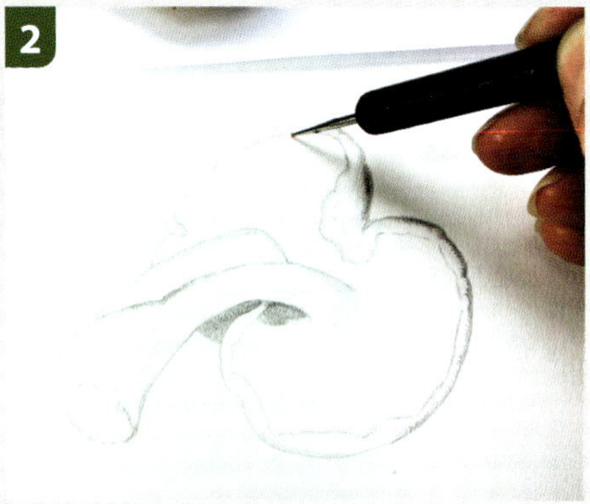

I then started to come in with the HB pencil adding tones, mainly using contour hatching strokes around the curve of each surface, following its form. Then, I decided to experiment with the Derwent indenting tool. I indented thin lines for the pale edges of the gills in some areas, but not everywhere.

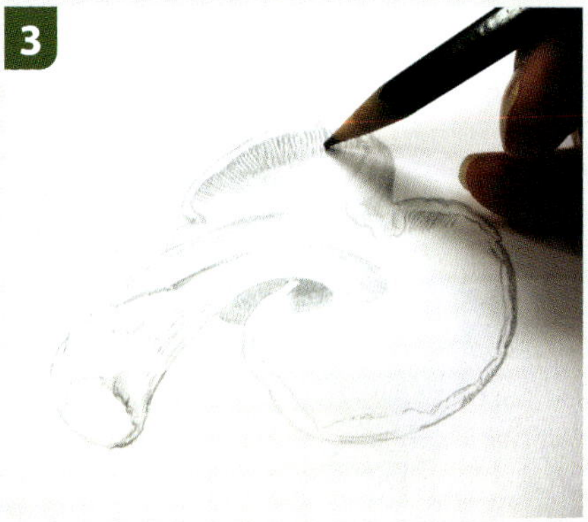

Then I shaded over the indented lines to create those pale gill edges. I think it worked quite well, but it's good to practise these things first before embarking on a finished piece of work. You may be able to see the indented lines in the lower left-hand corner of the cap.

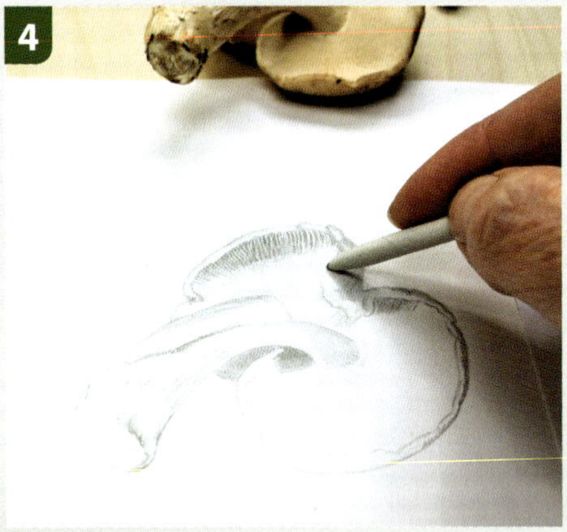

I used a tortillion to even out the graphite tone as it was a little grainy, but not pressing too heavily. I had also previously added the darkest area of tone – I squinted my eyes to see where the darkest area was and added it in. The eraser pen swept out any highlights where they were needed to be re-established.

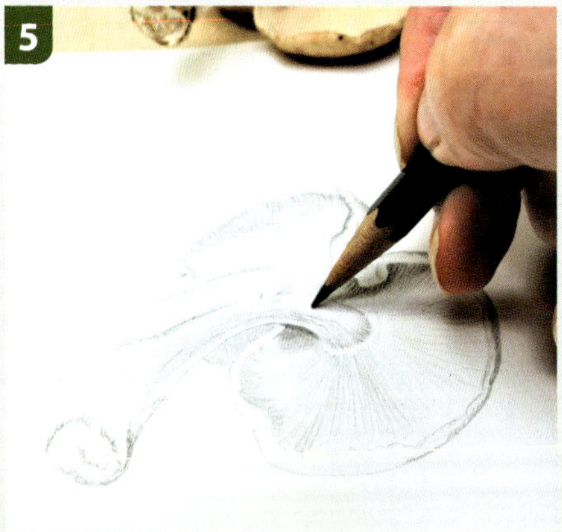

The tone was laid in, covering all areas and increasing depth to the shadows with B, 2B and 4B pencils. Then I started to refine with a sharper tipped pencil and also a mechanical pencil, adding texture and detail to the fibrous stipe. The sharper points neaten edges and allow finer details to be added.

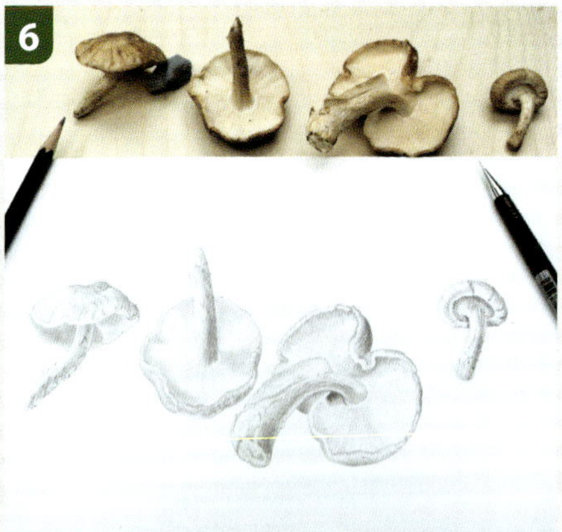

The finished study of shitake mushrooms, with different sizes and viewpoints. This Bristol vellum paper does have a bit of texture to it and during this study, I found that I would prefer a smoother paper for graphite work, so would opt for a cartridge paper or Bristol smooth/plate surface next time.

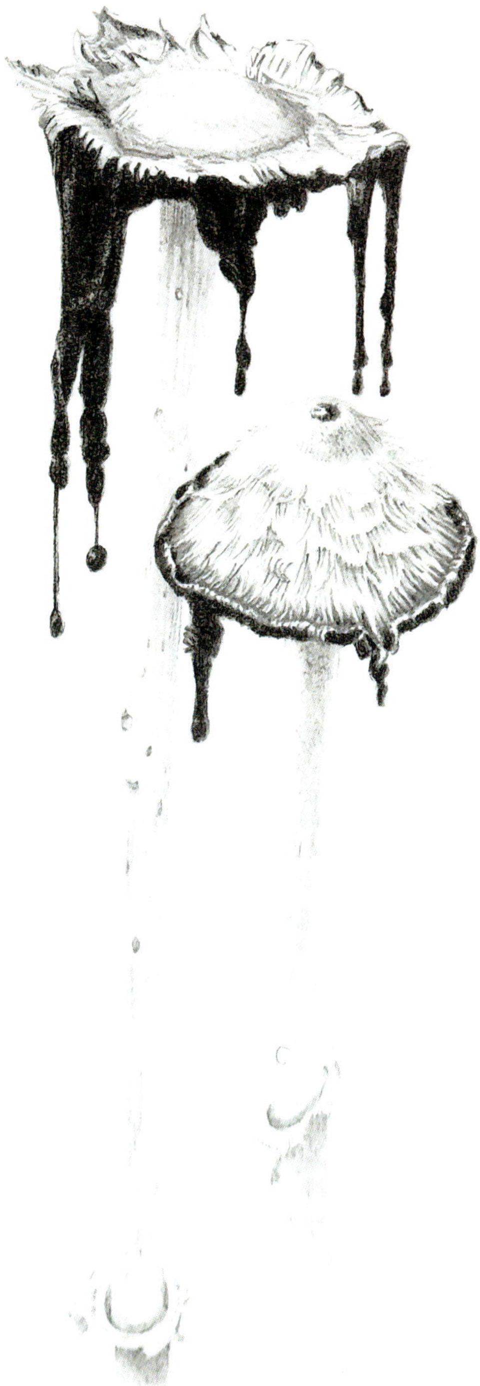

Inky caps by my friend and botanical artist, Polly O'Leary. With Faber-Castell 9000 graphite pencils, she started with 2H, then worked through HB, B, to 2B; 4B was needed for those tiny areas of dark to make them pop. But to get the real intense inky blacks, she used a Carb Othello Black Pastel pencil. This avoided getting the annoying shine associated with darker graphite pencil. (© Polly O'Leary)

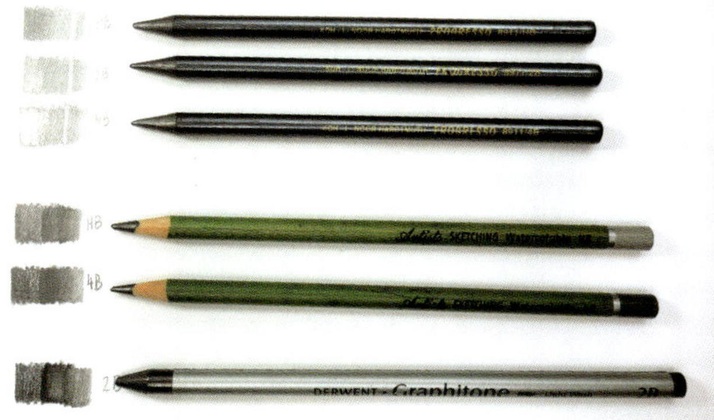

Swatching out my miscellaneous graphite pencils. The graphite sticks at the top and the water-soluble graphite below. The latter swatches are seen half dry and half blended out with water. In the top swatches you can see the graphite shine.

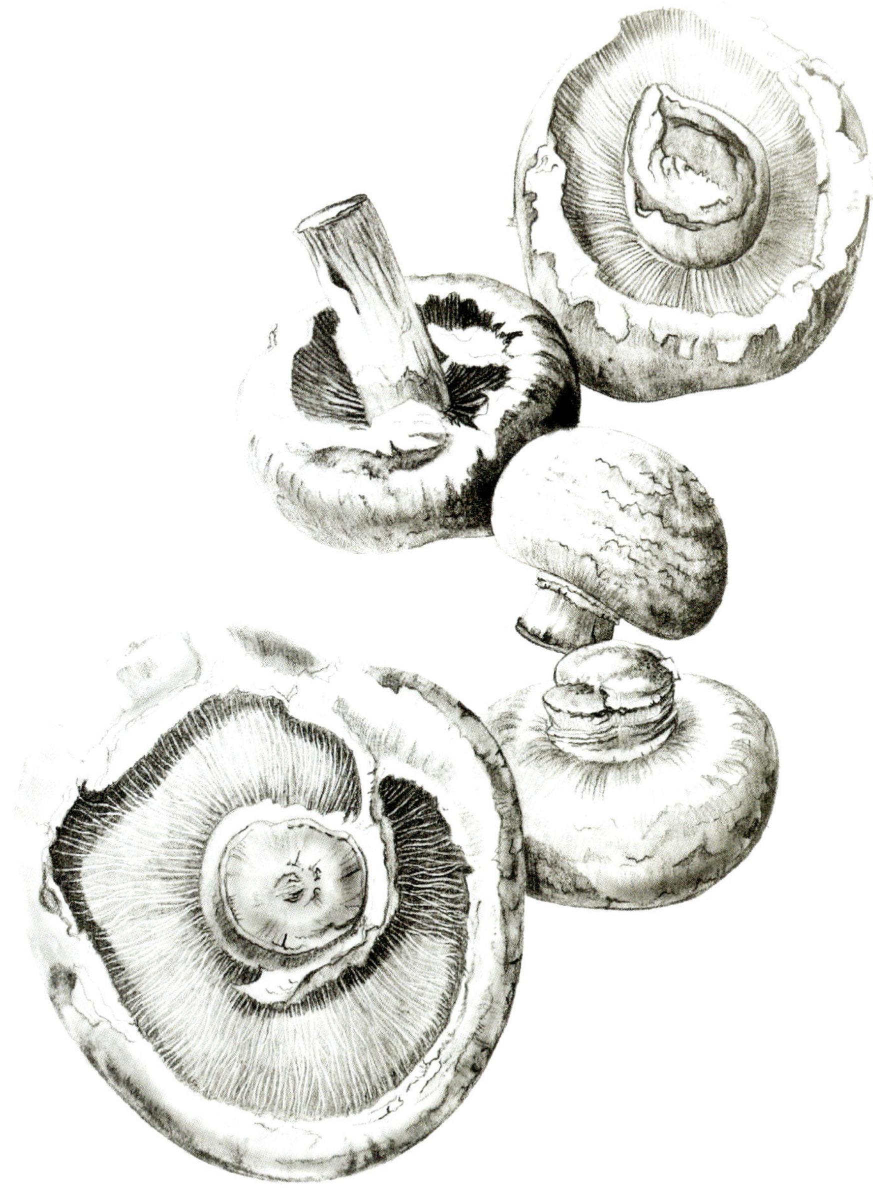

A study of supermarket mushrooms in the sketchbook using water-soluble graphite and usual graphite. The gills on the bottom mushroom were indented again as before but the top gills were just drawn in with a sharp pencil. The paper is cartridge and has a much smoother finish, but sometimes paper that is too smooth or slick can't take many layers.

SCULPTING FORM

Australian artist, Sharon Field, specialises in sculpting the intricate forms and patterns of her subjects in detail. She shares her inspirations for her drawing of fungi from 2020, called *Vignette – Opal colours that glow and fade*. She reveals, 'This little fungus I found under some eucalypts; in life it is only a few centimetres high. Orange in colour with dark broken stripes over its dome, I found it when it was slowly returning to the soil. I decided to draw it without colour, focusing on the patterns and sculptural beauty. While fungi are like opals, coming in many, beautiful colours, they do not survive in a showy form for very long.'

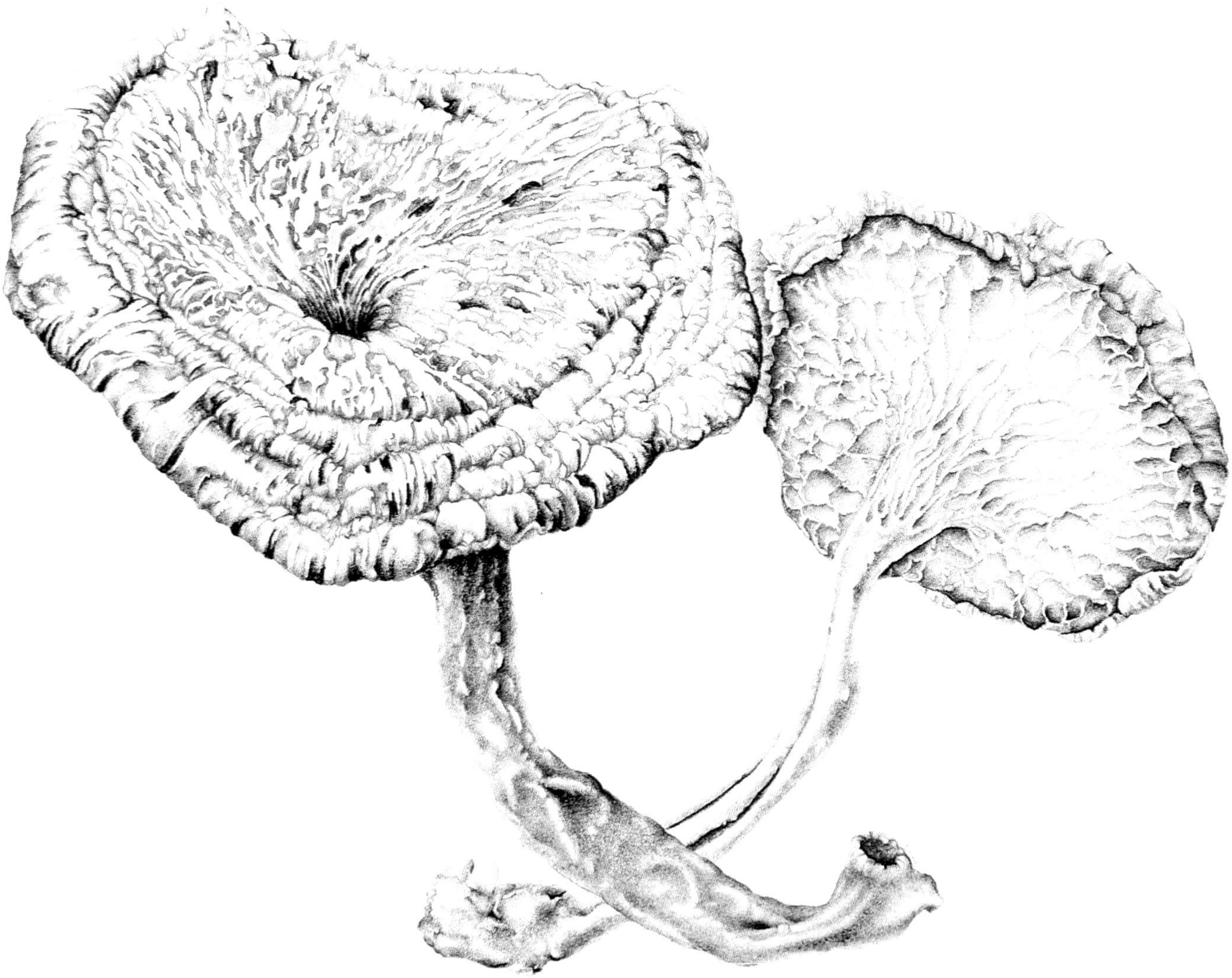

'Vignette' by Sharon Field. She begins her work with a hard pencil (6H) building up the tones with sharp pencils towards the 'B' ranges. The final dark highlights are done with a very sharp soft pencil. When she works with graphite, she considers that she is painting with pencil! The title for this work comes from a line in the poem 'The Colours of Light' by well-known Australian poet, Dorothea Mackellar. (© Sharon Field)

Charcoal and Carbon

When using charcoal pencils, you can use some of the same techniques as used for graphite drawing. The small, elliptical movements as in the continuous tone method will give an even consistency to tonal shading. Hatching and cross hatching will give quick, gestural shading. Stippling will not be successful due to the larger tip and rougher nature of charcoal.

Charcoal can be erased just as graphite can, but I find it's still best to leave some highlights as the white paper as charcoal and carbon pencils are harder to lift than graphite and you can never quite get back the white paper. The softest charcoals and willow or vine charcoals are the easiest to erase.

When drawing, you can cover the paper underneath your hand to protect the paper surface and this can also avoid any unwanted smudging. Glassine paper is a good option for this. For finished drawings, a light spray of graphite or pastel fixative can protect the artwork from smudging but always use outdoors preferably or with a mask.

Sharpening Pencils

Graphite pencils are easily sharpened with a barrel or handheld, metal sharpener. But for other types of pencil, you may not have as much success. Sometimes the tips break off or it can be a struggle to get a decent point, so you can try using a craft or X-Acto knife. This can be a good way to get sharpened tips to any type of pencil, although coloured pencil artists would be better off using a desktop sharpener such as the Rapesco 64 or perhaps a battery-operated one for efficiency. You need to be patient when sharpening with a knife and it can also be a strain on the hands to sharpen a lot of pencils. Using sandpaper is a good way of gaining a finer point. This can be purchased specifically for pencil artists or fine grade sandpaper can be obtained from a hardware store and could be just as effective and possibly cheaper too.

Some artists like to expose a little more of the graphite or charcoal so as to be able to sweep in larger areas of tone using the pencil on its side.

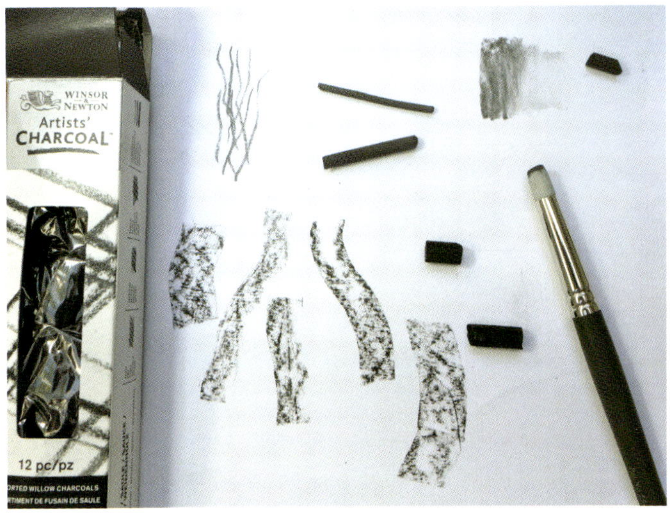

Testing out willow charcoal sticks – the thicker sticks are used on their sides and can make the shape of a mushroom stipe in one go. The thinner sticks create expressive linework; great for warming up or loose tonal studies.

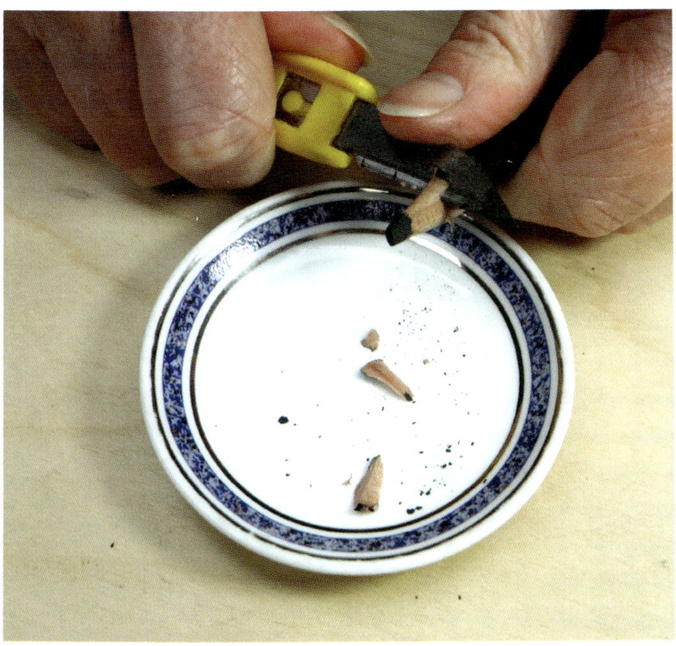

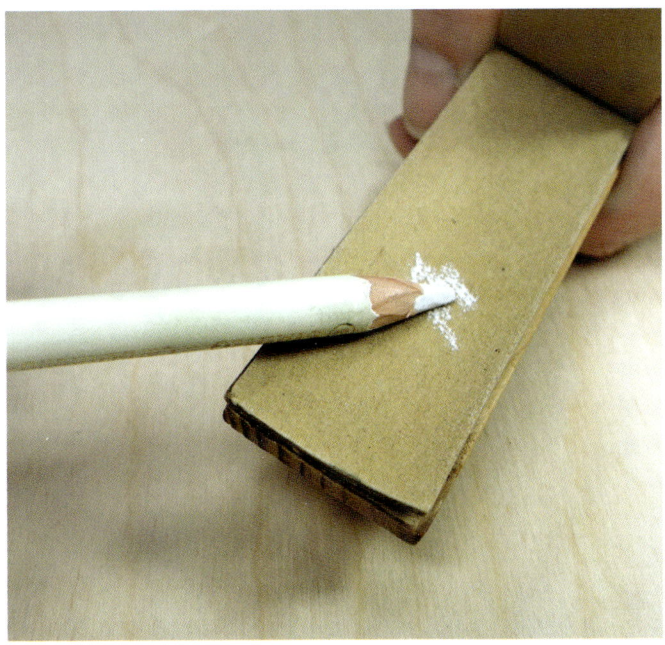

Left: Using a craft knife to sharpen a charcoal pencil. The knife is held with the right hand and it is gently but firmly pushed with the left-hand thumb to carve the wood down carefully so as not to gouge out chunks. Right: Using a Derwent sandpaper block to gently shape a finer point to a pastel pencil.

STEP-BY-STEP: DRAWING A CHESTNUT MUSHROOM WITH CHARCOAL

Using charcoal is a great warm up and a much faster way of achieving a tonal drawing than using graphite. It can also be a looser way of drawing. The Strathmore vellum paper is perfect with just the right amount of tooth to grab the charcoal and gives a subtle texture that suits the skin of these chestnut mushrooms. The packs of willow charcoal contain many different sizes and thicknesses of charcoal stick, so you can add in smaller areas of tone with the thinnest pieces if you don't have a charcoal pencil. Willow charcoal is much easier to erase if it goes over the outline.

MATERIALS USED:

- Strathmore Bristol Vellum 400 paper
- Winsor & Newton willow charcoal pieces
- Derwent flat silicone tipped blender
- Conté à Paris 2B charcoal pencil
- Spray fixative

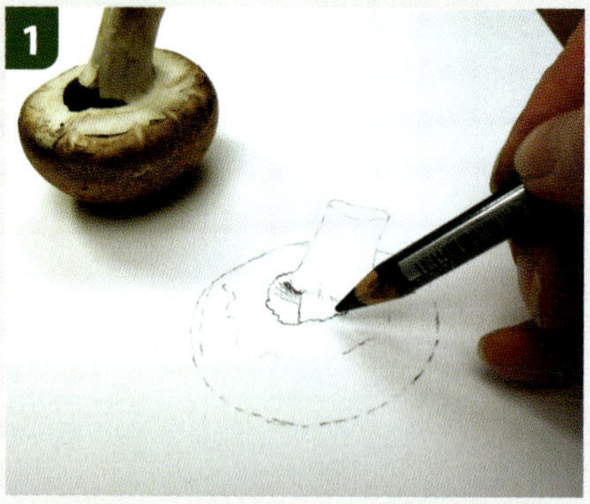

Very lightly and with broken line draw in the outline of the mushroom taking care with proportions. You could also draw lightly with an H graphite pencil before going over it with the charcoal pencil to be sure of an initial accurate drawing as the charcoal pencil is harder to erase if you make a mistake.

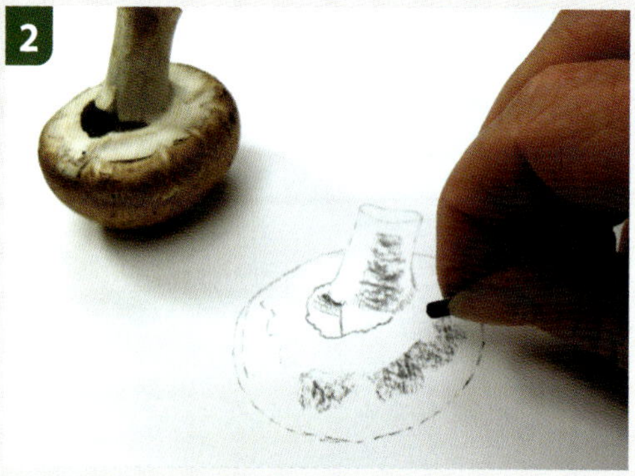

Break off a small piece of the willow charcoal to fit the size of the mushroom and sweep in the areas of shadow with the piece on its side to follow the contour lines on the surface. It does create a lovely textured look that is seen on the mushroom. Willow charcoal is the easiest to erase if it goes over the outline.

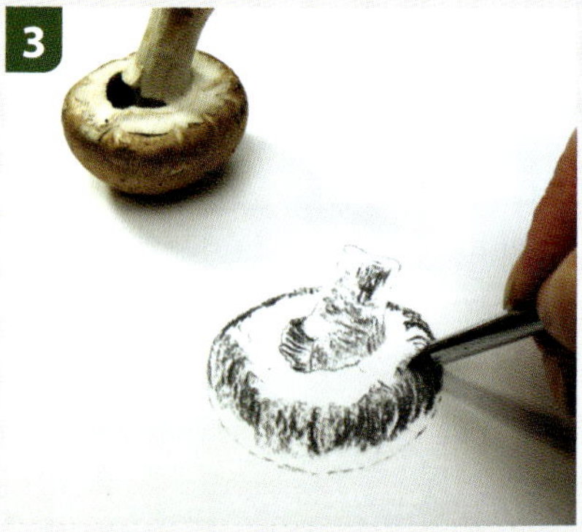

Then blend out some of the tones with the silicone-tipped blending tool going with the contour lines again. These are great tools for blending the looser mediums of charcoal and pastel. Try not to smooth it out too much at the front of the mushroom as it's very easy to lose that lovely texture.

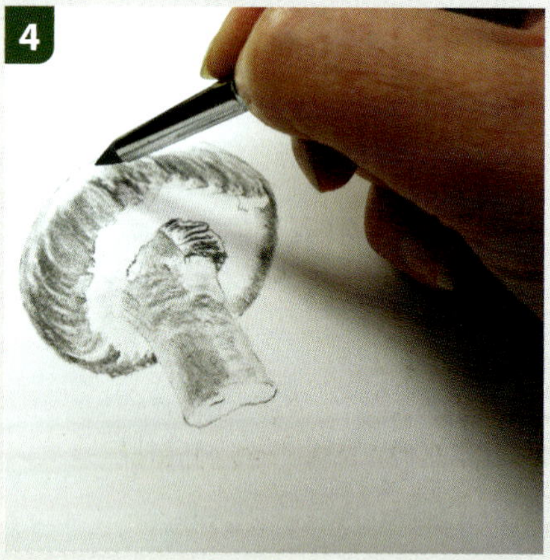

When adding the paler tones, you can take advantage of the charcoal residue that is already on the blender to add them in and also blend out darker areas into lighter areas, turning the paper around to work from the best angle.

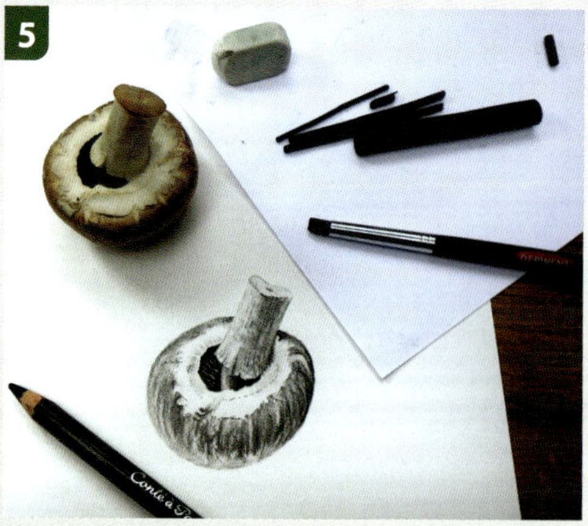

Finally, go in again with a sharp charcoal pencil to refine edges, enhance details and add the darkest tones. You can sharpen charcoal pencils gently with a craft knife and then use some sandpaper to get a good point. Derwent has a special sandpaper block for pencils shown on the previous page.

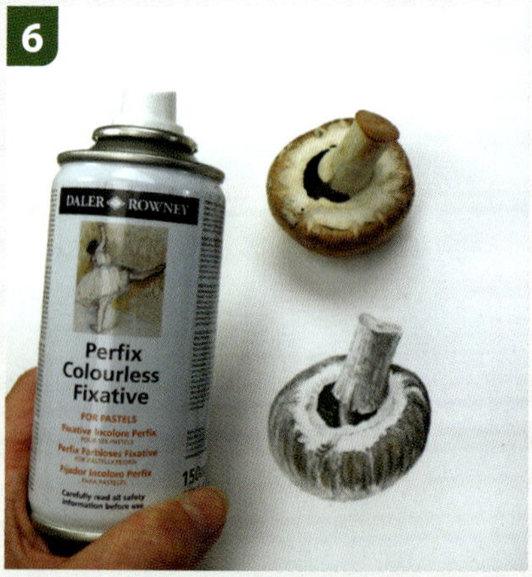

When happy with the result, give a light spray of fixative to protect from smudging – use it in a very well-ventilated room or outside and it's important not to hold the can too close to the drawing while spraying. Fixative can darken the tones if too much is applied, so a light spray or two should be sufficient.

PEN AND INK TECHNIQUES

Using pen and ink is a very rewarding medium. It is fantastic for showing textures, rough and smooth alike and as there is no distraction of colour, it depicts tonal contrast very well. It can be used for monochrome studies or with a watercolour wash (pen and wash) for added colour and softening.

Techniques for pen are similar to the other drawing mediums that we've looked at, hatching lines and stippling being the most commonly used (*see* the earlier graphite section). When using stippling, it's important to keep your dots consistently rounded and similar sized as it can become a little untidy if rushed.

Dip pens will give you a wide variety of line and choice of inks and colours. You press the nib lightly for a very thin line and press harder to create a thicker line. With the fibre-tipped pens of course you will need to have a range of different sizes of nibs to gain more variety in the line.

The best paper for pen and ink drawing is a smooth paper so a hot pressed watercolour paper or Bristol smooth surface will work well. Start with a light pencil drawing of the subject as a guide, making sure that the proportions of the subject are correct and making a note of where the darkest and lightest areas are. Then begin working with the pen to draw the outline in. Go lightly using broken or intermittent line and dots so as not to draw anything too definite or heavy, and then work into the shadowed areas with your chosen mark-making techniques. Leave the highlights free of marks and be careful as ink can't be erased easily. If you're feeling brave you can go in without the aid of a pencil underlay.

It's worth reiterating how important using a quality paper for finished artworks is, as it can be very frustrating trying to work with a cheaper paper that bleeds, making your little stipples swell in size!

Pen can also be mixed with watercolour washes. *See* Chapter 6 for more on this technique.

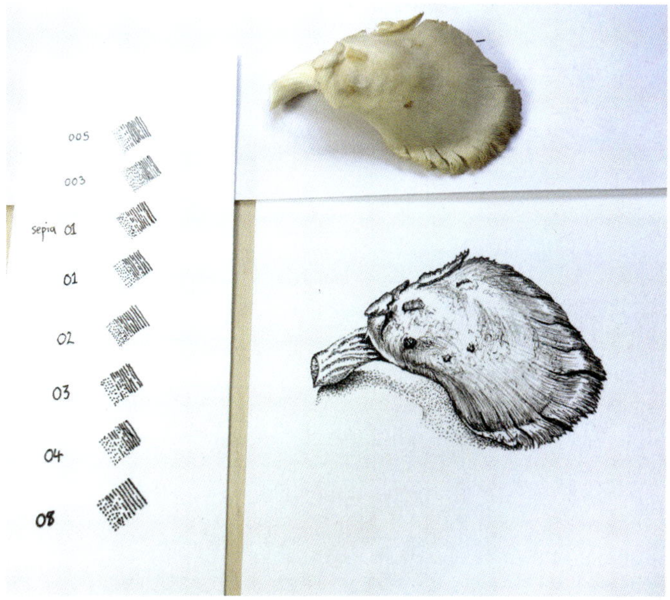

A pen test chart is a good idea to see what the different thicknesses of nibs can achieve, using the Pigma Micron range. The oyster mushroom sketch was completed using stippling and hatching and the faintest marks were made using an old 003 pen that was running out to give a fainter mark.

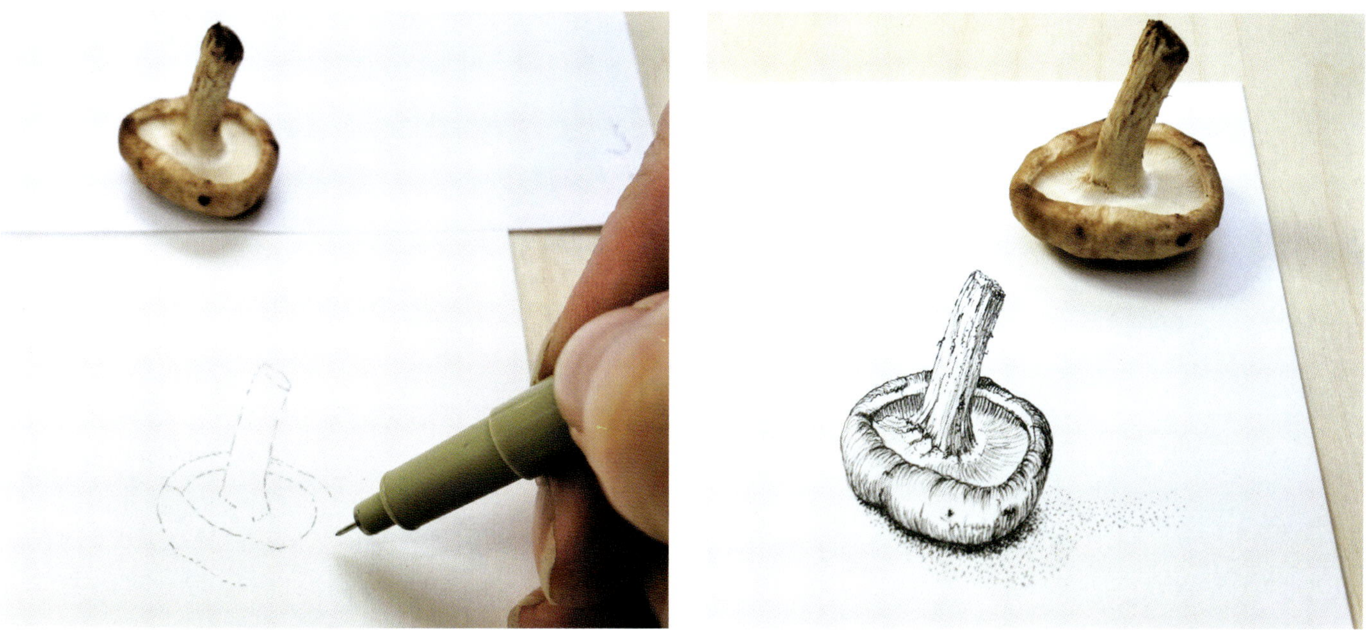

Using a Pigma Micron 003, the drawing was started tentatively as there was no pencil underlay, using little dots and strokes of the pen so that if a mistake was made it could be gone over and hidden. The drawing was finished rather quickly using contour hatching for the main body and stippling for the shadow.

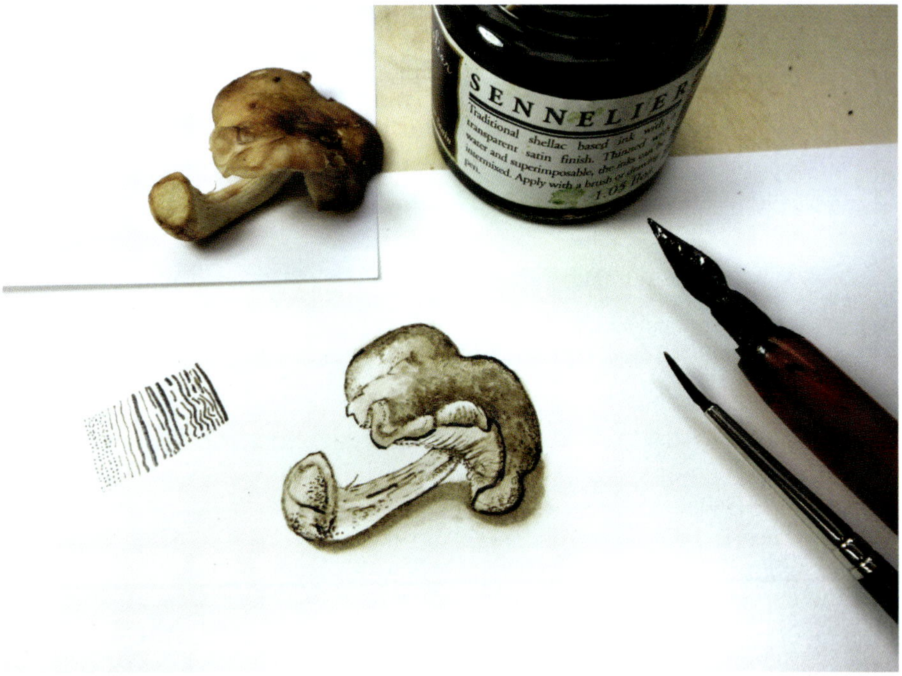

A shitake sketch using my very old dip pen (that I have had for thirty-seven years!) using Sennelier walnut ink. The ink is water-soluble so can be diluted into a beautiful wash perfect for hinting at the shadows. The Pigma Micron and many other fibre-tip pens are waterproof.

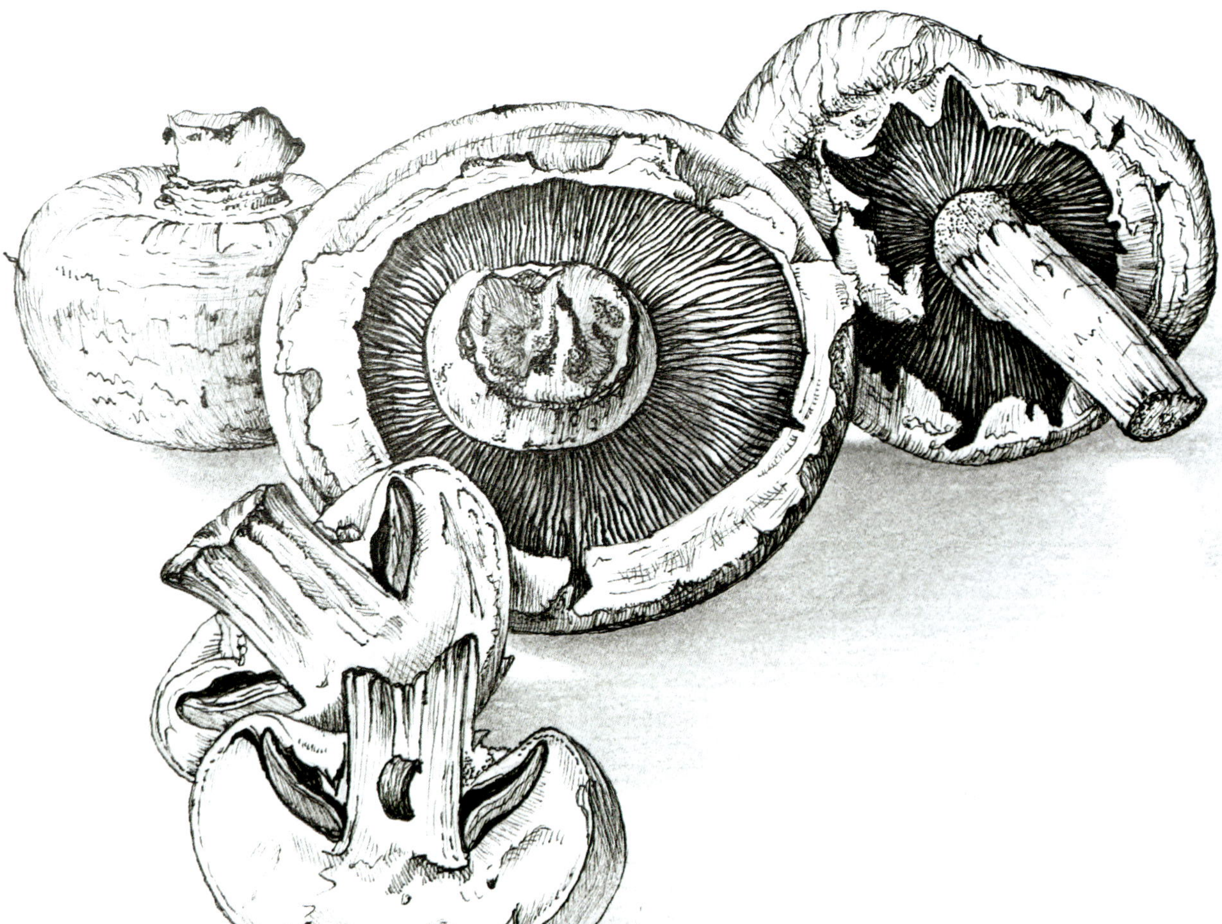

Baby portobellos and closed-cup mushrooms in pen in the sketchbook. I used a Pigma Micron 003 and 01 and a 2B graphite pencil blended with a tortillion for the shadows.

DRAWING ON TONED PAPERS

Working with toned papers is a great way of extending your drawing skills and experience when it comes to working with tone. There is a multitude of toned papers on the market today, ranging from black to cool and neutral greys to warm tans and beiges. You can even experiment with toning your own papers by staining with coffee, tea or inks or even a smooth layer of willow or vine charcoal gently rubbed into the paper with a tissue or soft cloth (if you're feeling brave, as it's quite messy!).

Think about the look that you want to achieve and how the subject will look against that background colour. For instance, a white mushroom would really pop out and be a little easier to depict against a black or grey background. *See* my black paper step by step further on.

When you draw on white paper you work from light to dark; you are starting from the extreme of the highlights. So, working on toned paper could make working out the tones a little easier as on toned paper you start with the mid tones, and you are able to push it either way tonally, towards the highlights by adding opaque whites or towards the shadows by adding darks. It can lead to some really interesting artworks that can have good visual impact.

In the Renaissance Period, great artists such as Michelangelo and Rubens sometimes used toned paper with inks and charcoals. Leonardo Da Vinci also toned his papers and then used white, red – sanguine and black chalks on them for initial studies.

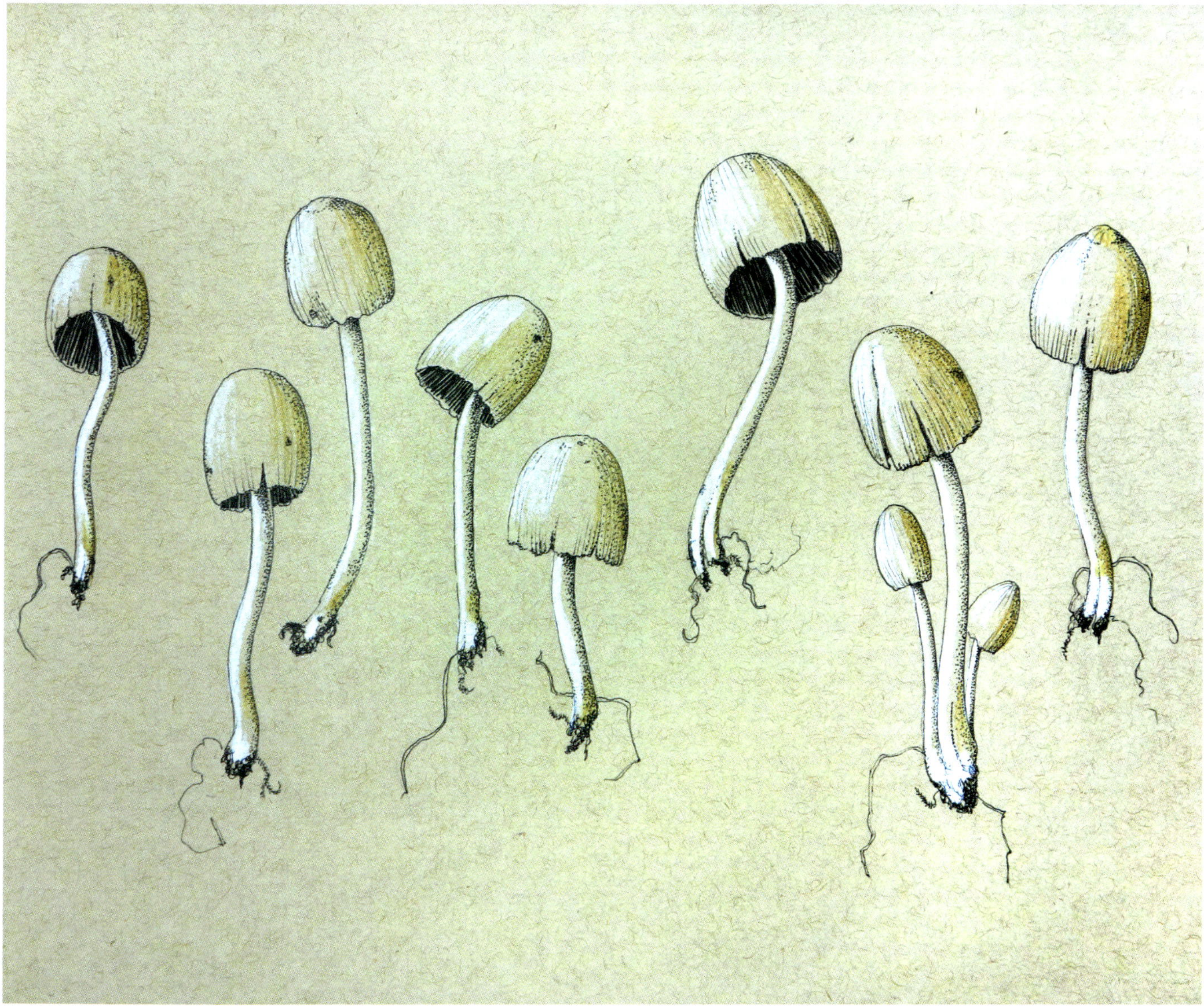

Dancing Inkcaps – *Coprinellus micaceus* – drawn on Strathmore toned tan sketchbook paper with pen stippling using Pigma Micron pens in sizes 003 to 01, Derwent Chinese White coloured pencil for highlights and also a touch of brown coloured pencil on the shadow sides.

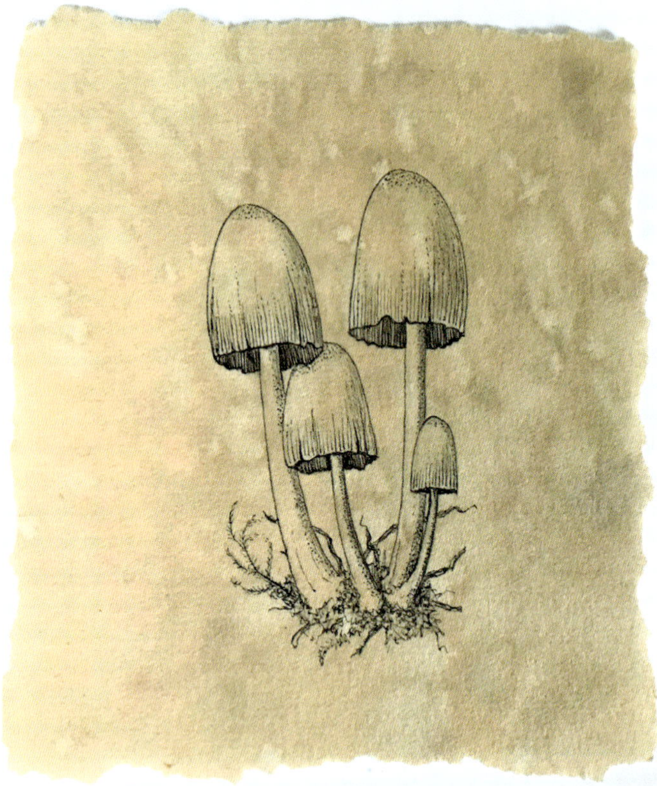

More inkcaps drawn in pen on coffee-dyed 140lb watercolour paper with salt textures. The paper was dunked into a large dish of a strong coffee brew and then laid out. I then sprinkled a small amount of table salt onto the paper while the background was still wet and left it to dry completely.

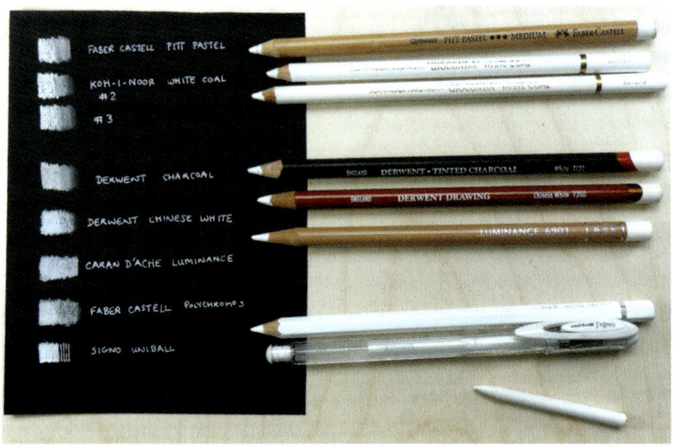

Testing out different white media and seeing how they perform on black paper. From top to bottom: pastel, charcoals (Koh-I-Noor and Derwent), coloured pencils (Derwent, Caran D'Ache, Faber-Castell) and last the Signo Uniball gel pen.

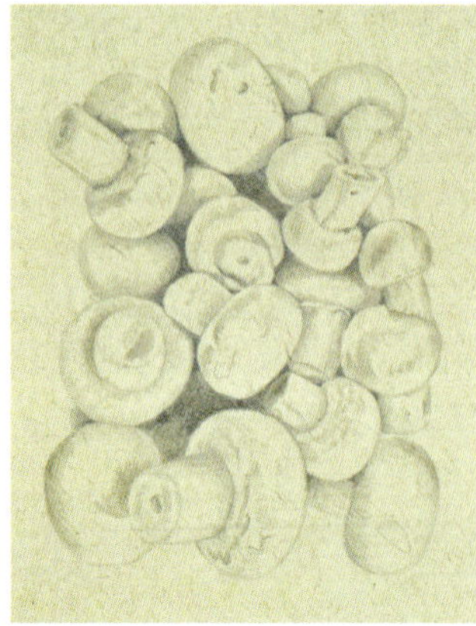

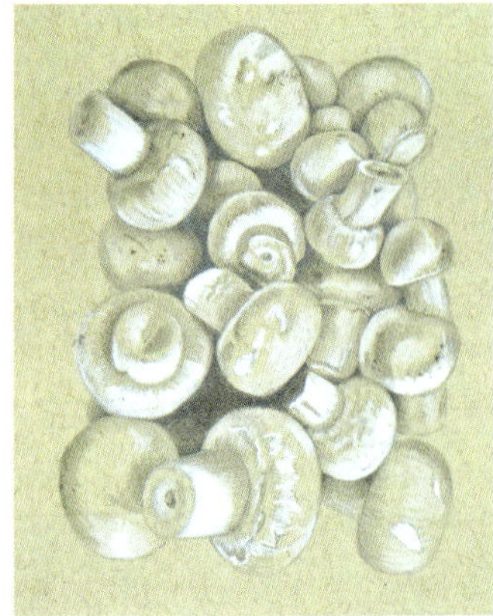

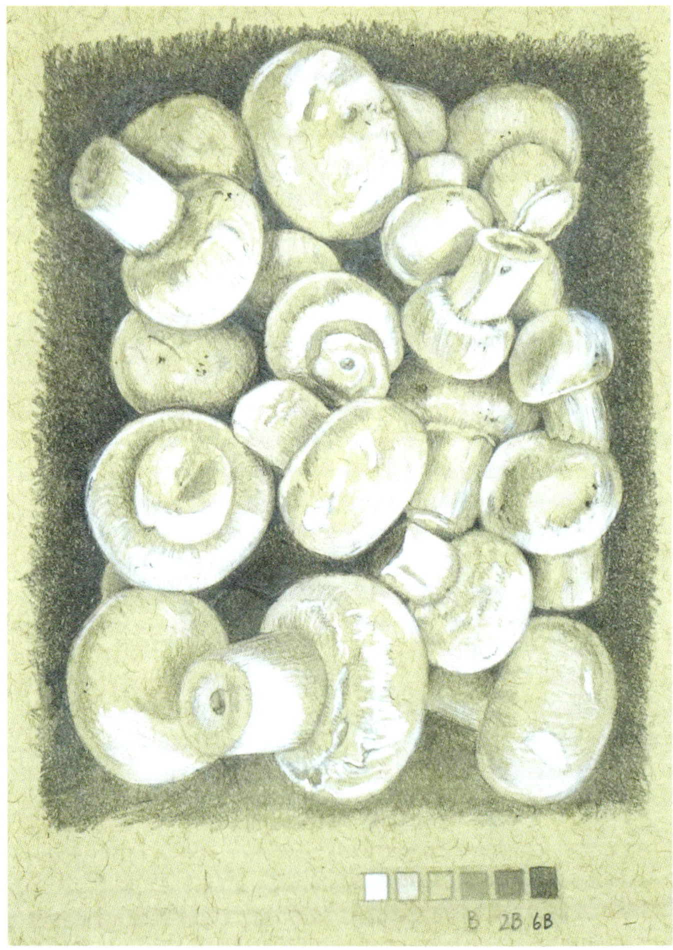

A collection of mushrooms drawn on Strathmore toned tan paper. After drawing the initial outline, the shadow tones are added in B and 2B graphite. The darkest little areas of negative space are cut in with a 4B and 6B. The tan colour of the paper is the mid tone and the highlights are added after in white pencil. The background was shaded in with a 4B Koh-I-Noor graphite stick.

STEP-BY-STEP: DRAWING A WHITE MUSHROOM ON BLACK PAPER

Drawing an ordinary, white, closed-cup mushroom bought from the supermarket is a great introduction to drawing on black paper. Again, the chalk is similar in application to the willow charcoal; looser but much quicker. On black paper you can work back and forth with the white and black charcoal pencils until you're happy with the finish.

MATERIALS USED:

- Piece of white chalk
- Derwent white tinted charcoal pencil
- Derwent dark charcoal pencil
- Faber-Castell kneadable eraser
- No. 2 flat chisel colour shaper silicone tool
- Black paper from Stillman and Birn

1

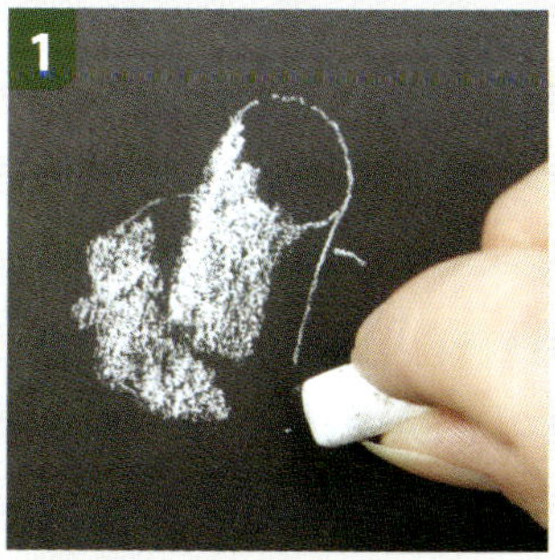

I started by lightly drawing in a faint outline of the stalk and upper area in the white charcoal pencil, then I decided to use the whole side of the chalk to quickly carve out the top body of the mushroom. This was a piece of ordinary chalk that is used for blackboards, you could also use a pastel stick.

2

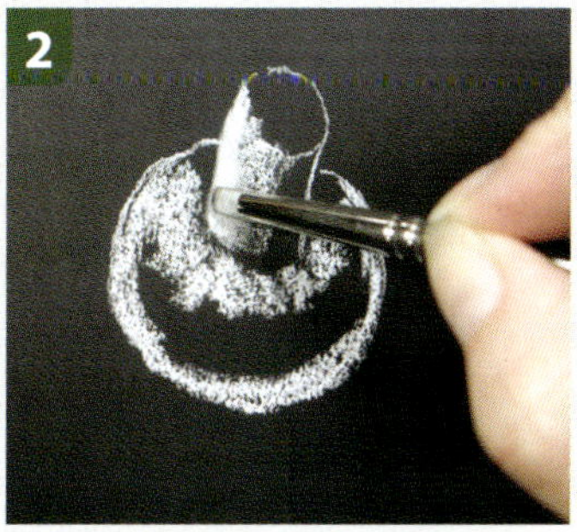

Then I drew in the base outline of the body with the tip of the chalk. Note that I left the right side of the stalk and the central body area as the black paper to effectively interpret the shadows; it's advantageous to utilise the black paper for the dark tones. When the shape was mapped in, I used the colour shaper blending tool to create the rounded form of the stalk and body, taking care to always work with the contour lines of the subject to create a three-dimensional look.

3

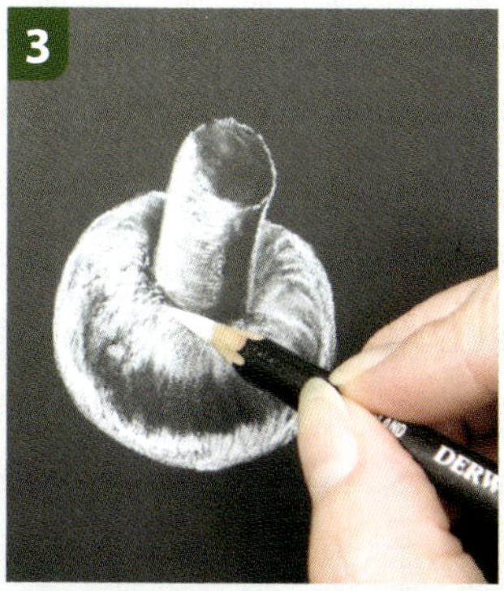

When the whole mushroom had been shaped with the blender, I used the white charcoal pencil to refine and neaten up edges, starting to add a little detail and texture.

4

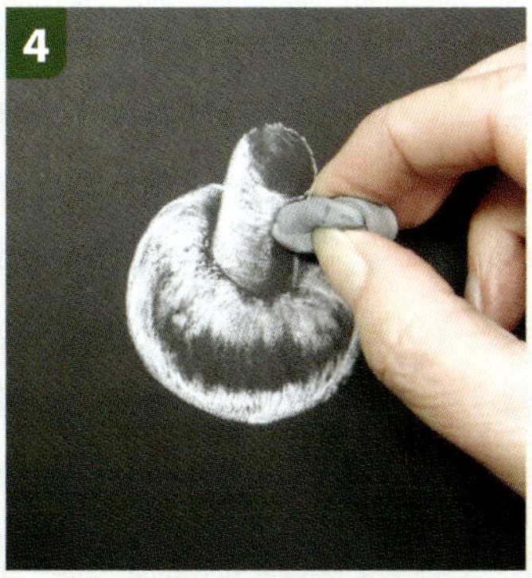

Areas that needed taking back to the dark paper were lifted with a small piece of kneadable eraser, so it is a very forgiving medium.

5

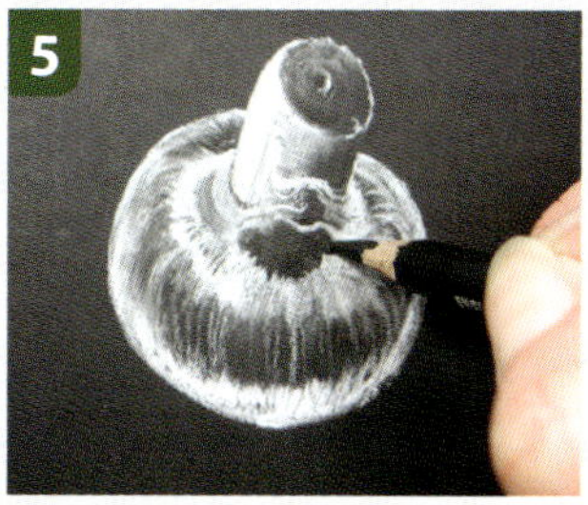

In the centre of the mushroom I used the sharp black charcoal pencil to cut into the dark areas negatively, where the gills are hidden underneath the rim of the white cap. This was very effective for creating that edge. I used both the black and white charcoal pencils in a few other areas to add details and textures.

6

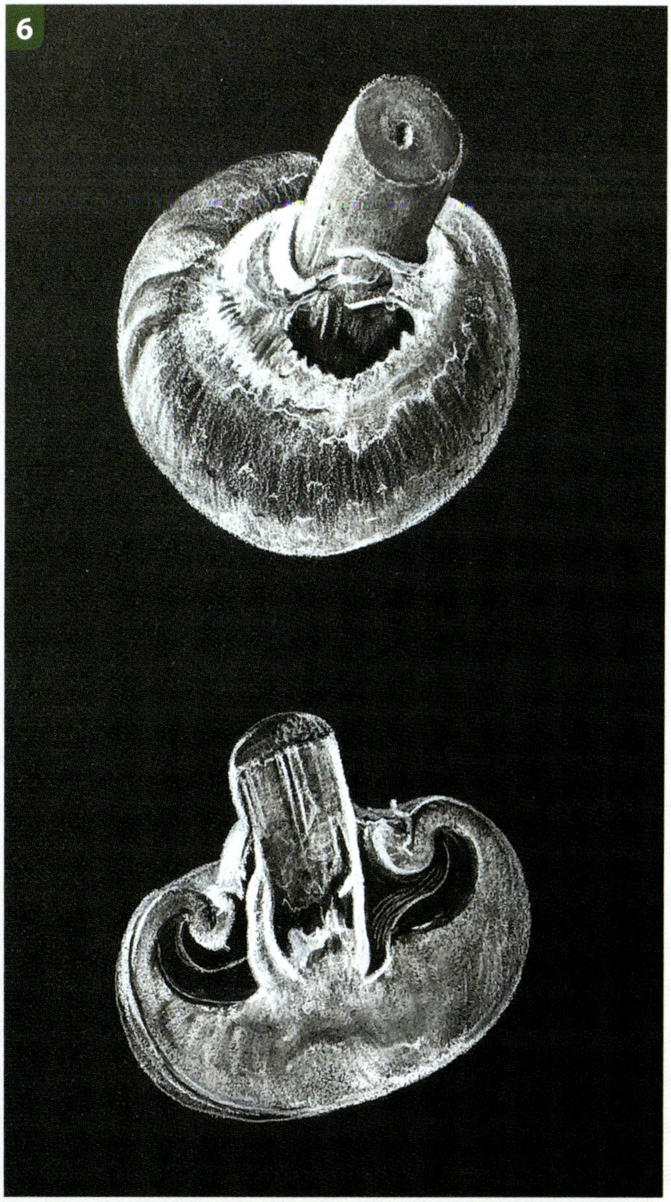

The white pencil was used to add finishing details, neaten up the outside edges and add the contour lines that flow over the darker toned central area to depict the textural surface that is seen. I used the black and white pencils to go back and forth refining details until I was happy with the look. I then decided to cut the mushroom in half to explore the interior, which I drew in the same ways as previously shown, starting with the piece of chalk and white pencil.

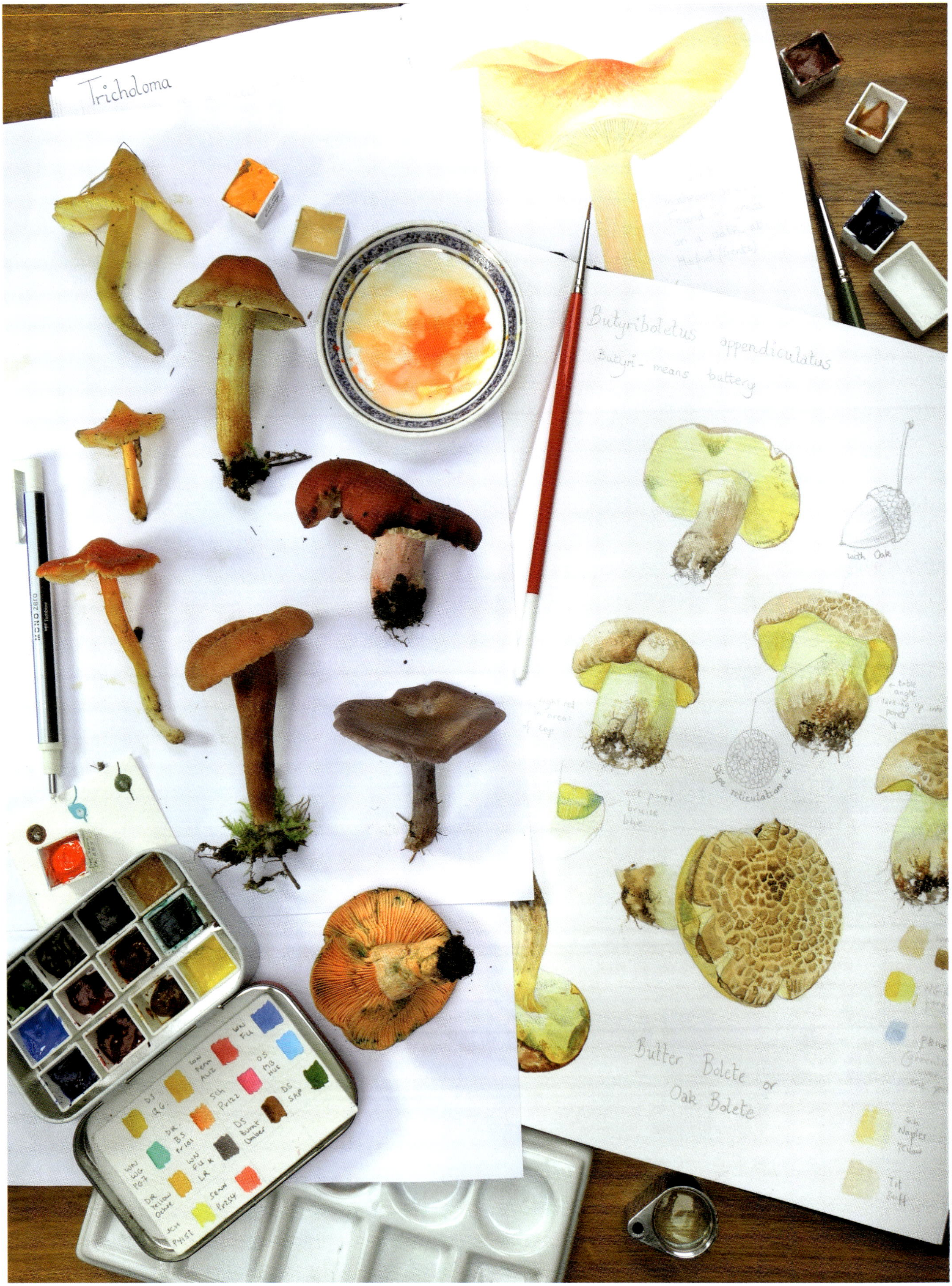
Tricholoma
Butyriboletus appendiculatus
Butyri- means buttery
with Oak
cut pores bruise blue
Stipe reticulation x4
Butter Bolete or Oak Bolete
Naples Yellow
Tit Buff

CHAPTER 5

USING COLOUR WITH DIFFERENT MEDIA

'The first of all the simple colours is white, although some would not admit that black or white are colours, the first being a source or receiver of colours, and the latter totally deprived of them.'

LEONARDO DA VINCI (1452–1519)

Colour means different things to different people and cultures, and it can evoke many feelings and emotions – like red evokes heat and fire; it is energetic and the blues are cool and serene, with a calming effect. Colour is relative and our perception of one colour changes in relation to the colour adjacent to it. This chapter will start with the basics of colour theory that are helpful and interesting for artists to know about and to recap on. Colour theory can be a difficult subject for beginners, but a little study and knowledge goes a long way.

THE PHYSICS OF COLOUR

Each wavelength of light is a particular colour and the colours we see are a result of these wavelengths of light being reflected back to our eyes from a subject. White light is actually made up of all of the colours of the rainbow because it contains all of the wavelengths. Objects appear different colours because they absorb some colours (wavelengths) and reflect other colours. White objects reflect all colours back, and black objects absorb all colours.

Isaac Newton offered a proper scientific study of colour around 1660. It was in his famous experiment where he split a beam of white light into the seven colours of the rainbow with a prism, proving that white light was made up of those different colours.

We still use the Swiss artist and teacher, Johannes Itten's (1888–1967) twelve colour-sphere today, which is based on the RBY (red/blue/yellow) system of primary colours that we were taught in school. CMY (cyan/magenta/yellow) is the system used by printers. We should be able to mix any colour using just these three primaries. Looking at the colour wheel will help you to understand colour.

Secondary Colours: These are green, orange and purple and they are formed by mixing the primary colours; blue and yellow makes green, yellow and red makes orange and so on.

Tertiary Colours: Yellow-orange, red-orange, red-purple, blue-purple, blue-green and yellow-green. These are the colours formed by mixing a primary and a secondary colour. That's why the hue is a two-word name, such as blue-green, red-violet and yellow-orange.

Complementary colours are colours that are opposite each other on the colour wheel, such as blue and orange, yellow and purple and red and green. These colours when mixed together will neutralise and cancel each other out. Yet when placed next to each other in a painting, they will create a vibrancy and colour contrast that stands out. Colours in nature show us this, for example, the red of holly berries against their green leaves. This is the concept of colour harmony, and it can help us use colour in a way that is pleasing to the eye.

Painting a collection of colourful mushrooms.

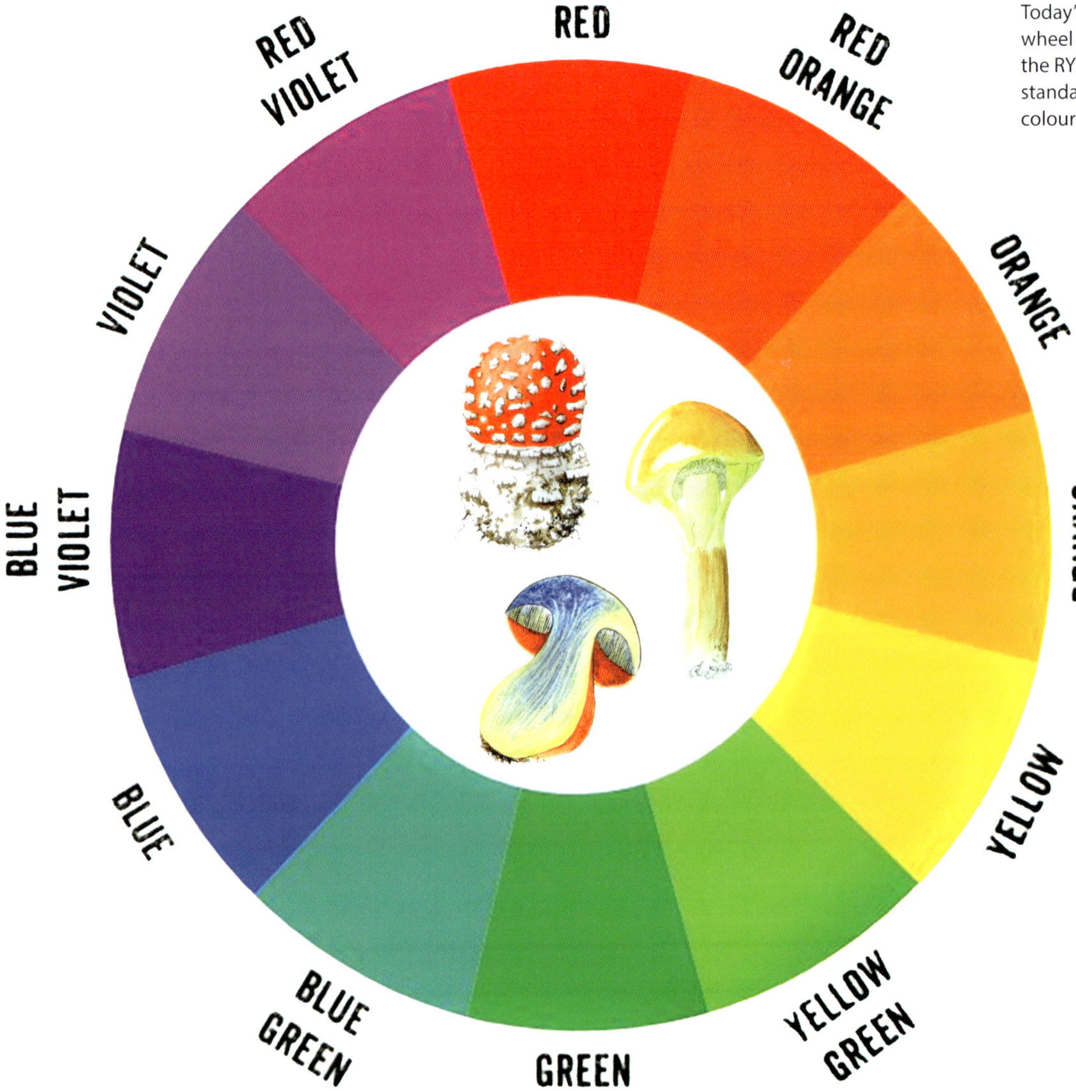

Today's commonly used colour wheel of twelve colours based on the RYB (red, yellow, and blue) colour standard. You can easily see all the colour relationships at a glance.

Complementary colours create vibrancy and intense contrasts if placed close together in a painting, but when mixed produce neutral tones of grey and brown. When choosing shadow colours, you can sometimes look to the colour wheel for guidance, for example, a warm yellow can be shaded with a cool violet.

Harmonious colours or analogous colours are any three or four colours that are next to each other on the colour wheel, such as green-yellow, yellow, and orange-yellow; they're in the same family, if you like. This creates a calm and serene look with usually one of the three colours dominating the scheme.

Monochromatic colour schemes are made with tones, tints and shades from one single hue that can be used for a subtle and simple look. It can be useful when learning to paint to use a single colour, which allows tonal values to be easily seen.

Triadic colour schemes are a triangle of three colours that are evenly spaced on the colour wheel, but with one colour dominating.

THE ATTRIBUTES OF COLOUR

Hue – This is the basic or local colour visible in a subject or pigment in the mid tones. In essence, it's just another word for colour.

Saturation – This indicates the strength of any colour that's seen, and it is lessened when the colour is paler, greyer or darker. This can be done by adding a little neutral tint to the basic hue to reduce its brightness. Also known as chroma or intensity.

Tonal Value – This dictates the lightness or darkness of the colours that are seen. When a colour is stripped of pigment you are left with its tone, so therefore tone is just as important as colour. Yellow is the brightest tone, with purple and indigo the darkest.

Tint – A pale, pastel colour with a low saturation and a high light value; a pigment diluted with lots of water or with white in the case of other media such as gouache or acrylic.

Shade – A darker, shaded tone of hue. This will have a lower saturation and light level. Adding a neutral tint, grey or some of the complementary colour to the hue will lower the shade value.

COLOUR TEMPERATURE AND COLOUR BIAS

We know that colours on the red half of the colour wheel are warm and colours on the blue half are cool, but colours also have a temperature bias; the primaries can be warm or cool as well. Being aware of this will help with clean colour mixing.

COLOUR BIASES WITH MATCHING PIGMENTS

- Cool yellows lean to green or blue – lemon yellows, green golds
- Warm yellows lean to red or orange – Indian yellows, new gamboge
- Cool reds lean to purple or blue – permanent rose, quinacridone magenta
- Warm reds lean to orange or yellow – scarlet lake, vermillion hue
- Cool blues lean to green or yellow – cerulean blue, phthalo blue – green shade, turquoise
- Warm blues lean to red or purple – French ultramarine, phthalo blue – red shade

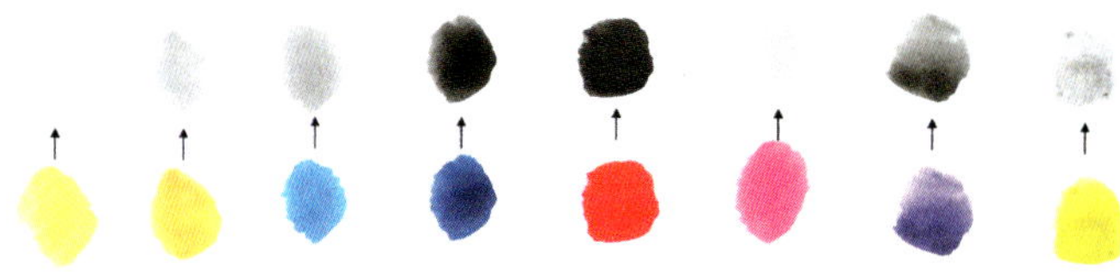

You can see the tonal values of each colour by converting some paint swatches to black and white using photo software. Darkest toned colours are dark blues such as Indigo and Indanthrene, Winsor Violet, and some reds. Lightest tones are yellow hues.

Beginners in watercolour may like to start off with only six colours on the palette: one of each of the cool and warm primaries listed previously. You can mix all colours with just these primaries so it may be easier to learn about colour mixing this way, then you can add further colours and evolve your palette as you become familiar with the pigments.

COLOURS FOR FUNGI

Colours for fungi bring to mind autumnal hues, of browns, siennas, umbers, caramels and buffs, echoing the russet and golden shades of the turning of the trees. All of these neutral beiges, taupes and earthy tones are essential to be able to mix, but many mushrooms are brightly coloured too. Look at the Waxcap family (*Hygrocybes* spp.) with their vibrant oranges, reds, pinks and yellows, even greens that shine in the autumn meadow like gems. The pink waxcap also called the ballerina, dances through the meadow wearing a pink tutu and the parrot waxcap shimmers with a vibrant green and sometimes other colours, just like a parrot. Another green fungus is the tiny green elf cup (*Chlorociboria aeruginascens*) that can be found on old oak or beech logs. The green stained wood is used in old traditional woodworking techniques such as Tunbridge ware to bring colour to pieces of furniture.

Another colourful group are the *Russula* family, with all manner of reds, yellows, burgundies and browns; indeed, the Latin name *Russula* means *russus* for red. And for other reds there is the obvious choice of fly agaric (*Amanita muscaria*) with its wonderful scarlet red and white spotted cap. Jewels of the spring woodlands are the scarlet and ruby elf cups (*Sarcoscypha* spp.) – ascomycetes that are hard to identify to species level. Another brightly coloured ascomycete is the orange peel fungus (*Aleuria aurantia*) which doesn't need much explanation; you may well walk past it thinking it's just a tossed orange peel along a footpath. The apricot jelly or salmon salad fungus (*Guepinia helvelloides*) is peach-coloured and jelly-like with a resemblance to slices of salmon and of very similar colour. The wrinkled peach – *Rhodotus palmatus* – is a beautiful pink mushroom mainly found on rotted elm logs. They all have such wonderfully descriptive common names.

For blue mushrooms there is the blue roundhead, *Stropharia caerulea*, although it has more of a turquoise colouration. Amazingly, some boletes can bruise bright peacock blue which is stunning to behold, such as the cornflower bolete (*Gyroporus cyanescens*). Magic mushrooms such as *Psilocybe cubensis* also turn an indigo blue in colour when they are cut; this is the active chemical *psilocin* reacting with the air. In eastern US, central America and eastern Asia, you can find a beautiful fungus called the indigo milk cap (*Lactarius indigo*), that is such a vibrant blue, it's quite unbelievable. All milk caps exude a milky substance when cut open, but this seeps a blue milk that changes to green in reaction to the air.

For the purples we have the wood blewit (*Lepista nuda*), amethyst deceiver (*Laccaria amethystina*), the

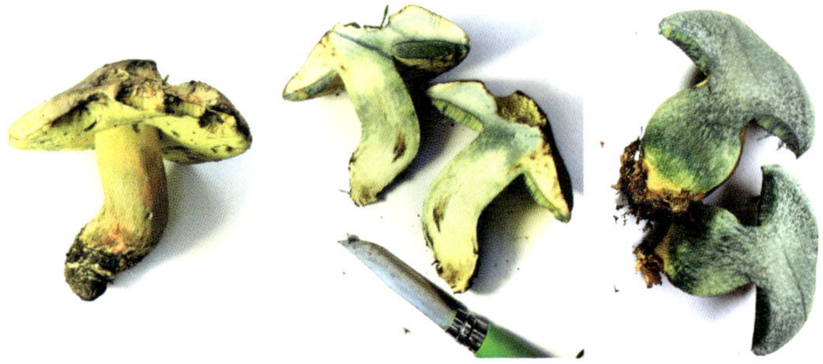

Here are two of the so-called blue boletes that have flesh that turns blue when in contact with the air. On the right you can see the blue reaction has happened after cutting the mushroom in half with a knife.

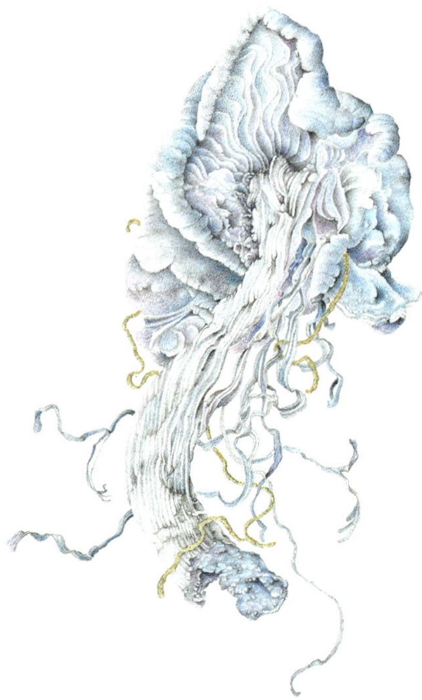

Much I Marvelled by Sharon Field ©. She says, 'This fungus was so interesting in its decaying form that I decided to add colour and wanted to try a colour opposite to what it was in life – an earthy brown/grey.

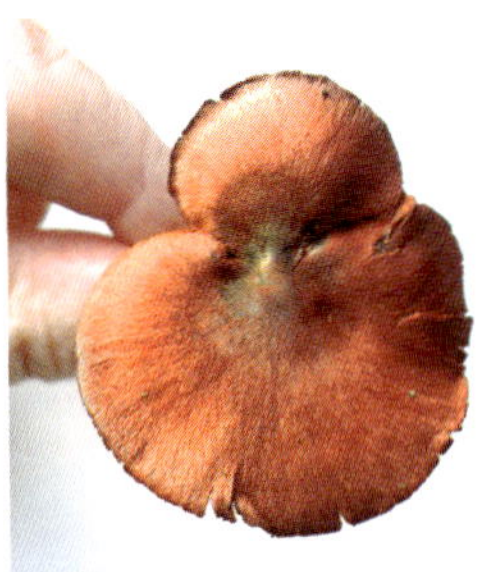

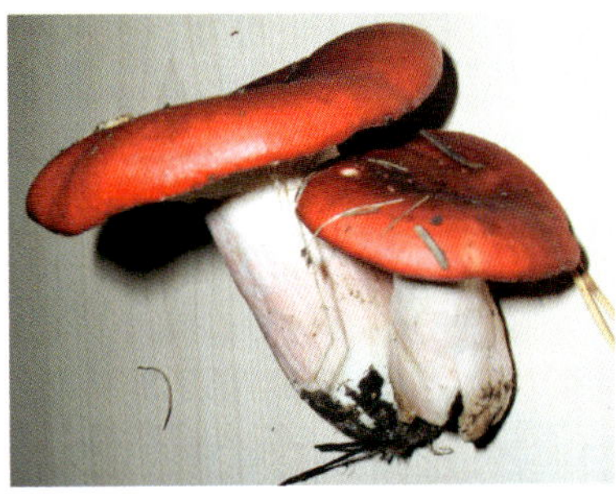

The dusky red cap of *Cortinarius sanguineus*, and a brightly coloured *Russula* species with a cherry red cap and stipe flushed pink.

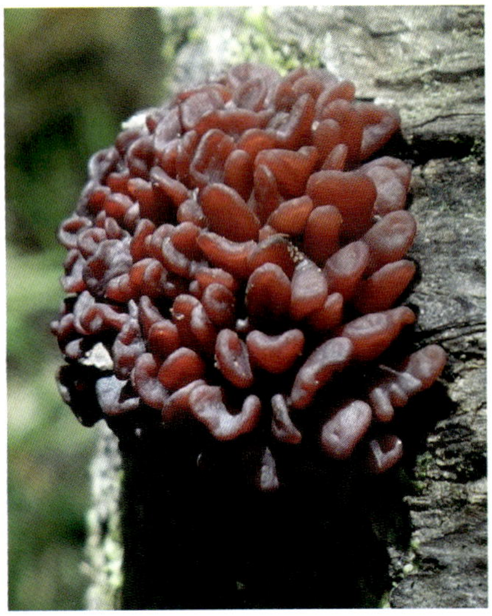

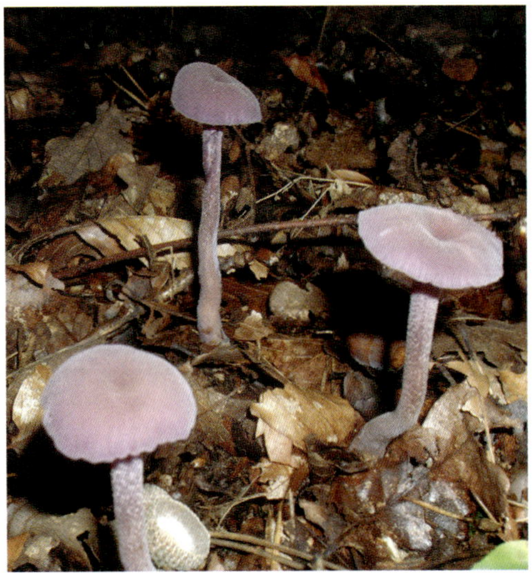

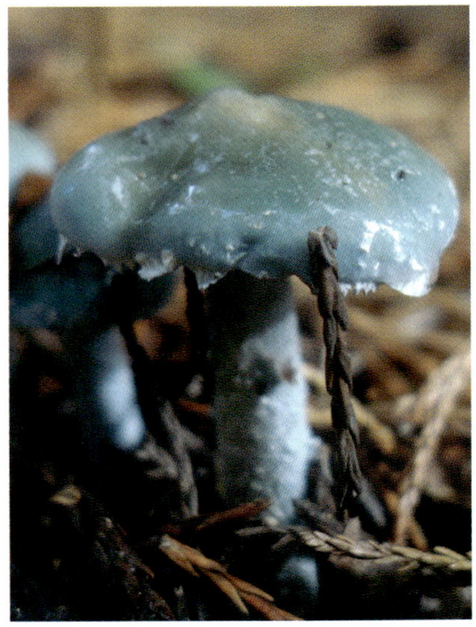

The amazing purples and violets of purple brain and amethyst deceiver and the vibrant turquoise of the blue roundhead.

violet coral (*Clavaria zollingeri*) and violet webcap (*Cortinarius violaceus*) all with beautiful shades of violet.

Then we mustn't forget the many white, beige and creamy coloured fungi that there are. They can give us painting challenges, such as portraying a white subject on a white background and also give us opportunities to use tinted papers.

The painting *Much I Marvelled* by Sharon Field demonstrates that you don't have to paint your subjects in their usual colours, but you can be free to use artistic licence. Sharon reveals the inspirations for her colourful painting. The title was inspired by the poem, 'The Raven' by Edgar Allan Poe. She says, 'After long anxious seasons of drought, fire, and floods in Australia, it was a miracle to see mushrooms coming up through the soil. While in life, this mushroom was not blue, it seemed to glow in a special way as it got on with the business it was programmed for. I decided to experiment with the blue hues because it took me back to our 'blue planet' and how important it is for us to look after what we have. The gold threads (also watercolour) tell me that these little organisms really are gold in our ecosystem. Our connections with nature in all its forms reinforce our close bond with the plants, animals and insects around us.'

PIGMENTS AND PAINTS FOR FUNGI

There are a few good pigments and paints that could suit the colours of fungi including Naples Yellow, Raw Siennas, Raw Umbers, Davy's Grey, Lemon Yellow (PY53), and Buff Titanium. As you'd expect they include a lot of earth colours. Some of the more opaque pigments, such as Naples Yellow and PY53 can fit with the opaque nature and denser qualities of a lot of fungi where translucency is not as essential as when painting petals and certain fruits. However, some mushrooms do have translucent properties, especially the viscous varieties as seen in the waxcap family, where transparent watercolours will work best.

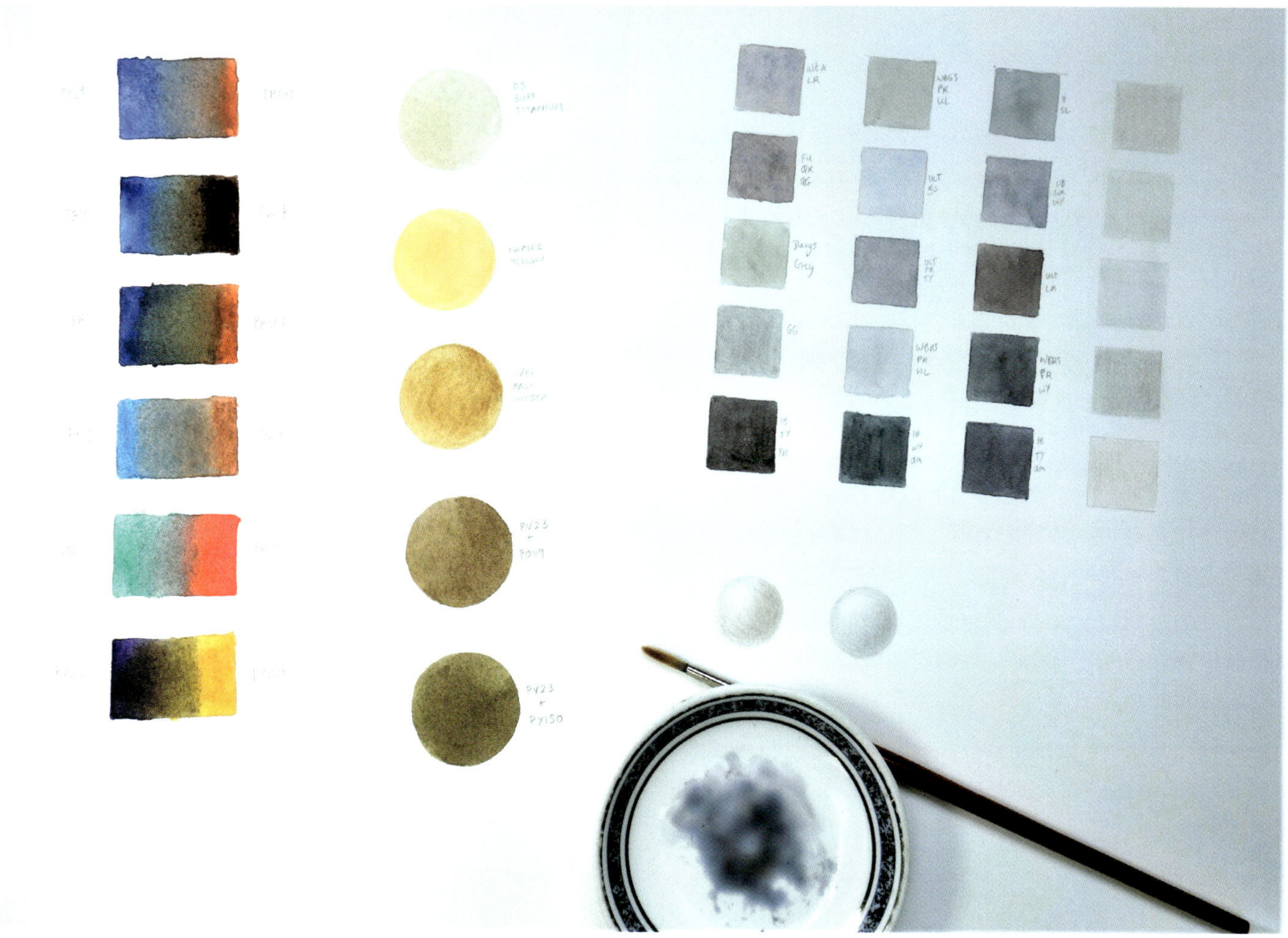

Various neutral mixes, from top to bottom. The paints are all from Winsor & Newton unless otherwise stated. Ultramarine and Light Red (PR102), Winsor Blue – red shade and Burnt Umber, Indanthrene and Burnt Sienna, Cerulean and Burnt Sienna (Daniel Smith), Viridian and Scarlet Lake, Winsor Violet and Transparent Yellow. Several grey mixes to the right all using different primaries.

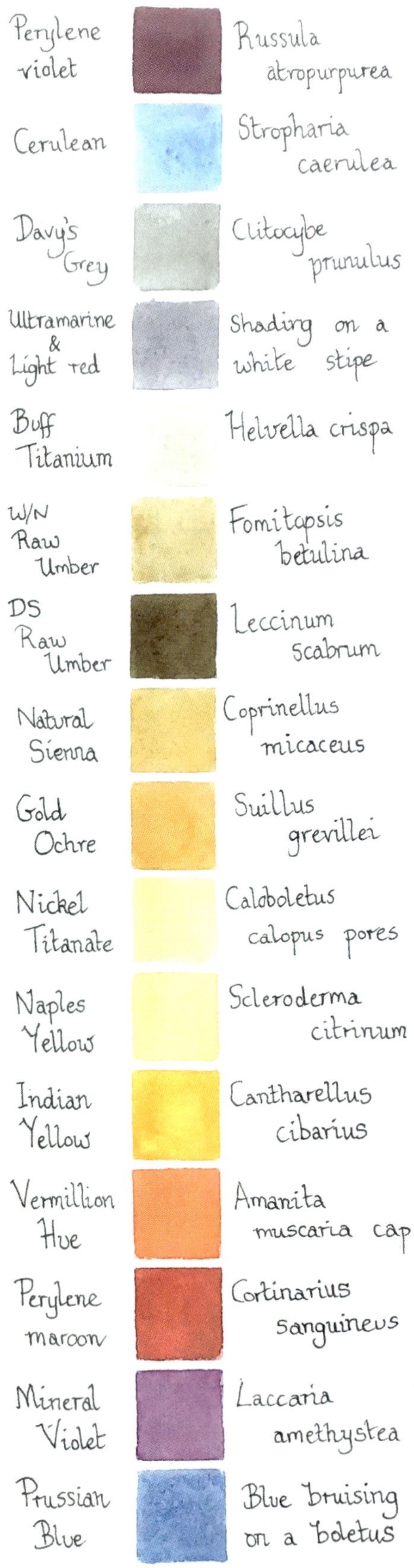

Just for fun: a fungi colour chart with colours that are associated with fungi and an example of a species with that colouration. Sometimes if you are stuck with a lack of motivation or inspiration to work then a colour chart can be a way to just play.

One thing to always remember when using transparent watercolours is to use them alone or on top of opaque paints and let the colours shine through each other using their transparent properties. It can be easy to forget this sometimes; you could split your transparent and opaque pigments to remind you of this.

Paints such as Payne's Grey, Sepia and Neutral Tint have a black component in them usually Lamp black (Pbk6) made of soot from burning oil. If you're vegan, you'll have to give Ivory Black (Pbk9) a wide berth as it's made from burning animal bones. These 'Pbk' pigments can create uninteresting, opaque layers and can give a sooty look (sometimes you'll want that look – for instance, when painting *Xylaria* sp.). On the whole, I tend not to use black pigments very often in fungi or botanical illustration, preferring to mix my own neutrals. Subtly tinted greys and lively browns that have so much more life to them can be mixed using home-made neutral tints. These are greys that have no warm or cool bias to them; they are neutral. They are composed of different combinations of the three primary colours, in varying proportions; more blue and red with less yellow will create different shades of grey, and more red and yellow with less blue will create the browns, tans and umbers. Each mix can easily be altered with a bit more red to warm it up or a bit more blue to cool it down.

Mixing your own neutrals is especially useful when you need to have a transparent colour, as many convenience neutrals are opaque or with black pigments in them. Although not essential, convenience darks can be handy to have around when the need arises for extra dark values in small areas and for efficiency while sketching in the field. I recommend experimenting to find greys and neutral mixes that you prefer, perhaps creating a colour chart for future reference.

GRANULATION

The pigments you choose will produce different effects, for instance, granulating pigments such as French ultramarine, and cerulean will create textured washes. Granulation textures may look great on mottled fungi caps, logs or tree branches, lichens and decaying, autumnal subjects. But, if you have a lovely smooth fungi cap to portray then you'll want a flat, even wash so you'll need to pick a paint that doesn't granulate, such as a phthalo, quinacridone or perylene colour. It pays to think about the look that you want to make and choose the pigments wisely; get to know them.

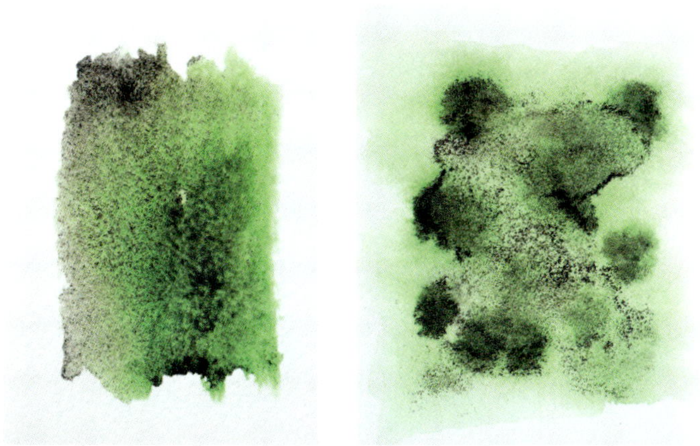

The textural effects of granulating watercolours, sometimes sought for but generally unwanted in botanical art. The left picture shows this effect on cold press paper. The right picture shows it on hot press paper.

For an ultramarine that doesn't granulate as much as others, I use ultramarine finest made by Schmincke, who are a quality German paint manufacturer. They also have a range of super granulating colours, as do Daniel Smith. These paints are quite expensive and not essential as you can mix your own super granulating paints or paints that split into two-tone colours. For a two-tone effect, just choose a granulating pigment such as burnt umber, Potter's pink or Mars black and mix it with a modern staining colour such as a phthalo blue – the colours will split out and create interesting effects. When using granulating colours, for a really textured effect use more water or for interest to a background, add drops of water onto a drying wash.

You can also buy a granulating medium from Winsor & Newton that can create textured effects when dropped onto washes and allowed to mix and flow. This is all great fun to experiment with for looser styles of artwork and to create interesting backgrounds.

WATERCOLOUR PAINTING TECHNIQUES

Wet into Wet

This technique is essentially using wet paper with wet paints and to be successful at it takes a lot of practice. You must be quick to blend the different hues while the glaze is still wet. The first washes of a painting are best laid on to paper that has been pre-glazed with water. This initial priming of the paper softens the size on its surface and helps the paint be accepted to produce a smooth and even application with no hard edges.

Brush a water glaze onto the paper evenly and after a few moments, check the surface of the paper. Timing is everything with watercolour; you have to wait until it is no longer really wet and shiny but just has a dulled sheen. This means that the water has been absorbed into the paper core leaving it just damp, the best time to confidently add the wash.

One, two or more colours can be dropped or charged into the water glaze carefully but quickly and blended together with the tip of the brush. While it is still wet, a clean, damp brush can carefully lift out any unwanted paint to create areas of paler tones or highlights. When lifting paint off the paper, the brush must be drier than the painted paper so that it absorbs the paint readily – a thirsty brush.

If the paper is starting to dry, then it is best to stop and let it dry completely. You can always add further washes on top to deepen tones and even out washes. Putting the correct dilution of paint on when quite wet, but not too wet, is the secret, it's a balancing act. If it is too wet, the paint will diffuse out too readily and you will lose those subtle differences of tone and hue. If it is too dry you will not be able to blend the colours wet in wet on the paper before it dries and you'll get a streaky look. Because watercolour is translucent, it is best to work from light to dark – laying down the palest tones first, with the white paper left for the highlights and then working the darker tones on top.

Wet on Dry and Layering Washes

The painting progresses with the build-up and layering or glazing of successive washes to reach the wanted levels of tone and shading. These next washes can be laid on wet on dry; this is a wet wash onto dry paper. It really is essential to allow each layer of paint to dry before another is laid over it. If it is not dry, the brush can lift the paint up from the layer below, potentially ruining the look or mixing the paint up into 'mud'. It is so important not to fiddle, as the

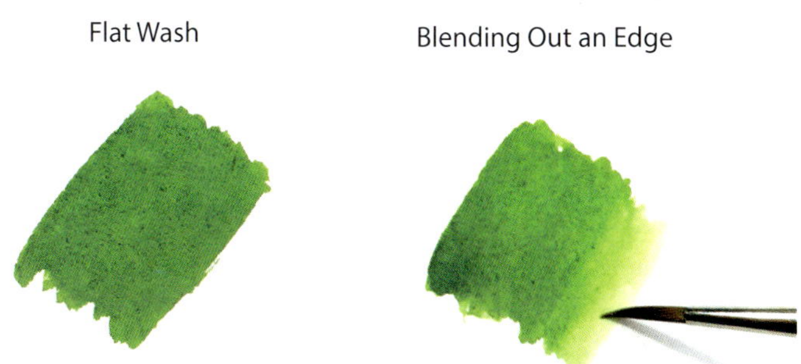

Watercolour techniques 1: A flat wash is the most basic method of applying paint to the paper; the aim is to create as smooth a look as possible. 2. To blend out an edge, use a clean, damp brush to stroke along it to pull and fade the colour out. Rinse and blot the water from the brush after each stroke.

Things to Avoid

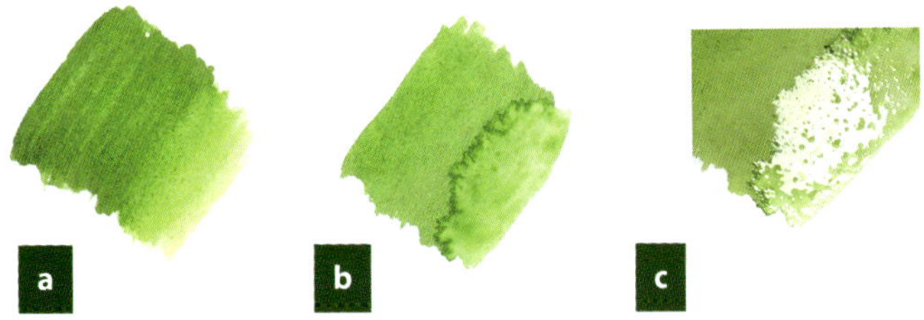

a. Streaks can occur if the wash starts to dry between brush strokes so enough dilute paint on the brush gives a smoother wash. Make sure the brush is large enough for the size of wash. **b.** Too much water on the brush can cause backruns or 'cauliflowers'; water control is an essential skill. **c.** If the glaze is very shiny, let it absorb or lift some out with a damp brush before adding paint to avoid possible dark lines around edges or too much dilution.

Wet into Wet

Wet on Dry

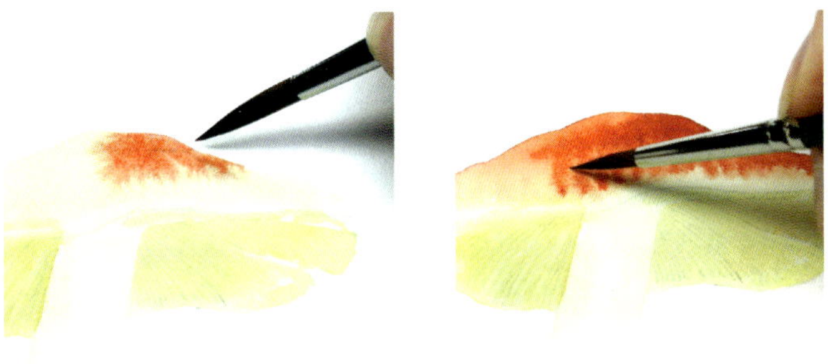

Wet into wet disperses the paint out onto the wet to damp paper surface creating lovely soft edges on this example of a plums and custard – *Tricholomopsis rutilans*. Wet on dry technique uses wet paint on a dry surface to create hard edges but gives more control. Hard edges can always be softened out using the blending out technique.

repeated brushing and disturbing of wet paper increases the loosening of the wet fibres at the surface, which makes it appear fuzzy and so dulls the painting. Bright, clean colour is achieved by confidently applying the paint in one stroke and letting it fully dry.

Lifting Colour

To lift colour where a lighter tone is needed or where paint is not wanted, dry pigment can be loosened with the tip of a clean, damp brush and blotted with a tissue to lift paint. This is a good technique for lifting out light striations and spots and also for creating areas of high, low or reflected light. The paint is lifted off with the brush to reveal the white paper beneath and so produces a soft lifelike effect. A small flat brush, size No. 2, synthetic, is good to use for this purpose. The result will, of course, depend on the staining qualities of the pigment used so this can be thought about before starting work.

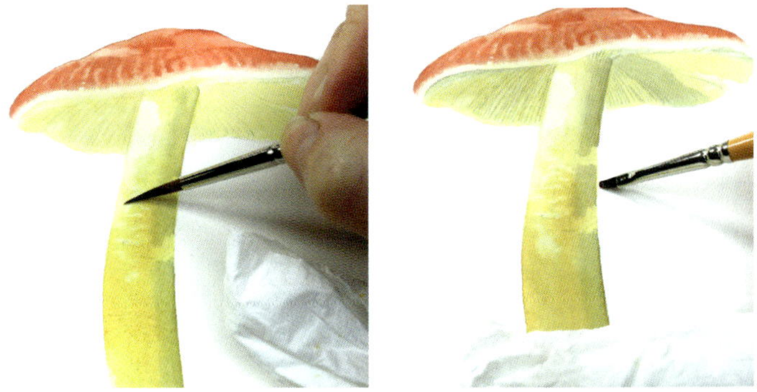

Left: Lightening areas on the stipe by loosening the paint with the damp brush and then lifting out with a tissue. Right: Cleaning an area on the edge of the stipe where the paint went over the pencil line. Using a flat brush to very gently scrub to lift and then dab with a tissue again.

Dry Brush Technique

After the initial layers that have built up tone and form are added, it's time to continue with drier and more concentrated paint on top using the dry brush technique. This is used to intensify tonal contrasts and add detail and pattern. It can also be handy for covering a messy area. It is a slower and more controlled method of working than wet in wet wash work. The brushes used are smaller and not completely dry but damp.

Dry brush is generally painted on top of wash work but can be sandwiched between layers of washes. This helps to soften any harsh dry brush like veins or fibres and so on, and can give a more natural appearance. The paint is usually applied in small strokes and blended together to lose hard edges. It is perfect for the building up and modelling of heavy shading to increase tonal contrasts. A good tip is to let a wash dry out on the palette and then use it for dry brush.

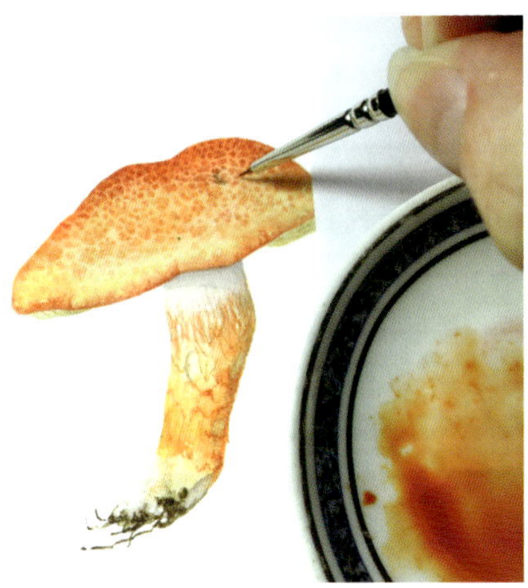

Dry brush finishing technique is being implemented on a dappled webcap – *Cortinarius bolaris*. A thicker consistency of paint is stippled on with a small size 0 brush in little dots to build up tone as well as the cracked texture seen in these caps.

TIPS TO REMEMBER

- Always keep your tones varied, otherwise the painting will look flat and try to never lose the highlight.
- Watercolour always dries lighter so remember this when applying washes.
- Lift and blend paint with a damp but **not** wet brush, so after cleaning the brush in water, dab the brush on kitchen roll to soak up excess water then use to lift out paint.
- Keep a spare piece of paper under your painting hand to protect the work from splashes.
- Mix up enough paint when making a wash so as not to run out.
- Keep old brushes for mixing paint and use a synthetic flat brush (size 2) to lift paint or stains and to tidy up edges.

DIFFERENT TECHNIQUES TO CAPTURE FUNGI FORMS AND TEXTURES

This is the most fun part of painting fungi; assessing the subject for textural qualities and then figuring out how to recreate that look with your painting materials, preferably experimenting in the sketchbook first. Many surface textures such as dark fibres or the intricate cracking seen on some caps, will be added using the dry brush technique on top of wash work.

Highlights and Lowlights

If the fungi are very wet or slimy, termed as viscous, you can show this when painting by leaving very bright and sharp white paper highlights. The surrounding wash is blended out into the white highlight with clean water and a damp brush to form a sharp contrast between dark and light, the same as when painting any shiny subject.

This effect is superior to using white paint for highlights, but that may be used as a last resort if highlights are lost, all too easy in watercolour. Sheen can be described as a softer shine or lustre that has less contrast between light and dark, so adding a very pale wash to dampen down the highlight could help give this softer look.

A couple of drops of gum Arabic can be added to a wash (use cautiously – not too much) to increase transparency of the paint and create a little added shine when dry. It can reduce the staining effects of pigments, acting as a barrier on the paper to stop paints being fully absorbed into it and so makes them more liftable. It also slows down the drying time of the paint allowing more time to work with the washes. A lifting preparation can also be purchased to help lift staining colours but I've had more success with gum Arabic than this product.

A diffuse, low light will suggest a dry and matt surface. These effects of light are softer and duller than the bright highlights and can be achieved by blotting the wet paint with a tissue to create a cloudy, lowlight effect. Lowlights can also be created by lifting out the areas to be lightened, after painted washes have dried with a damp brush or damp cotton wool bud. This creates a soft and lifelike effect.

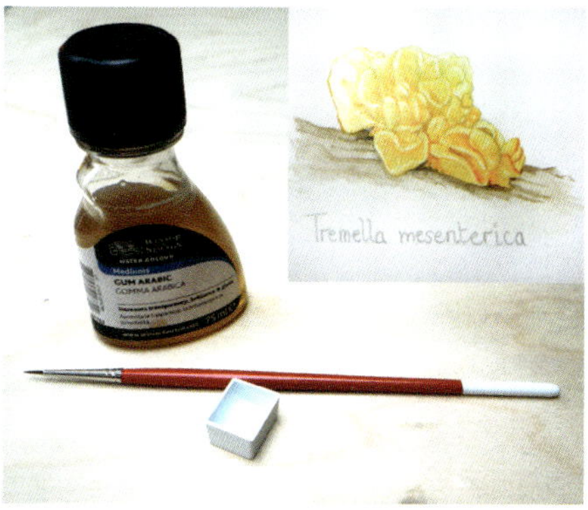

The little painting of yellow brain – *Tremella* sp. here was coated with a thin layer of gum Arabic diluted down in water. It gives the subject a glossy shine for a look of wetness. Experiments to find the correct amount are needed; it's best not to use too much as it can be very sticky.

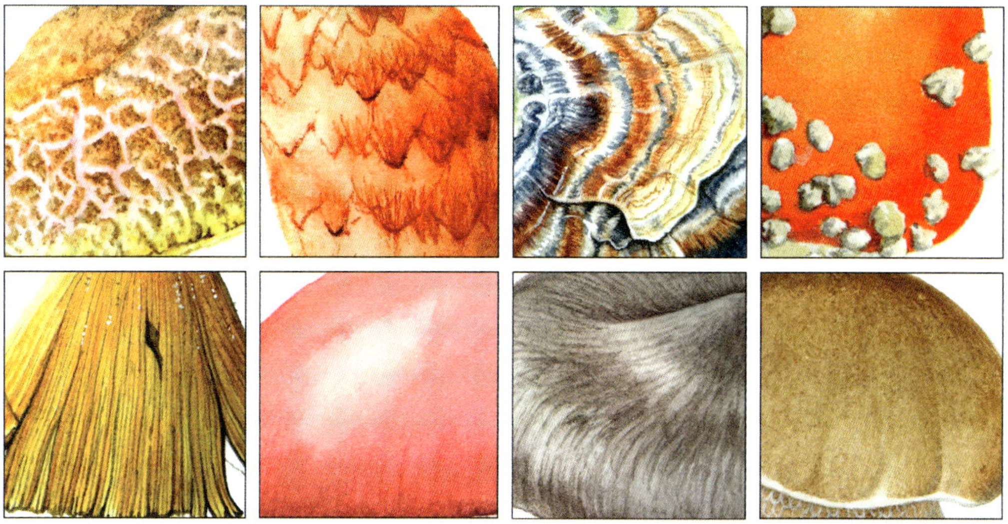

Assorted painted textures and details seen on many fungi subjects, clockwise from top left: rough/cracked, fibrous, velvety striations, hard-edged shapes, velvety smooth, silky sheen, smooth shine and striate.

FOCUS STUDY: CAPTURING TRANSLUCENCE AND SHINE – PARROT WAXCAP

Translucence means allowing light to pass through something, so it seems obvious that you'll need to use transparent paints to capture this effect. Adding cool violets and blues to the reflected lights can also give the effect of light shining through the translucent cells of the viscous waxy cap and an effect that is often termed the 'disappearing edge'. This can help to give rounded subjects their form. For the bright shine seen on the main highlighted areas, the white paper is reserved but no masking fluid is needed. The aim is to create a sharp contrast between the highlight and the surrounding area.

MATERIALS USED:

- Stonehenge Aqua HP 140lb paper
- Manganese Blue Hue (Daniel Smith), Indian Yellow by (M. Graham – PY110), for the violet mix – Ultramarine Finest (Schmincke) and Permanent Rose (Winsor & Newton), and Sap Green (Daniel Smith)
- No. 2 Raphael fine tipped brush

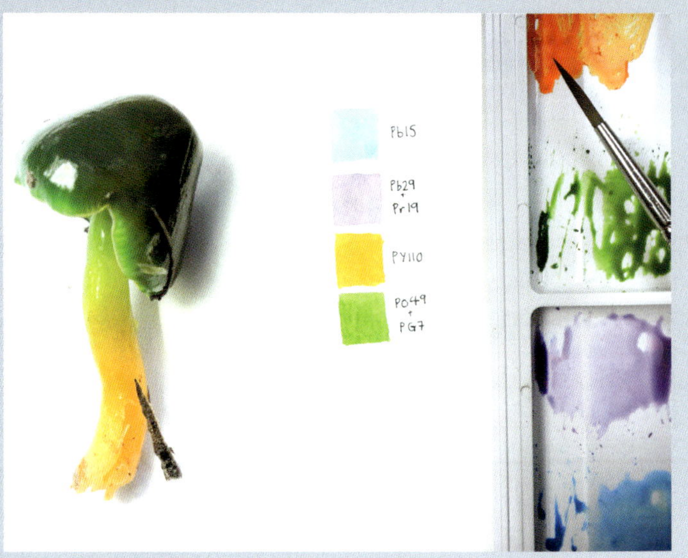

The parrot waxcap – *Gliophorus psittacinus* is the perfect example of a mushroom with a very wet-looking, viscous cap and stipe. *Gliophorus* is Greek for 'glue-bearing' referring to its thick 'gluey' coating. It glistens with bright green, yellow and orange hues with cool blue and violet in the reflected light and centre light.

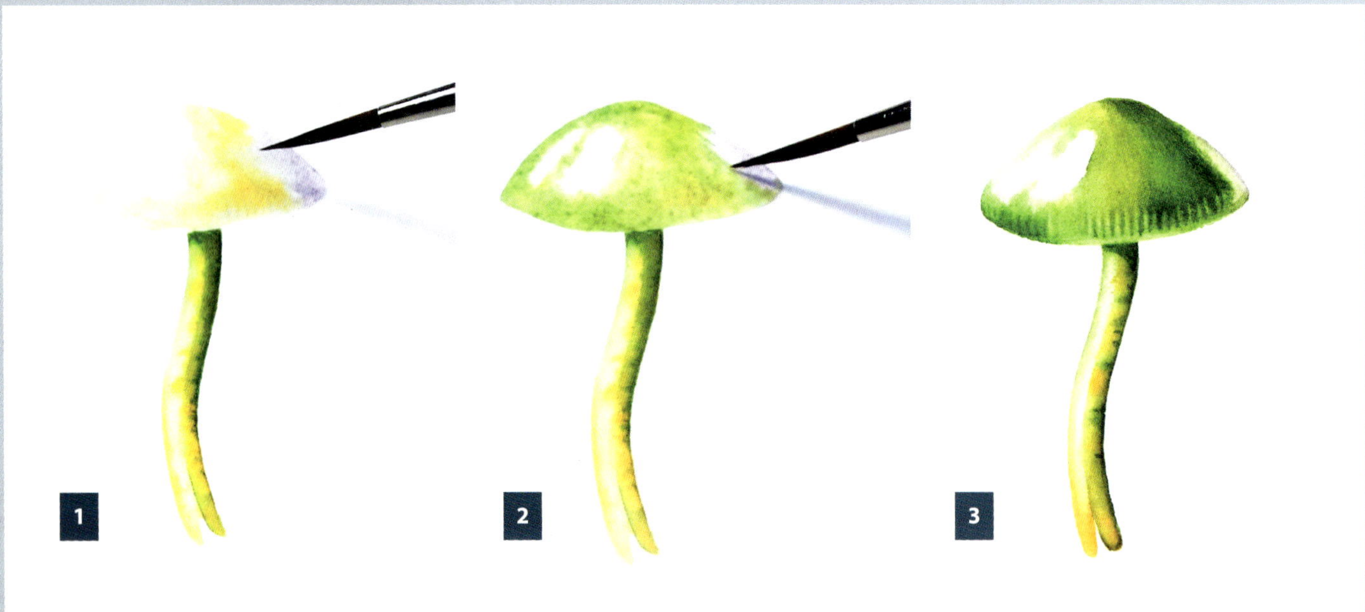

In the first wash on the cap, multiple pre-mixed colours were dropped into a plain water glaze wet into wet after allowing the water to sink into the paper a little. The pale blue was added to the centre light seen above the highlight, Indian Yellow was added into the centre for the orange cap underlayer, and the violet was dropped into the reflected light area. I made sure I painted around the main highlight leaving it as white paper but trying not to make it too circular or regular.

When dry, the green mix was added carefully painting around the highlight again and leaving some violet reflected light showing. A little stronger orange was also added in the centre. These washes were blended into the lights with a clean, damp brush to fade out. This was allowed to dry, trying not to fiddle with the wash!

More green was added as a stronger mix, wet on dry, blending out to lose hard edges, except by some of the highlight edge – that gave a crisp, sharp contrast between light and dark and a look of shine. Stronger green was added with a drier brush to add striations where the gills are seen through the translucent cap and further shading applied to the right side of the cap. Some striations were also created using a clean, damp brush and a tissue to lift pigment. The left side to the base of the cap was reshaped using a dry brush to form the rounded contours seen in the subject.

STEP-BY-STEP: VELVET TEXTURES – *AMANITA* CAP

Some caps have a velvety or silky texture and this can be suggested by glazing thin layers when dry with different transparent colours. This layering technique can be described as optical mixing and will add greater depth and richness to the colours. Then a careful stippling technique or tiny hatching lines with the brush in the final layer can help to create a velvety look if needed. I used Naples Yellow in the first layer which is a more opaque colour, fine for a first layer on fungi, but leave out of the subsequent layers where transparency is wanted.

This blusher's cap was a great example of a cap that glowed with these different hues of golds and maroons; good to demonstrate a velvety texture that can be worked up in layers. Usually, most *Amanitas* have scales on their caps but there were no scales on this cap – they had all been washed off by rain.

MATERIALS USED:

- Stonehenge Aqua 140lb hot press
- Naples Yellow (Schmincke), Quinacridone Gold (Daniel Smith), Perylene Maroon and Burnt Sienna (PR101) (both Winsor & Newton), and Ultramarine Finest (Schmincke), browns mixed with the Ultramarine, Perylene Maroon and Quinacridone Gold
- A size 2 round brush

1

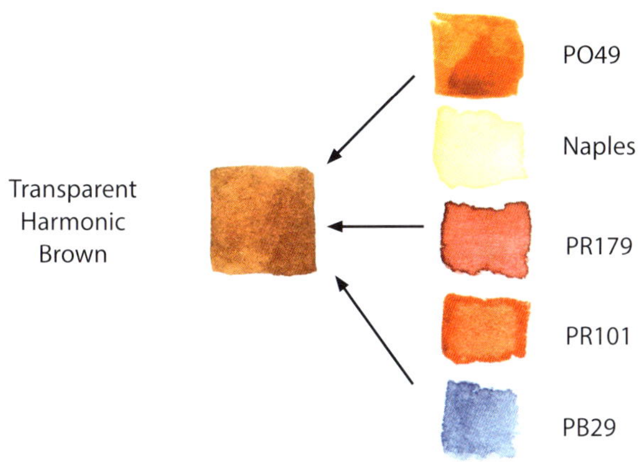

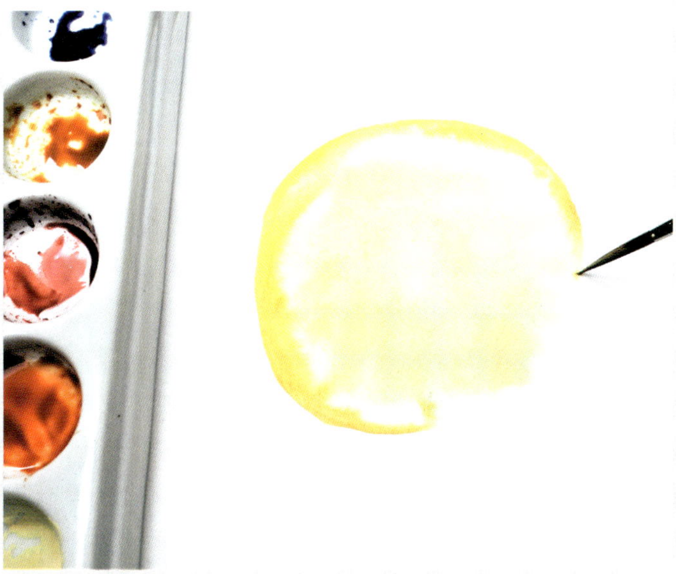

The cap is studied to identify the colours seen within it, trying to see which colours lay underneath. Then all the chosen paints are premixed on the palette ready; a wash of Quinacridone Gold and Naples yellow is added wet into wet to an initial water glaze then allowed to completely dry.

2

Then the area is reglazed with water and all the various colours are charged into the glaze, wet into wet. The rich colours flare out to create beautiful softly blended patches. Again, it is allowed to completely dry.

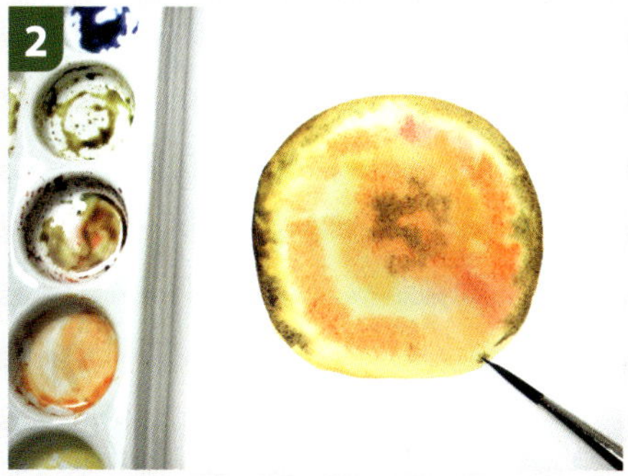

3

A rich wash of Quinacridone Gold is added over the top, but no water glaze is needed, it's just added on wet on dry. This Daniel Smith pigment is the old formula of this colour, (PO49), which unfortunately has now been discontinued.

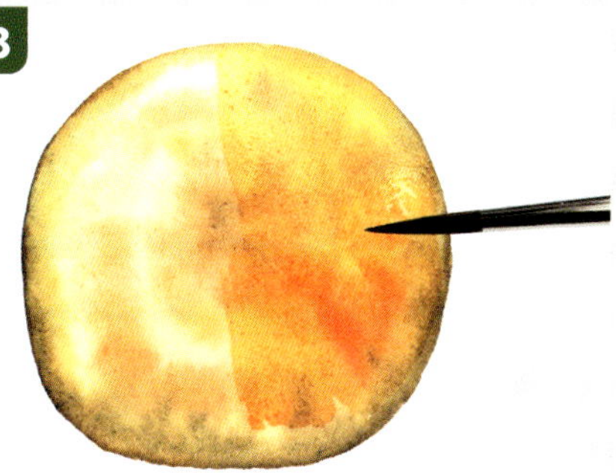

4

When that layer is dry, a final top layer of the golden-brown local colour (made with the Ultramarine, Perylene Maroon and Quin. Gold) is added. The colours will shine through the layers thanks to their transparency.

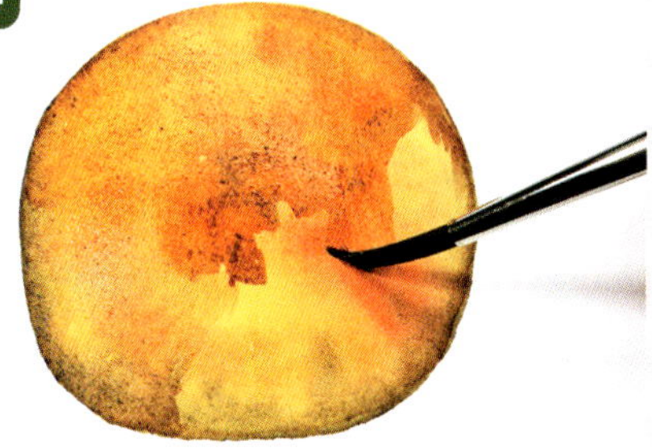

5

Additional darks can be stippled in while the wash is still damp, Indanthrene blue can give a darker tone to the browns if that's needed. The cap ought to be smooth and velvety looking with good depth of colour from the layering.

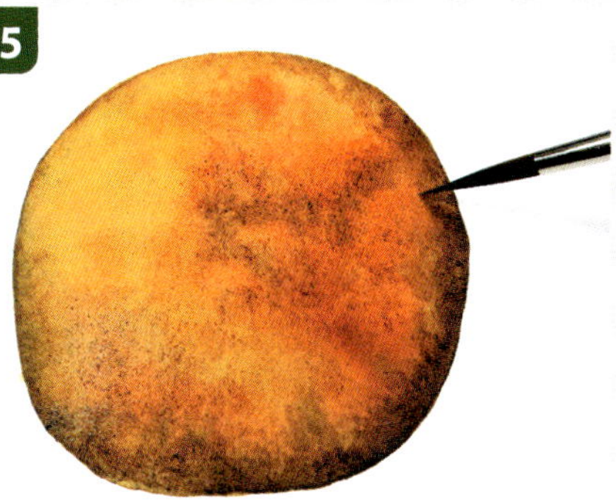

Fibrous Textures

Fibrous stalks and caps are quite a common attribute on many fungi species. It can be depicted well using a sweeping dry brush technique, where the hairs on a size 2 or 4 damp brush are splayed or spread out, just using the fingers to compress them. Then it's dipped into drier paint and lightly swept onto the paper, giving the impression of the individual fibres. You need to always brush in the direction of the fibres.

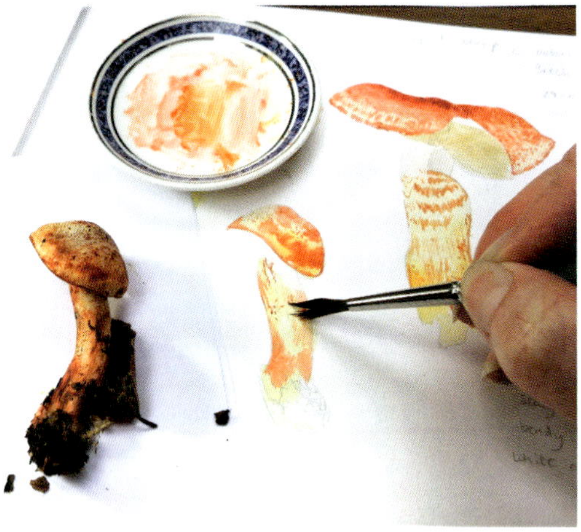

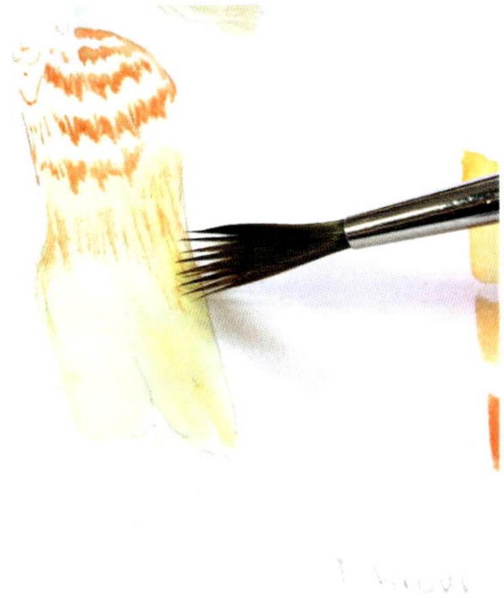

Load the brush with quite concentrated paint, then splay the hairs out to give an irregular edge. Try out the textures this creates on a spare piece of paper as you may need to dab out any excess moisture; you want to create a dry brush, textured effect.

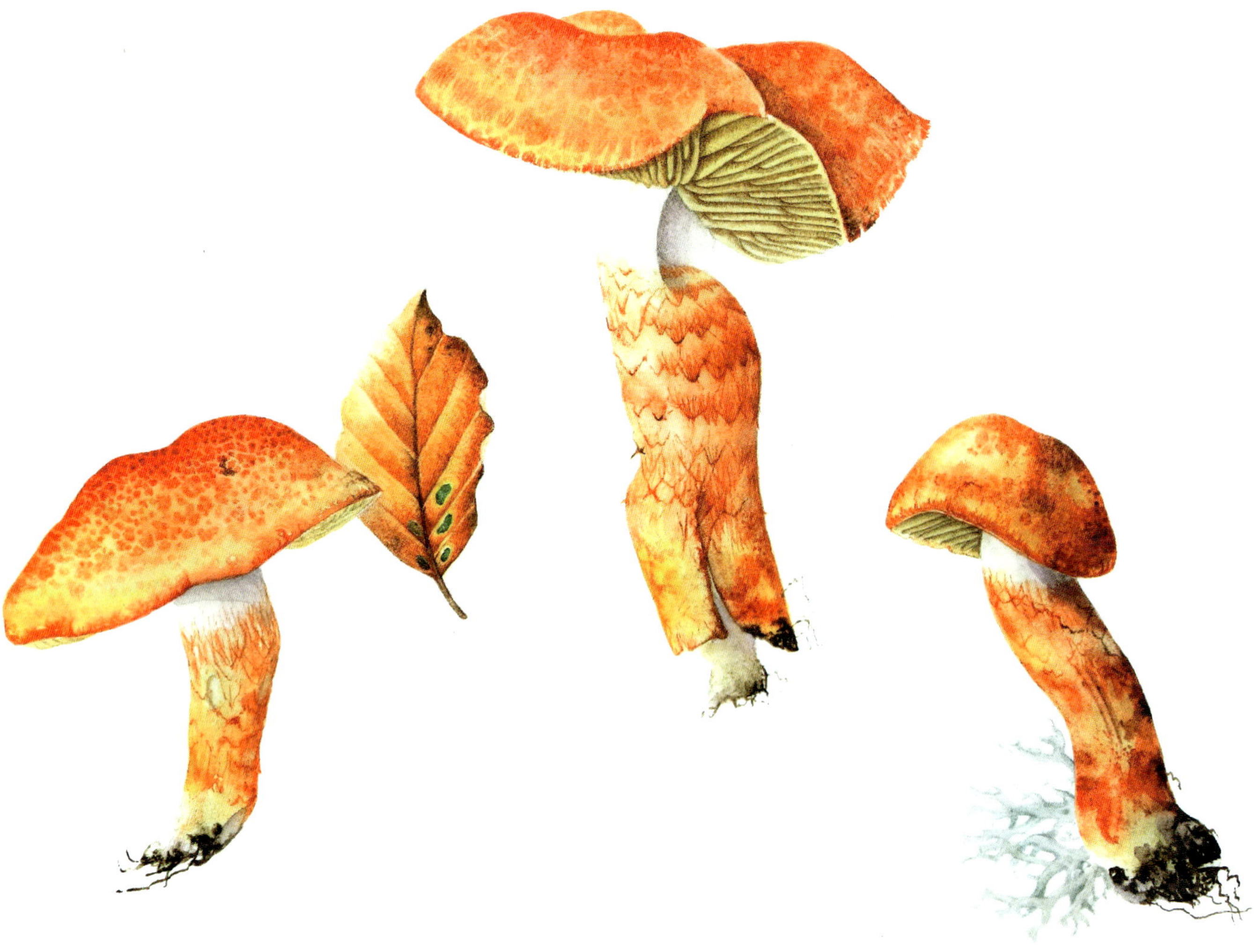

Dappled webcaps – *Cortinarius bolaris* have wonderful textures and a warm colouration, with fabulous, cracked effects and patterns to their older caps. The decaying leaf hints at their habitat of beech woodlands and the blue lichen gives a bit of cool relief.

Painting Gills

When painting the gills of fungi, you are most often going to be painting negatively and actually painting the shadows in between the gills. The gills at the centre point face on to you and will have the darkest shadows as you're looking straight down into the dark crevices between the gill structures. Then as you move out to the cap sides you won't be able to see into the gill spaces as much so the shading will become paler.

Gills can be carefully observed, noting spacing or other features listed in Chapter 2 on gills. Then drawn in using graphite at first, and after initial washes of local colour, they can be shaded in using wet on dry paint of an appropriate shadow colour and/or by using dry brush stippling or hatching to increase the tone of the shadows.

In this painting of a false saffron milkcap – *Lactarius deterrimus,* you can see a close-up of the gills and how the tone has been gradated from light to dark. This same attention to tone must be given to each gill according to the light falling on your subject.

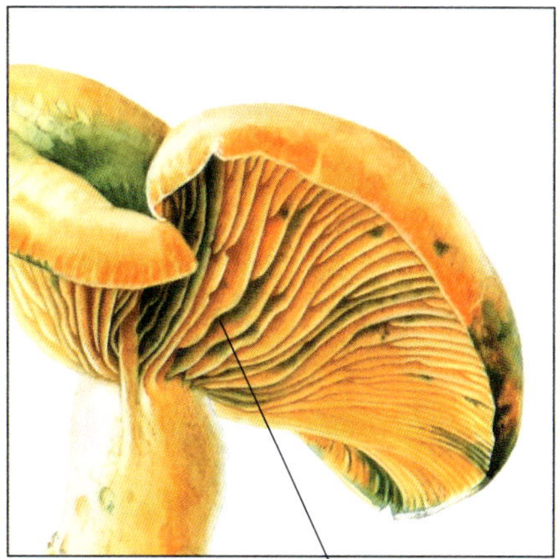

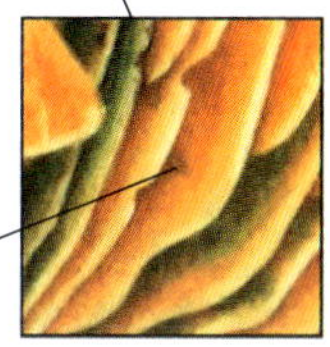

Blended, gradation of tone on the gill, from the pale highlighted edge to the darker, interior shadow.

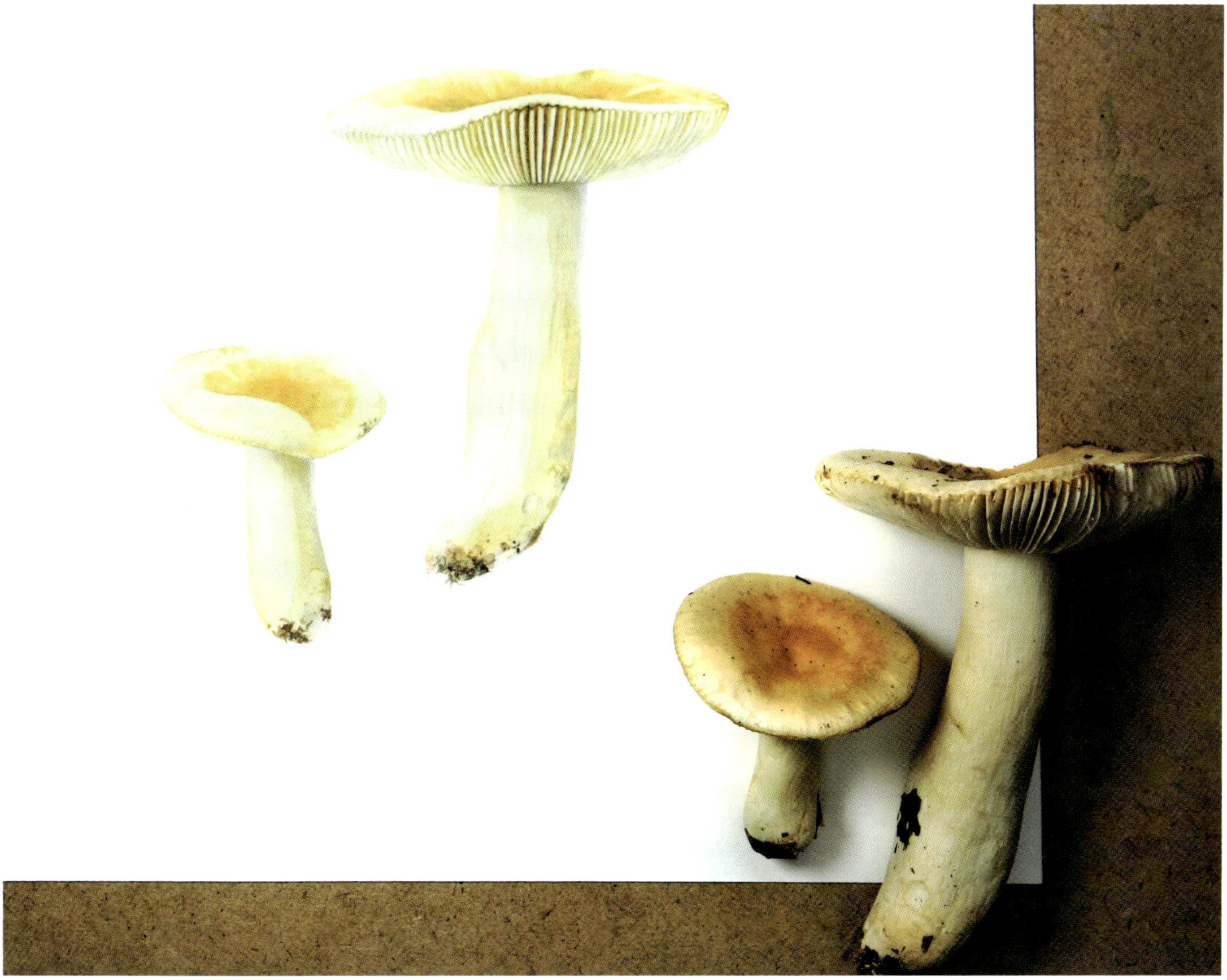

Geranium-scented Russula – *Russula fellea.* This painting demonstrates a good example of where you can see the dark shadows in between those gills exactly at the front.

STEP-BY-STEP: SCALES ON A FLY AGARIC

The scales on caps are easily done using masking fluid to protect and preserve the white paper and create hard edges which is perfect for depicting scales. The fluid can be put on using an old brush, a toothpick or ruling pen. Some brands of masking fluid have their own applicators. As mentioned before, always test masking fluid on your papers to see if there are any issues and don't leave it on for too long.

MATERIALS USED:

- Arches 140lb hot press paper
- Schmincke masking fluid and an old brush
- Size 2 round brush, Indian Yellow, Ultramarine Violet, Vermillion Hue (Daler-Rowney – PR255), Winsor Red Deep, Raw Umber (Daniel Smith), Buff Titanium (Daniel Smith), grey mix with Winsor Blue red shade and Light Red (PR102). The paints are all from Winsor & Newton unless otherwise stated

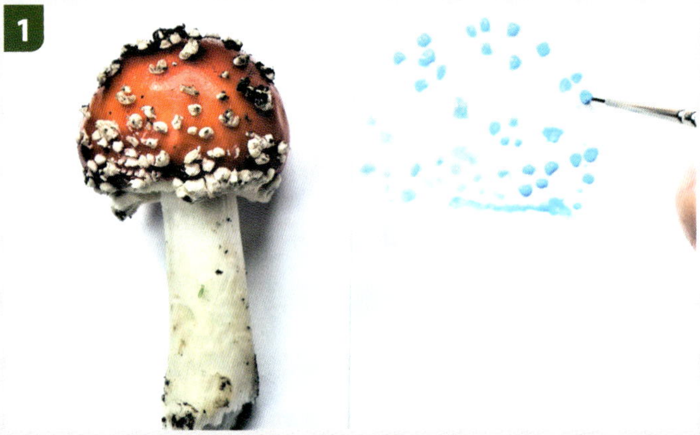

The masking fluid is painted on using an old paintbrush. Usually with other brands of masking fluid, I would coat the brush in soap or diluted washing up liquid to protect the brush hairs as the rubbery masking fluid ruins them. But here I'm using a new masking fluid from Schmincke that you can remove from brushes with water – it works but I still used an old brush! Then it's imperative to let the masking fluid dry, so I work on another painting while it dries.

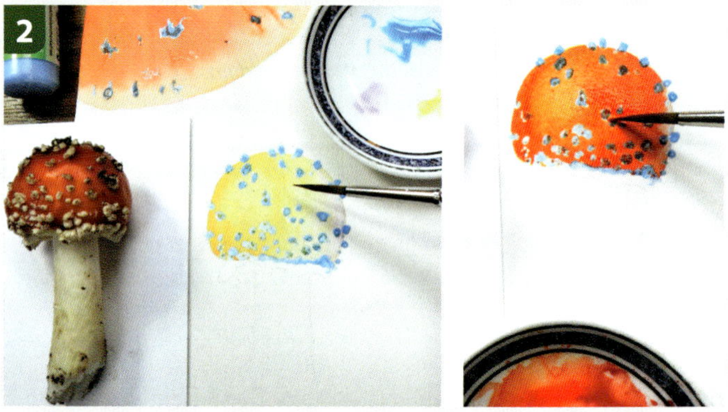

Then when it's dry, I look for any underlying colours that I see in the subject. Here it's a warm yellow undertone so I mix up some Indian yellow and a dash of violet for the reflected light and paint it on, wet on dry. When that layer is dry, I wash over a coat of Vermillion Hue mixed with the yellow for the bright scarlet colour. I blend it into the paler highlights and let it dry. Small amounts of dry brush Winsor red deep were added to deepen the red cap colour in the shadows.

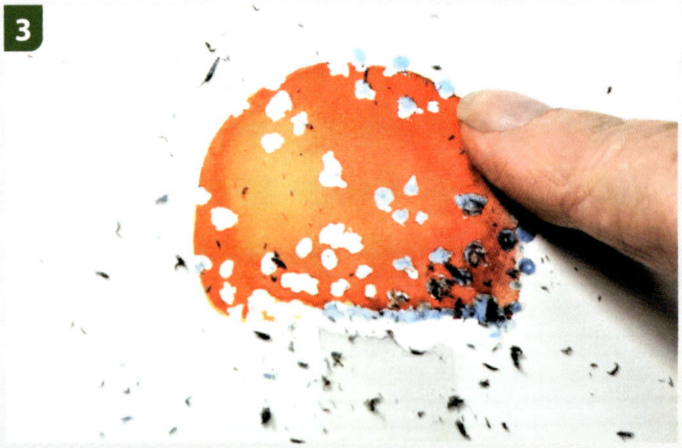

When I'm happy with the depth of tone on the painted layers of scarlet, remembering to keep a paler area to the left for the highlighted area, I rub off the masking fluid with a finger. You can buy a masking fluid rubber block to remove it if you use the fluid a lot, but I rarely use it. I have found that masking fluids can go off over time and become unusable.

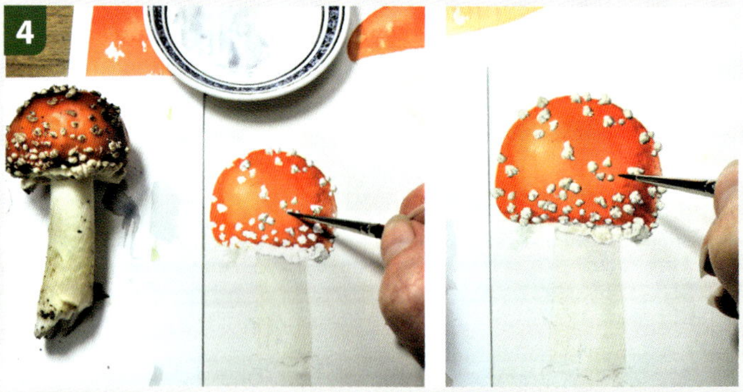

I painted each of the scales with Buff Titanium as they are not white but a dirty, off-white colour. If you don't have Buff Titanium, you can just add a dark Raw Umber like the one by Daniel Smith to some titanium white watercolour to tint it. Here you can see the individual scales being worked on with a drybrush technique with grey mixes to add the shading to give each one form. You can see that the scales are not flat at all, they really are quite lumpy.

PAINTING WHITE AND PALE FUNGI

White fungi can easily be painted with a background and masked out with masking fluid to preserve the white paper, as in the nature printing step by step in Chapter 6. But the challenge will be to paint a white subject on a white paper background; being able to show it up against the similarly toned backdrop.

The first thing to do is to analyse the subject for the type of white that you can see as they are never completely pure white. Really study and observe it for other colours that you may be able to perceive and try to describe them. For example, is it warm, cool, creamy-coloured, tinted green, or brownish tinged or other? Make sure you're in good, natural lighting to better judge the colours – bright sunlight and deep shadow may hamper your perception.

Next, mix up a base of a tonal grey using a homemade grey similar to Davy's or a neutral tint mixture, that you can then vary by adding the other touches of colour that you see in the subject too; perhaps you see a hint of violet or a trace of yellow. This will subtly alter and tint the grey mix to add realism and bring it to life. These mixes are used to model the form of the fungi and create the tonal

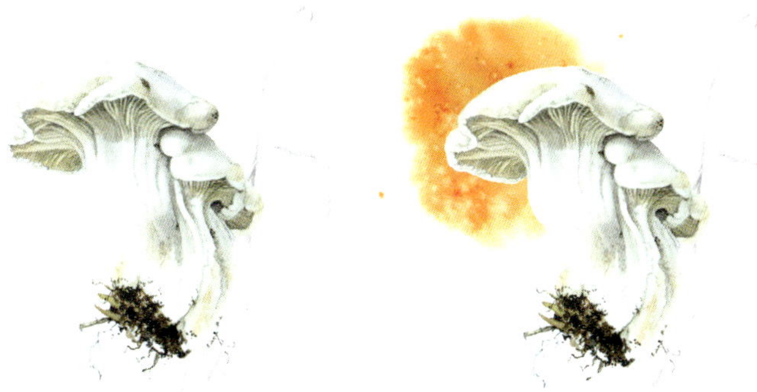

This little suede capped mushroom is called the Miller – *Clitopilus prunulus* as when young they smell just like fresh yeast!! To make the subject show up on white paper I used subtle grey mixes and pale Burnt Sienna (PR101) for the gills, made so due to its pinkish coloured spores. You can also experiment with splashes of colour behind your subject to inject some extra interest there and lose some of the white background.

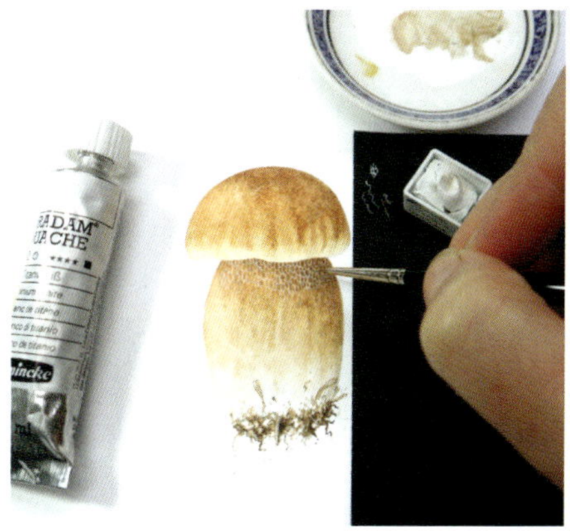

For adding the white reticulation detail to this little *Boletus edulis* study, little touches of white gouache were painted on with a small brush. The gouache can be tinted with watercolour if it looks very harsh.

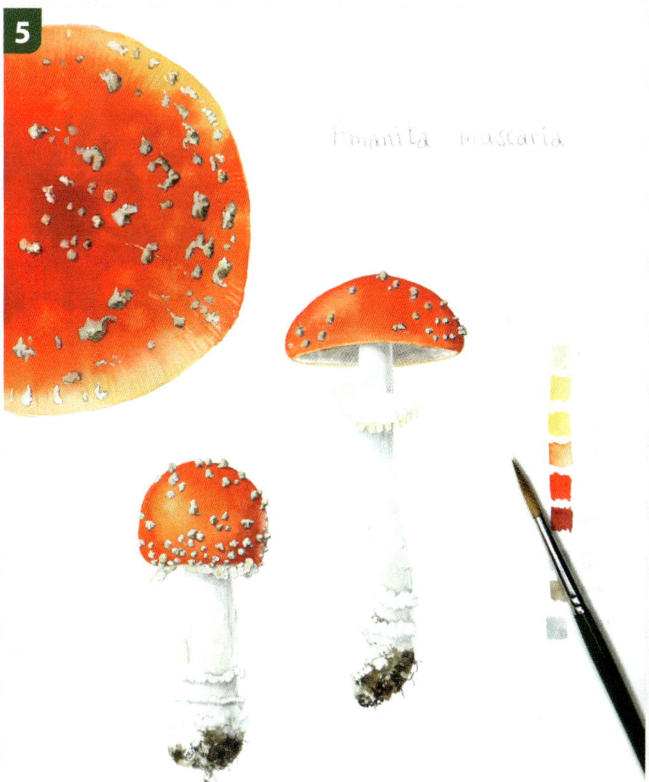

If you don't have masking fluid, you could try adding the scales on afterwards with tinted white gouache as in the smaller right-hand cap in this illustration. You could also try painting around the scales – obviously easier if you don't add too many!

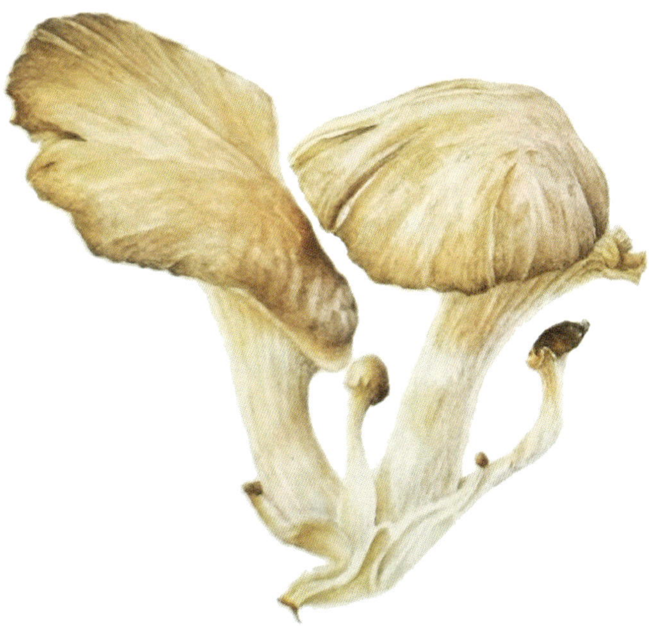

Oyster Mushroom by Jackie Isard. For the softly lit and muted tones of these mushrooms, Jackie has mixed warm, neutral hues mixed with transparent colours – such as Winsor Blue red shade, Transparent yellow and Permanent Rose. (© Jackie Isard)

shading for a three-dimensional look. The key is to leave the white of the paper for the majority of the mushroom to avoid it becoming too dark by painting it too grey. In any white subject the darkest shadows are still quite pale in comparison to other more colourful and deeper toned subjects. Be sure to carefully paint the gradation of the coloured greys into the white areas using a clean, damp brush to blend out edges. As with all watercolour techniques, practise and experiment first to see how it goes.

Some mushrooms can have a chalky, dusty bloom covering their caps or stipes. This is known by the term *pruinose*, and its depiction will lend itself to opaque gouache paints, which we will look at in the next section. Using white paint is good for adding certain details like little white fibres or that fine pale reticulation on the apex of a Cep's stipe or getting back lost scales on *Amanita* caps!

SHADOW COLOURS

The best colours for shading most subjects are the grey and neutral tint mixes biased towards the local colour of the subject as described in the section on 'pigments and paints for fungi' earlier in the chapter. As a general rule, you can try using the complementary colour for shading, especially for oranges and blues and violets and yellows, as they neutralise each other well, depending on the temperature of each colour. Green and red is the exception to the rule, as they mix to make a dull brown, so you have to adjust the mix with a little blue to get a suitable neutral grey. Sometimes no grey shading is needed at all, just the use of analogous, darker, cooler colours can be perfect. In Chapter 9 there are some experiments with different methods of shading a bright red subject.

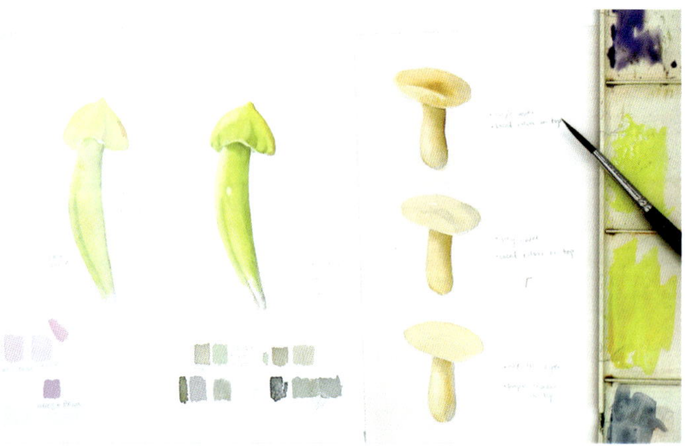

Experiments on watercolour paper with shading on warm yellow and cool yellow subjects using different violets, grey mixes and neutral tint mixes, very valuable experiments for future resources.

GOUACHE TECHNIQUES

Gouache is used in slightly thicker washes than transparent watercolour with a creamier consistency. As it is opaque it can be used on tinted paper or dark coloured board with great effect. Highlights are achieved with white paint instead of the white paper, just as in acrylics or oils and mistakes can be covered up. Unlike acrylics though, it is not permanent when dry and subsequent layers can be lifted, reworked, or disturbed if you are not careful when layering. Gouache also has the habit of drying differently than it appears when wet, so lighter colours tend to dry darker and darker colours dry lighter. It is also best to avoid putting on the paint too thickly as it may crack so this can be quite a frustrating medium. The key is finding the correct consistency – not too thick, not too thin.

In common with other opaque medium techniques, you can work from dark to light adding the whitest highlights as a final step, that always brings the painting to life. As previously stated, you can try mixing your transparent watercolours with white to give the paint covering power and make it opaque as was done in the past, but always keep that mixing area separate from your transparent watercolour mixing area to avoid contamination. There are two white pigments; Zinc White is a slightly more transparent white, often seen as the best for mixing as it is slightly more translucent and will not change the colour as much as using the more opaque Titanium White, that can turn every mix into a pastel colour. That is best for those final brightest highlights.

You can use the same brushes as you would with normal watercolours but dedicate them to one media or the other. Synthetics will be better than natural brushes such as sables as they are tougher and will last longer. Acrylic brushes may work well also. I sometimes keep my old watercolour brushes for use with gouache, remembering to keep them in a separate pot.

STEP-BY-STEP: USING GOUACHE ON A DARK BACKGROUND

I found some beautiful chanterelles; they are very common around where I live, and I see them as early as July sometimes going on until December. I thought that they would make a great subject for gouache as they do have a whitish opacity to them that lends itself to this medium.

MATERIALS USED:

- Stillman & Birn Black paper
- Schmincke Horadam white gouache, Winsor & Newton gouache paints in Cadmium Orange, Winsor Violet, and Spectrum Yellow, Indian Yellow transparent watercolour
- A white coloured pencil, piece of tracing paper
- Synthetic watercolour brushes – sizes 0, 2 and 4

1

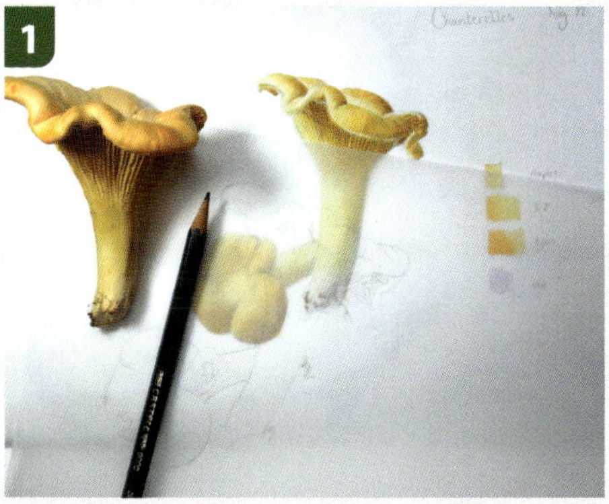

It's always a good idea to start in the sketchbook, playing with ideas for compositions and making colour notes as we've seen in Chapter 3, getting familiar with the subject. My original sketch was drawn out onto tracing paper, reworking it slightly to get a better angle until I was happy with the composition.

2

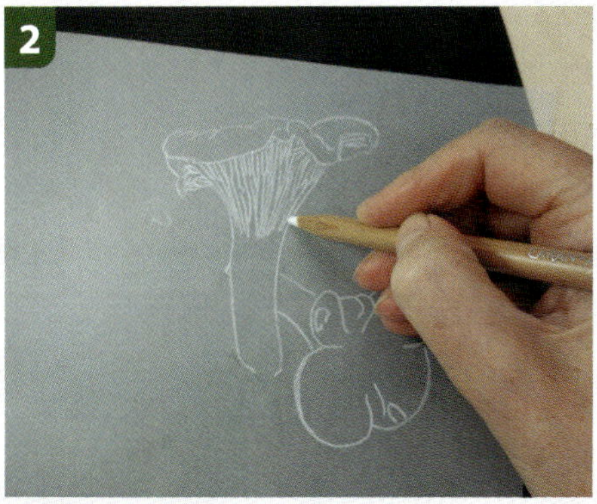

Then in order to properly see the drawing on the black paper, the image is drawn out again on the reverse side in a white coloured pencil.

3

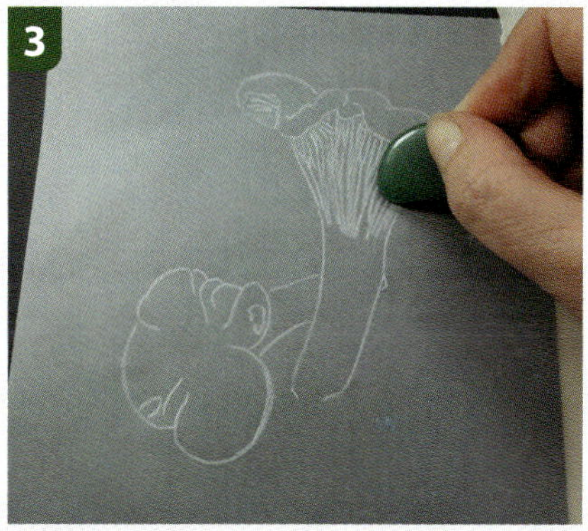

The tracing paper is flipped back over and taped down with low tack masking tape onto the final paper so that it doesn't move. I transferred the image by rubbing carefully with a polished gemstone checking to see how well it had been copied over. Sometimes you may have to redraw it again a little in places.

4

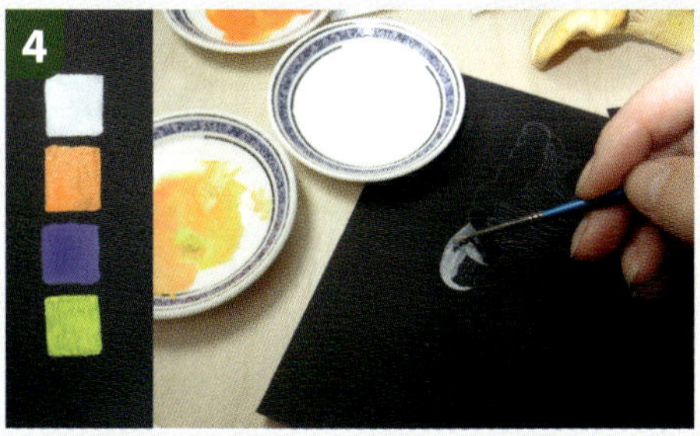

After mixing up some colours, I started with a first layer of white gouache making sure to follow the contours of the cap with my brush strokes. The orange, yellow and purple mix up to create browns or you could use an umber gouache if you have it.

5

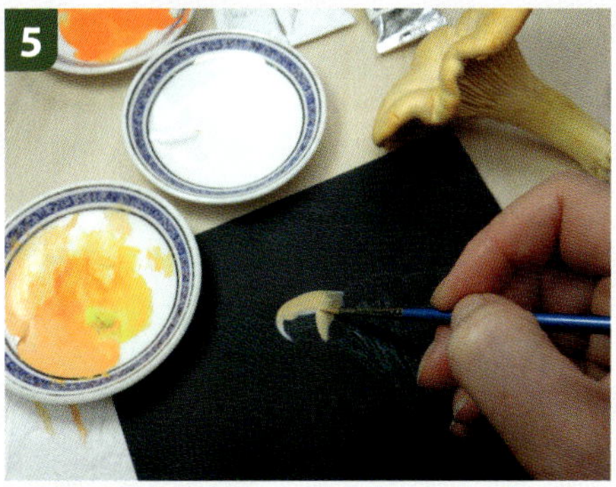

Now adding some colour to the white underlay. You have to be very careful so as not to lift the under layer too much. This can be a very challenging aspect to painting with gouache, so patience is needed. You could experiment with a white acrylic under painting if the gouache keeps lifting as that is permanent.

6

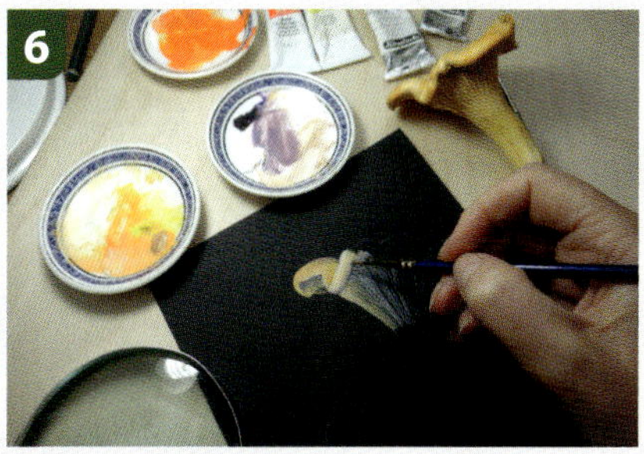

I do think in gouache that it's a good idea to start with the areas that are furthest back and work forward, so with this in mind I now began working on the gills as they finish underneath the cap. For the lighter areas on the gills, I added white and I've left the shadowed areas as black paper.

Continued on following page

7

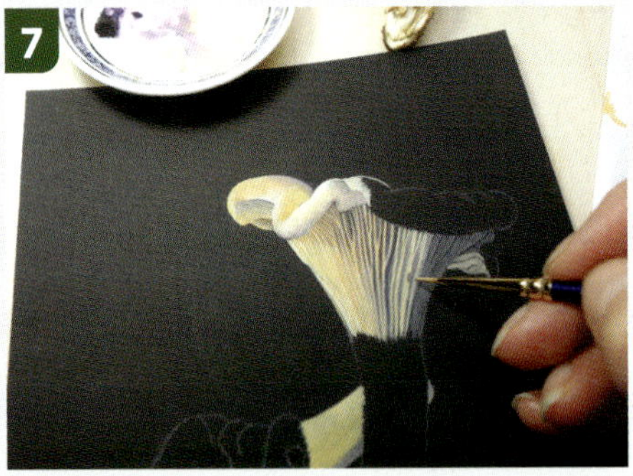

Adding volume to the gills – the light and shadow. In the shadowed areas, I added Winsor violet gouache and allowed the black to still be seen in the very darkest areas. Gouache is very forgiving if you've made a mistake; you can easily lift it out with some water and a tissue.

8

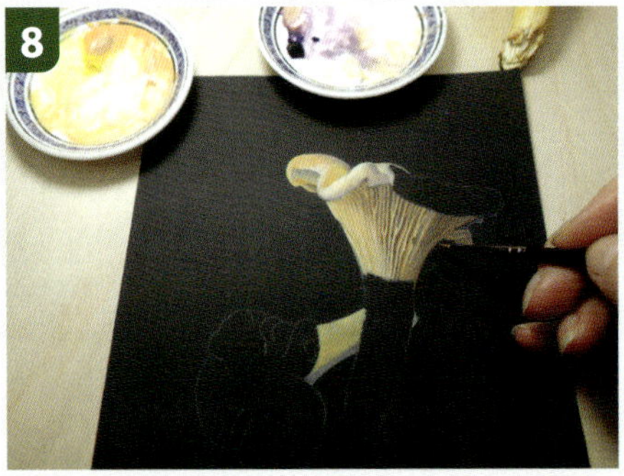

Adding the local colour of orange now by gently blending into the existing layers. Then the final touches to the gills are adding white to the edges where the light is catching them.

9

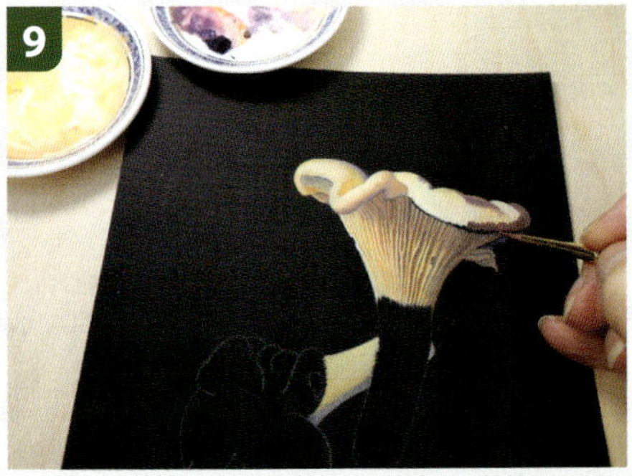

Finishing off the rest of the cap. You can see me adding the paint in blocks of light in yellow/white, local colour in orange and the shadows in purple/grey after the initial layer of white. It can then be blended together using gentle strokes of the brush always following contours.

10

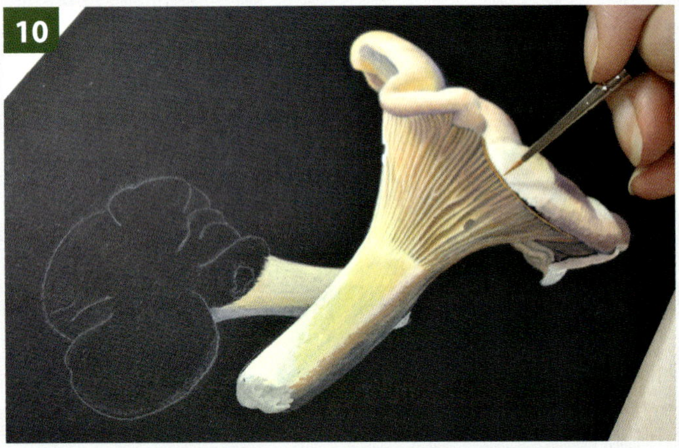

The stipe is added in the same way as the cap, with more white to the left and the thinner paint to the right to let the black help to act as a shadow. The smaller stipe was painted in first as it is behind. Here you can see me delineating the cap edge in orange, just refining and making sure that it is clean edged.

11

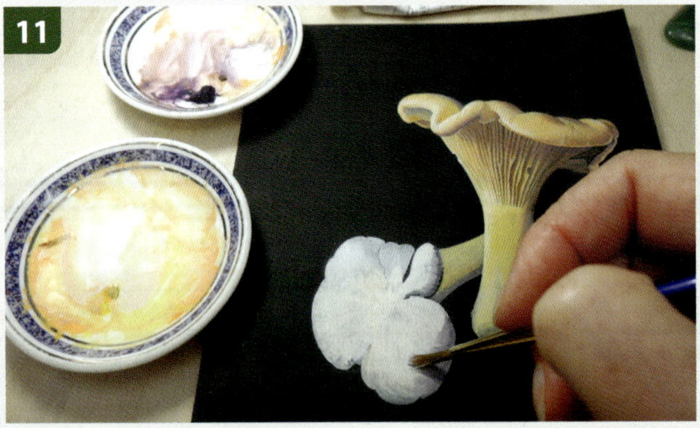

The second cap is painted in completely in white with some purple and grey paint in the shadows. I've swapped to a bigger brush to add this larger area of paint. This is a size 4 synthetic watercolour brush.

12

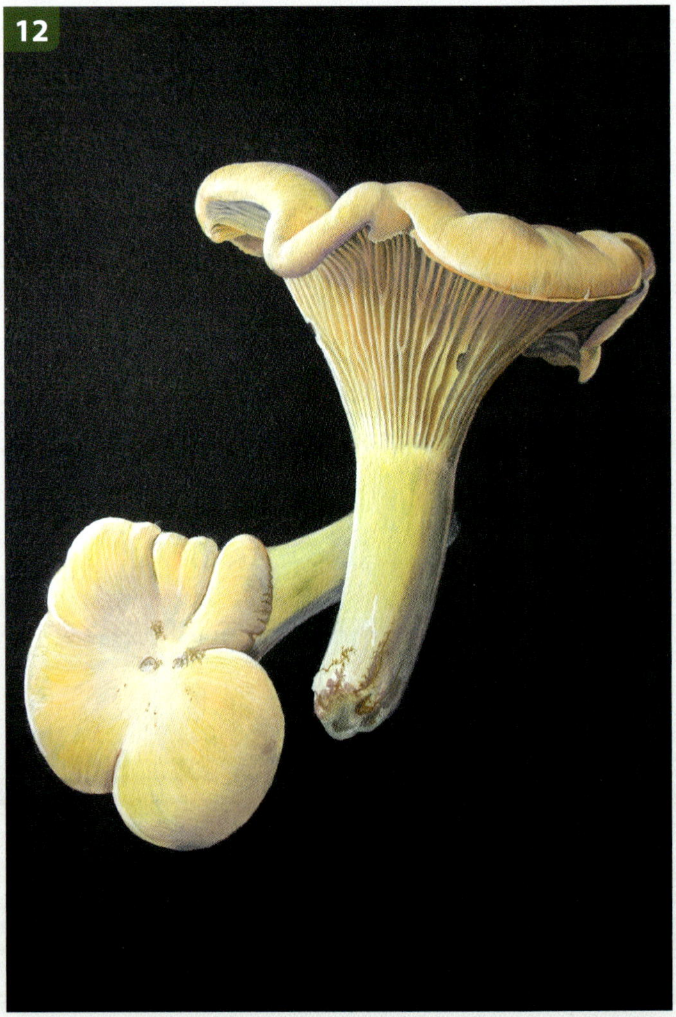

The finished painting. I added some very careful glazes of Indian Yellow transparent watercolour to brighten the colours; it's absolutely fine to mix ordinary watercolours with gouache and well worth experimenting with.

TIPS FOR PAINTING ON A DARK COLOURED GROUND

- Coloured grounds include acid-free mount board, black, toned or tinted papers.
- The initial drawing is completed in a white pencil to show it up better.
- As gouache is easy to lift, it can be frustrating work trying not to lift the under layers, so care and practice is needed. You could also try painting in the subject first with a white acrylic paint as an undercoat and then work on top. The acrylic is permanent and will not lift.
- Gouache technique uses more dry brush work not wet washes.
- After a few thin layers are in place, colours can be blended together for smooth gradations.

PAINTING ON VELLUM

Vellum has become popular in natural history illustration owing to the luminosity it brings to subjects painted on it. Colours seem to glow more jewel-like, and the unique finish of natural vellum can bring a beautiful texture and warm colouration to the background. It seems quite apt to paint fungi on a vellum skin seeing as fungi are more closely related to the animal kingdom than to Plantae.

The botanical artist Jean Emmons is an experienced colourist capturing the vibrant jewel-like tones within her subjects. She explains her technique for painting fungi on vellum. 'I like to paint from life when I can, as I see more colour that way. I paint in watercolour and gouache on vellum. I use a Raphael Designer's Series 8408 size 2 Kolinsky sable brush. While requiring a much drier touch than watercolour paper, I find vellum so versatile in terms of making lots of changes. They can be changes to colour or changes to composition. I don't have to do as many preliminary drawings. In the case of fungi, I am often changing the perspective of the gills, or in the case of boletes, the perspective of the tubes. I lift and sand paint off, again and again, repainting multiple times, until things look right to me.'

Vellum is very forgiving as it is non-absorbent and so paint sits on the surface. But because of this it won't be able to take very wet washes and requires a drier brush technique. Little strokes or stipples of paint can be added to deepen layers and strengthen tones but carefully so as not to lift underlying layers. Kelmscott calfskin vellum is often thought of as the best quality and easiest to work on, with a creamy colour. Some natural vellums can have a dark coffee colour and lots of blemishes and textures that can be incorporated into a painting.

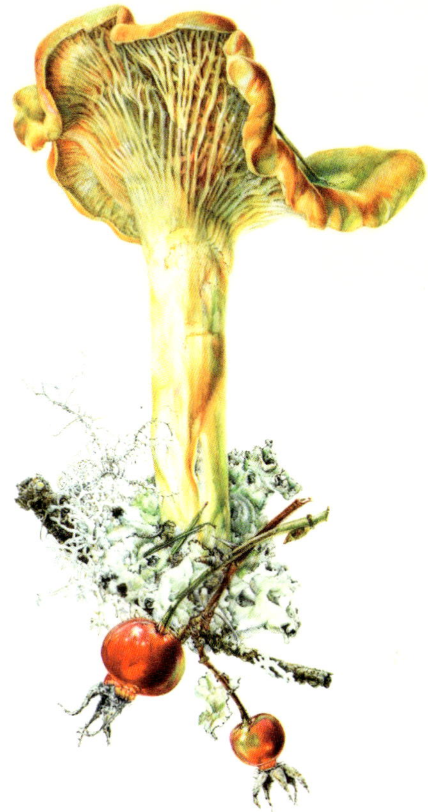

Pacific Golden Chanterelle – *Cantharellus formosus* by botanical artist Jean Emmons. Watercolour and gouache on Kelmscott vellum, 17 x 10cm (6¾ x 4in). You can see different colours reflected onto the mushroom and the warm glow of the vellum in the background. (© Jean Emmons, 2021)

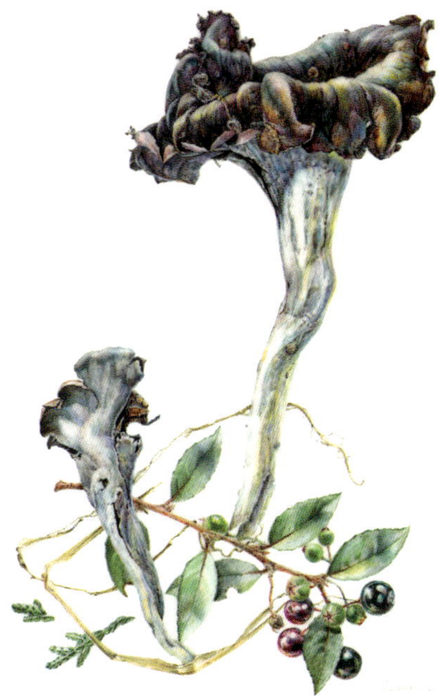

Horn of Plenty – *Craterellus cornucopioides*, by Jean Emmons. Watercolour on vellum stretched over panel, 17 x 13cm (6¾ x 5in). The vellum creates such a vibrant luminosity to the colours on this interesting, funnel-shaped black mushroom. Jean says, 'This one is edible and delicious!' (© Jean Emmons, 2020)

Vellum needs storing with care as it is sensitive to humidity and heat and even when mounted it can react to changes in the atmosphere, so it's important to keep it or hang in dry environments, behind glass.

COLOURED PENCIL TECHNIQUES

As with other pencil techniques, the drawing is worked up in layers. They can be worked from light to dark or dark to light. As in watercolours, a *Grisaille* technique can be used to render the initial shadow tones in the first layers with greys, violets and neutrals and then the local colour built on top.

They can be used on any paper, but smoother papers such as Bristol paper, board and hot pressed watercolour paper are the best to use for more detailed and realistic artworks. Drawings can have a textured, grainy look, especially if using a more textured paper and so some blending will be needed to push the pigment into the tooth of the paper. This technique is called burnishing and can be achieved using a colourless blender or a pale-coloured pencil that is added on top of the layers of pencil. However, it's best to not press too hard to start with or you may be in danger of flattening the tooth of the paper so that no more layers can be added; coloured pencil technique usually needs lots of layers.

Erasers can be used with most coloured pencils and battery-powered erasers may be especially useful. Coloured pencil can be used in conjunction with solvents such as odourless mineral spirits for artists, which dissolve the pigment to give a more painterly look, settling the pigment into the tooth of the paper without the need for burnishing. You will need to make sure that you've added enough layers of pigment before using the spirits to achieve the best look. Alternatively, you could lay on a watercolour base, then add detail, shading and pattern on top with the pencils.

A good functional sharpener with a strong spiral core will be needed for artists working in this medium and a recommended make is the Rapesco 64 that can be clamped onto a desktop. These sharpeners are cranked by hand.

Watercolour pencils are great as they explore both worlds of wet and dry media; you can use them dry for normal coloured pencil effects or brush out with water to dissolve the pigment into a wash. If using with water, care must be taken as the colour can sometimes be a little too bright or overwhelming. So, experiments are important to determine the amount of pigment needed to achieve the finish that you'd like. You can mix on a paper palette by drawing a patch of pigment out and then picking up on a brush and mixing with it. You can also shave off little scrapings of pigment onto a wet surface to create interesting, textured effects for looser studies.

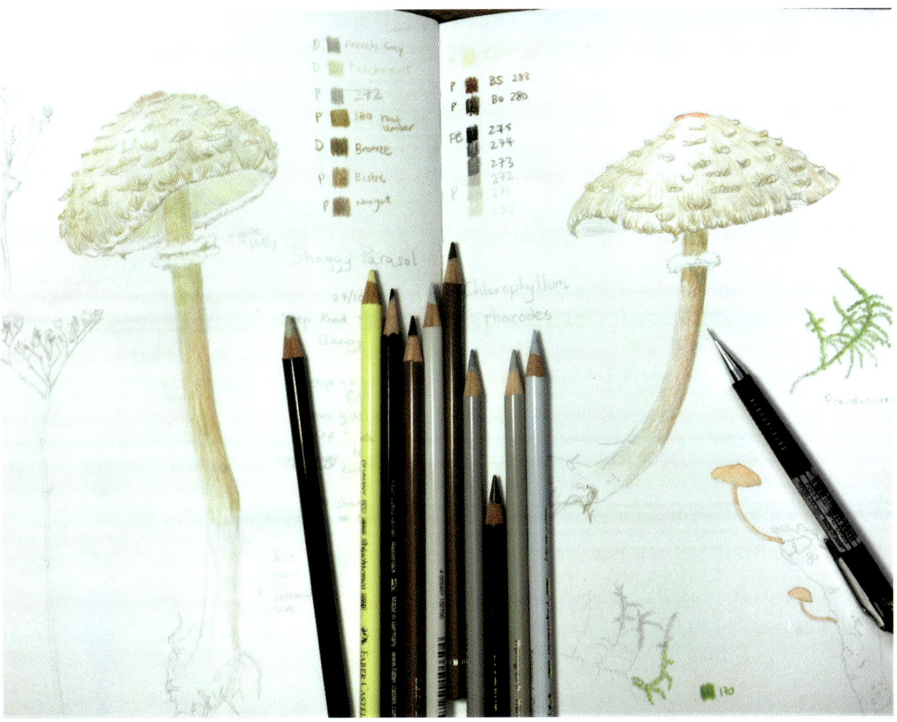

Drawing Shaggy Parasols – *Chlorophyllum rhacodes* in the sketchbook. They have such a dry, hairy, tasselled look so I thought using coloured pencils would be very appropriate. I made colour notes in exactly the same fashion as I would with watercolours.

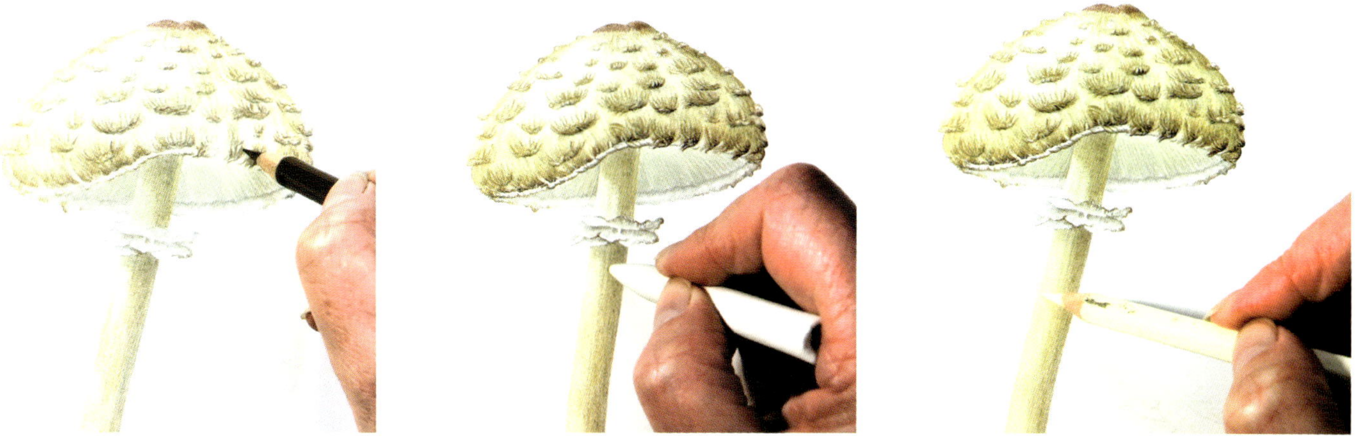

Drawing those Shaggy Parasols on Arches HP with the Faber-Castell Polychromos coloured pencils. Here I built up many layers of colour and then I tried burnishing the layers to blend them together with a tortillion paper stump and a white pencil. You can purchase burnishing pencils and colourless blenders specially for the job, but I made do with these here.

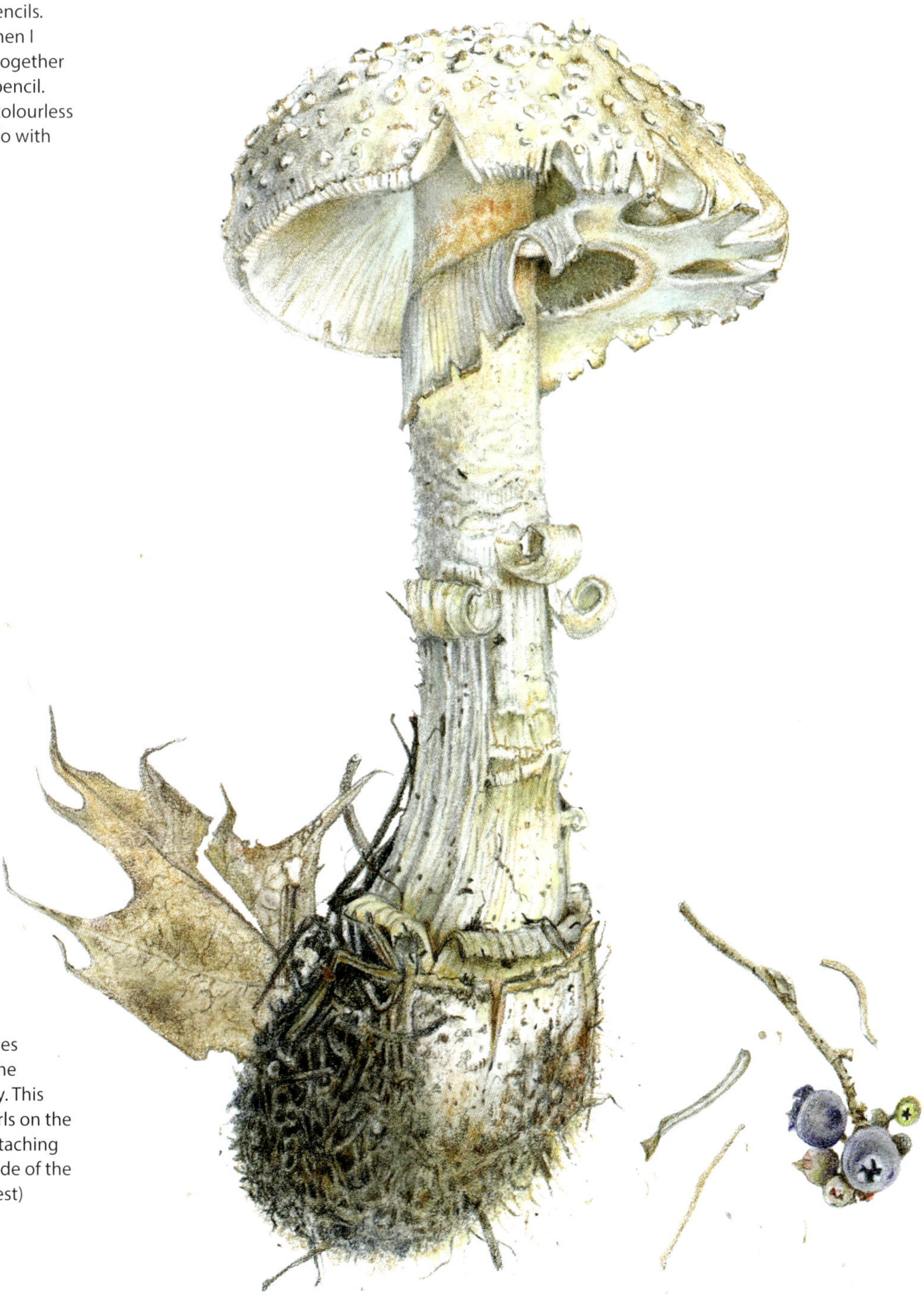

Amanita multisquamosa in coloured pencil by botanical artist Margaret Best. Sometimes called the white panthercap, you can see the classic characteristics of the *Amanita* family. This mushroom has real personality, with its curls on the stipe and the way that the partial veil is detaching its protective seal from around the underside of the cap and is forming the ring. (© Margaret Best)

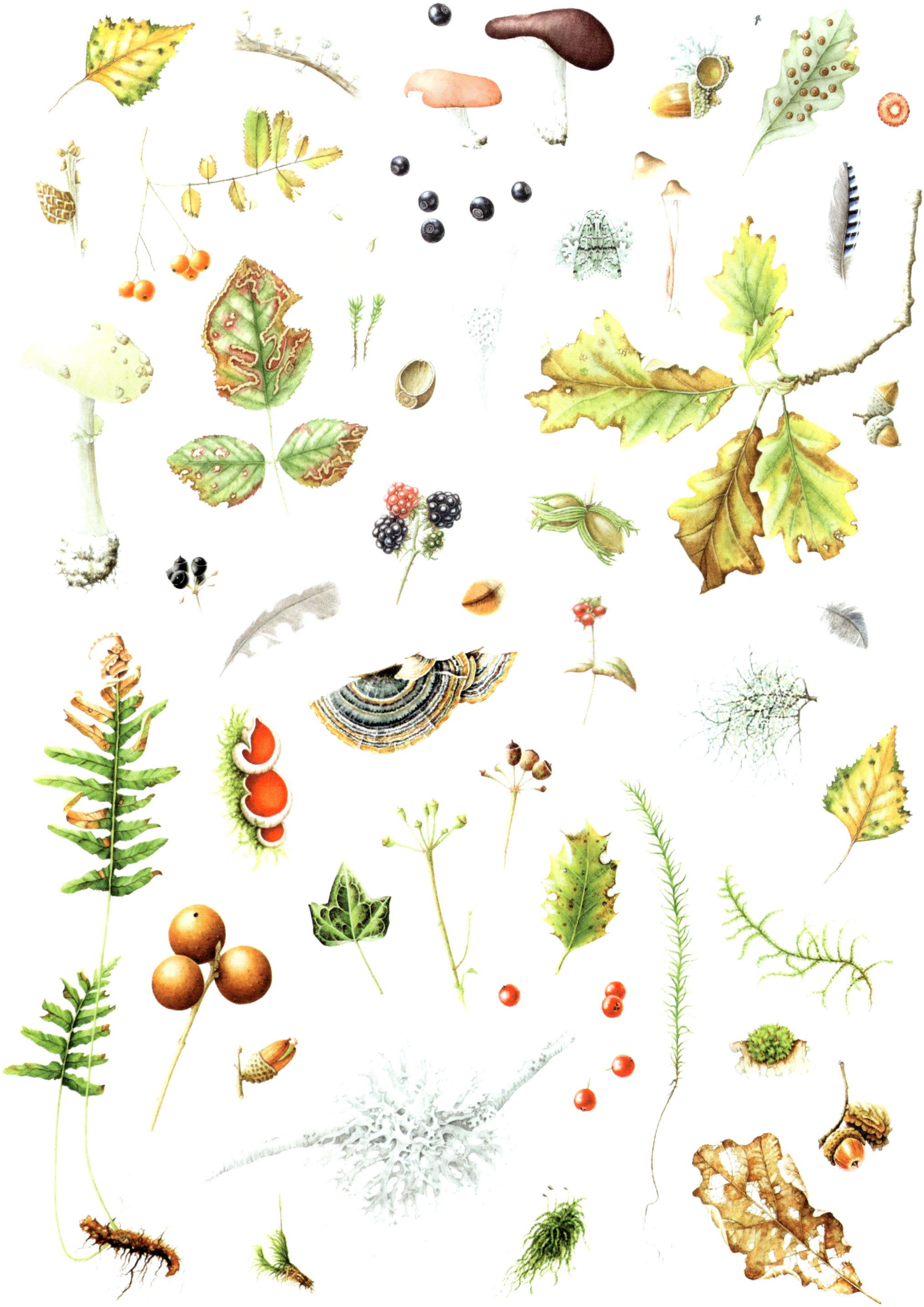

CHAPTER 6

COMPOSITION, BACKGROUND ELEMENTS AND OTHER TECHNIQUES

'Even in front of nature, one must compose.'
EDGAR DEGAS

Composition is the design element of an artwork; the way the subjects are placed to lead the eye and guide it around a painting. Good composition is the aspect that grabs our eye and makes us come in and take a closer look. Designing an artwork or composition is quite an understudied topic but incredibly important.

It is vital to get this right at the beginning, so preparation is key. Many a time I have rushed in, focusing on perfecting technique and not considered the composition enough, only to find that the design is somehow wrong! It can be a very subjective topic; each person may have their own ideas about design and what works for one person may not for the next. But each artwork should always warrant this pre-thought, especially when being painted for exhibitions or shows.

INITIAL CONSIDERATIONS

- What aspects are relevant to the artwork or illustration? These could be features to help with identification. Is it to be scientific or decorative?
- What format do you want it to take? The most obvious formats are portrait and landscape of differing proportions, but you could also consider square or circular. An open format is a cropped off image that continues outside of the frame. This gives a more contemporary feel to the artwork whereas a closed format is the more traditional look of a subject placed in entirety within the frame.
- What compositional aids could be used to help guide the eye around the picture? This could be simply adding diagonal or circular aspects that could make the design more interesting and add movement. Straight lines appear more static.
- Where will the focal point be and do you need one? Most pictures usually contain a focal point, which is the most prominent part of a painting. A composition can lead the eye to this point by use of line and/or bright colour, contrast or detail.
- Thinking about the negative space around the subject which can act as a rest for the eye and the balance of the positive painted space to this negative white area.
- Use of odd numbers and triangles creates harmonious compositions and also colour and depth can bring further dimensions. The addition of a splash of red in the picture could add warmth and contrast to the colour composition. Colour transference, such as a pink colour carried through aspects of the painting, creates unity and harmony.
- To think about the balance or visual weight of all the features that you'd like to add and arranging them in a way that looks good and feels right.

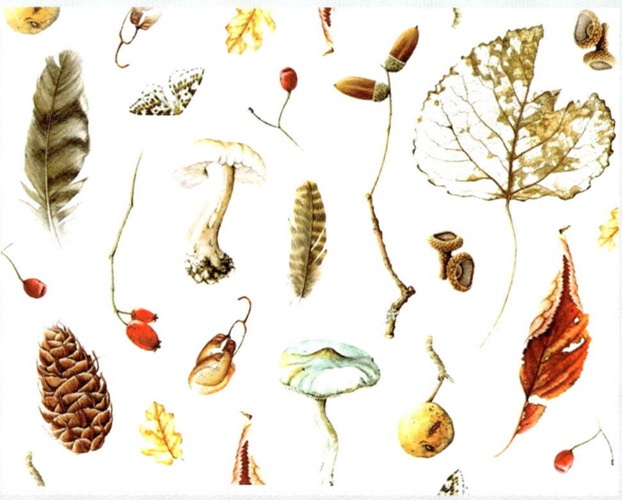

The repetitive pattern of this compilation of autumnal subjects could make a good design for fabrics or wrapping papers or even gifts such as tea towels.

Collection of autumn and winter findings from the oak woods of the Rheidol Nature Reserve in Wales.

MORE AIDS TO COMPOSITION

Methods that can help form the underlying structure include the rule of thirds, which is probably the most used aid to composition in any genre of art and I expect you are familiar with it. It comes from a very old concept called 'the Golden Section' which is based on a mathematical formula, supposed to represent beauty; the ratio of 0.618, which is found in many places in nature, so we may be subconsciously drawn to objects embedded with this ratio. It is basically where the picture plane is divided into nine squares, or thirds. Where the lines intersect is called a 'sweet spot' and they are where (or close to where) to best place a focal point in the painting for an aesthetically pleasing look.

Preparation for a design should include lots of rough thumbnail sketches in a layout notebook or sketchbook. This can help to test out and see your ideas and the arrangements of elements quickly and simply within the frame and consider if they could work.

CHECKING A COMPOSITION

To test if a composition will look right especially if it is complex and multi-layered, you can draw the sketches out on to some transparent tracing paper and move them around on another piece of paper until you can find an agreeable design. Then a more detailed sketch can be carried out when a good design has been found. Using tracing paper to transfer your sketches will also protect the paper surface from the overuse of erasers by cutting down on making mistakes.

An adjustable mount or viewfinder can help to frame a picture to see if it could work; you can make these easily or buy them in art shops. A good way to check a design is to hold it up in front of a mirror. The reverse image can sometimes show up inconsistencies in the balance of a composition, bringing it to your attention.

It's also a good idea to leave the work for a couple of days and then come back to it with fresher eyes, looking at it from a distance.

THINGS THAT YOU CAN CHECK

- Variety is important to add interest, so check sizes, colours, tones, shapes, and textures.
- Is the picture or subject balanced?
- Is there movement, a focal point?
- Does it have all the relevant elements within it?
- Could you add depth using aerial perspective for more interest?

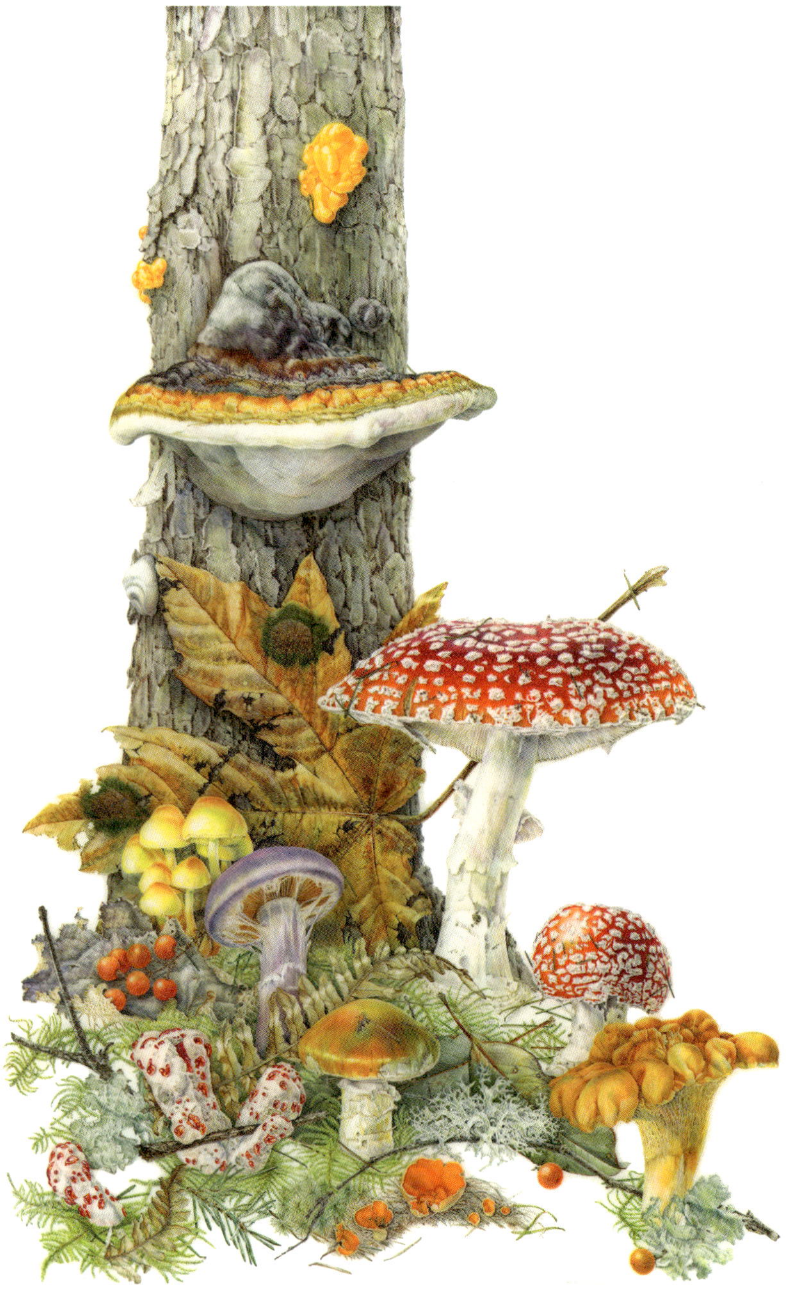

Pacific Northwest Mushrooms by Jean Emmons. A complex composition of fungi from Jean's award-winning RHS exhibition in 2021. The fungi are *Hydnellum peckii, Cortinarius traganus, Hypholoma fasciculare, Rhytisma punctatum, Fomitopsis pinicola, Dacrymyces palmatus, Amanita muscaria, Cantharellus formosus,* and *Aleuria aurantia.* (© Jean Emmons)

MIXED COMPOSITIONS

For fungi illustrations the choice for compositions is mainly of whether to focus on painting a single species or a mixture of many different species to show diversity, variation of size, texture and colour, or perhaps a group with a shared common attribute such as edibility or medicinal qualities. When painting a single species, one could be drawn at each stage of growth from button mushroom stage to fully grown, such as in the Death cap painting in Chapter 2, along with a longitudinal section to show the interior structure. You could also add a suite of autumnal accompaniments (or other season of growth), adding bits of vegetation that are found with the mushroom such as tree leaves, acorns, mosses, pine needles and cones. This can determine the habitat that the species is found in, and also highlight any mycorrhizal relationship with particular trees. These additional elements can also help to balance compositions, fill up any annoying gaps and add interest, texture and colours.

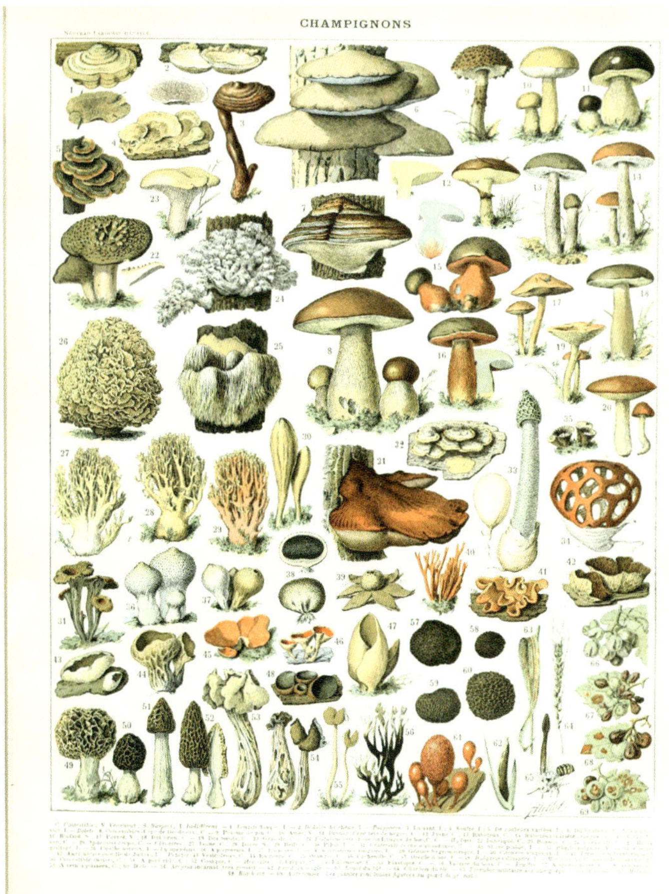

Champignons. One of the many large, mixed, natural history illustration compositions from the French artist, lithographer and entomologist Adolphe Millot (1857–1921).

Another option could be to scale up your subject, perhaps twice life-size or more if it is very small. This is a contemporary way of composing a subject and a great way to focus in on tiny details, really bringing them to the viewer's attention.

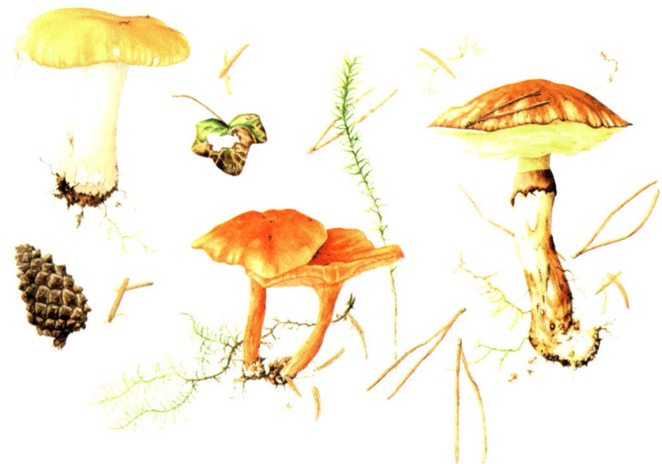

A walk in the woods – 2010 – *Russula ochroleuca, Hygrophoropsis aurantiaca* and *Suillus luteus* with lots of vegetative coniferous accompaniments that were found with the fungi. These additions help to fill up any gaps on the page.

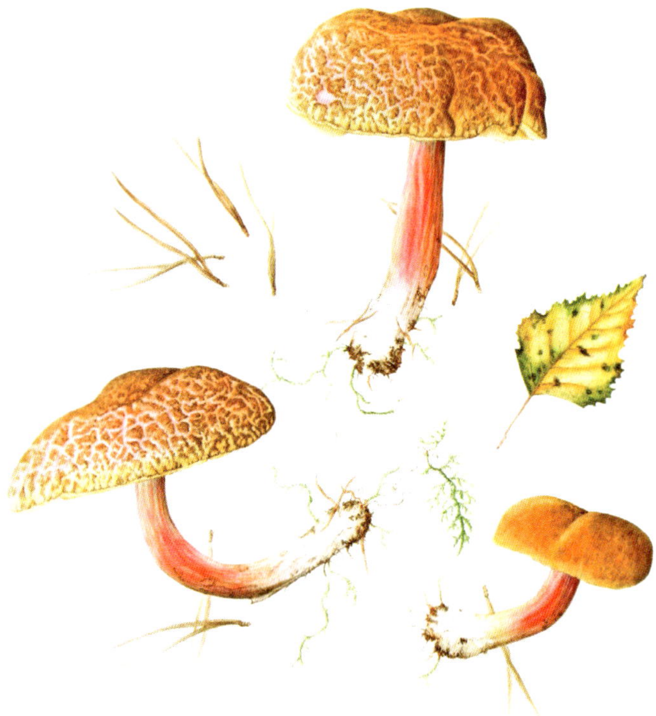

Red Cracking Bolete – *Xerocomellus chrysenteron,* 2011. In this painting I've added habitat elements but on reviewing the painting, I realised that I had not given a view of the beautiful primrose yellow pores, a lovely feature of this mushroom. This shows the importance of checking relevant details before commencing an illustration.

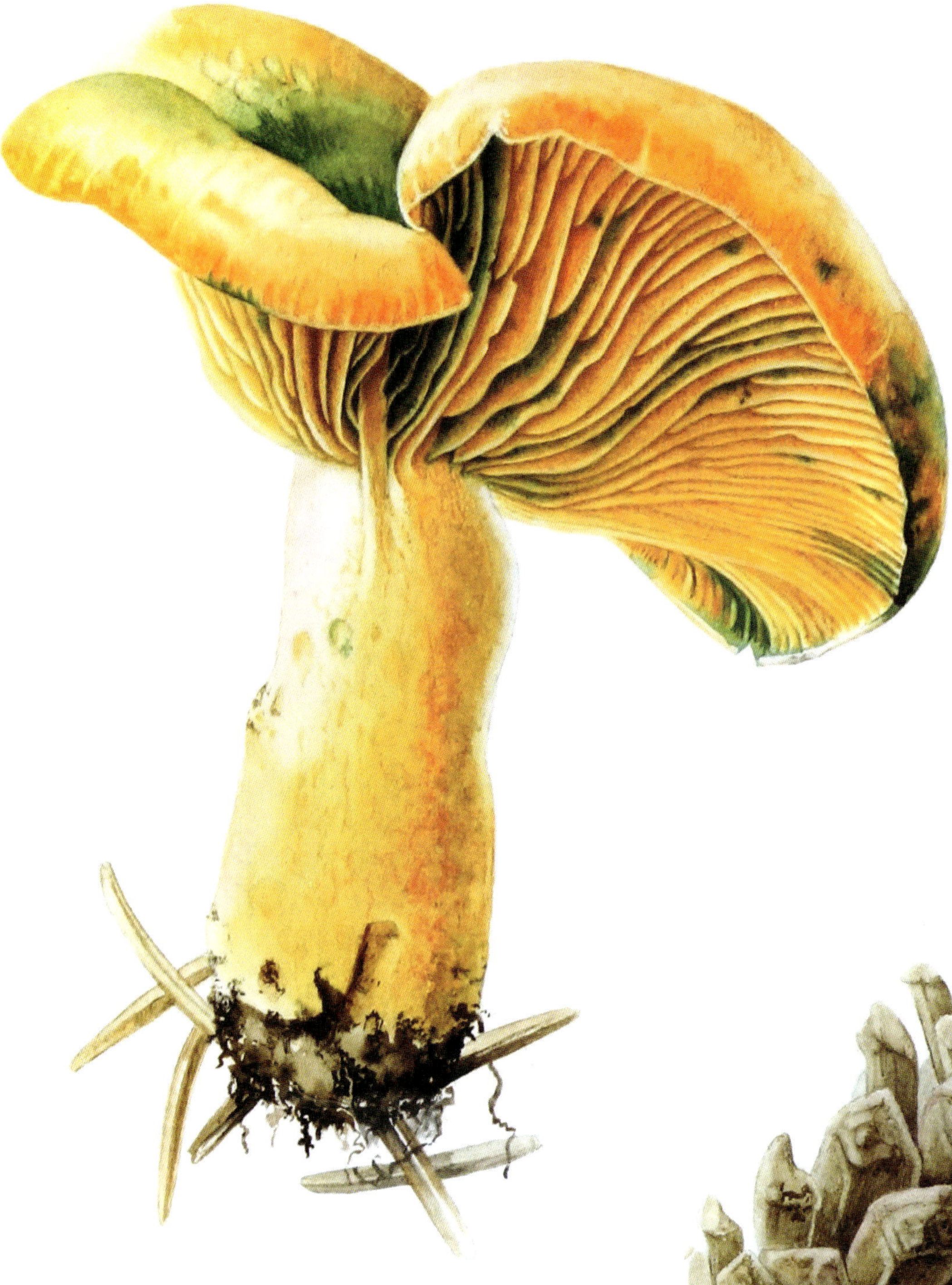

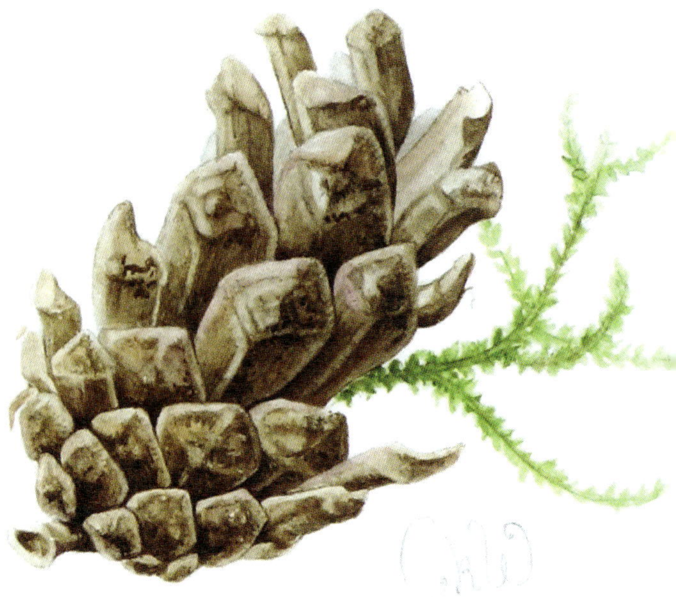

Portrait of the False Saffron Milkcap – *Lactarius deterrimus* twice lifesize. Scaling up a subject is a great way to show up the tiniest details. This is a colourful mushroom, with its carrot orange and bright turquoise hues. Found in coniferous woodlands, it has a smoother stipe than the Saffron Milkcap which has a pitted one.

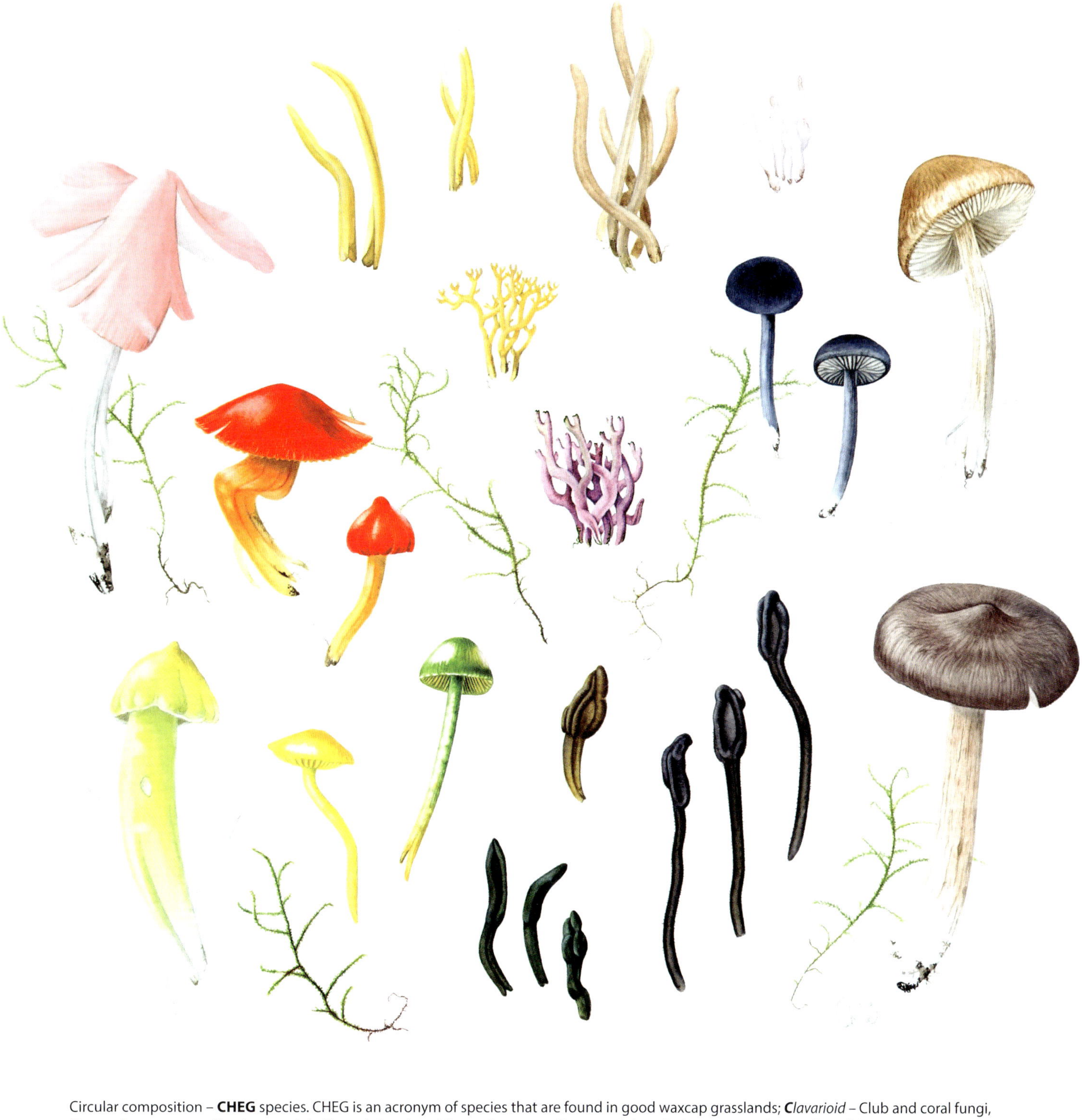

Circular composition – **CHEG** species. CHEG is an acronym of species that are found in good waxcap grasslands; ***C****lavarioid* – Club and coral fungi, ***H****ygrocybe* – waxcaps, ***E****ntoloma* – pinkgills and ***G****eoglossoid* – earthtongues. Surveys of these habitats count the number of these CHEG species in order to evaluate the biodiversity of the site.

CHEMICAL COMPOSITION

An interesting addition to compositions is including the chemical structures of any curious molecules that certain species contain. I really like the visuality of these scientific forms. Here we have psilocybin and musimol from the psychedelic mushrooms, coprine from the common inkcap and Cycloprop-2-ene carboxylic acid – a toxic molecule present in *Russula subnigricans* and *Tricholoma equestre*. This last chemical also has the funkier name of triangulenic acid and I've also heard it called Tinky Winkenic acid due to its shape! This particularly nasty chemical is responsible for poisonings in Japan and the east, with these mushrooms unfortunately being mistaken for edible ones. The common inkcap (*Coprinopsis atramentaria*) contains coprine which is poisonous if consumed with alcohol, up to twenty-four hours before or after. It can give very unpleasant symptoms, similar to a severe hangover.

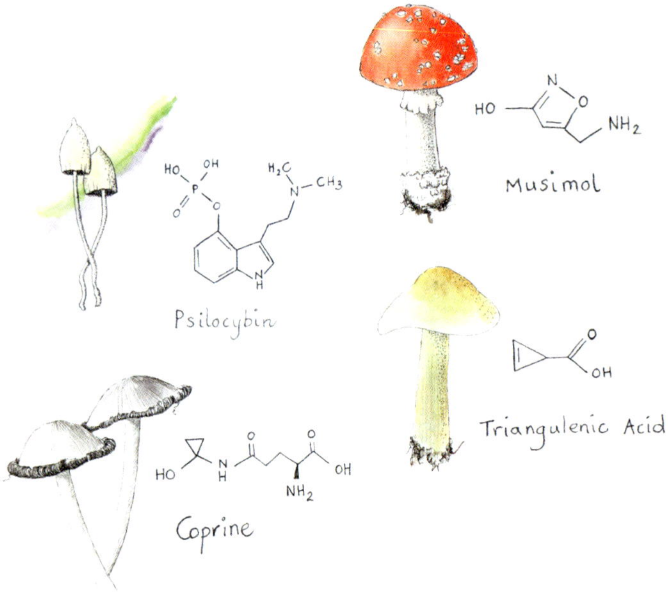

The Chemicals within – Psilocybin and Musimol, the magic in magic mushrooms and fly agaric, Coprine is the anti-alcohol drug in the inkcaps and Tinky winkenic acid is found in the Yellow Knight. This rather whimsical and stylised illustration is in pen and coloured pencils.

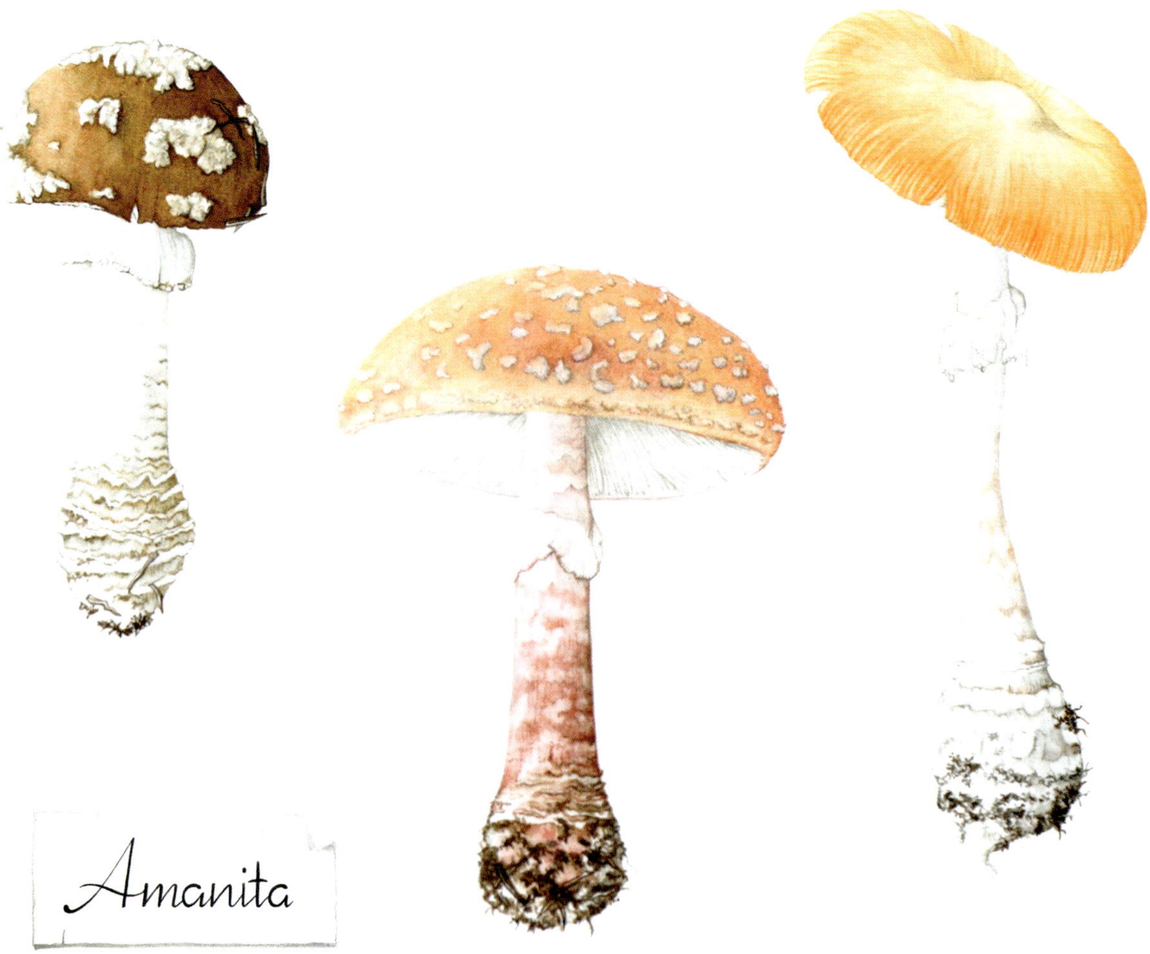

Adding Text – perhaps a title or the species names could be written in to fill the page; some beautiful calligraphy could add elegance and finish off a piece of work very well. This addition could help to balance out a composition also.

BACKGROUND ELEMENTS

Adding a background can turn an illustration into more of an artwork. It will really embed a subject into an environment and will give information about its habitat. It can also be a chance to loosen up and have a bit of fun with textures or fluid watercolours. Textural effects can be created using all sorts of items from around the house, such as salt, cling film or bits of string – the imagination can fly here! These can all lend qualities of bark or moss and create interesting forest-scapes in a piece of work and give an opportunity to experiment.

Another option could be the addition of digital backgrounds, whether it's just a plain colour or a complex one like in the image. It can be a helpful tool for experimenting to see if a black background for instance would look good and then it could be painted in afterwards.

The top study painting with a plain white background and below, the addition of a background in Photoshop Elements, photo editing software. It can be fun to experiment with digital backgrounds on your paintings, either plain, dark grounds or something a bit wackier like this!

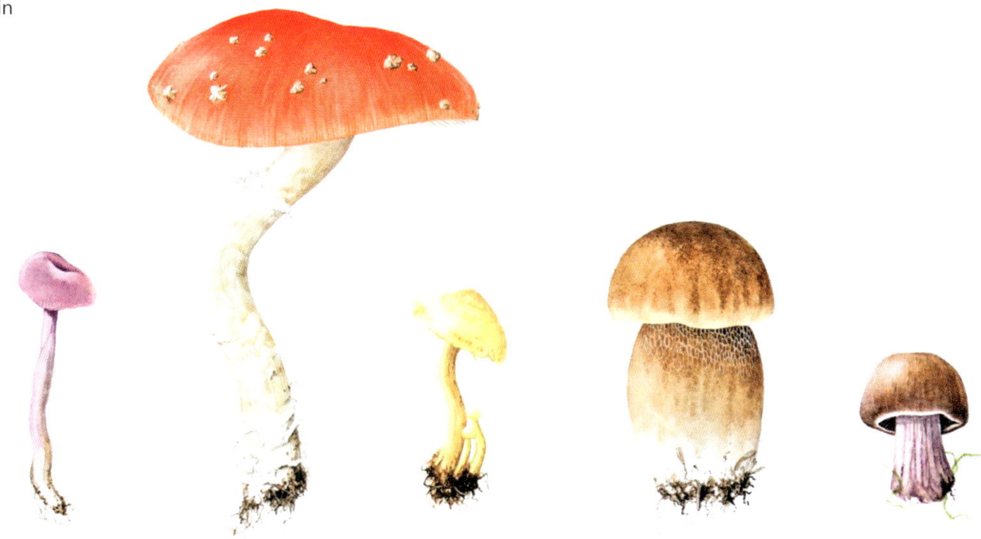

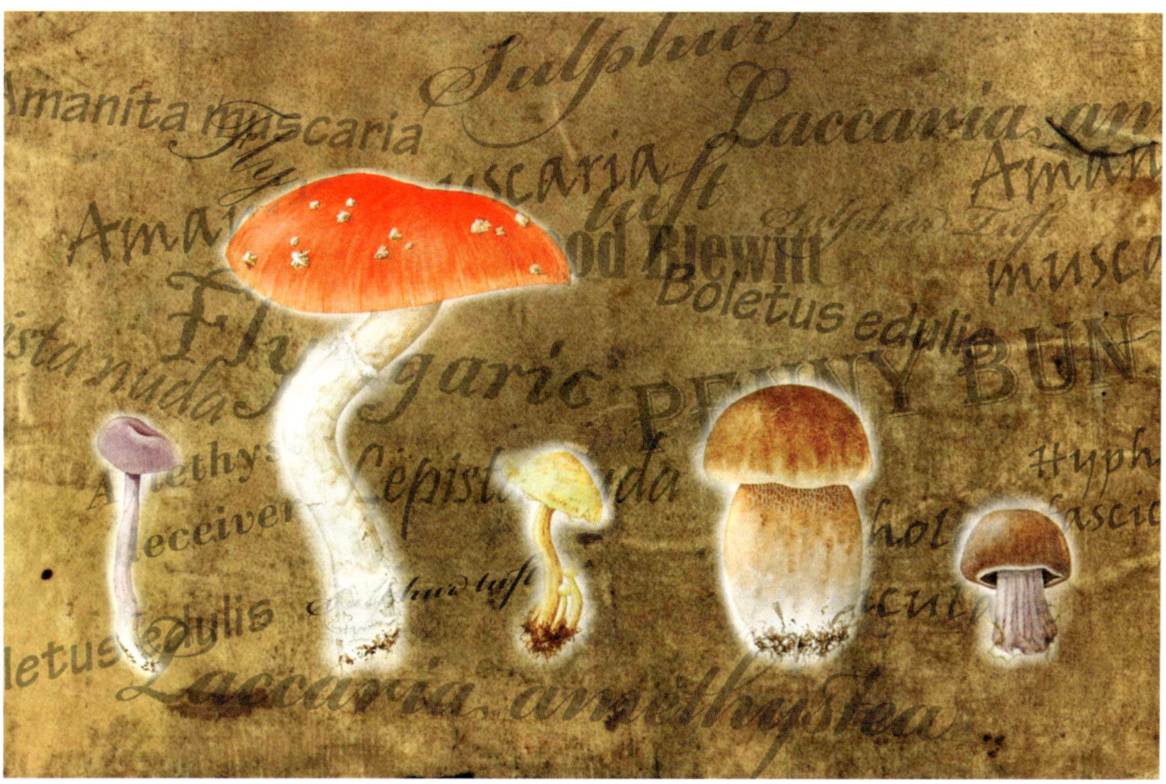

FOCUS STUDY: THE BIRCH TREE AND BRACKETS

This is an approach to adding a fluid background using watercolours and masking fluid.

The birch is a stunning tree, one of my favourites and good to paint or draw. The older trees are cracked and gnarled with bright green, velvety moss cascading from the bumpy surface of the textured bark. The Birch Polypore, *Fomitopsis betulina,* that I previously made the paper from (*see* this in Chapter 1), is found growing upon the birch tree. So, while out on a hunt for them, I found a beautiful tree as a subject to paint. It made for some great photos looking up towards the blue sky.

For the first painting, I worked very quickly using a Pigma Micron 003 pen to draw the tree and brackets and then watercolour washes on top. The paper I used was Fabriano Artistico 140lb hot press but it is important to note here that when using a large wet into wet wash for a background, it may be a good idea to use a heavier weight paper or to stretch the paper first. As I rarely paint very large washes, I never stretch my paper first. I used Winsor Violet, Indian Yellow and a Daniel Smith Primatek paint called Green Apatite that splits into

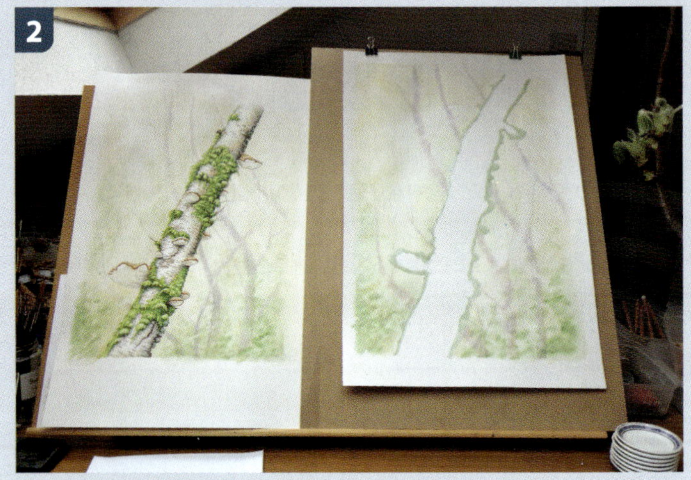

The first pen and watercolour painting that I didn't like is on the left and then on the right is take two, with the tree edges masked out and the background washed in with a pale wet into wet watercolour wash.

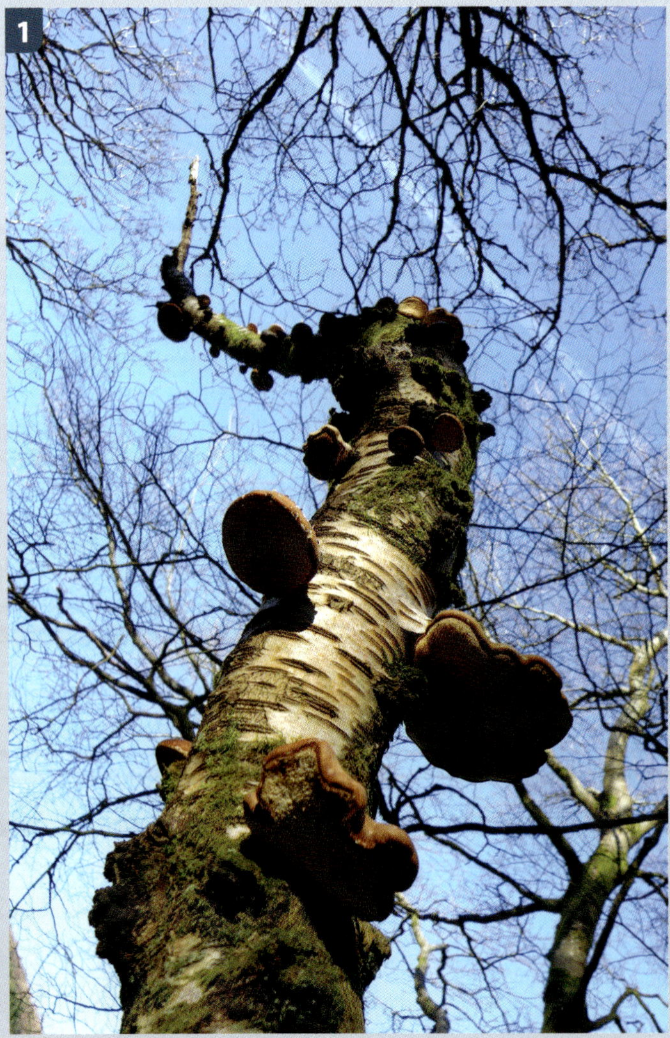

Looking up at the brackets on the birch tree – this is an excellent viewpoint and gives a different and interesting perspective against the blue sky.

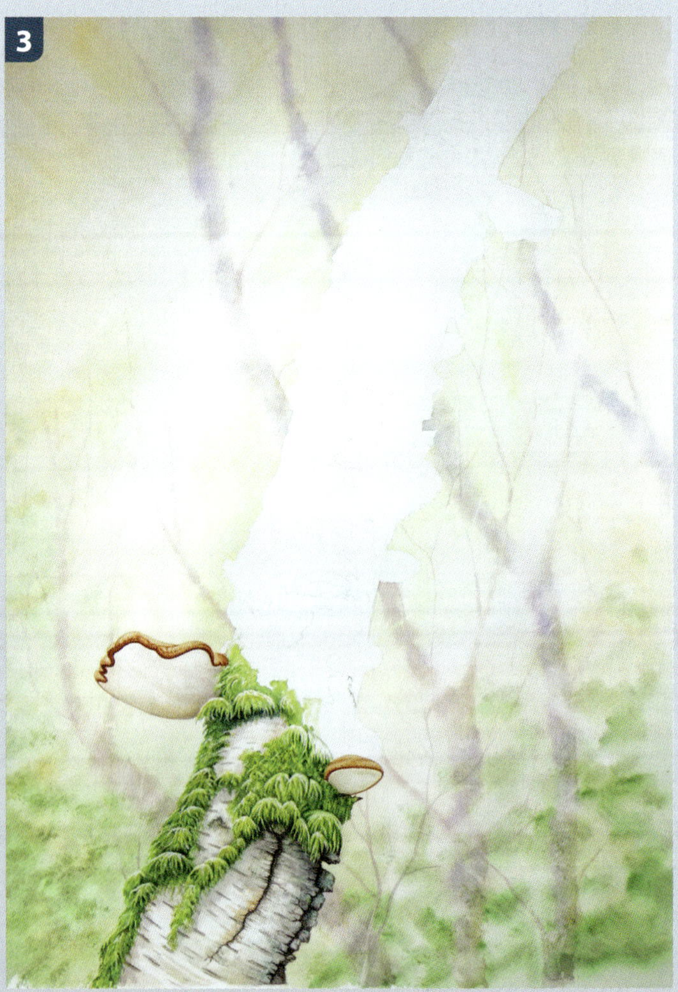

The masking fluid was rubbed off and the tree details were then started. I worked up the tree completing small sections like this fully at a time. In retrospect, I probably didn't need the masking fluid at all as the background came out very pale, but it allowed me to loosen up and to not worry!

a lovely green and brown speckled wash. I love these granulating paints for work like this or landscapes. They include many textural and interesting, earthy colours made from minerals, but they can be expensive.

When completed, I didn't like the shape of the trunk; it didn't have the sinuousness that I liked in the tree's shape. So, I decided to do it again, but this time just using watercolours. I used masking fluid to mask out the edges of the trunk so that I could work on a quick wet into wet background. I used the Masquepen type masking fluid and quite like it. I have had issues with this masking fluid on Stonehenge Aqua paper, where it ripped the paper when being rubbed off. I think it is the very soft surface of this brand of paper, so it is advisable to experiment with different papers first as to how well they work with masking fluid.

This second painting took five days, much longer then the first one. For the beautifully textured birch bark, I used mixes of Raw Sienna, Ultramarine Violet and Cerulean Blue (all Winsor & Newton paints), making sure not to lose the pale bark. The little marks and cracks were painted on using dry brush. I used a touch of gouache to get back the highlights on the moss, which was especially difficult to paint convincingly. I think this subject could be good for painting in oils and other opaque mediums.

4

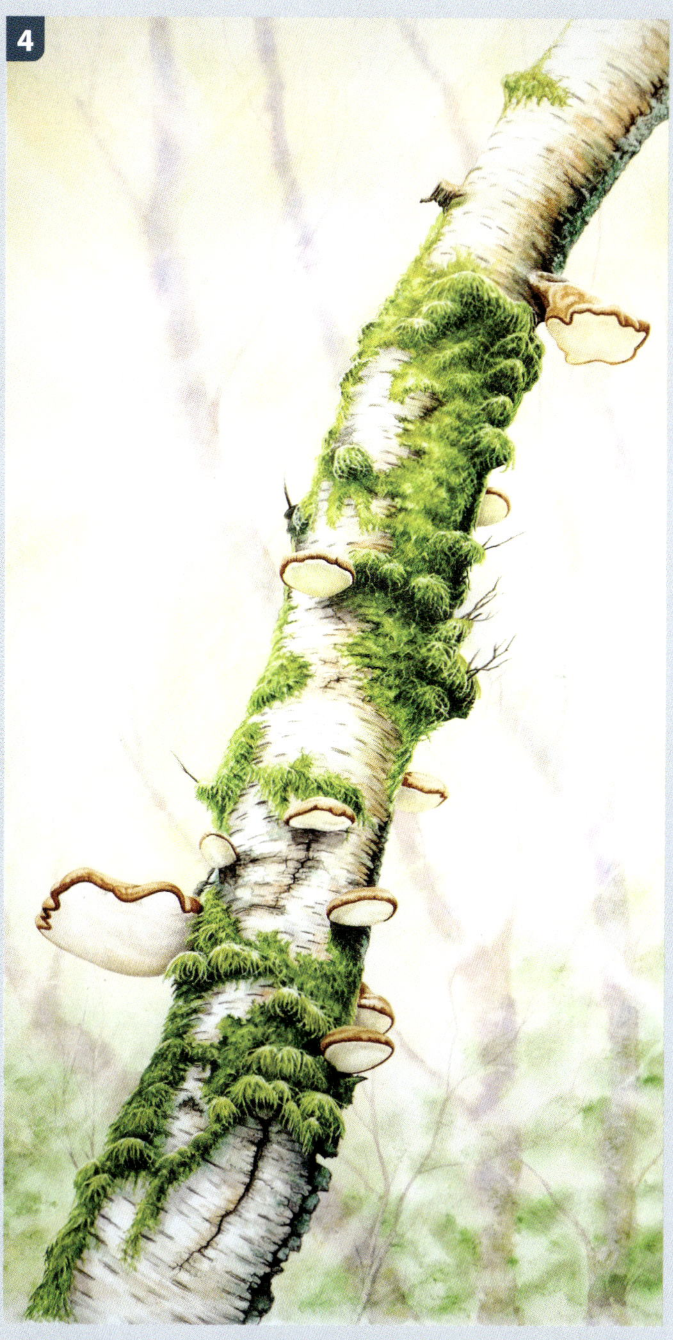

The final painting; I much preferred the shape of this tree to the one in the first painting.

DRAWING BARK AND MOSS TEXTURES

If you are embarking on a realistic portrayal of a species that grows from a tree trunk such as a bracket fungus, then you'll need to capture the characteristics of the tree bark. This can be quite different from tree to tree, from the smooth bark of the beech, the rough, almost elephant skin look of the oak to the silvery pale tones of craggy birch bark. Each species of mushroom or bracket may only grow on one specific type of tree, such as the previously illustrated Birch Polypore, or the Porcelain Fungus – *Oudemansiella mucida* that only grows on beech trees, so it does need some consideration. Bark often has crevices and cracks that can be depicted really well in most media especially using pen, ink or drybrush painting techniques as in the preceding birch painting.

Mosses can be illustrated in intricate detail, with their tiny leaflets and bright green colouration, often with colourful stems on some species. Painting mosses can be described as drawing with the brush, using a small round brush with a very good point to get that fine detail. For looser painting, a rigger brush can be used and for very loose, expressive painting styles or background habitats and foliage, moss can be hinted at using a little table salt scattered into a variegated green wash and allowed to dry. This can give a wonderfully starry texture that creates a great mossy look. Any good sap green can be used, I especially like the one made by Daniel Smith, but you can mix your own mossy greens with most blues and yellows, naturalising with a dash of scarlet red.

STEP-BY-STEP: IMPRINTING NATURE

I have always been very inspired by the work of Claudia Nice and Ann Blockley, who both use mixed media and textures in their watercolours. So, in this step by step I go about using foraged ferns from the garden that I can print onto a painting to form a loose background that hints at a forest scene. For inspiration, I flicked through my sketchbook and found a little mushroom on a twig that I'd sketched a few days before and thought it would make a good composition with a background. I used Arches hot press paper as it really is a tough paper that can take the masking fluid. I'm not sure of the species of mushroom but it could be an *Alnicola* sp. with its light brown spore print. I wasn't sure on the twig species, but think it must be an alder as *Alnicola* spp. usually grow with alders.

MATERIALS USED:

- Arches 140lb hot press watercolour paper
- Artist's masking tape
- Plexiglass sheet
- A spare piece of cheap printer paper
- Large mop brush
- Small size 0 brush
- Masquepen masking fluid
- Green Gold and Light Red (Winsor & Newton), Sap Green, Deep-sea Green, Burnt Umber and Buff Titanium (all by Daniel Smith), Aquarius Green (Roman Szmal)
- Foraged ferns
- A black fine liner pen and a white gel pen

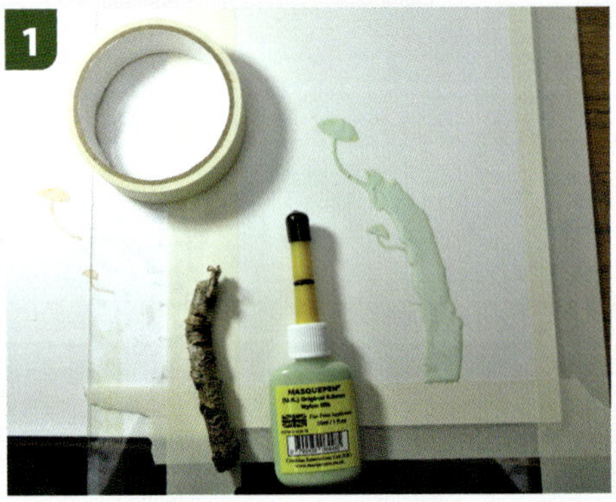

I taped my watercolour paper down onto the plexiglass sheet with masking tape. It's important to use low tack tape to avoid ripping the paper when removing. I drew the mushroom twig in pencil, then masked it out completely with masking fluid, just using the applicator on the bottle, and let it dry.

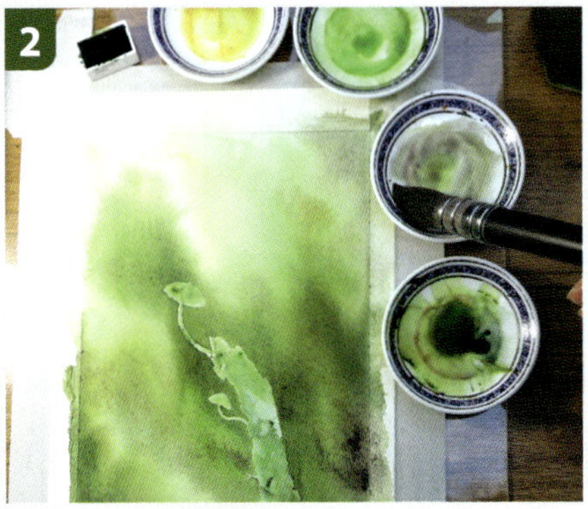

I got the various juicy watercolour washes ready in small dishes. The paints are listed in the 'materials used' section, but any greens and browns would suffice. I gave the paper a water glaze with the large mop brush and then added the washes into the glaze wet into wet to create lovely, variegated colours.

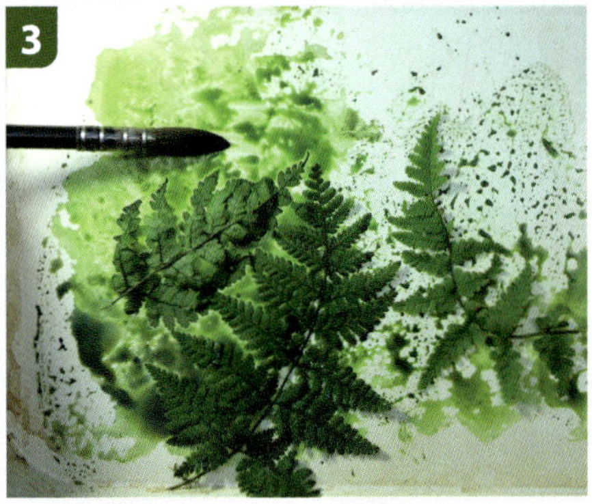

I'd collected some fresh ferns from the garden, took one and painted it with quite thick watercolour in a spare tray. I used Aquarius Green and Sap Green for this, but any green mixes would be good.

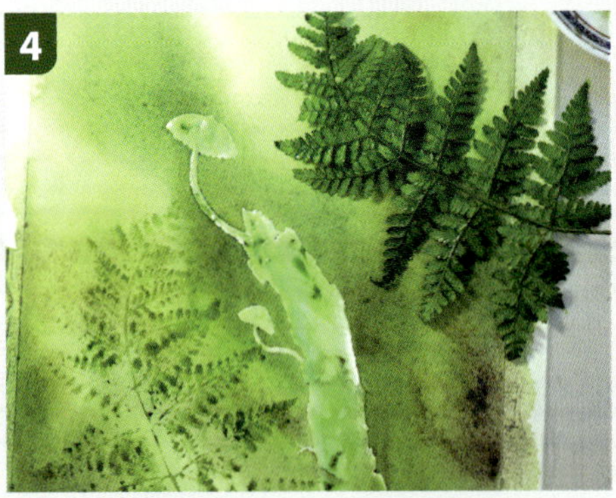

Then when coated with paint I carefully placed the frond onto the painting when it was dry, where I thought it'd look good, pressed a sheet of printer paper on top so that the paint would adhere to the paper and then peeled the fern off.

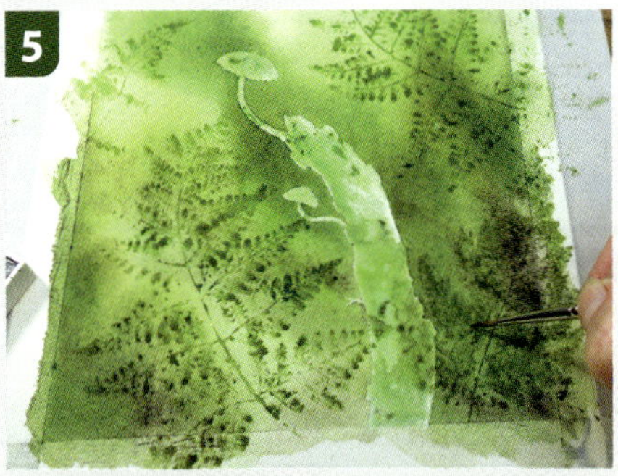

When the fern prints had dried, I used a small paintbrush to add to and touch up areas in the fern prints with a dry brush technique and the same colour as the ferns. I didn't add too much to the ferns as they are in the background and so shouldn't have too much detail.

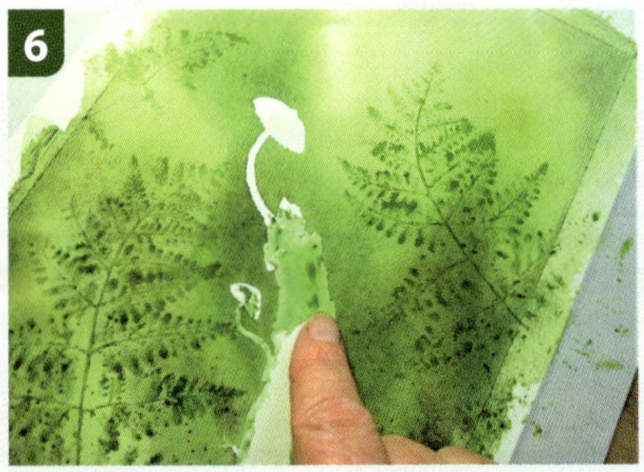

When the paper was completely dry, I started to peel off the masking fluid. A word of warning here; the Schmincke masking fluid (previously used in Chapter 5) does not work with lots of watery washes, this was painting take two, as when I added the water glaze, some of the masking fluid got washed away leaving bits on the paper!

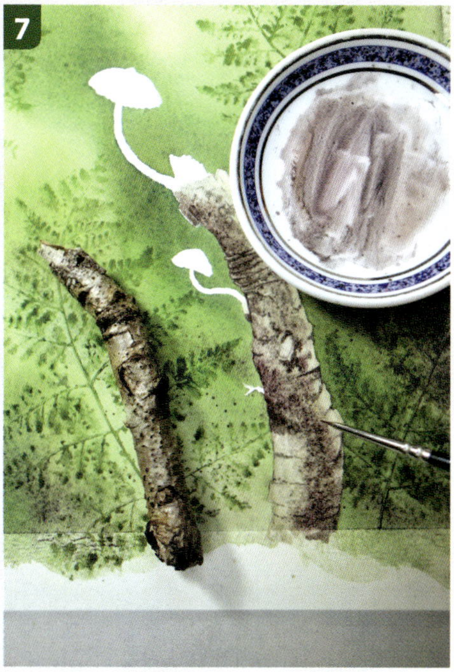

I started to add watercolour washes to the twig to model the light and shadow first. Then when dry, I added textures and details using a dry brush technique with thicker paint. Granulating paints are great for adding these textures.

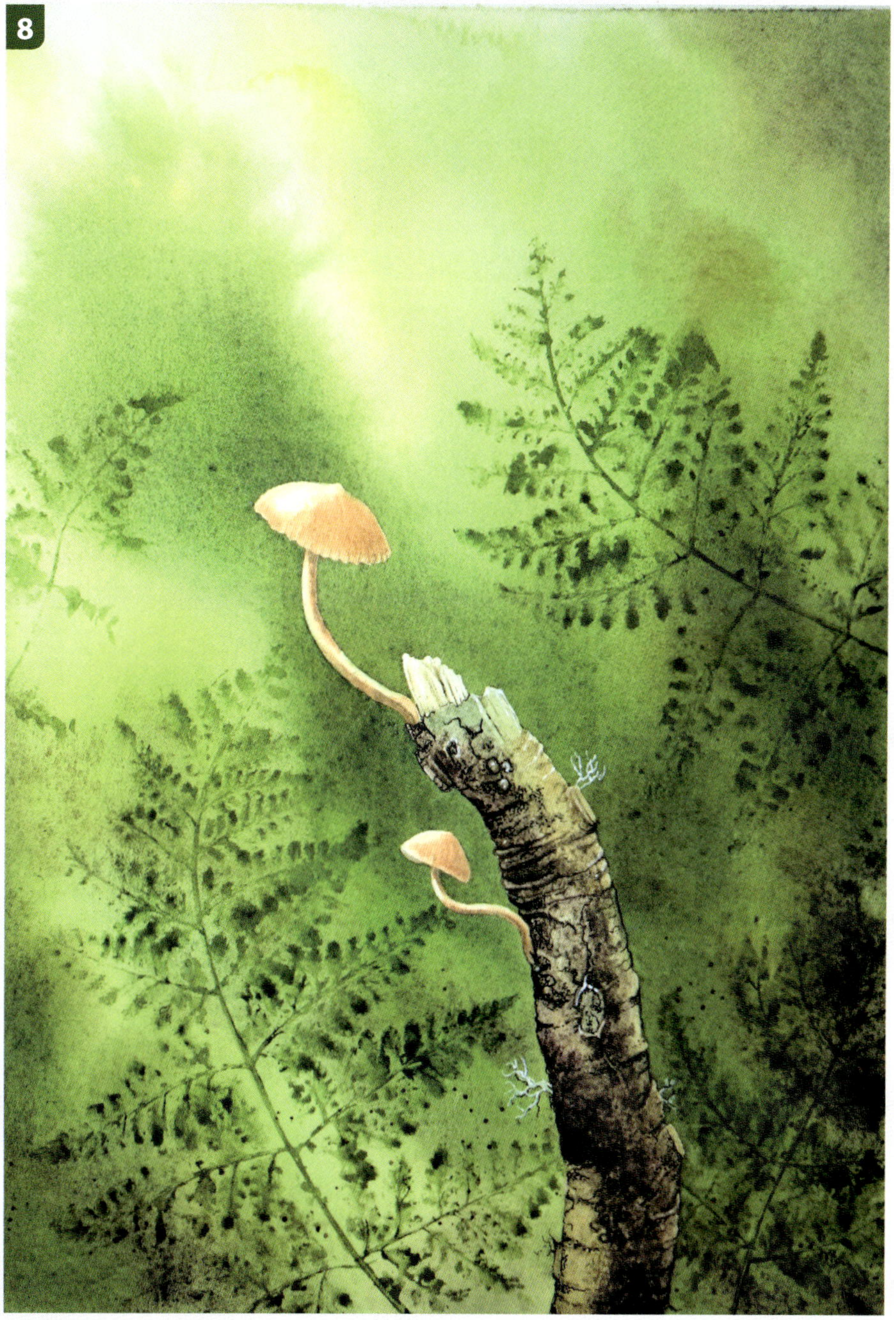

The little pink/beige mushrooms were painted last using Buff Titanium and Light Red. A bit of pen detail was added to the twig, to darken the contrasts and add more texture. The white gel pen added a few highlights and fruticose lichens. The masking tape was carefully pulled off to reveal the clean edges.

MIXED MEDIA

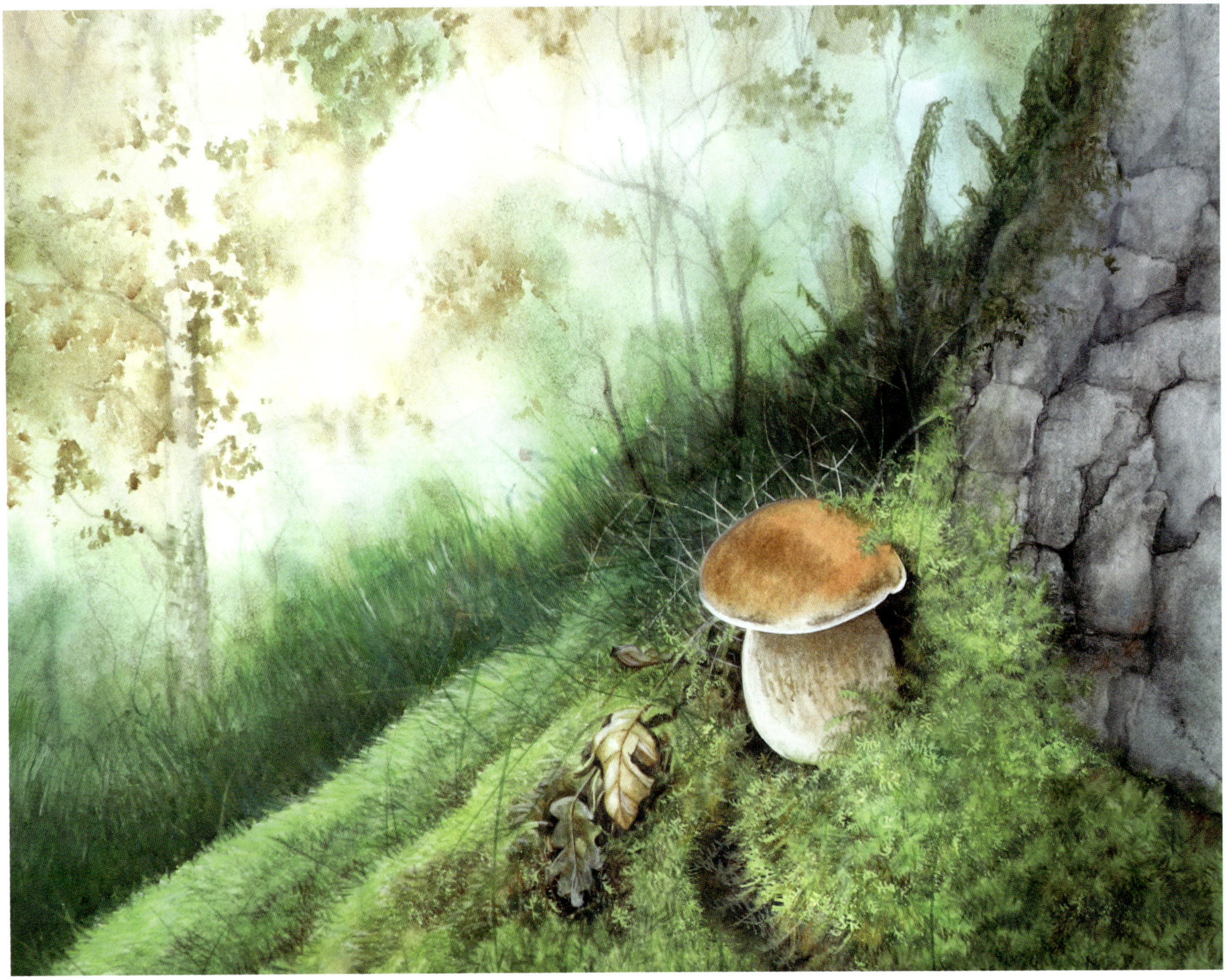

This study of a penny bun bolete nestled in its bed of moss at a sweet spot, according to the compositional rule of thirds, was completed using a mixture of watercolour, gouache and water-soluble coloured pencils. These mediums all play quite well together but it's too easy to go overboard on all the details.

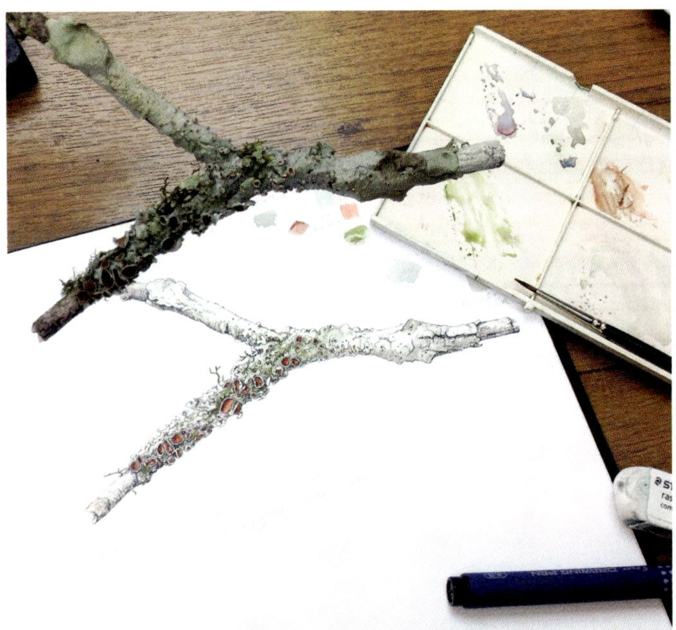

Pen and Wash

This is a popular technique where the pen gives the main form and tones of a subject and light, transparent water-colour washes give colour to the work. You can work with the pen detail first and then go on top with the washes or work the other way around, it really doesn't matter. In fact, some pen detailing can work wonders on a watercolour painting that you're not happy with.

This lichen study of *Lobaria virens* was completed in the sketchbook and then pen details added on top as I wasn't happy with the paint finish. I do much prefer it with the added pen detail.

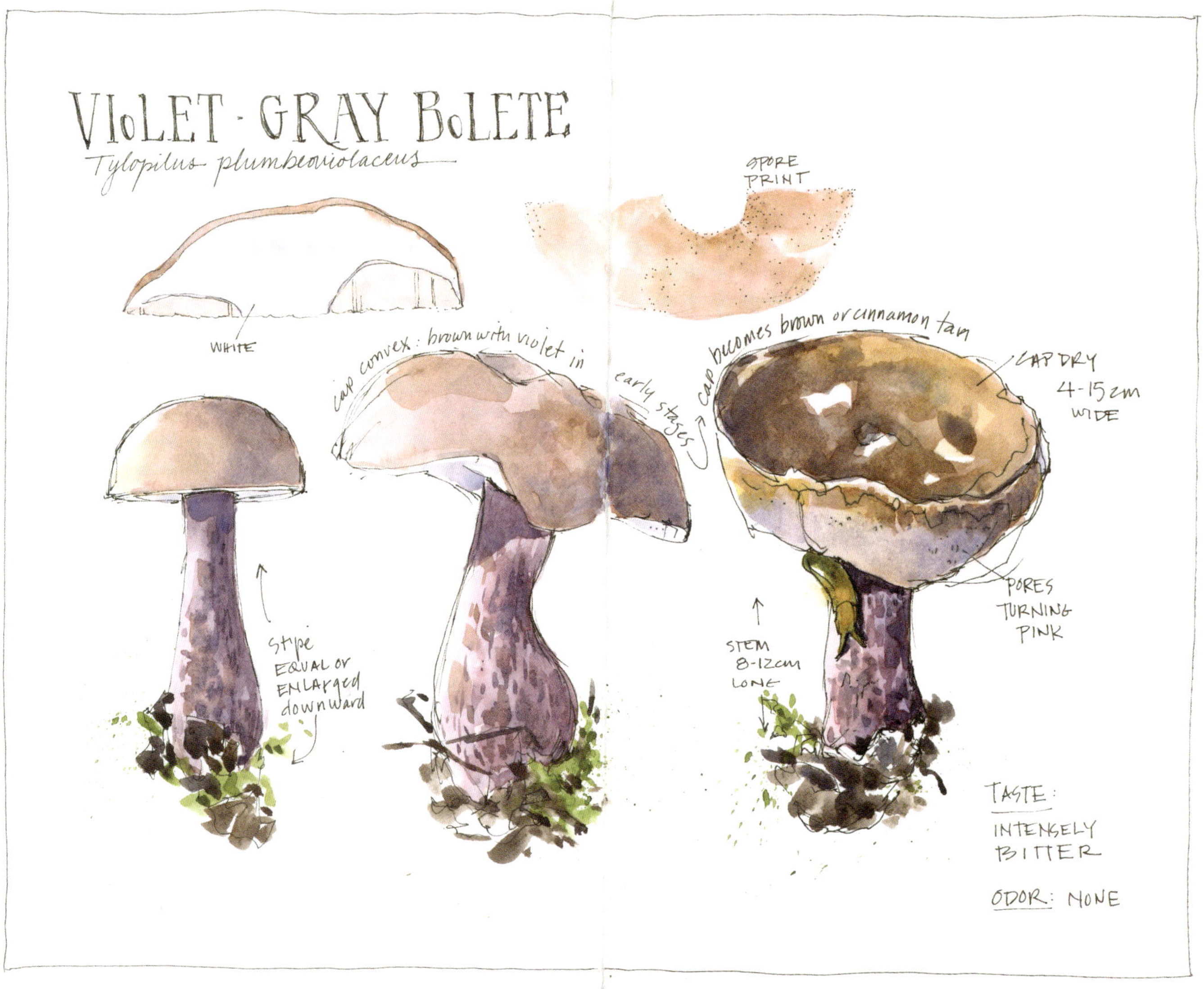

A lively and expressive pen and wash journal page of this US species, the Violet Grey Bolete – *Tylopilus plumbeoviolaceus* by Jean Mackay, a writer, artist and naturalist from New York. (© Jean Mackay)

Watercolour and Graphite

This could be construed in two ways, either watercolour painted over a tonal graphite drawing akin to pen and wash or a watercolour painting of a subject with separate graphite elements or a background in graphite. This latter technique adds delicacy and a subtlety and can enhance depth in a piece of work.

I've found that it is best to use a harder graphite pencil such as a 2H when using watercolour for very detailed work. A softer pencil into the B ranges would leave too much graphite and may give the washes a dirty look. The pencil is best laid down using the continuous tone shading method so that there are no marks unless of course, you want to show texture.

FOCUS STUDY: USING PEN AND WASH

Velvet shanks – *Flammulina velutipes* is a beautiful orange-capped little mushroom seen from late autumn through the wintertime. They grow in large groups on the boughs of broad-leaved trees such as oak and beech. Their stipes have a darker, velvety base and this gives them the common name of velvet shanks.

They are edible and are related to the mushrooms grown in Japan known as *Enoki* or *Enokitake (Flammulina filiformis);* those white, tiny-capped mushrooms with delicately elongated stipes that can be bought at markets. They are grown in the dark and the stems are force-grown in collars so that they elongate. There has been some research to show that they have possible anti-cancer properties as well as many other health benefits. Unfortunately, there are similar-looking mushrooms that are poisonous, but the fruiting time over winter, the fact that there are no rings on their dark-based stipes and the white spores should help to identify them.

I found this clump growing on a beech tree one January and had to draw them. I decided to use pen stippling and the thousands of tiny, stippled dots seemed apt to represent the millions of spores that would be released from those gills. The initial drawing was completed using a grid method on a photograph seen in Chapter 3 using graphite.

MATERIALS USED:

- Stonehenge Aqua 140lb hot press watercolour paper
- Pigma Micron pens – sizes 005, 003, and 03
- Uni-ball white gel pen
- Quinacridone Gold (Daniel Smith), Transparent Yellow and Burnt Sienna (Winsor & Newton)
- Size 2 brush
- A magnifying glass

1

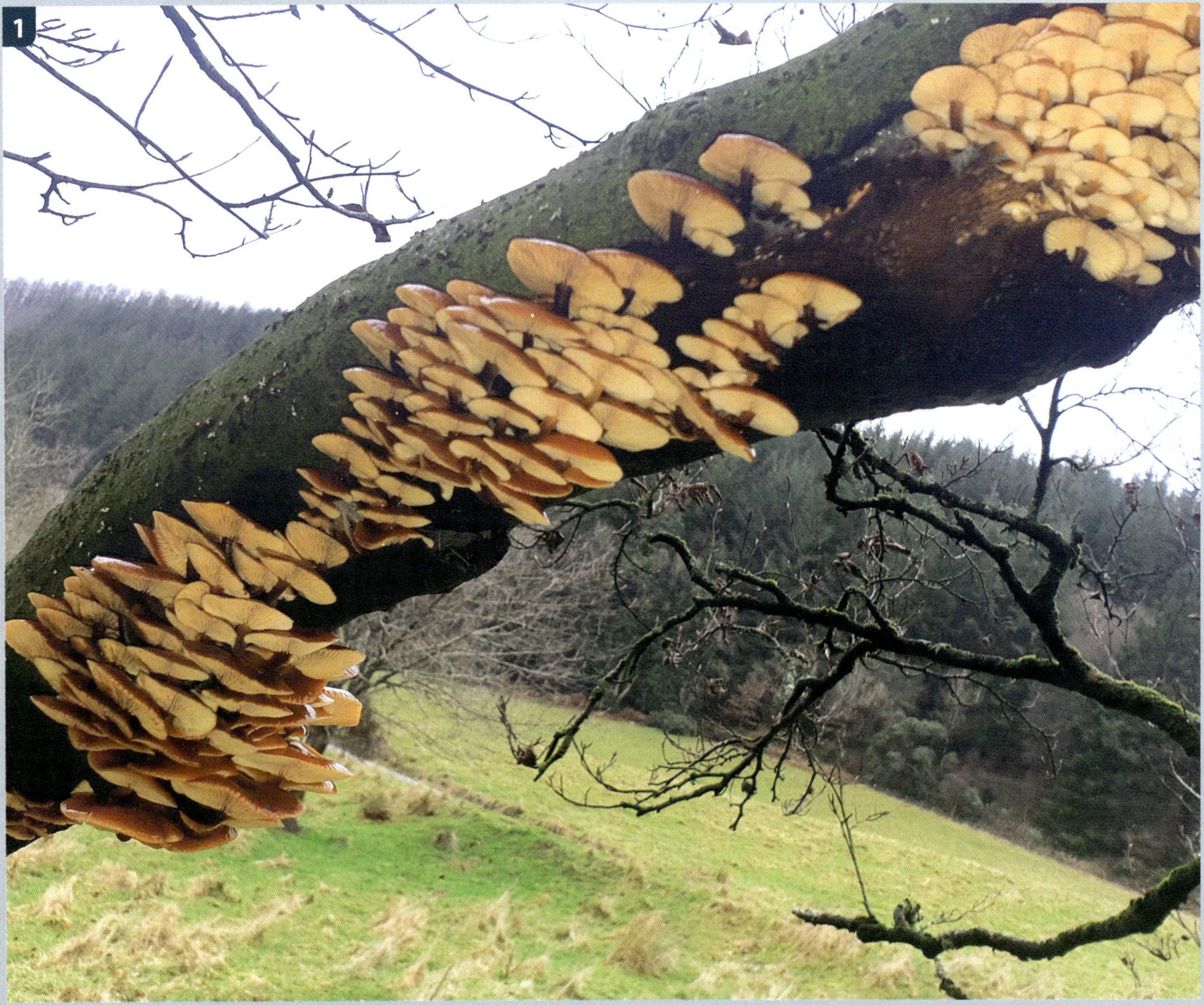

A very large and impressive cluster of Velvet Shanks that I found one January growing on the underside of an old beech tree.

2

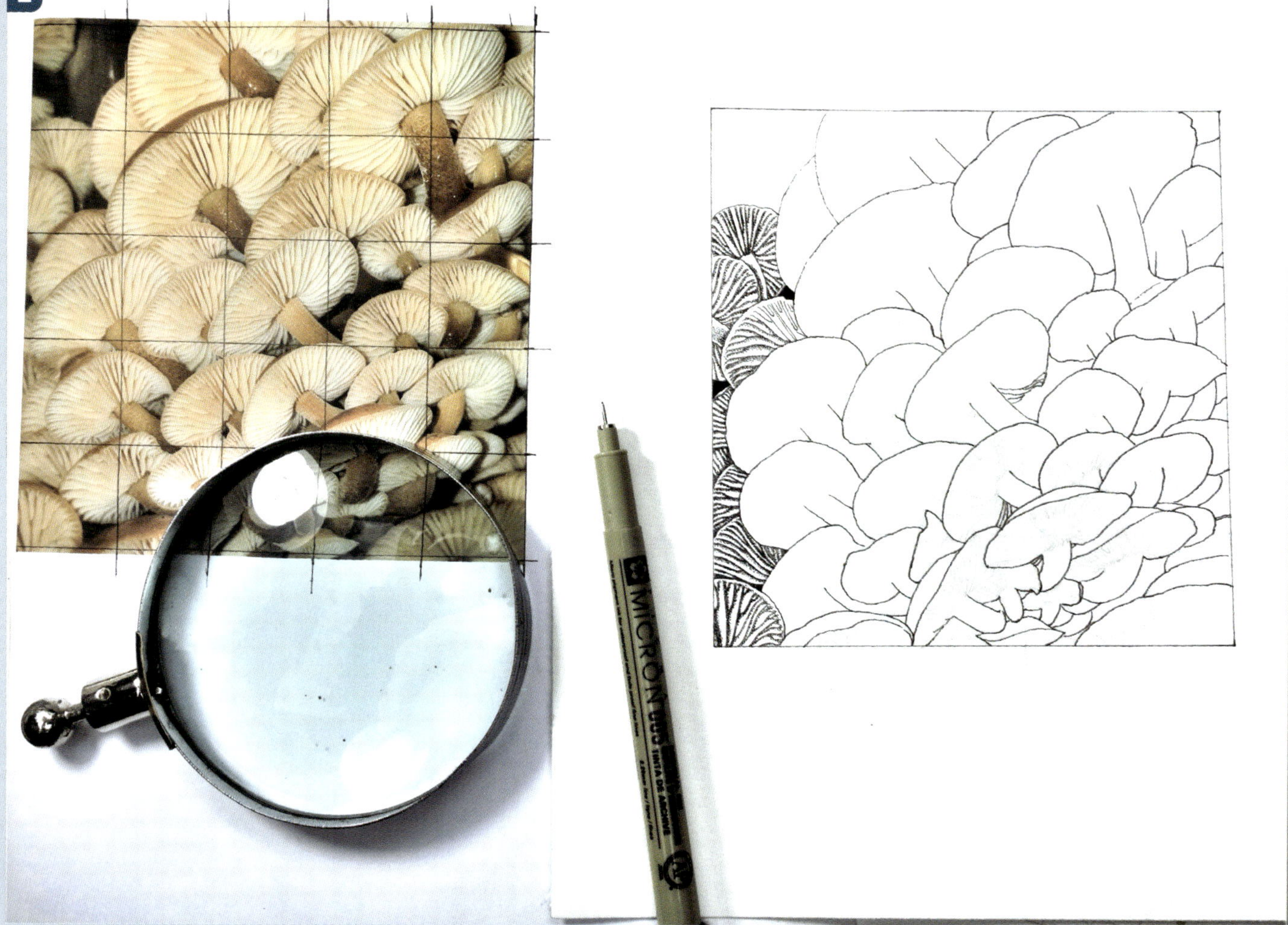

My velvet shanks composition that was drawn out in Chapter 3. I decided to work with pen and wash for this study. Here you can see that I've just gone in marking round the outlines quite lightly with a size 005 Pigma Micron fibre tip. Then adding the shadows with a stippling technique.

3

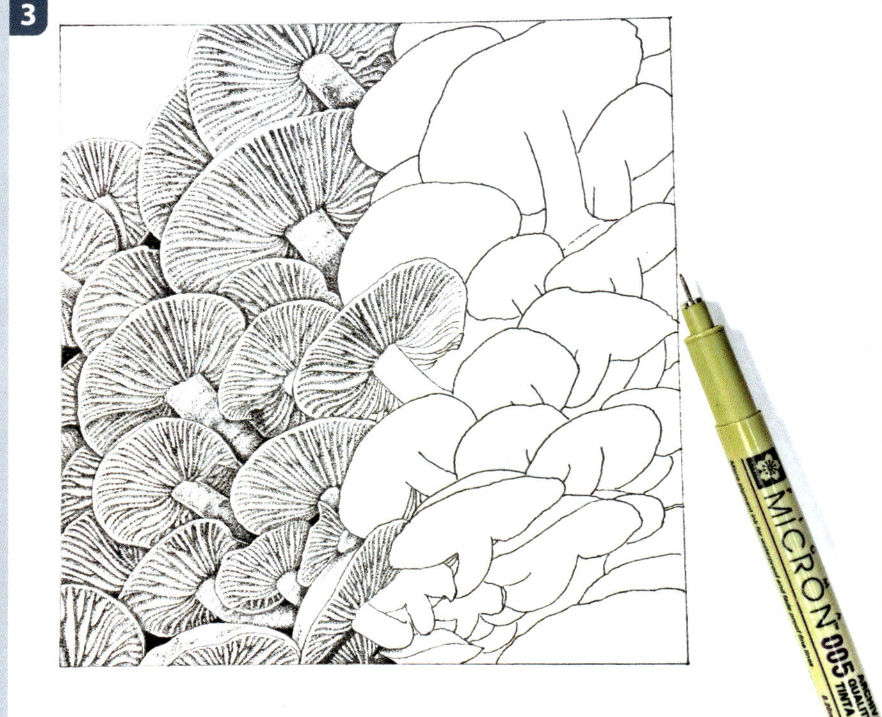

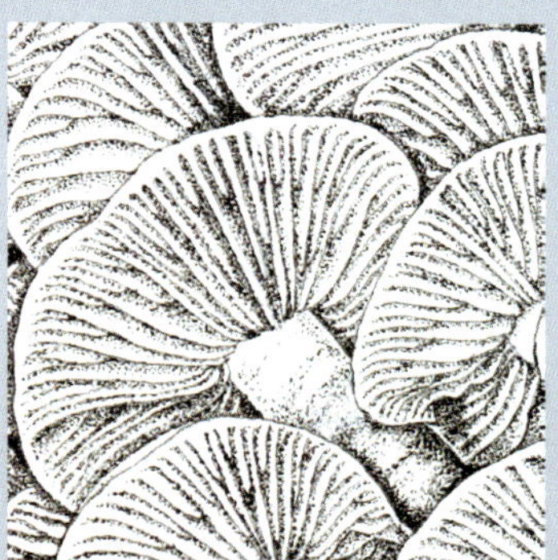

Slowly, slowly adding more stippling to the tones. I use a magnifying glass to get close in on the details (above). This amount of work took two days, so it is a slow process that requires some patience with a good audiobook and I needed lots of breaks to rest the eyes!

Continued on following page

4

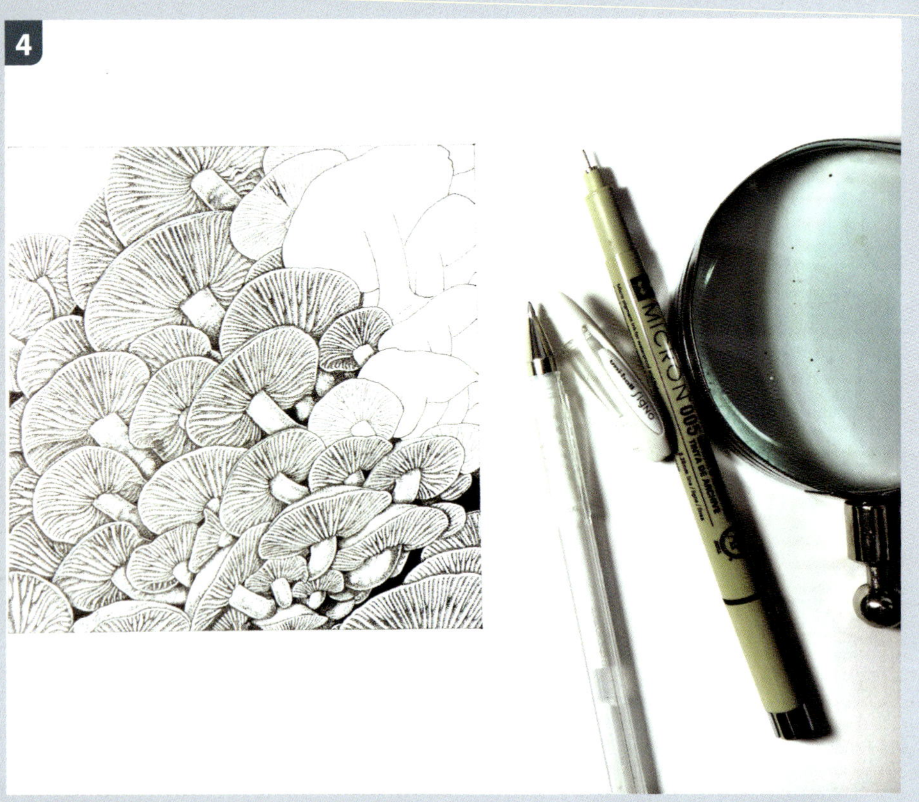

Nearly finished here but it's so easy to lose patience and rush things at this stage, best to step away for a while! I filled the top left area in with a larger nibbed 03 Pigma Micron. I also used the white Signo Uniball gel pen pictured here to cover over little mistakes. It worked quite well with a couple of layers.

5

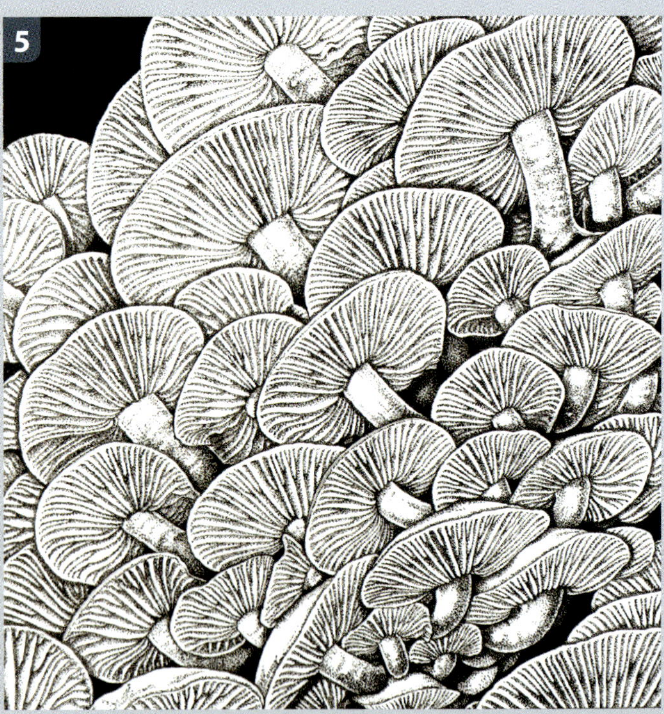

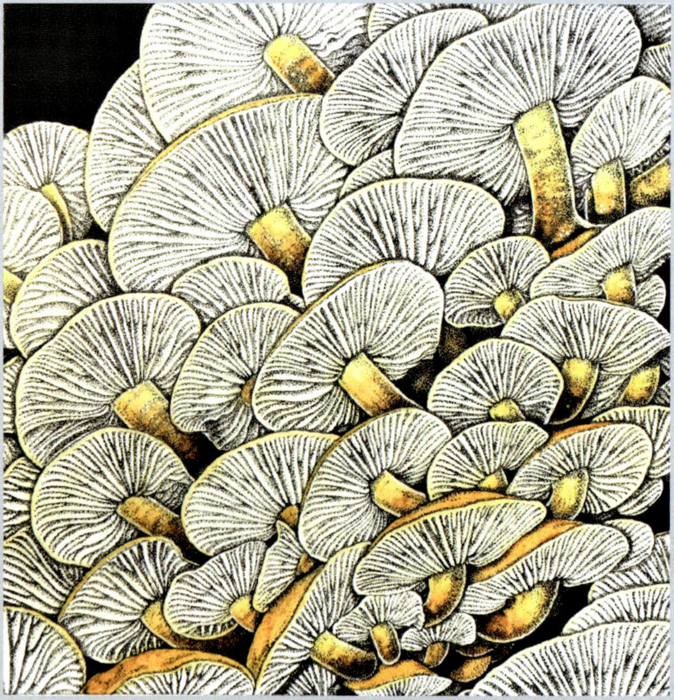

When completed, I mixed up some golden hues using Quinacridone Gold, Transparent Yellow and a touch of Burnt Sienna. I then washed them over the top, keeping the gills very pale and the caps and stipes more strongly coloured.

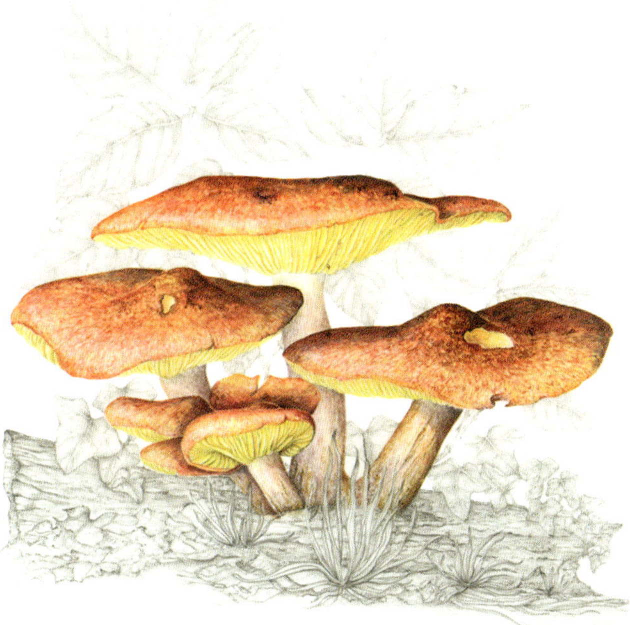

Plums and Custards – *Tricholomopsis rutilans* by botanical artist Sheila Etchingham. Sheila has used watercolour for the mushrooms and then added the background leaves in graphite. It really puts the focus onto the colourful mushrooms with their reddish hues on the cap and stipe and bright yellow gills. (© Sheila Etchingham)

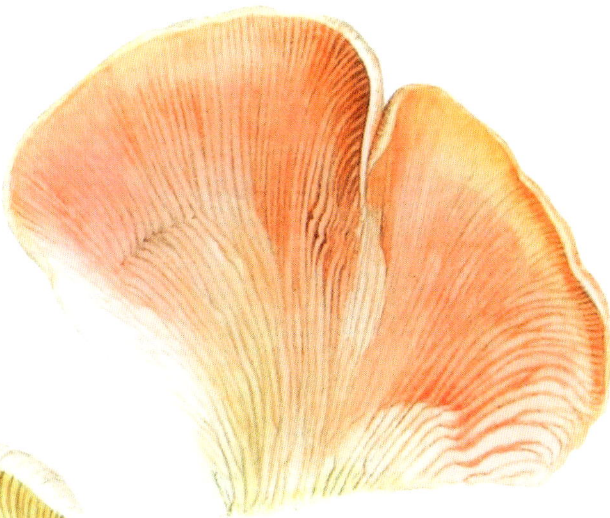

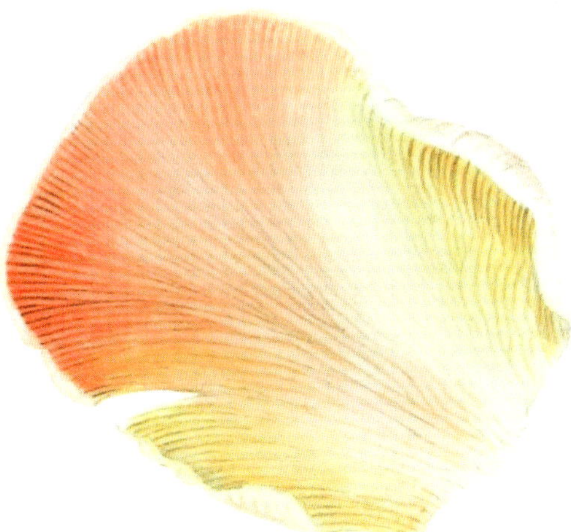

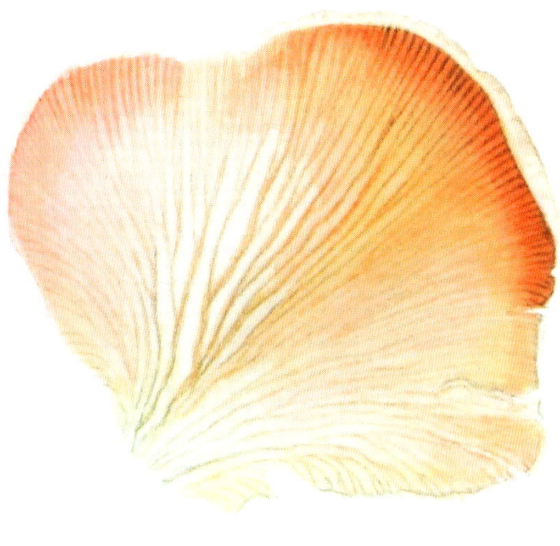

Pink Oyster Petals, in watercolour over graphite pencil on Arches HP. I purchased a pink oyster mushroom growing kit for me to draw. They do really look like pretty pink petals; fungi can sometimes be just as pretty as flowers!

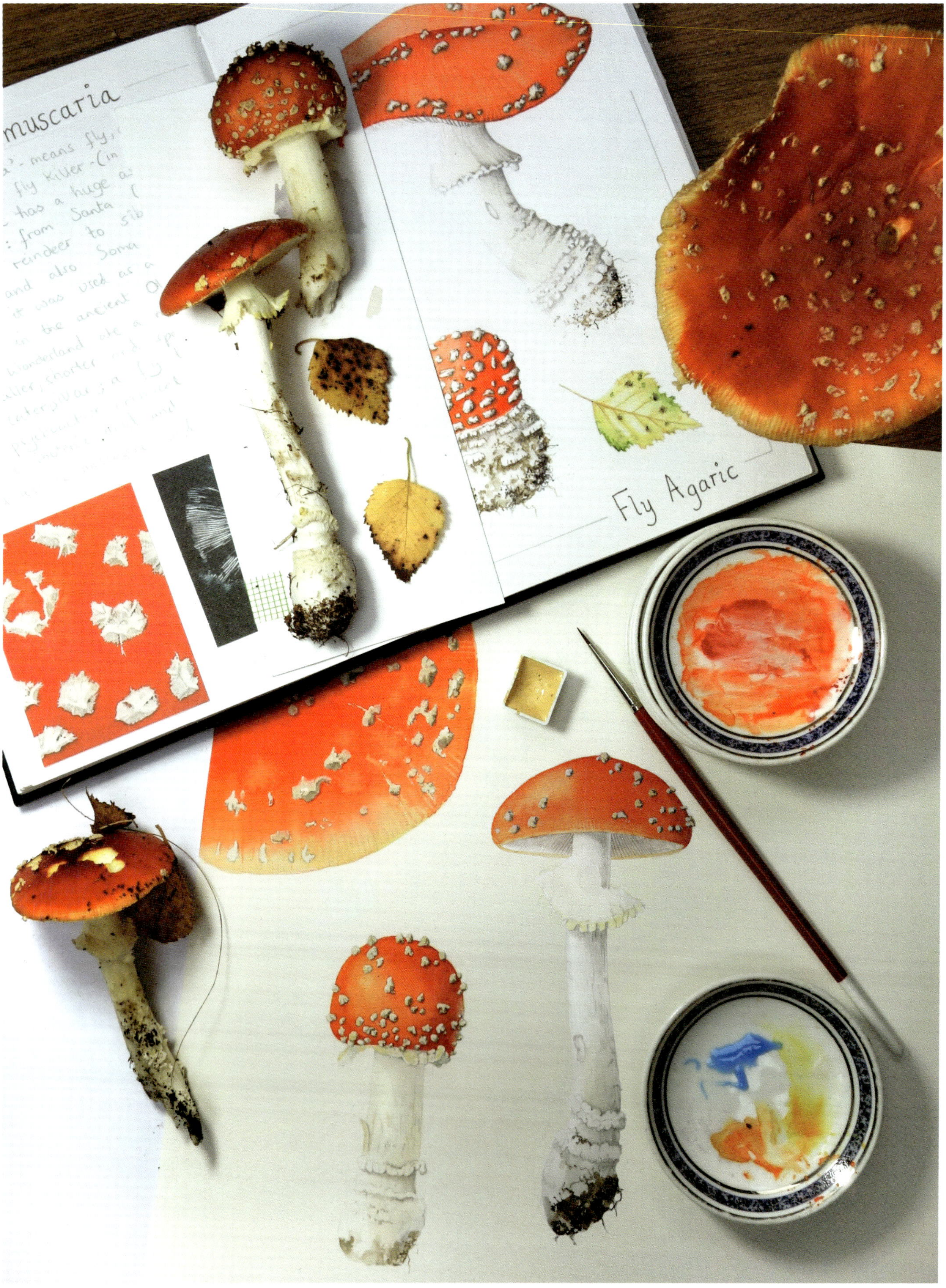
muscaria
Fly Agaric

CHAPTER 7

BASIDIOMYCETES – 'THE CLASSIC MUSHROOM'

The Basidiomycota is a large division in Kingdom Fungi with around 30,000 species recorded. It is subdivided into three further groups: the mushrooms, rusts and smuts, and so it is incredibly diverse. This chapter concerns these higher fungi or the 'club' fungi, which have the familiar form of the mushroom. These fungi reproduce sexually using cell structures called *basidia* that are club-shaped and form basidiospores; *Basidium* is Latin for club. The spores are released from the *hymenium*, which is found on the surfaces of the gills and spines or within the pores of the boletes. All the varying spore-releasing structures have large surface areas to be able to release a substantial number of spores, some as many as 30,000 released per second in pulses. Fungi do not have male and female sexes like the X and Y chromosomes we see in other organisms. Instead, they have much simpler sexes called mating-type loci and many more of them. A single spore can create a new mycelium and when two compatible mycelia meet in the soil, they combine to form mycelium that can produce fruiting bodies.

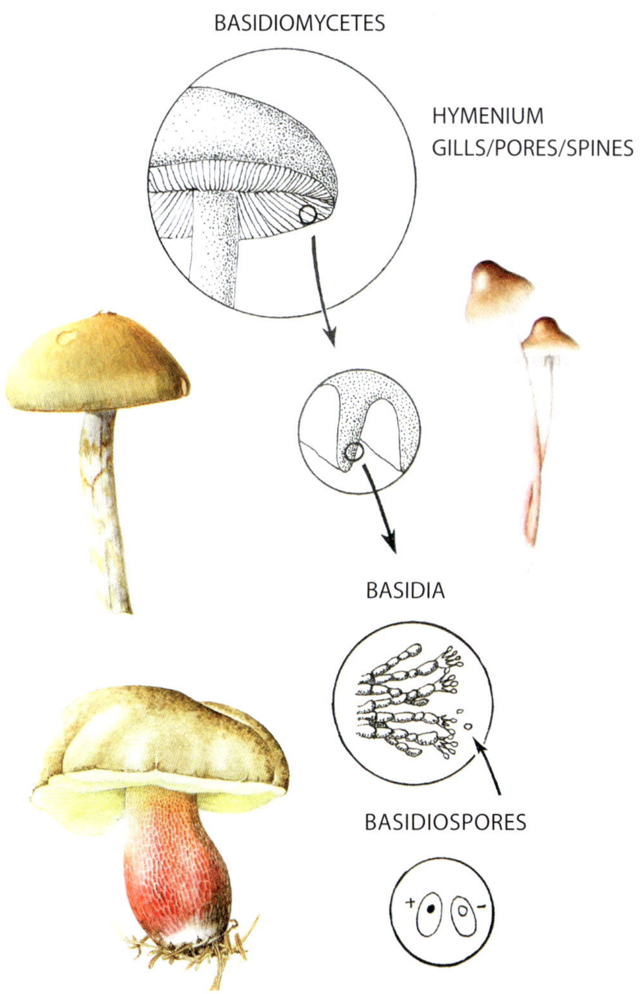

Diagram showing the characteristics of the Basidiomycete group of fungi. The spores are formed on the *basidia* in groups of four and released to catch the air currents.

Studying the Fly Agaric – *Amanita muscaria* – a classic basidiomycete mushroom.

FUNGI WITH GILLS

The majority of mushroom species have gills, those intricate membranes of spore dispersal. The following species are just a few of the fungi that I and other artists have been most drawn to for illustrating and as you can imagine, they tend to have the most colourful and highly textured forms or have the most fascinating stories to highlight.

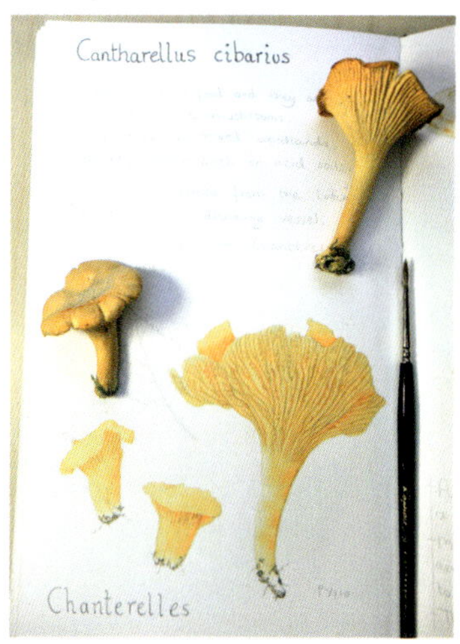

A few species of fungi have what are called false gills that have a folded and wrinkled appearance rather than gills that can be removed individually. This includes species in the *Cantharellus* family, such as these apricot-hued chanterelles.

AMANITA SPP.

A genus to be respected as it contains some of the most poisonous mushrooms, including the death cap and destroying angel. But it also includes the edible *Amanita caesarea* found in Europe, the very similar and beautiful *A. jacksonii* found in the US and the blusher – *A. rubescens*, among many others; indeed, there are around 600 species worldwide. They are on the whole large mushrooms, but some can be slender too, and most have rings on the stipes but a few do not. This family has some colourful and stylish members, great for painting subjects, such as the fly agaric – *Amanita muscaria*. This is probably one of the most well-known and iconic mushrooms of all time, with its bright scarlet cap speckled with creamy scales. It is a joy to find and to illustrate. Featured in tales of folklore, magic and legend, it is often pictured with fairies or gnomes and was once used in religious ceremonies to commune with the ancestors, due to its psychoactive properties. These come from the active mycotoxins of muscimol and ibotenic acid, but they are not fatal like the toxins found in the death cap and others within the *Amanita* family. The quite similar looking panther

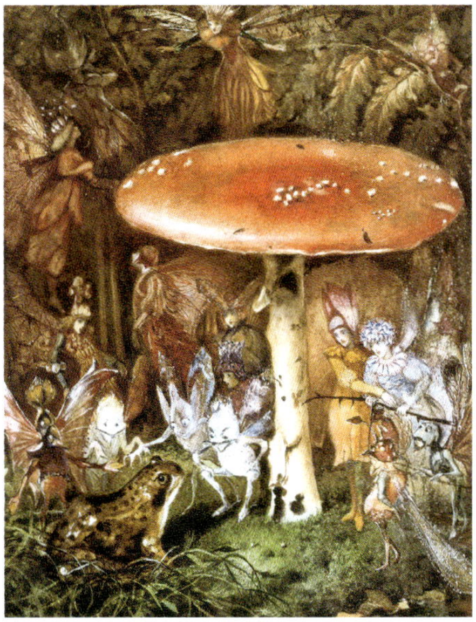

This painting by John Anster Fitzgerald (1819–1906), called *The Intruders* depicts the Victorian love of the fly agaric and its association with otherworldly realms.

cap – *Amanita pantherina* – has a brown cap with white spots and is also loaded with these chemicals. *A. muscaria* was also used as a fly killer, which explains the common name. Pieces of the mushroom were placed in milk to steep to then attract and poison flies. In the Arctic circle, reindeer are keen to eat them and are said to jump and

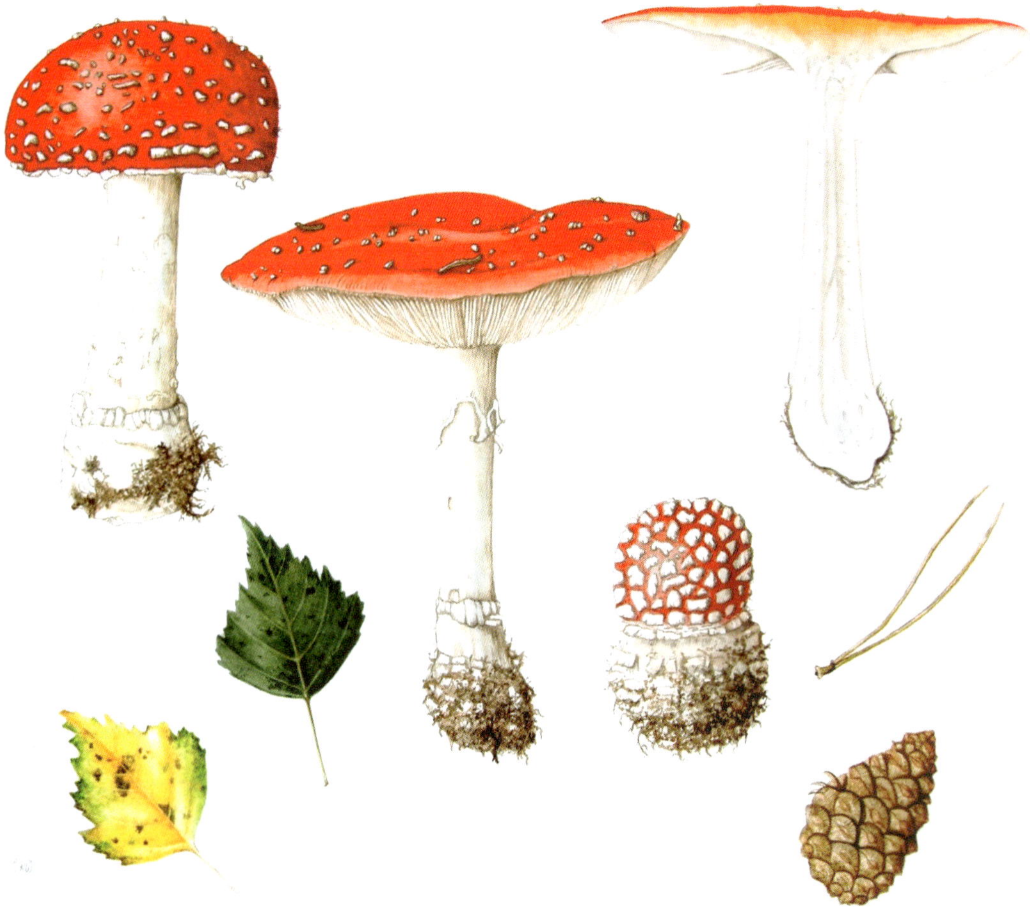

This illustration in watercolour from 2009 depicts the lifecycle of the fly agaric with a cross section to show the gill and stipe structure, and birch leaves and conifer needles tell the mycorrhizal tree partners.

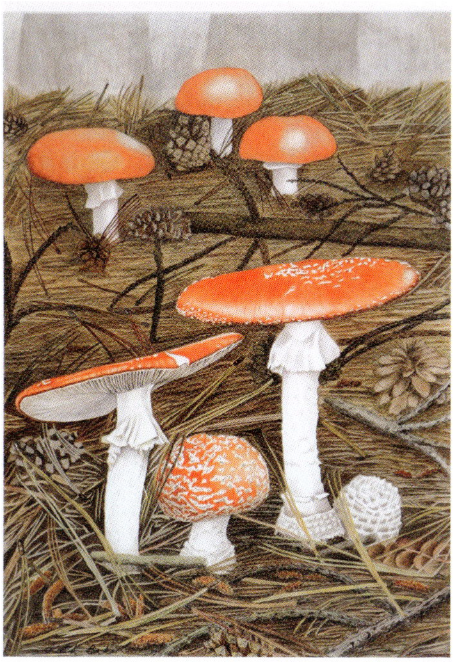

This painting of Fly Agarics by Kathleen Baker perfectly illustrates the profusion that you can often find these stunning mushrooms. Kathleen has painted in the forest floor littered with pine cones, which reveals one of its habitats of coniferous woodland. (© Kathleen Baker)

prance around after ingestion, so this may be why reindeer relate to flying in Christmas stories. And apparently under the influence of the active compounds it seems that you can have the actual feeling of flying. After ingesting this mushroom, as well as some really nasty toxic effects, it can apparently alter your perceptions and give you the feeling of being incredibly large or very tiny; akin to scenes from *Alice in Wonderland* by Lewis Carroll. It is a fascinating mushroom with an interesting history and also rather common to find, usually growing abundantly with birch or conifer trees.

The whitish scales can be simply masked out using masking fluid to preserve them while the scarlet colours are washed on top. There is a step by step of this technique in Chapter 5.

Waxcaps – *Hygrocybe* spp. are a colourful family that I think of as the gems of the autumn meadows and are probably the genus of fungi that I have studied the most, not only due to their wonderful colours but also as they have a stronghold around where I live in Wales. Saying that, some members of the genus are now very rare and some are becoming rarer. They are indicators of ancient meadows and will grow most commonly in grazed pastureland where there is no trace of fertiliser or ploughing, but disappear when these farming practices are employed. Snowy, meadow and blackening waxcaps are the most common in the UK. They can be found growing in woodlands in the US. The genus name comes from the Greek meaning 'water-head' due to their often viscous, shiny, wet look. Some members from the *Gliophorus* genus of waxcaps such as the parrot waxcap are incredibly viscous and coated with quite a slimy glue-like substance making them glisten and shine.

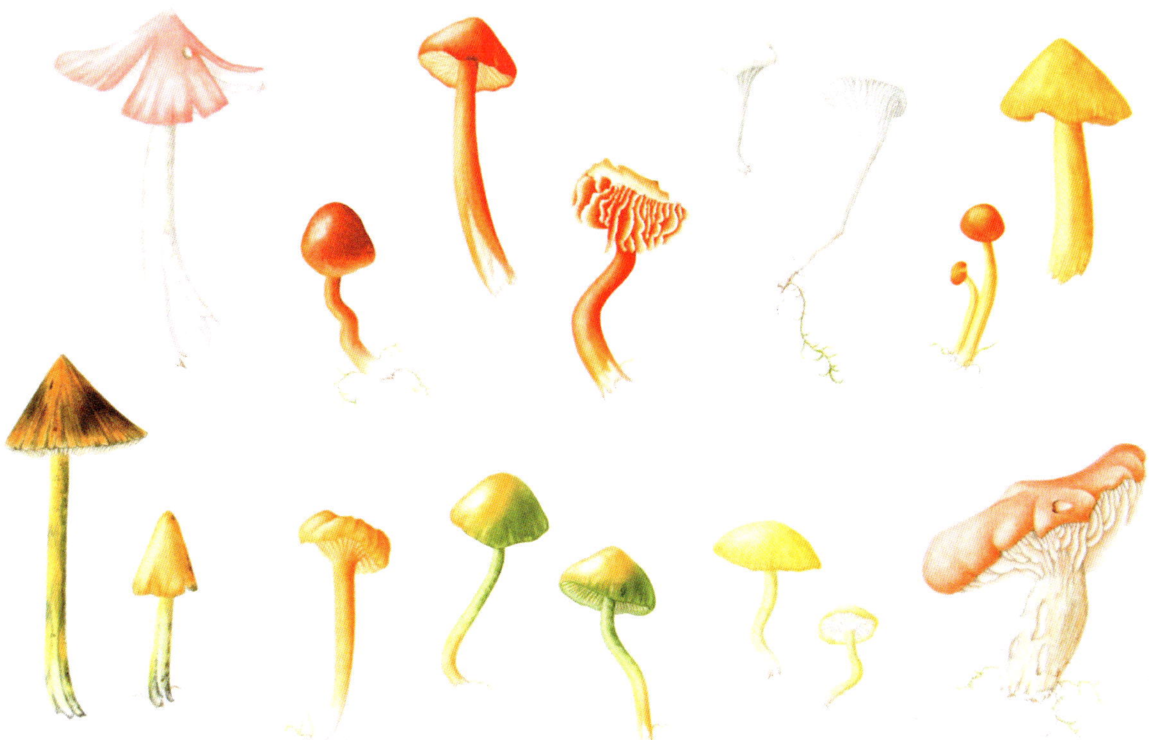

A Rainbow of Waxcaps in watercolour, painted in 2012. A few of the colourful Waxcap species that can be found in my local meadowlands and graveyards growing among the moss.

Russulas are another large and colourful family of mushrooms that go by the common name of brittlegills owing to their delicate and fragile gills and flesh that breaks easily. This is due to the rounded structure of their cells called *sphaerocysts,* a characteristic that they share with the closely related family of the milkcaps – *Lactarius* spp. They really don't hold together as well as the typical oval cells of other fungi and so a stipe can snap like a piece of chalk (and with the same colour) – some are worse than others such as the Fragile Russula – *R. fragilis.* The charcoal burner – *Russula cyanoxantha* is one of the family that isn't as brittle and this is a good way to identify it for sure – the gills are actually flexible. Otherwise, they can be hard to identify to species level as the caps and colours can be quite variable. There are often some interesting smells among them, like geraniums, stewed apples, crabmeat and cheese, so a delight for the senses.

There are no deadly poisonous *Russulas* in the UK, but there are a few that make you ill most notably is *Russula emetica.*

There's an interesting edible mushroom found in the US called the Lobster Mushroom. This is a mushroom usually from the genus *Russula* or *Lactarius* that has been parasitised by an ascomycete fungus called *Hypomyces lactifluorum.* The parasite completely takes over the host changing its colour to the bright orangey red hue of a lobster and apparently imparting it with a delicious, seafood flavour – fascinating!

Inkcaps – *Coprinus/Coprinellus/Coprinopsis* spp.
There are many lovely inkcaps to be found from the stately lawyer's wig and sprawling troops of fairy inkcaps to the rarer and stately, monotone splendour of the magpie inkcap. They are all a joy to find and draw.

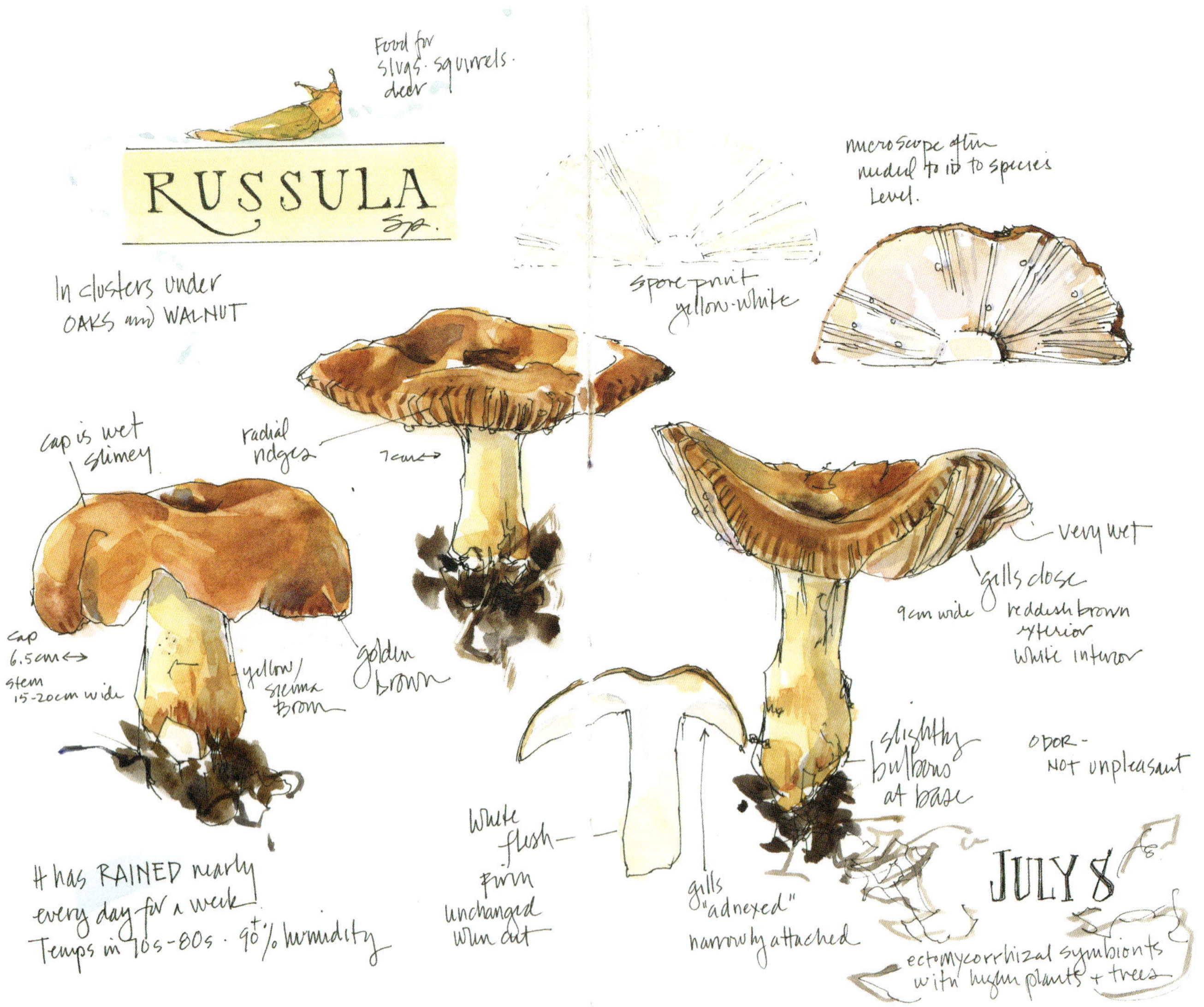

Pen and wash journal page of an unknown species of *Russula* by US artist Jean Mackay. Jean has included so much information here including the weather, odour, spore prints, partner tree species, even critters that dine on the mushrooms. (© Jean Mackay)

The shaggy inkcap or lawyer's wig – *Coprinus comatus* – is a common large mushroom that can actually push through asphalt along the edges of roads. It is edible when fresh, which isn't long before it turns to black ink. It is after the fly agaric, perhaps one of the most commonly illustrated mushrooms.

Glistening inkcap – *Coprinellus micaceus* – are lovely little mushrooms found growing on tree stumps and wood in often quite large groups. I've drawn these a lot. *Micaceus* refers to the tiny granules that glisten like mica on young caps, the remains of the universal veil. They can be washed away by rain so are sometimes not found on older specimens. They can be found from spring right through to autumn and sometimes in mild winters. There are similar inkcaps that it can be confused with including the trooping or fairy inkcap, which is smaller and the firerug inkcap, which has a bright orange, fuzzy mat of mycelium called *ozonium* sometimes found at the base.

Fellow botanical artist Sally Pond describes her influences for her fungi paintings, she says 'I was very heavily influenced as a child by the illustrations in the books I read. Those gorgeously rich images of trees and fungi

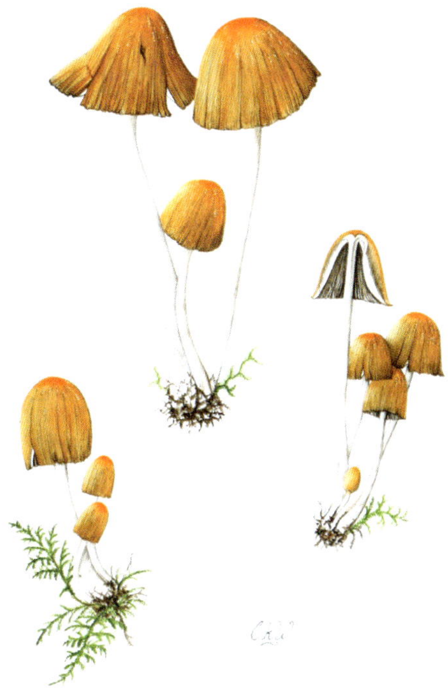

Glistening Inkcaps – *Coprinellus micaceus* – 2006. These mushrooms have sienna-coloured caps that are very striate, and this can be added on with drybrush detailing. The little granules on the cap can be added using white gouache. When young and fresh the stipes are white so may be good depicted on a toned paper.

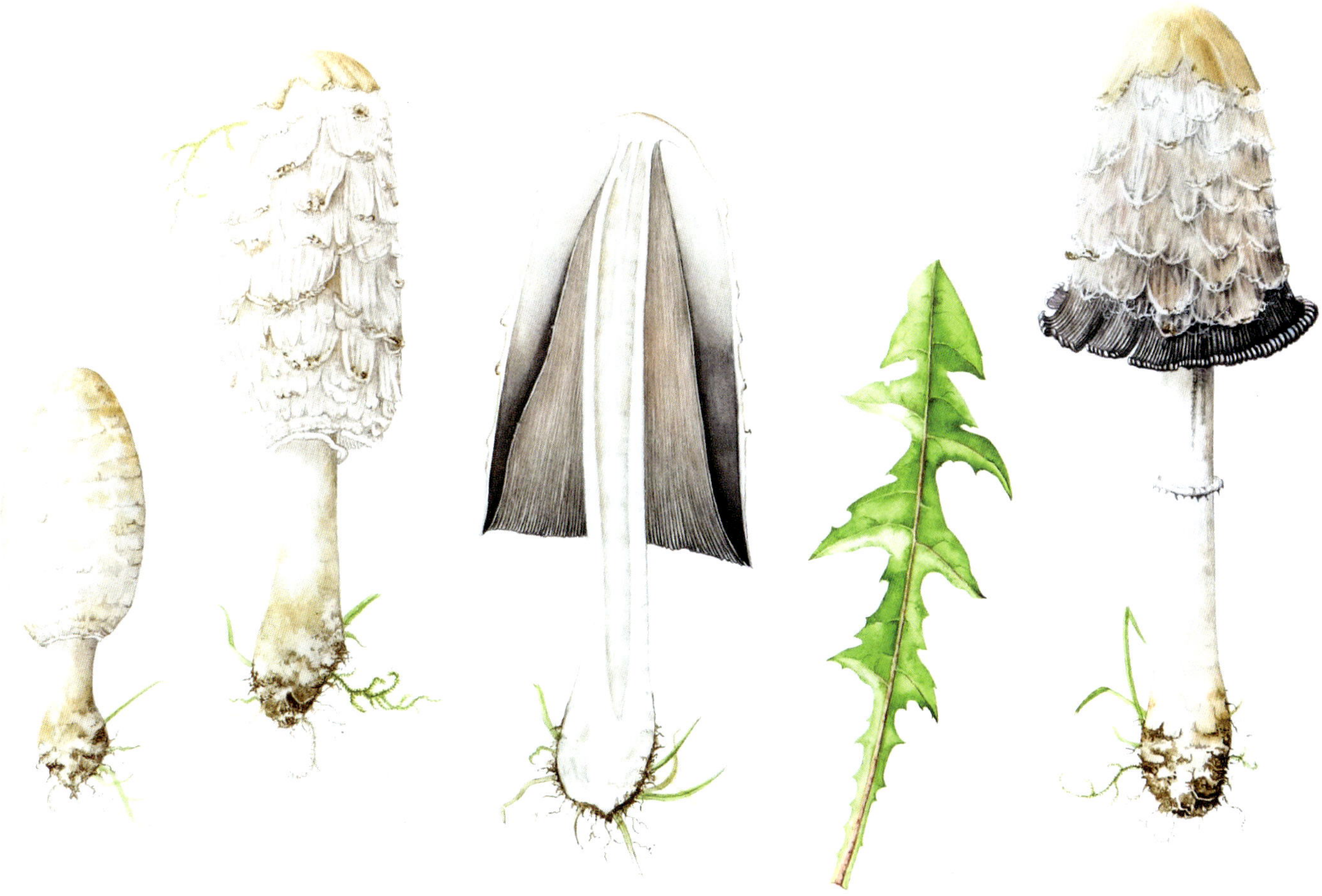

Shaggy Inkcap – *Coprinus comatus* 2014, this species epithet means hairy to denote its shaggy scales. It also has the common name of lawyer's wig inkcap. This illustration shows the lifecycle of this mushroom, and the dandelion gives a hint to its grassland, verge and lawn habitats.

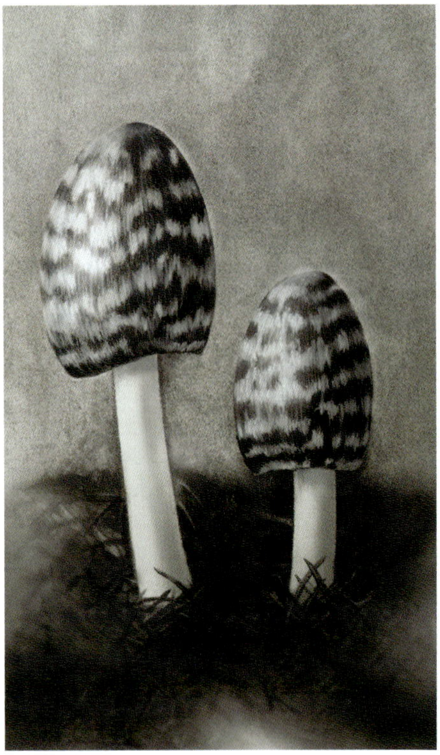

Magpie Inkcaps – *Coprinopsis picacea*. I think these are really attractive mushrooms and as their common name suggests they are black (actually, a very dark brown) and white after the magpie bird – which has the Latin name of *Pica pica* hence *picacea*. This drawing was completed using charcoals and Conté Pierre Noir pencils to suit their monotone nature.

populated by imaginary little people done by artists such as Arthur Rackham, Dulac and the Robinson brothers. Quite often sinister and dangerous but always captivating. There were those marvellous paintings and drawings in the nature study books too which had me searching hedge and woodland for the hidden things. Years later I'm still looking. When I paint fungi, I try to recapture some of the wonder I felt as a child. Maybe I'm still looking for the fairies but that frisson of magic I associate with them is still there.'

The webcaps – *Cortinarius* spp. are thought to be the largest genus of mushrooms in the world with possibly as many as 2,000 species, maybe even more. As previously mentioned, they have a web-like partial veil made of very fine threads that protects the gills called the cortina (meaning curtain) that gives them their common name. Some are deadly poisonous containing the toxin orellanin, which is actually fluorescent. All webcap species form mycorrhizal relationships with trees and some are really colourful and can be used in dyeing.

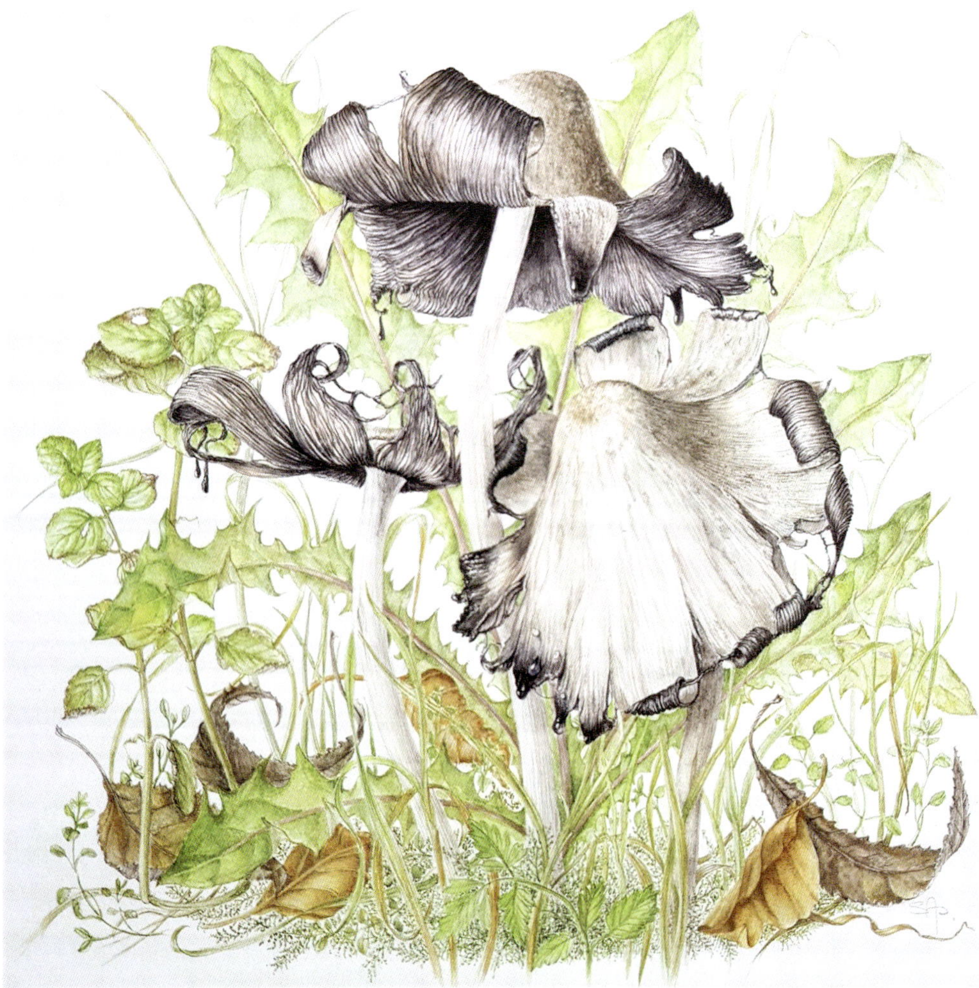

Common Inkcap by Sally Pond. She says, 'Use caution when painting inkcaps. I left a toadstool on my table overnight undisturbed. I'm used to flowers dropping pollen and apart from a few sneezes it's fine. This time however everything on my worktable was covered in a film of black spores. Fortunately, my painting was raised up on a board and was saved but cleaning up was lengthy resulting in bowls of black, inky water taking ages to clean. Be warned!' (© Sally Pond)

Cortinarius austrovenetus by artist and biologist Anna Voytsekhovich. On this colourful webcap you can see the cobwebby material left over by the partial veil that is called the cortina in this genus. The little red accents in the painting set off the vibrant green colour of these stunning mushrooms. (© Anna Voytsekhovich)

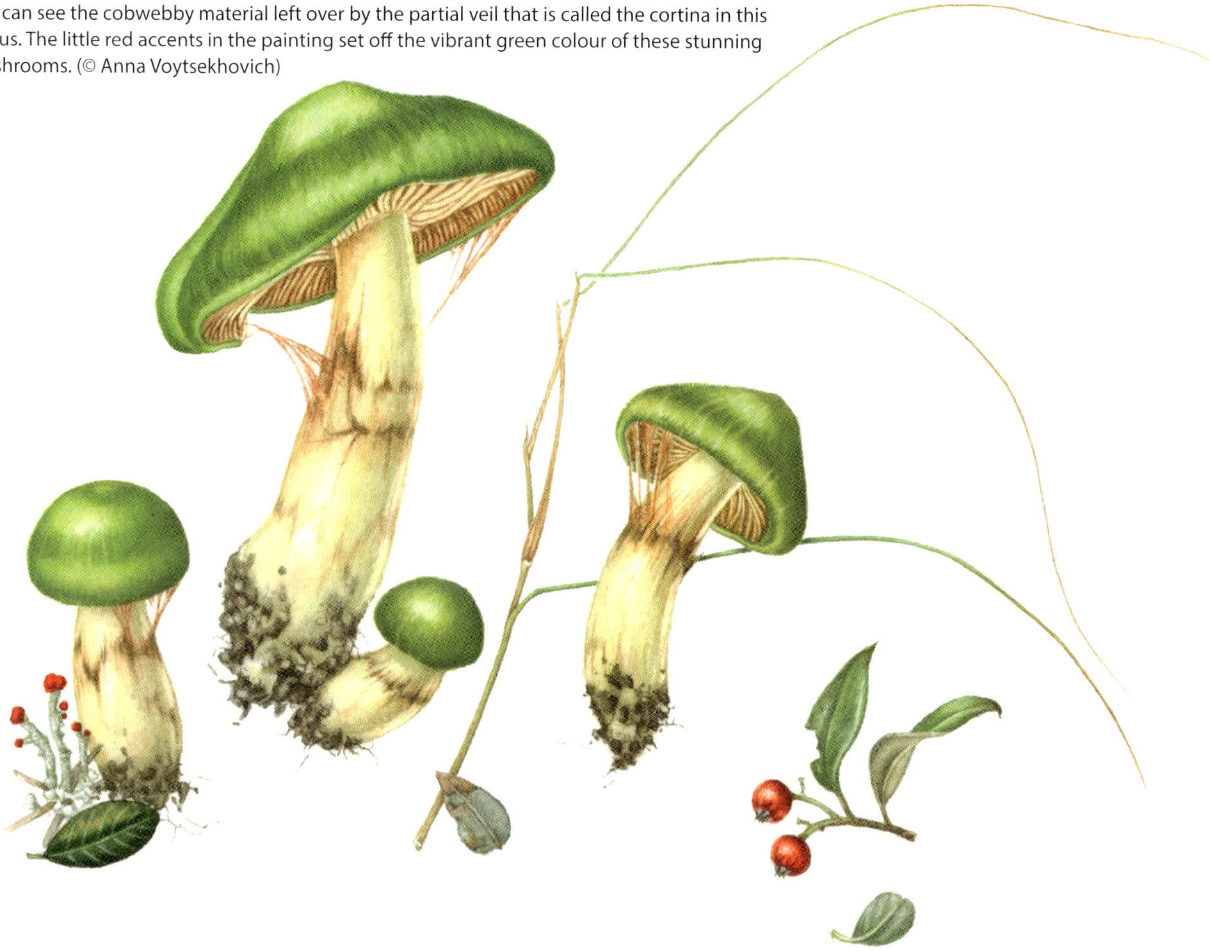

Honey Fungus – ***Armillaria mellea*** is the most destructive of all tree parasites and is one of the commonest fungi found on tree stumps. It can attack a selection of garden plants, as well as trees. Spores of the fungus do not directly infect trees, instead strands of mycelium, called rhizomorphs, which have the appearance of black bootlaces, gain entrance via cracks in the bark or through wounds. Rhizomorphs travel through the soil to infect other trees. Dead wood containing the mycelium gives out a bioluminescent glow and in olden days, when trees were worshipped, it was thought that possession of some luminous root would bestow on its owner creative ability, enabling gold to be produced by magic, for example. There are several accounts of dead, infected wood being employed during the war as a source of light for the troops. Luminous wood stuck in steel helmets was used in the trenches of the western front.

Other species of Honey Fungus include the rare Marsh Honey Fungus – *Armillaria ectypa* – which is on the red data endangered list in the UK. It doesn't have the pernicious bootlace mycelium and lives secretly in marshland and bogs. Perhaps the tales of 'will-o'-the-wisps' and 'fairy

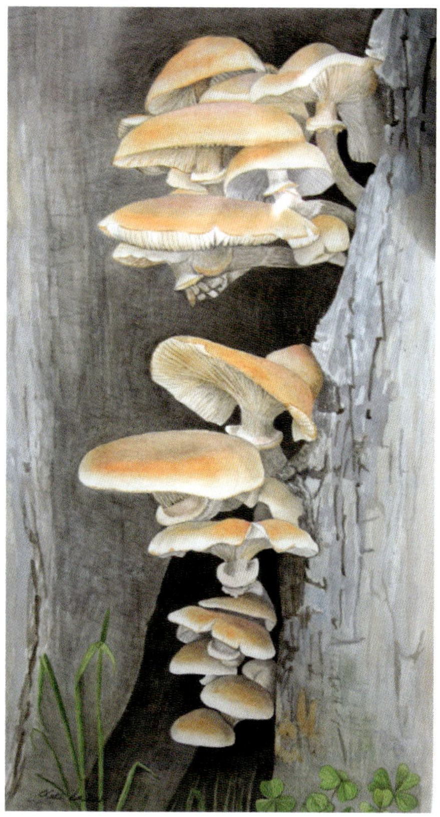

Honey fungus – *Armillaria mellea* by botanical artist Kathleen Baker who is also based in Wales. The ubiquitous honey-coloured mushrooms are sprouting from the decaying wood. (© Kathleen Baker)

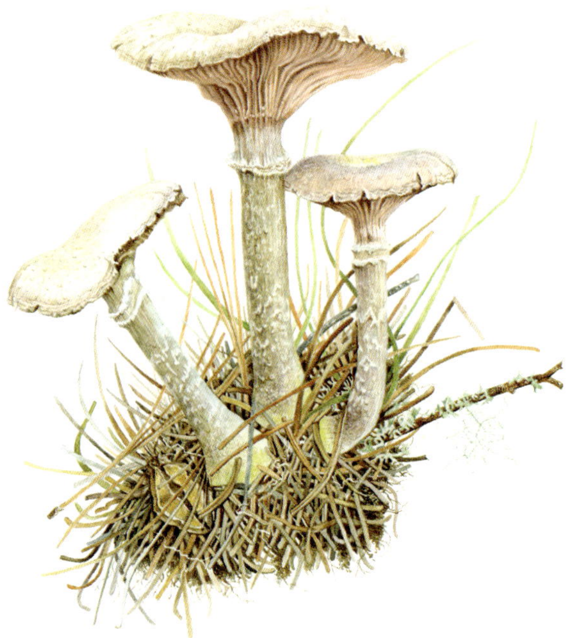

Honey fungus by botanical artist Margaret Best from Nova Scotia. These have been painted in watercolour with soft and subtle muted neutral tones and pastel hues with lots of texture. (© Margaret Best)

lights' in old bogland are the bioluminescent glow of this little mushroom along with other natural phenomena.

Parasol mushroom – ***Macrolepiota procera*** is a large, edible and impressive mushroom – *procera* means tall. It is seen quite commonly in late summer in pastures, verges, stable dunes and open woodlands. They have an interesting zigzag pattern on the stipe, reminiscent of snakeskin, which is wonderful to illustrate and is a good identification characteristic.

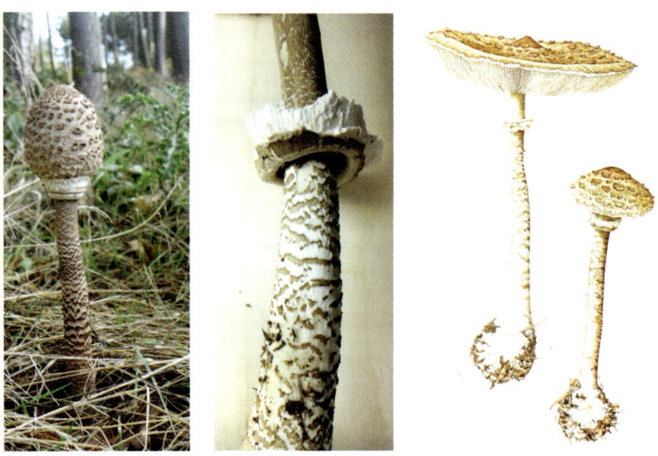

Parasol mushrooms – *Macrolepiota procera* – are lovely to find and illustrate. Here you can see the size difference as the cap swells with age, the movable ring, and the strong brown band patterning on the stipe. The cap is covered in scales and has quite a textured look so great for detailed drybrush.

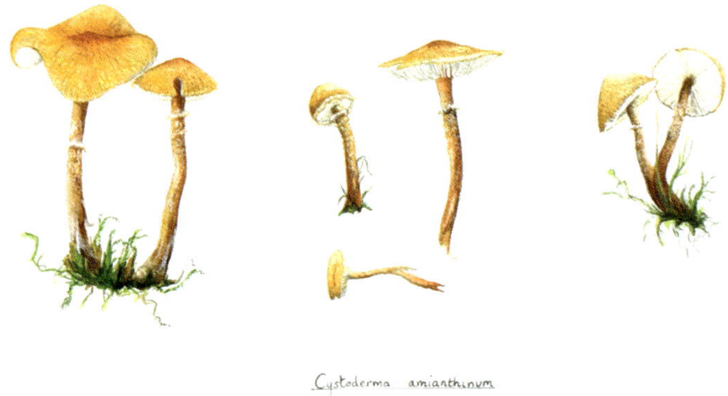

Saffron powdercap sketches in watercolour on cold press paper. You can see the paper has more texture to it making it robust, but it can still take some fine detail, so hot press doesn't always need to be used for detailed work. The cap and stipe both have a granular texture, and the stipe also has a ring, so they're quite interesting to paint.

Saffron powdercap – ***Cystoderma amianthinum*** – is an attractive little saffron-coloured mushroom that I've illustrated a few times as it's quite common in local meadows. This mushroom is interesting as it is parasitised by another mushroom menacingly called the powdercap strangler – *Squamanita paradoxa* – that takes it over by actually growing through the stem of the powdercap to replace the cap with its own. The lower stem remains the saffron colour of the host mushroom and the cap becomes the brownish violet colour of the new mushroom, making it distinctly two-toned. It is a fascinating species and very rarely recorded but worth keeping an eye out for.

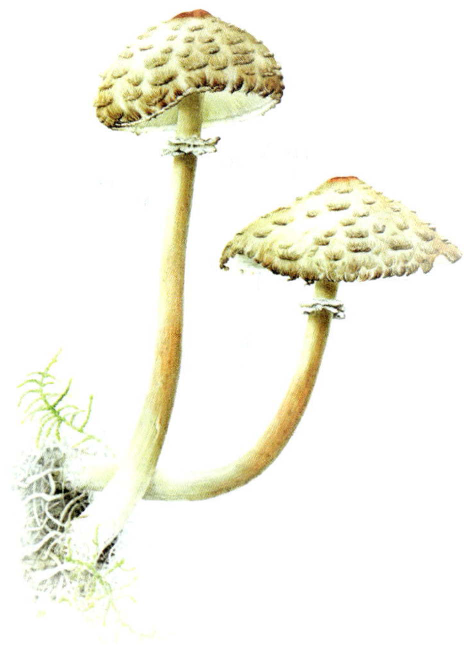

Shaggy parasol – *Chlorophyllum rhacodes* in coloured pencil. Driving along one day I noticed these fine-looking specimens growing in a road verge due to be pruned. I had to stop the car and gather them as they looked so beautiful. I thought the shagginess of the cap could be portrayed well using a dry media such as coloured pencil.

STEP-BY-STEP: USING A LIMITED PALETTE AND ENLARGING YOUR SUBJECT

Plums and custard – *Tricholomopsis rutilans* – is a beautiful mushroom that I have often found year in year out, sometimes in great profusion in plantations but then in others, hardly any. The cap is textured with scaly reddish, maroon-coloured dots over its yellow flesh and bright custard yellow sinuate gills. There is a similar mushroom called prunes and custard – *Tricholomopsis decora* – but it's not quite so colourful nor as common.

MATERIALS USED:

- Arches hot press 140lb
- Sheet of tracing paper
- Maths set dividers
- 2H graphite pencil
- Raphael 8404 brushes size 0, 4 and 6
- Perylene Maroon and New Gamboge – both Winsor & Newton – and Schmincke Ultramarine Finest

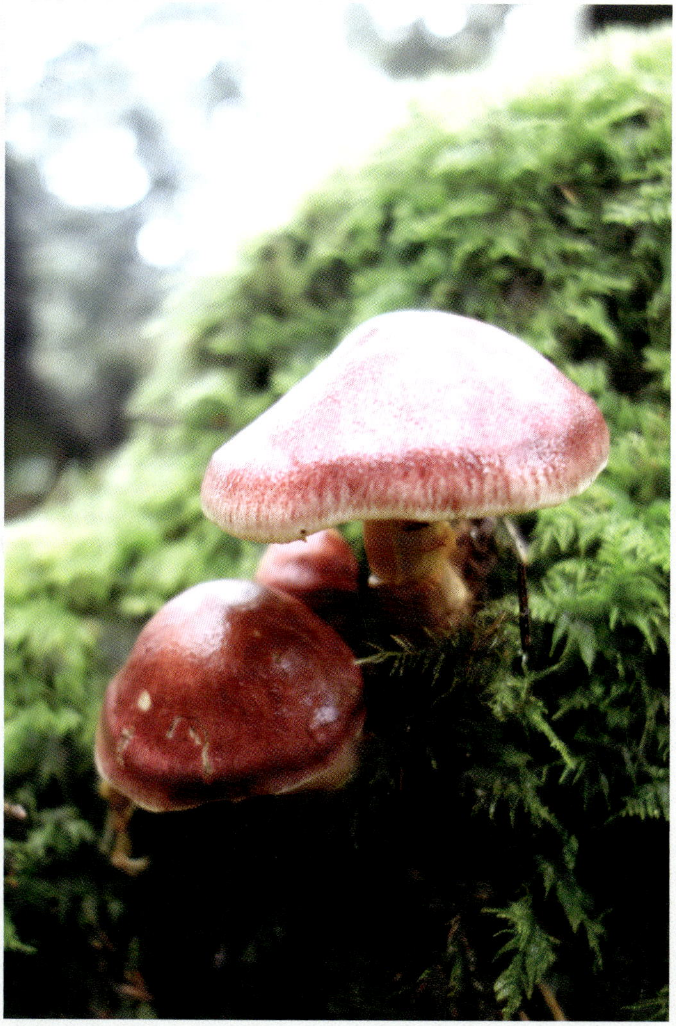

Plums and custard – *Tricholomopsis rutilans* is an attractive mushroom that graces coniferous woodlands. It likes to grow on mossy stumps, and some can get quite large. As the common name suggests, it has colours of warm custard yellow and plum red but despite their tasty name, they are bitter and inedible.

1

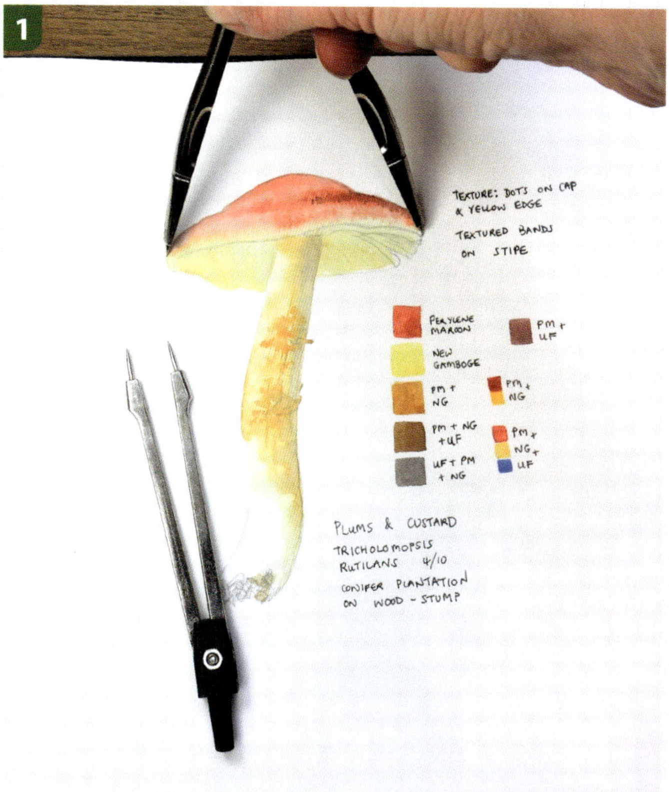

I initially drew the specimen from life in my sketchbook, drawing at life-size and capturing accurate colour notes. I wanted to enlarge it up to make a portrait of it as this is one of my favourite mushrooms. I took a couple of reference photos on my iPad also as my specimen would be long gone before I managed to get around to completing the actual painting.

When I was ready to paint, I used a pair of dividers to measure each width and height proportion and then sized up to twice life-size by 'walking' each measurement out twice onto tracing paper and then plotting out. If I wanted to draw at three times life-size, I would 'walk' the dividers out three times and so on. Then with enough marks plotted out, I drew the mushroom again, this time enlarged and referring to my initial sketch. Then I could transfer to the watercolour paper.

I also decided to try to paint it using a limited palette. I typically use a lot more than this so thought I would enjoy the challenge. The three chosen colours are one each of the primaries, so all greys and browns can be mixed using the three paints in different proportions. You can see the colour notes in the image and the different colour mixes achieved with the three paints. I think it made for a painting with more harmony and purity.

Continued on following page

2

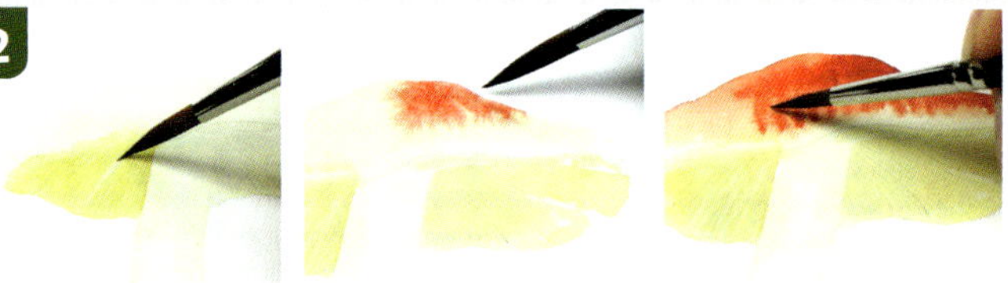

After transferring the original sketch to watercolour paper (you can see that I drew out the gills in detail as a tonal framework) with the size 6 brush, I laid on the washes with the yellow mix first using both wet into wet and wet on dry techniques. The Perylene Maroon was added on top of the yellow, again wet into wet then wet on dry to increase depth of colour.

3

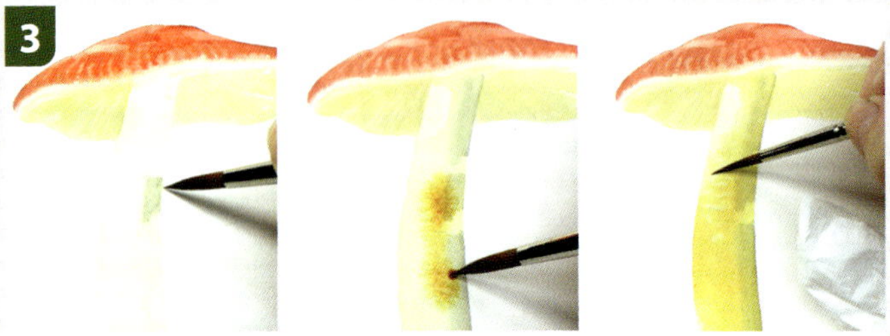

The grey mix was added wet on dry to the stipe's shadow side and then blended out into the highlighted side with a clean damp brush. While painting the grey shadow colour on top of the yellow, it was important to not have a grey that was too blue as the colours would optically mix to create a green shadow, not ideal!

Next the yellow and brown mixes are added wet into wet with some lifting out using the size 4 brush and a tissue to depict the textural stripes.

4

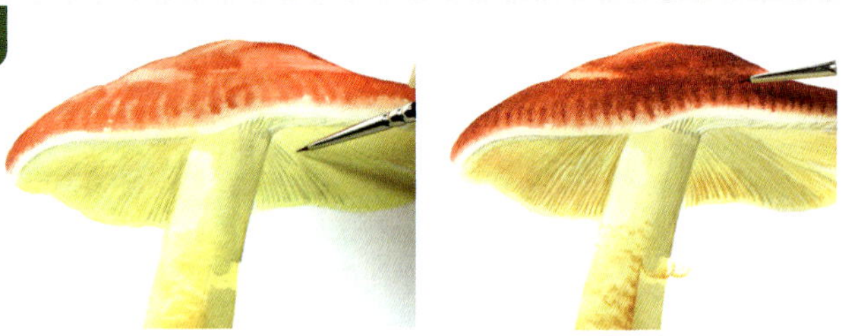

Working on the dry brush techniques next. The shadows between the gills are strengthened with the grey mix using the size 0 brush. I completed the detailed dry brush work of the cap and stipe textures with the help of the reference photos I had on my iPad, as it's so easy to enlarge to the right size. A thicker consistency of paint is stippled on with a small size 0 brush in little dots to build up tone, as well as the dotted texture seen in these caps.

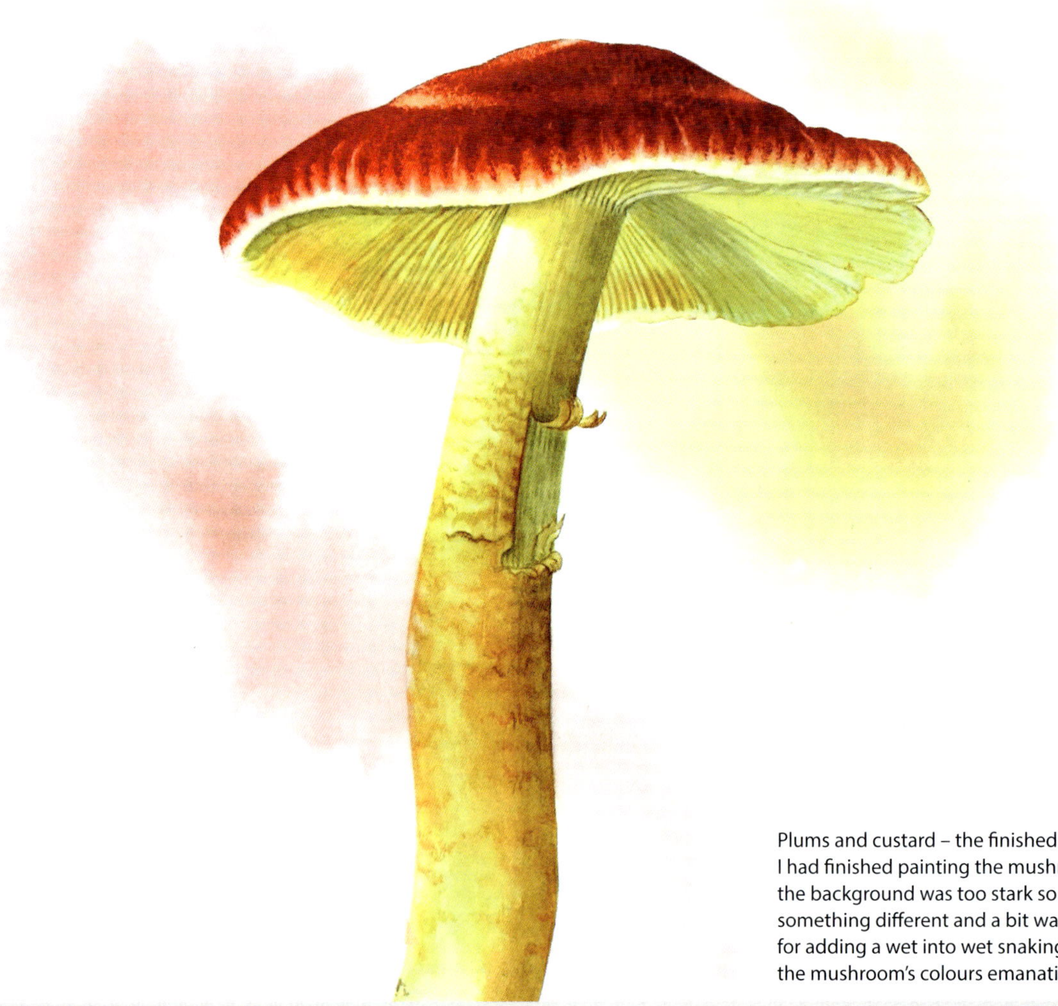

Plums and custard – the finished portrait. When I had finished painting the mushroom, I felt the background was too stark so for fun and something different and a bit wacky, I just went for adding a wet into wet snaking pattern with the mushroom's colours emanating from it.

FUNGI WITH PORES

Having spongelike pores instead of gills, many of these fungi belong to the *Boletus* family. The name comes from the Greek; *Bolos*, meaning lump of clay and referring to the clay-like colour and texture of the caps. When observing boletes, make a note of the size of their pores, as some will be large and angular while others will be much smaller.

There is only one known poisonous bolete in the UK, the devil's bolete – *Rubroboletus satanas*– with bright scarlet red pores and stipe and sometimes a large pale almost skull-like cap. This is one I'd love to find and paint but so far, I've not found it yet as it likes chalky soils and warmth and apparently it does not smell good up close!

For colourful subjects to paint, there are a few attractive boletes such as the scarletina bolete – *Neoboletus luridiformis* – that has red dots on the stipe and the lurid bolete – *Suillellus luridus* – that has a reddish reticulate stipe; plenty of scope in this group for depicting texture and layering watercolour techniques for portraying their velvety caps. For extra colourful interest, they both have quite a strong blueing reaction when cut, that eventually fades a little.

The bitter beech bolete (*Caloboletus calopus*) is a stunning mushroom with a pale velvet cap over primrose yellow pores and a beautifully reticulated stipe of reddish hues. Indeed, the prefix *calo* comes from the Greek word meaning pretty. I first came across these mushrooms in 2006 in a conifer woodland where they were having a bumper year. There were so many of these beauties growing up from the mossy forest floor and some were a really good size, so I took two specimens home to draw. They also bruised blue slightly when I cut them open, so made for a fascinating study. As the name implies, they are incredibly bitter to taste but there was not a beech tree in sight, just spruce trees in a plantation. The trees have since been thinned out after forest operations and sadly I've never seen them since in this place. I hope that the mycelium is still alive within the soil and some day they will grace the woodland again.

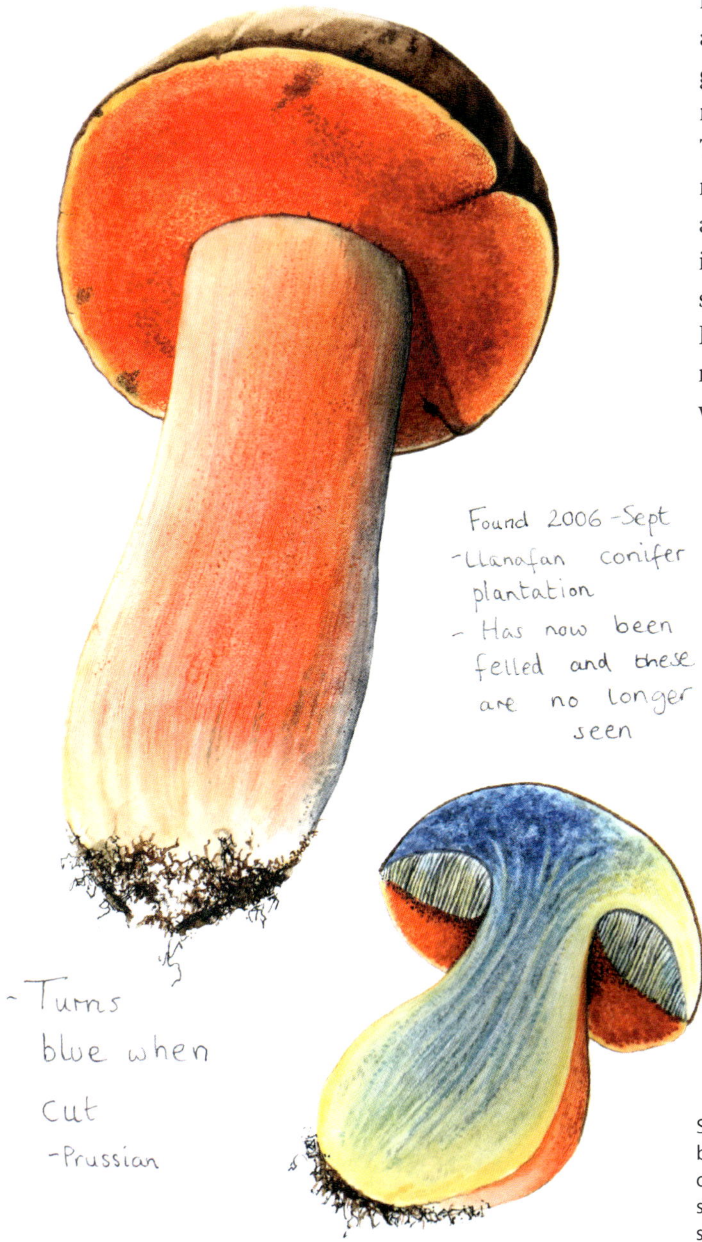

Sketchbook study page from 2006 of the wonderfully coloured scarletina bolete – *Neoboletus luridiformis*. It graces acidic coniferous forests and is often with bilberry. Up close you could see the individual red dots on its stipe but when painting, I just hinted at a few in the mid tone area. The strong blue reaction was painted using W/N Prussian.

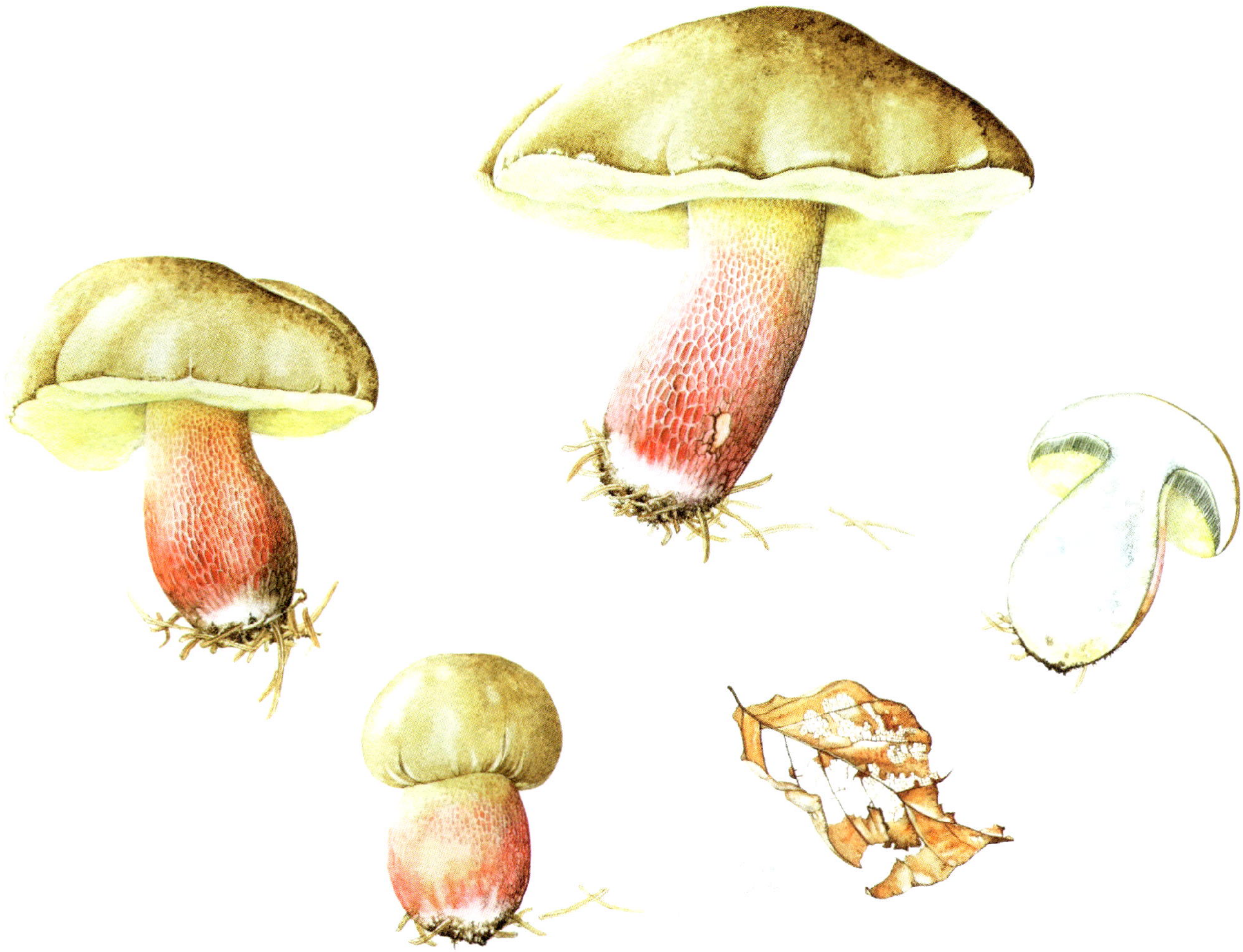

Bitter beech bolete – *Caloboletus calopus* is one of my favourite mushrooms, *calopus* means 'pretty foot' and you can see the beautiful carmine coloured reticulation here on the stipe. These and other boletes were more common in my area but many spots for it have disappeared due to forest thinning in the plantations, which can often look so destructive afterwards.

The penny bun, porcini or cep (*Boletus edulis*) is a most magnificent species that has several common names due to its sought-after nature as a very well-known edible mushroom. It can grow very large, with a thick, stout stipe that can have a lovely white reticulation on it. It grows most commonly in relationship with beech and birch, but is also seen under oaks, conifers and rock rose species in Southern Europe.

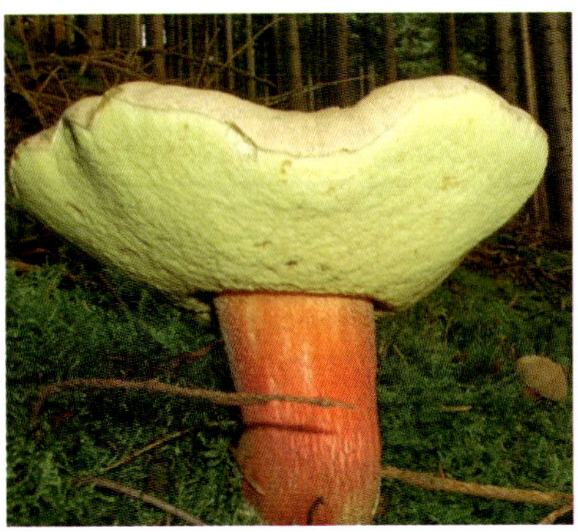

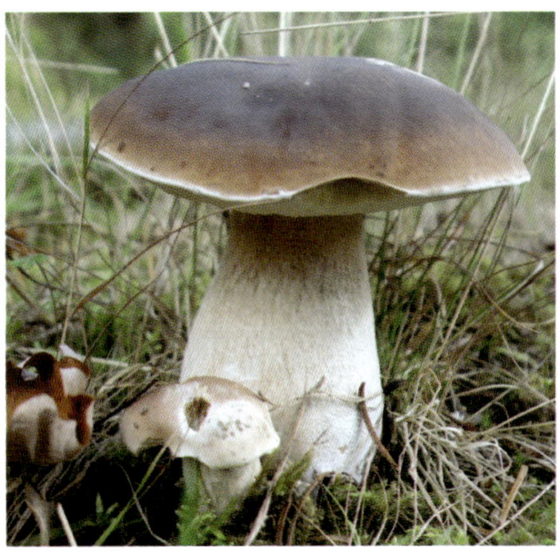

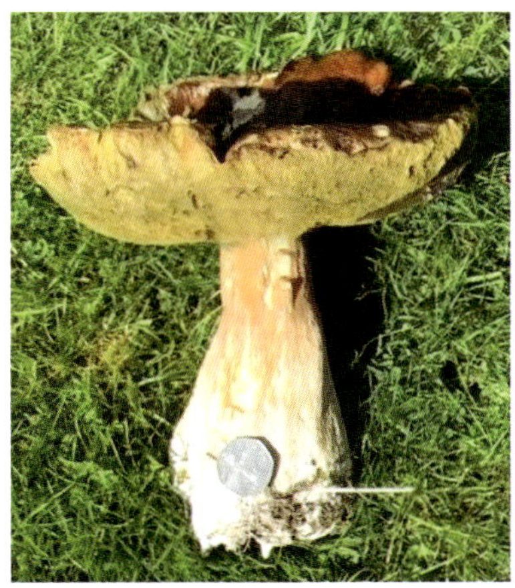

On the left is the bitter beech bolete – *Caloboletus calopus* and in the centre, the penny bun – *Boletus edulis,* both growing in conifer plantations. Some boletes can grow very large, as you can see with the 50p coin for scale in the image on the right.

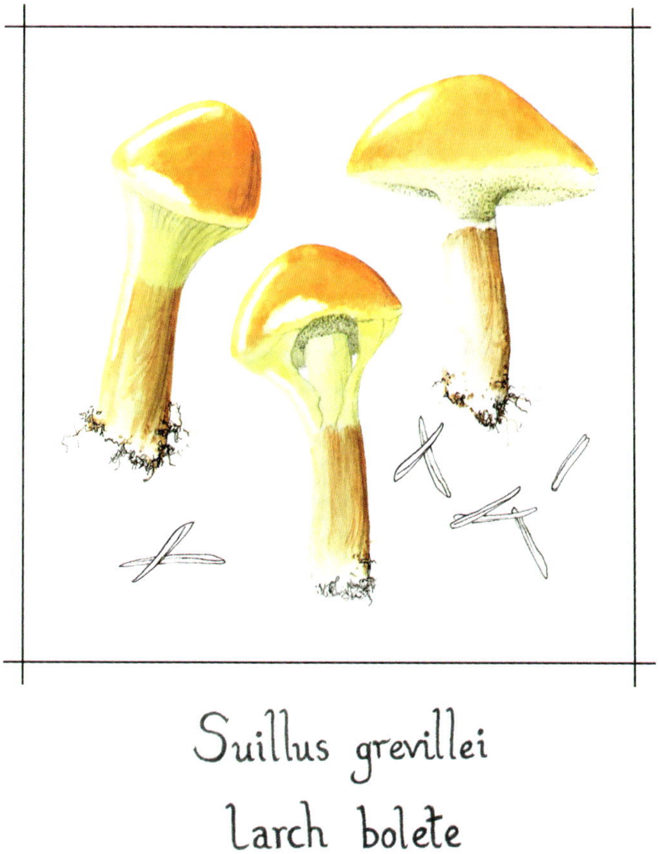

Larch boletes have a lovely bright egg yolk yellow cap and the shiny, viscid look has been depicted by leaving the white paper. Larch needles, name titles and an outline frame have been added in Pigma Micron black pen.

The larch bolete – *Suillus grevillei.* The generic name means of pigs/swine possibly because of the sticky, slimy and viscid look. The species epithet was named after the Scottish botanist and mycologist Robert Kaye Greville (1794–1866) and he was also an accomplished botanical artist. They are mycorrhizal with larch, and I wonder how they will fare after so many larch forests have now been felled in the UK owing to disease.

Peppery bolete – *Chalciporus piperatus*. This is quite a small mushroom for a bolete and it has large and often quite angular pores under a dry cap. When cut in two, its flesh is a vivid bright yellow so makes a great study showing this feature. I am fascinated with this little bolete as it seems to appear alongside groups of *Amanita muscaria* and so it seems there is a relationship there. This is one of the few mushrooms that I have tasted apart from *Russulas* and waxcaps and it truly lives up to its name of the peppery bolete, with a very hot and fiery taste. Apparently, the hot taste is lost with cooking but it's not such a good edible mushroom.

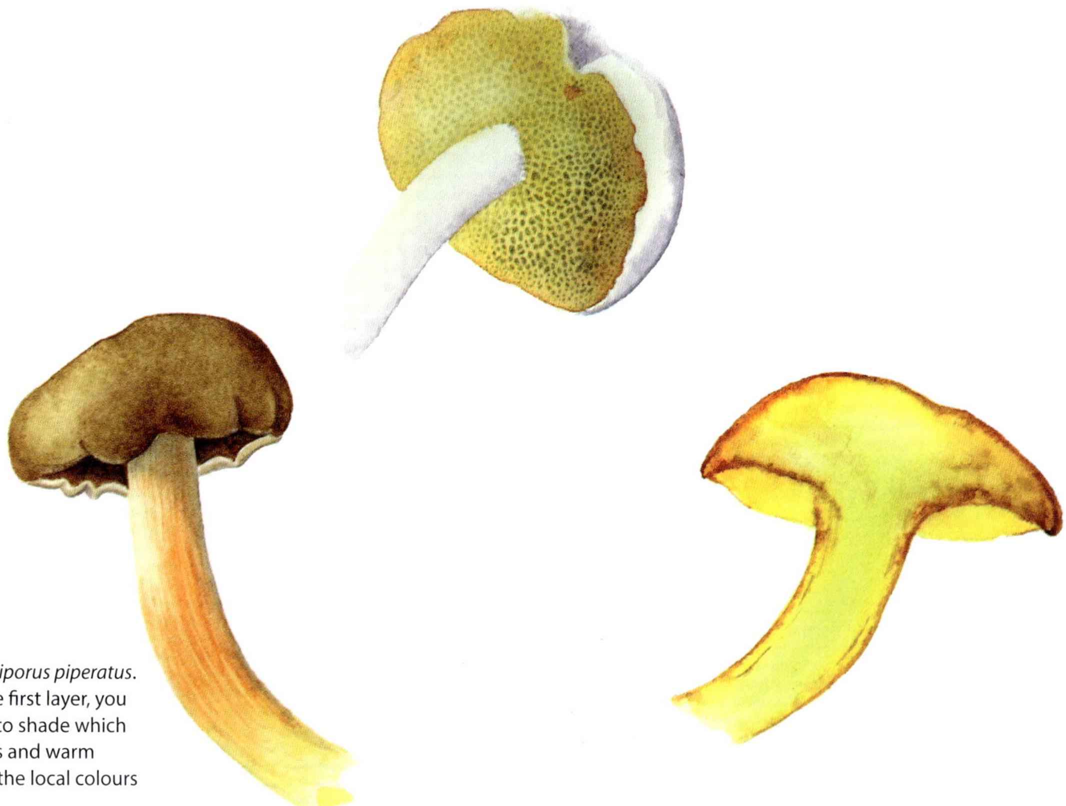

Painting peppery boletes – *Chalciporus piperatus*. Here on the top mushroom in the first layer, you can see that I used Winsor Violet to shade which is a good way for shading browns and warm yellows. When dry you can wash the local colours over the top.

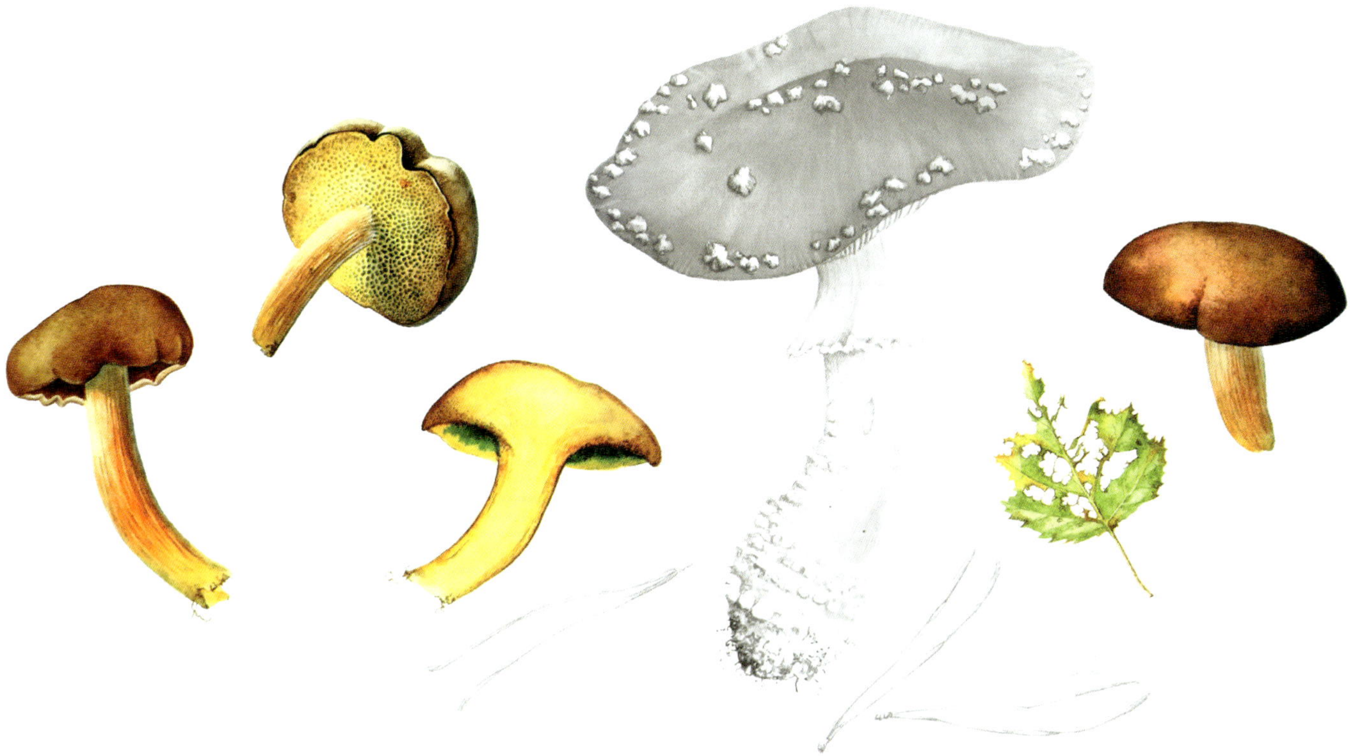

Silent Partners. The peppery bolete can be nicely coloured with maroons, cinnamons and golden yellows and the pores stain blueish when bruised as seen in the longitudinal section. I have only ever found them growing alongside fly agarics and it is thought to be parasitic on the mycelium of that mushroom, hence the addition of it here, depicted in monotone.

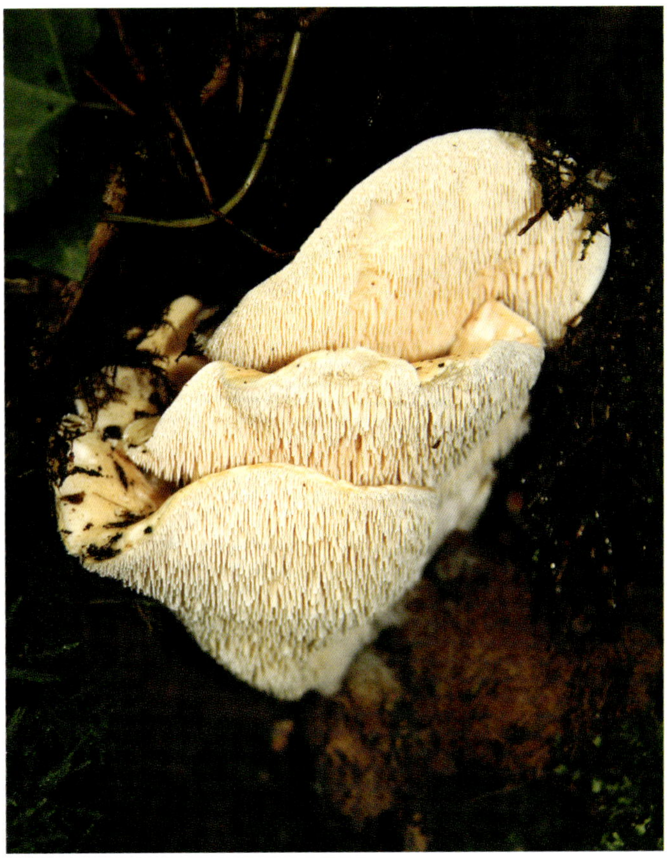

FUNGI WITH SPINES

There are a few species with spines, also known as teeth fungi, which are intriguing. These include the hedgehogs – *Hydnum* spp. and the *Hericium* spp. that includes the rare medicinal lion's mane mushroom.

The earpick fungus, *Auriscalpium vulgare* is a small, brown mushroom that grows on pine cones. It has spines for gills and an incredible hirsute texture covering its kidney-shaped cap and thin stipe.

Auriscalpium comes from the Latin *auris*, an ear, and *scalpare*, to scratch and *vulgare* means common. It doesn't have the nicest name, but it is a lovely find. I prefer to call it the pine cone fungus as that is its substrate.

Hedgehogs – *Hydnum repandum* are a lovely find in mixed woodlands with intricate little teeth and supposed to be a tasty edible.

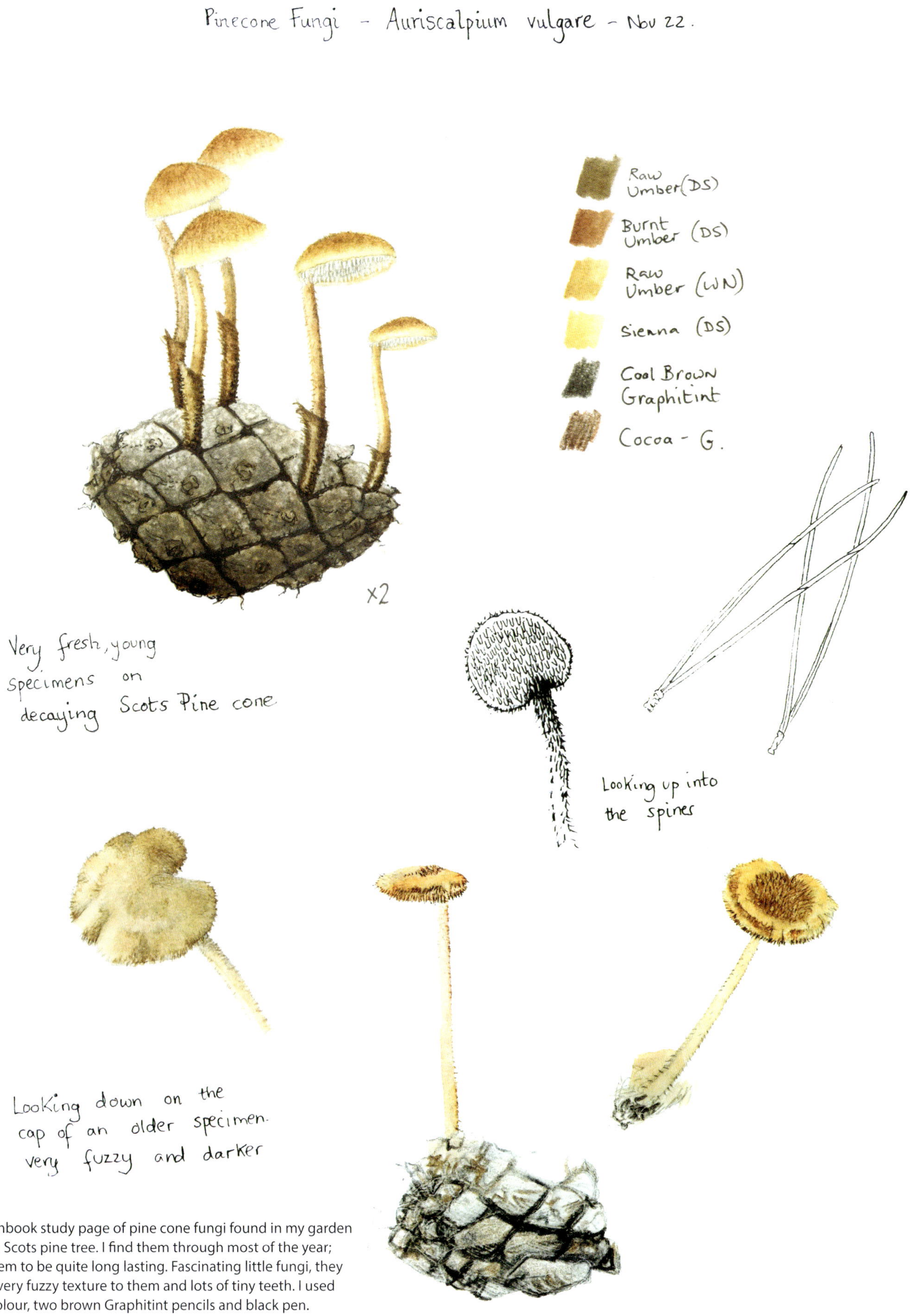

A sketchbook study page of pine cone fungi found in my garden under a Scots pine tree. I find them through most of the year; they seem to be quite long lasting. Fascinating little fungi, they have a very fuzzy texture to them and lots of tiny teeth. I used watercolour, two brown Graphitint pencils and black pen.

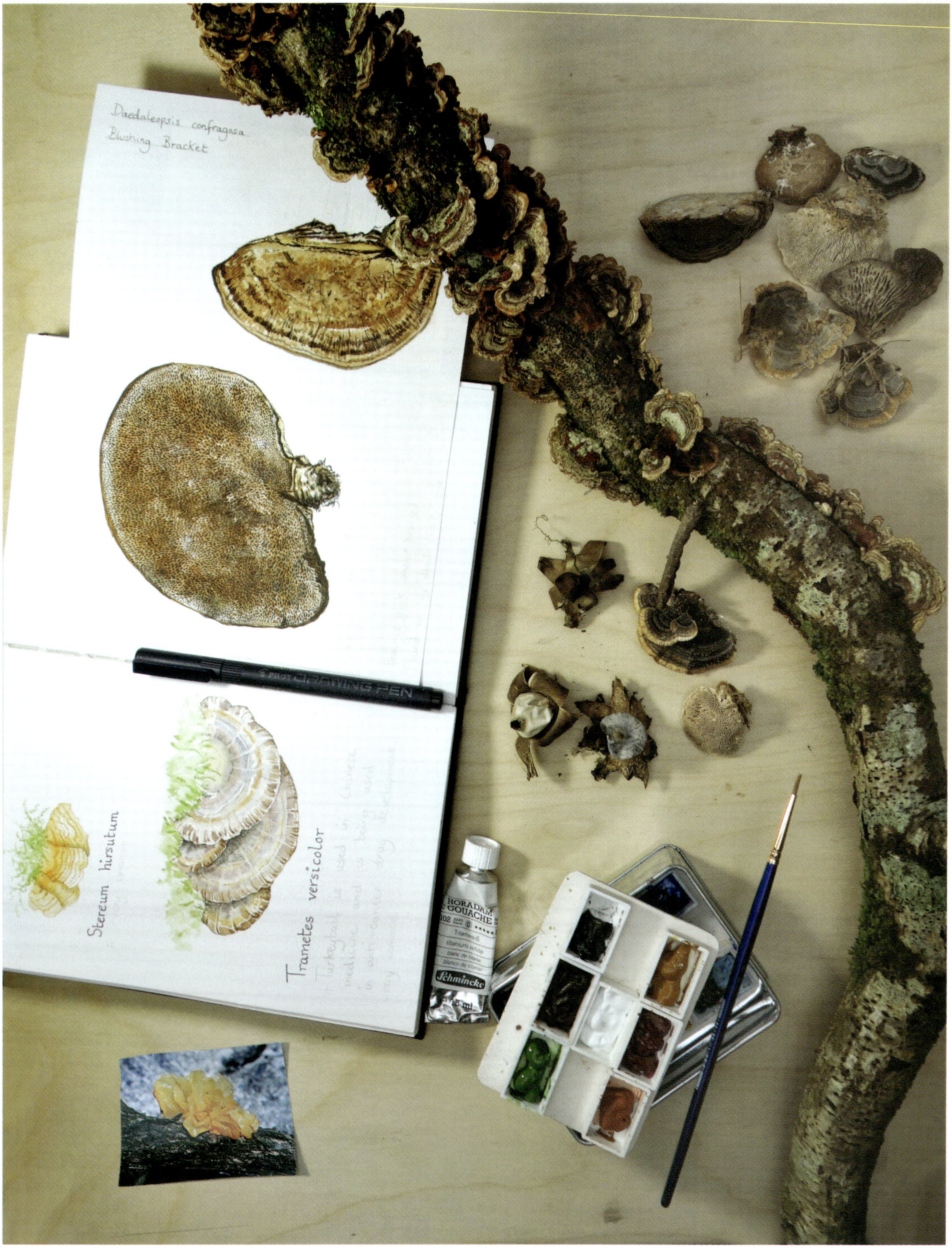
Daedaleopsis confragosa
Blushing Bracket
Stereum hirsutum
Trametes versicolor
DRAWING PEN
HORADAM
GOUACHE
Schmincke

CHAPTER 8

BASIDIOMYCETES – 'THE UNUSUAL'

This chapter will focus on the more unusual fungi that do not have the classic form of a mushroom, but are still classed within the *Basidiomycetes*.

BRACKETS

Bracket fungi or polypores are shelf-like fungi that grow upon decaying or dead trees or stumps. More robust than their ephemeral mushroom counterparts, they are tough and woody with often quite large fruiting bodies firmly attached to the substrate without a stipe. They can release millions of spores from the underside of their protruding bodies through their pore systems. The pores are variable in size, from the tiniest of holes and intricate tubes to large, elongated structures such as those of *Daedalea quercina* – the oak mazegill, that has very large, gill-like pores that resemble a maze. The tough, older brackets are conspicuous through most of the year and so can be great subjects when there is not much else around. You can often find brackets forming sturdy shelves in crevasses and hollows of old trees.

Sometimes you may come across brackets that have fused together in interesting ways, such as the turkey tails further on. You may even find some that have engulfed nearby twigs or grass so that they have become embedded within their bodies. This type of growth even has a name – *haptomorphosis,* but it is not something that I have illustrated yet.

Brackets may give an opportunity to work outdoors 'en plein air' capturing their growth on a tree trunk or dead stump perhaps within a landscape in different media.

The following species are just a few that I've encountered; there are so many more to discover.

A collection of brackets and earthstars, more unusual looking fungi but all are classed as *Basidiomycetes*.

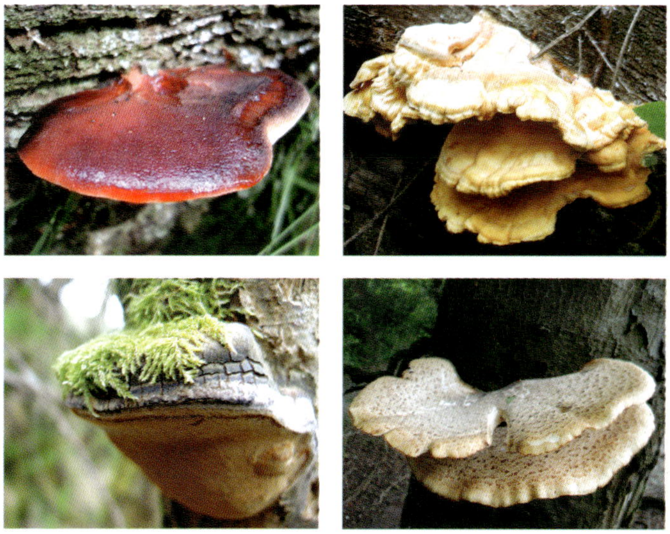

Top left: beefsteak fungus – *Fistulina hepatica* looks a little like a slab of raw meat hence the common name. Underneath, with its mossy cap, is the tinder or hoof fungus – *Fomes fomentarius*. Top right: The edible chicken of the woods – *Laetiporus sulphureus* and below it, the dryad's saddle – *Polyporus squamosus,* an incredibly large growing bracket.

The tinder fungus – *Fomes fomentarius*. Our ancestors used this fungus as a fire starter and as a way to hold and transport fire between camps, hence its common name. It is also called the hoof fungus as it has the shape of a horse's hoof. The bracket is persistent, adding a new layer upon the tough fruit body year after year. It's reported to have many medicinal properties also and it commonly grows on birch but may be found on other deciduous trees.

Birch polypore – *Fomitopsis betulina*. This large bracket is very common on dead or dying birch trees. Like the tinder fungus, it can also hold a spark that slowly smoulders and was used by early man to transport fire. Like many fungi, it produces an antibiotic as well as other chemicals and it is also antiseptic and anti-inflammatory. So, this bracket is a very interesting one in terms of medicinal use, but it is too bitter to be edible.

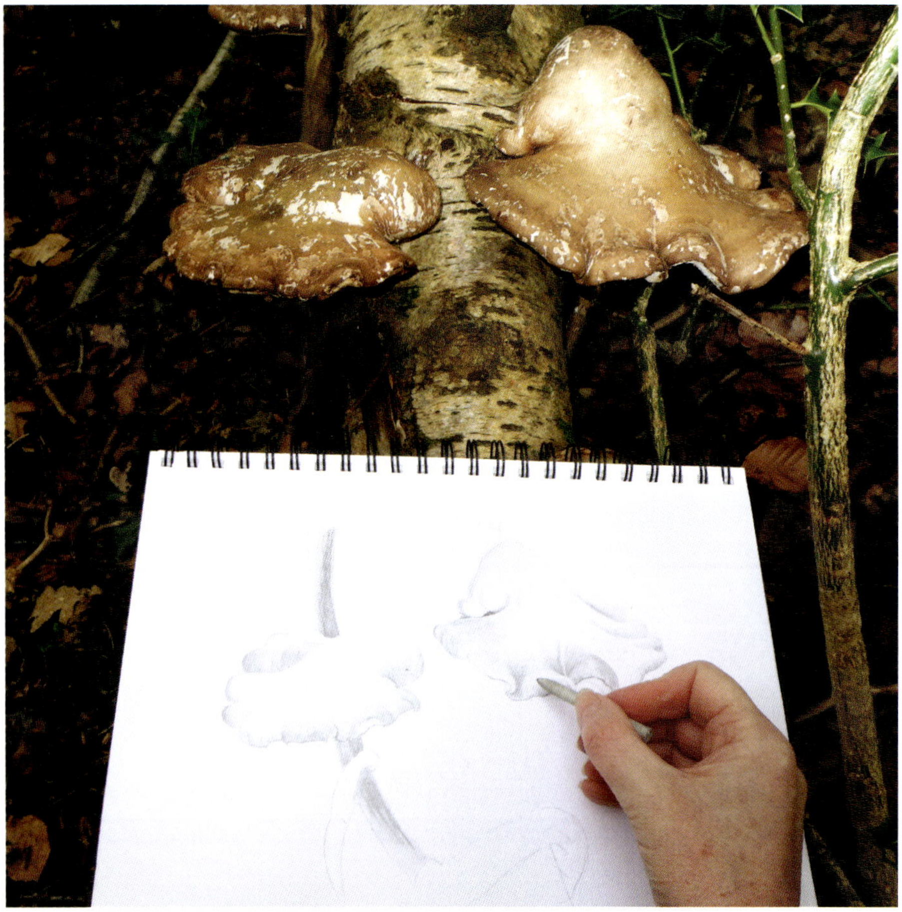

Sketching a couple of wonderfully curvaceous birch polypore brackets one spring day. It was very cold but nice to sit on a log listening to a bubbling stream and the birds singing, drawing with graphite sticks. I used a tortillion to blend out the graphite to try to create the smooth contoured surface of the brackets.

Oak mazegill – *Daedalea quercina* drawn in graphite on Stonehenge toned paper. You can see its labyrinthine pore structure. It was tricky to draw them accurately as it was very easy to lose your place in the pores, quite apt seeing as it is a mazegill! The highlights were added with white pencil and the darkest tones were the matt graphite 6B.

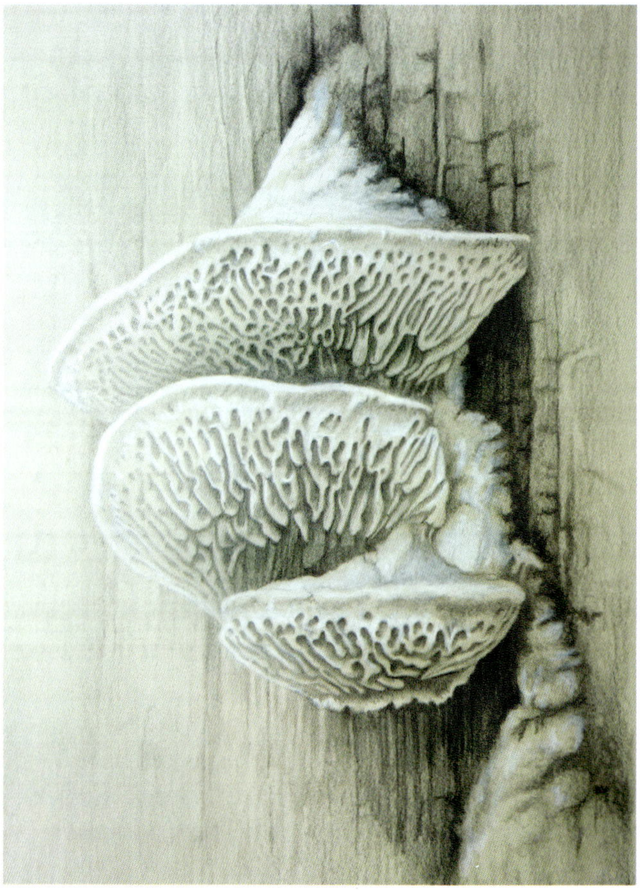

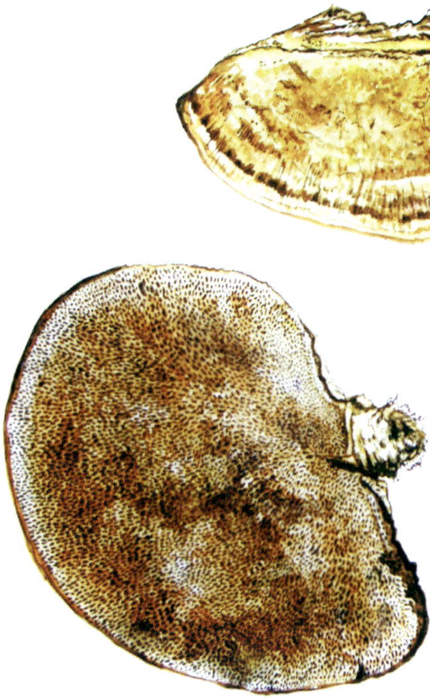

Blushing Bracket – *Daedaleopsis confragosa*, drawn in 2005, is a tough polypore often with pinkish tones that is found on broadleaf trees such as willows. Here it has been drawn in pen and wash; a labour of love, with every pore added in pen. *Daedaleopsis* means 'like a *Daedalea*' species (*Opsis* – is from the Greek for appearance).

Artist's fungus/conk – *Ganoderma applanatum* is quite a common bracket fungus that has creamy white pores that you can draw on to reveal dark marks. It grows on oak and beech, sometimes conifers too and is seen on fallen trees. It can grow to a large size as it is a perennial bracket and can often form shelves of brackets that look like stacks of pancakes! The *Ganoderma* genus includes the medicinal bracket called Reishi that has been used for thousands of years and has a wonderful shiny look as if it's just been lacquered!

Turkey tail – *Trametes versicolor*, is a common little bracket fungus found growing on wood. On fresher specimens, it can have beautifully colourful concentric bands on its surface, living up to its species name of *versicolor*, ranging from dark blue-greys and browns to golds and russets with a suede or velvety texture. You can tell if it is turkey tail and not a lookalike by examining the underside to see if it has a pore system with a pale cream colour; if it is coloured and smooth, it's not turkey tail. This fungus has also been found to help some cancer patients by strengthening the immune system when taken in conjunction with chemotherapy. It can sometimes have a strong, sharp chemical smell, quite medicinal and indeed it can be used to make a medicinal tea, but not so nice tasting!

Some turkey tail lookalikes are within the *Stereum* family of brackets, such as the wonderfully named hairy curtain crust – *Stereum hirsutum*, (*hirsutum* means hairy), which also has variously coloured striations. It sometimes forms a crust growing attached to the wood – this growth is called *resupinate* from the Latin for 'on its back'. If you look closer in, you will see how hairy this little bracket is. Under the

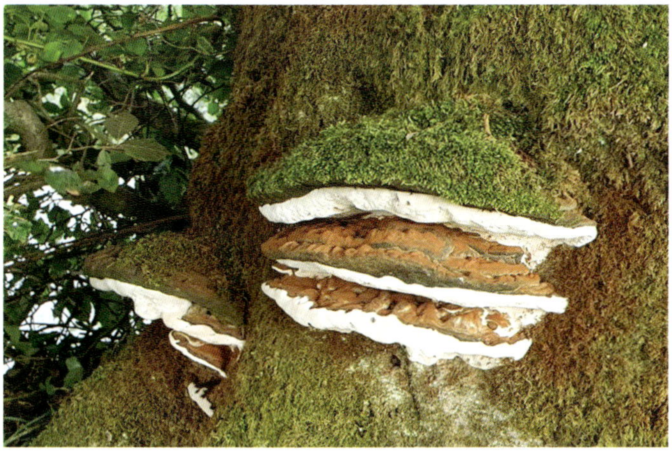

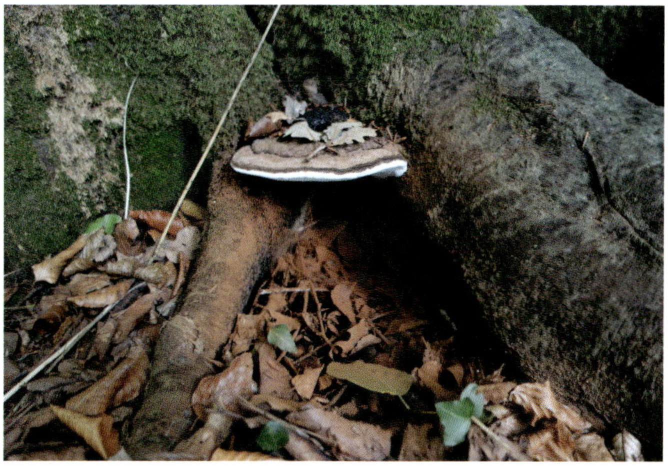

A *Ganoderma* bracket releasing its millions of spores, coating everything beneath it in a dusting of what looks like cinnamon or cocoa powder.

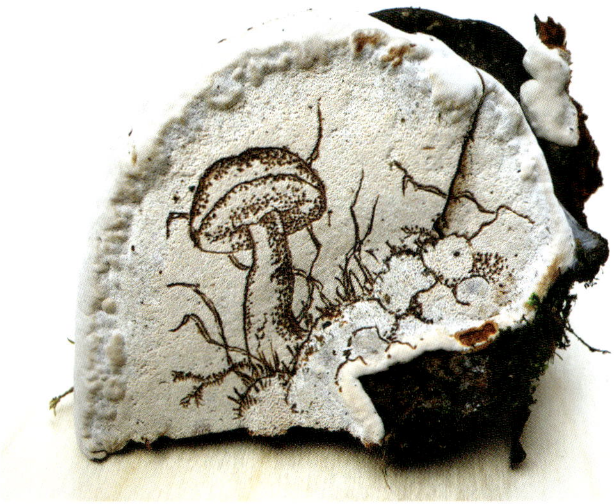

Boletus on a bracket. This little bolete study was drawn onto the Artist's Conk pore surface using a compass point. It seemed very apt to draw in little stipples with the sharp tip of the compass almost mimicking the little pores.

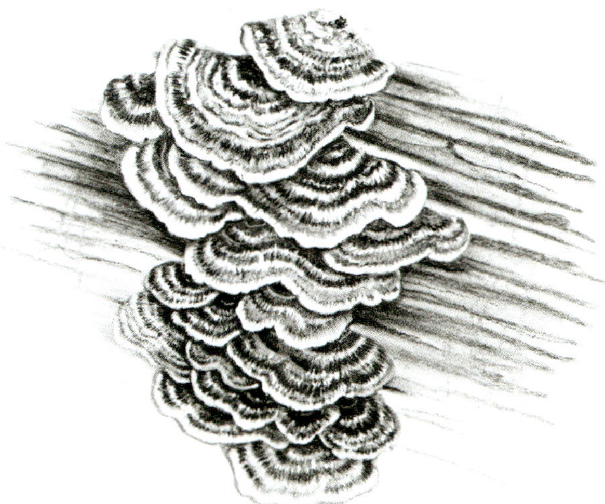

Turkey tail – *Trametes versicolor* study on wood, drawn on Strathmore 400 vellum paper with Derwent light and dark charcoal pencils and then blended in the direction of the vertical striations with a size 2, flat chisel silicone tool. Using charcoal is such a quick way of working, this only took about an hour.

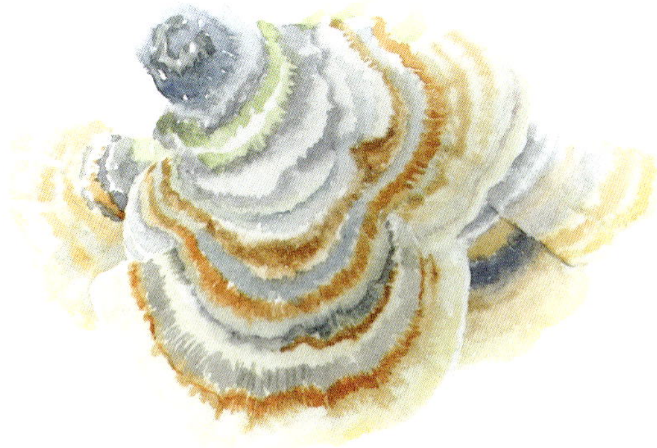

1

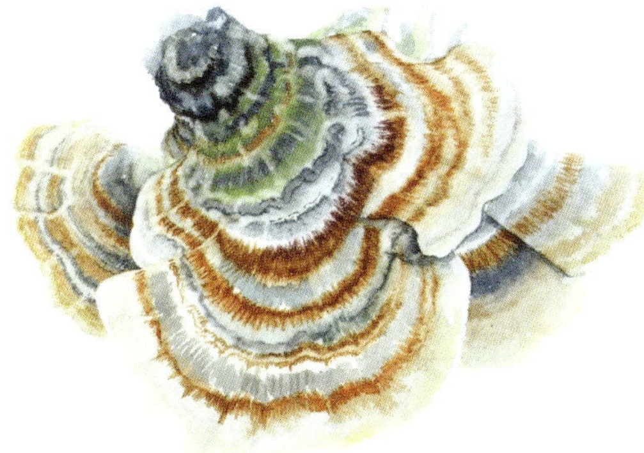

2

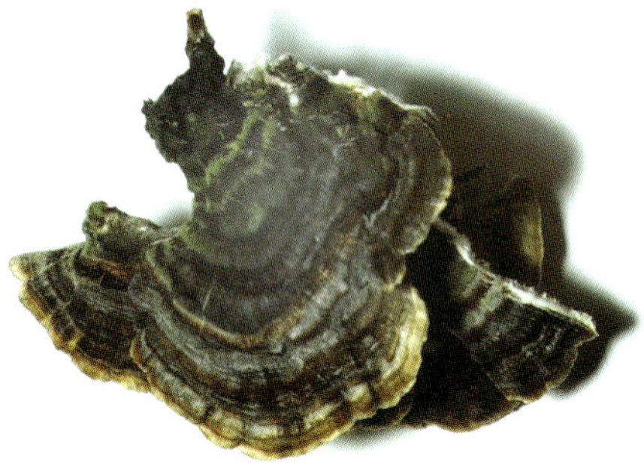

Turkey tail: picture 1. On Bockingford HP paper, the initial layer of watercolour is painted on, merging the many concentric zones of colour together. Picture 2 is the second layer painted with more concentrated colour using little strokes in the direction of the vertical striations. The actual specimen seen here had dried out a little and lost some of its vibrant colours over time.

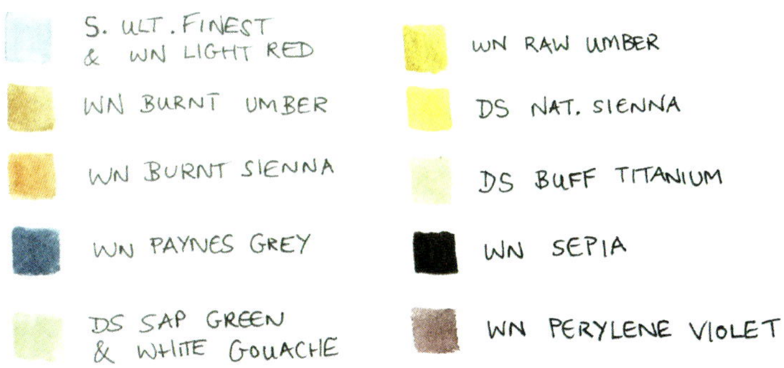

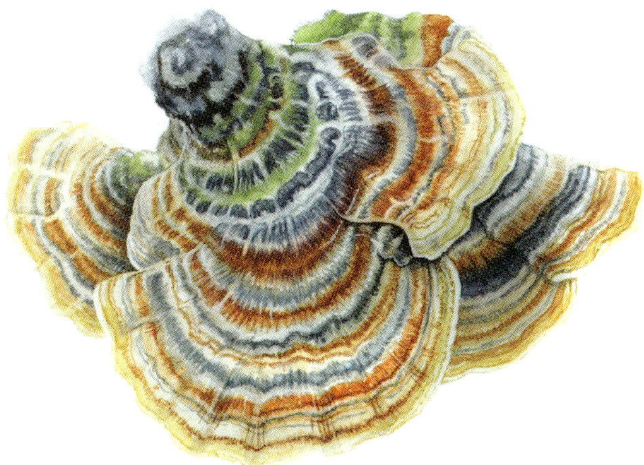

Turkey tail – *Trametes versicolor,* the finished study after laying on the final layers, blending together the concentric bands of colour to give the bracket the velvety, furry and quite opaque look that it has. Dry brush technique neatens the edges and adds some shading in the overlap and shadow areas to heighten the form.

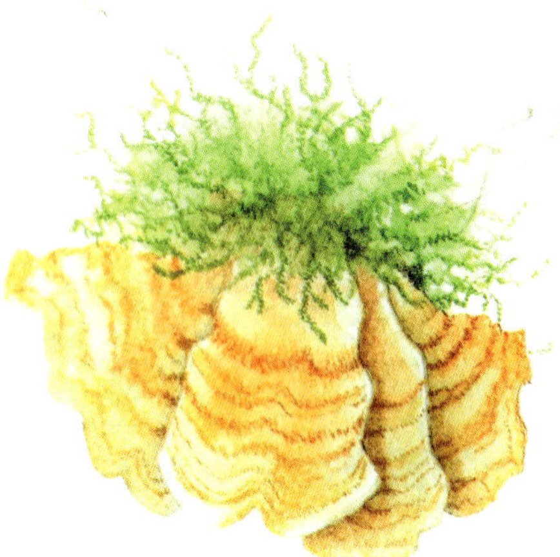

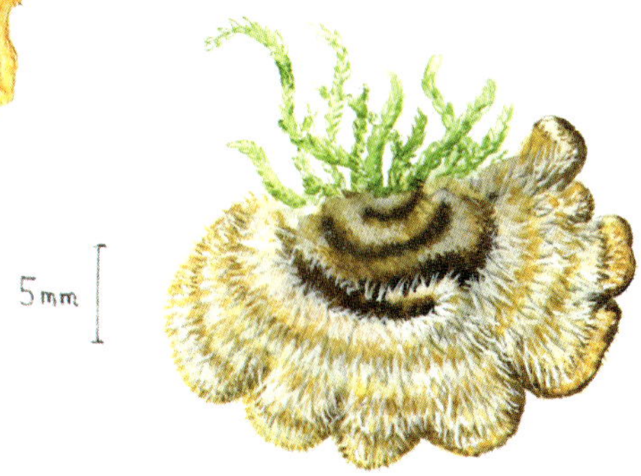

Hairy curtain crust – *Stereum hirsutum* study. The left-hand bracket is painted life-size in watercolour, the right-side bracket is painted twice life-size in watercolour and gouache to show up the hairiness.

hand lens, it actually looks a bit like a woolly rug! Also on the underside, there are no pores, just a smooth yellowing surface, so it is actually very different to turkey tail. The colours also tend to be more orange-coloured or ochraceous, and some of the older brackets turn a dark orange, almost red colour in patches. So, I think both of these little brackets would make lovely painting studies, especially with the addition of their woody substrates.

JELLIES AND CORALS

Wood ear or jelly ear – *Auricularia auricula-judae*. This common species can be found throughout the year. Shaped very much like ears, they grow on old wood, most commonly on elder trees but can be found on other hard woods too. It is an edible mushroom and was once used in traditional medicine.

Corals, clubs and spindles – *Clavarioid* fungi. These fungi can be found in so many bright colours from bright orange and deep yellows to creamy whites, grey browns and pinks. One such species is the violet coral – *Clavaria zollingeri*, which is a stunning fungus if you find it young and fresh. It has a deep violet colour and branching coralloid shape, as if it belongs under the sea. Like most *Clavarioid* fungi, they can be found in grasslands or woodlands, but I've only ever found the violet coral in graveyards and cemeteries. They are erratic in appearance and there's no guarantee that they'll be seen again in the same place next year. You can see an illustration of some coral fungi in Chapter 6 under CHEG species.

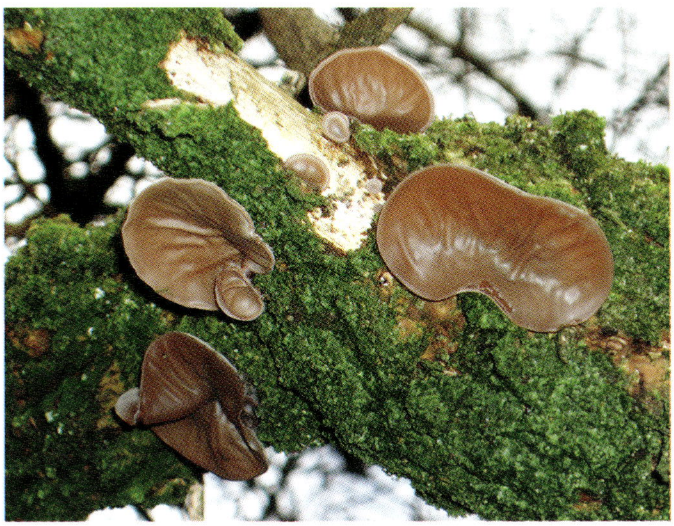

Wood ear can be commonly found growing on old elder wood. In this picture you can really see the resemblance to ears, and they have a tough, leathery almost plastic look. I've not got around to painting them yet, maybe one day!

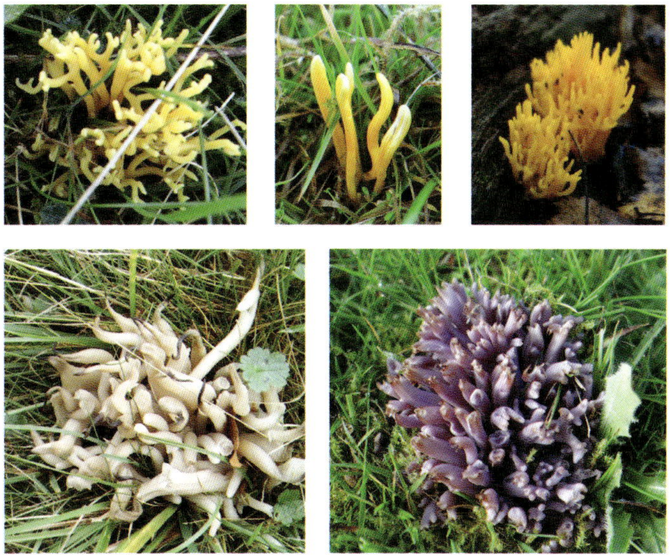

There are so many different colours of coral fungi. Some are found in large clumps, but others are just tiny spikes hidden amongst the grass in meadows. On the lower right is Violet Coral – *Clavaria zollingeri,* a beautiful fungus if you're lucky enough to find it. Top right is yellow stagshorn – *Calocera viscosa*. It is different to the others pictured here in that it is always found growing on wood.

GASTEROMYCETES

The Gasteromycetes are a group of fungi in the Basidiomycota, also known as gasteroid fungi, which literally means 'stomach fungi'. It encompasses species that enclose their spores inside an outer structure. They were once classed in the order *Gasteromycetales*, but this class has now become obsolete as it contains species that are not closely related, including puffballs, earthstars, and stinkhorns. In fact, some of these species are more closely related to the boletes and certain gill fungi, like

James Sowerby (1757–1822) produced a huge number of illustrations on natural history subjects including volumes called *Coloured Figures of English Fungi or Mushrooms*. These are the pepperpot earthstars, which have a multi-perforated top. It was thought to be extinct but was recently found fruiting in Kent, UK – great news.

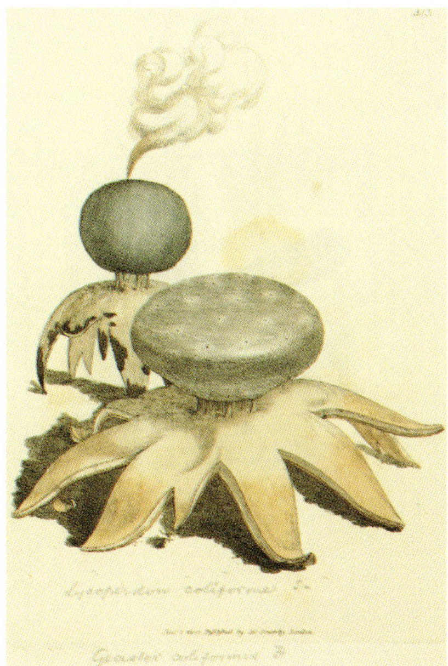

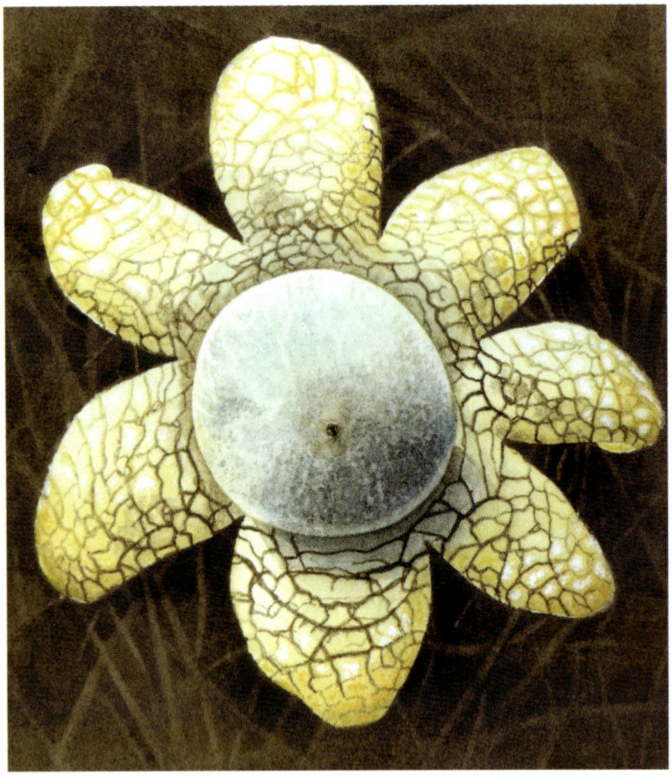

The barometer earthstar – *Astraeus hygrometricus* in watercolour. I was given permission to use a perfect photograph of this wonderful species taken by Alicia Joubert Culverwell in South Africa. I used granulating pigments such as French Ultramarine, Cerulean and Umbers on Arches HP, in many layers to create the textures seen in this amazing, quite flower-like earthstar.

Lepiota spp. I'm sure in the not-too-distant future, some of these species will change genera and find themselves in their true families.

One such species is the barometer earthstar or false earthstar – *Astraeus hygrometricus* – which is closely related to the boletes and despite its similar appearance, is not related to the *Geastrum* family of earthstars. It is a rare find in most of the UK but is found more commonly in the south of England, southern Europe and beyond. It is called the barometer earthstar as it is very sensitive to the weather and opens and closes its wonderfully cracked and textured rays in response to humidity in the atmosphere – the species name means water measurer.

Earthstars – *Geastrum* spp. – have truly weird and wonderful forms. Starting out as small round structures a bit like puffballs, they unfurl into stars crowning a delicate, round fruit body with a central hole called a *peristome* from where the spores are dispersed. Their rays curl back underneath their bodies and can actually raise them up away from the ground a little way. They open in response to moisture in the air and it's the pattering of raindrops on the central body that releases the spores.

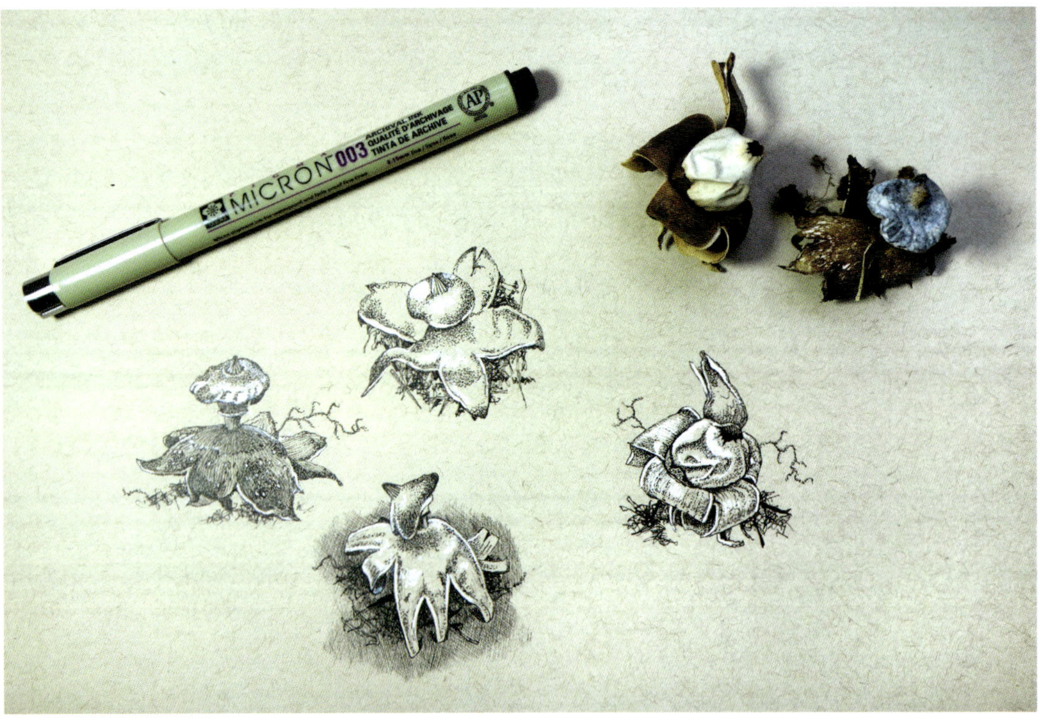

Earthstars in pen on Strathmore toned tan paper. The three on the left are the striated earthstars, as they have ribbed beaks and a collared neck underneath and the one on the right is a collared earthstar. They dry out, so keep well and make great drawing studies. They are certainly weird and wonderful, like strange little creatures.

Puffballs, earthballs and stalkballs – *Lycoperdon, Calvatia* or *Scleroderma* spp. These rounded fungi have explosive spores that are released into the air sometimes in such numbers that you can see them in a cloud above the fruit body. They have interesting textural surfaces that would make great mark-making studies. The puffballs – *Lycoperdon* – are edible when young, pale-coloured and fresh. Their Latin name is funny; *Lycoperdon* means 'wolf fart'!

Calvatia gigantea lives up to its common name of giant puffball as a fruiting body can be huge, up to 85cm (33½in) in some cases! The apt Latin name refers to its likeness to a skull.

Earthballs – *Scleroderma* – are a more golden, brownish colour. They look a little bit like a truffle but grow above the ground and are poisonous. If you cut them open, they will be very dark inside. Common earthballs – *Scleroderma citrinum* – can sometimes be found with a parasitic *Boletus* partner sprouting from them called *Pseudoboletus parasiticus*. It's supposed to be quite an uncommon species but I've come across it a few times in broad-leaved woodland.

Stalkballs, of which *Tulostoma brumale* is the most common in the UK, are just as the name implies – little puffballs on stalks and can be found growing in moss in dune slacks and sandy habitats.

Bird's nest fungi – *Crucibulum* spp. and ***Cyathus* spp.** look just as the name implies, like little bird's nests with eggs in them. They are very small and found on twigs and dead stems, so they are obviously very easily overlooked. When raindrops hit the eggs or *peridioles*, they are dispersed from the nest and the spores are released. To illustrate them, magnification is needed, and the addition of a scale bar will communicate how small they are to the viewer. You can add a x magnification factor, in the illustration it is 3x lifesize. If the image is to be reproduced, a scale bar is best used because it changes along with the size of the image.

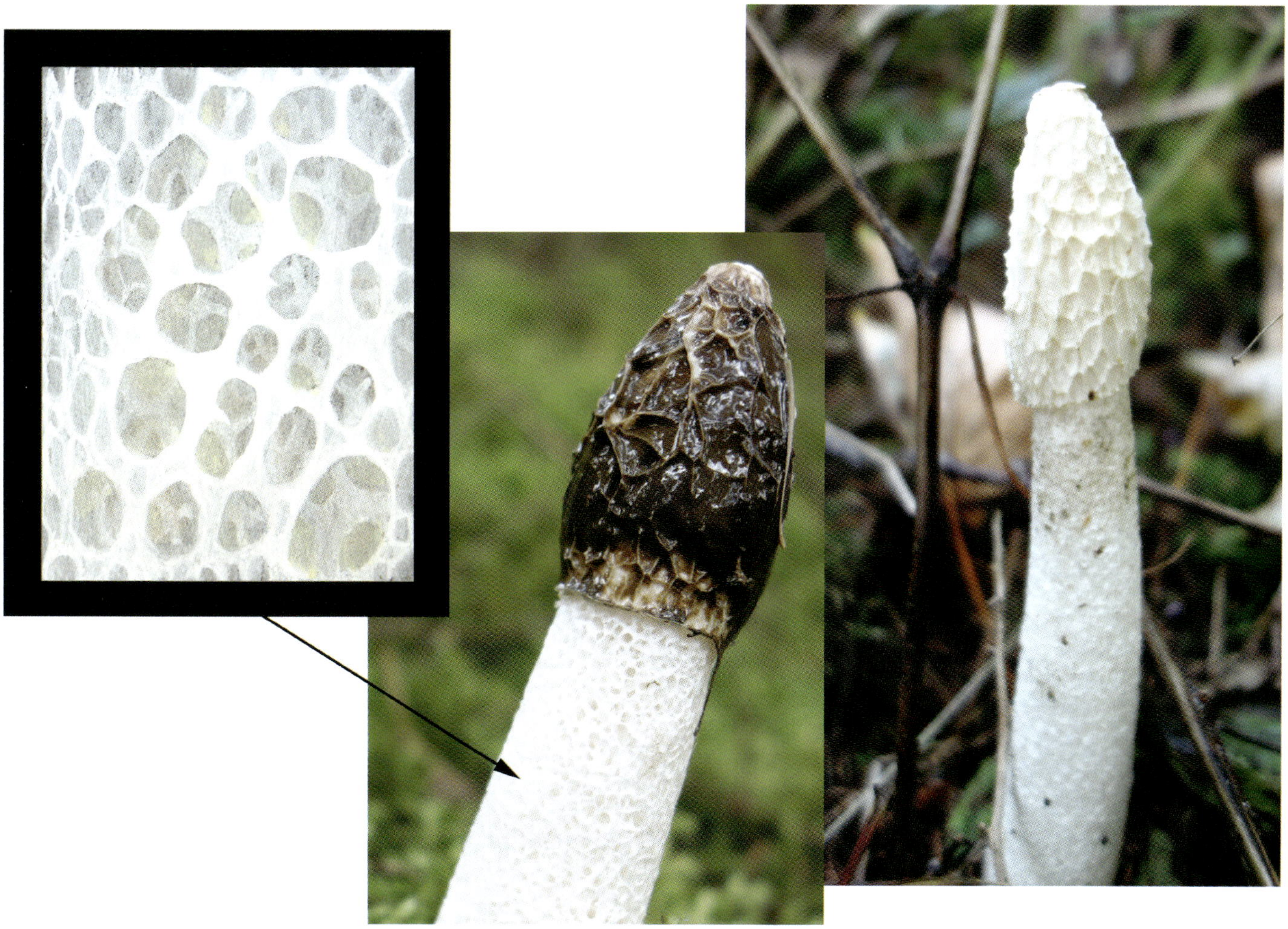

Common stinkhorn – *Phallus impudicus*, the Stinkhorn on the right has lost its dark coating of *gleba*, seen in the central photo. You can see the strange honeycomb structure here. I have illustrated it using tinted gouache on black paper.

Anemone Stinkhorn – *Aseroe rubra* by Anna Voytsekhovich, who is a scientific illustrator and biologist. This fascinating stinkhorn is quite common in Australia where Anna lives. It is a non-native in North America and southern UK, where it may come up on woodchip mulch. (© Anna Voytsekhovich)

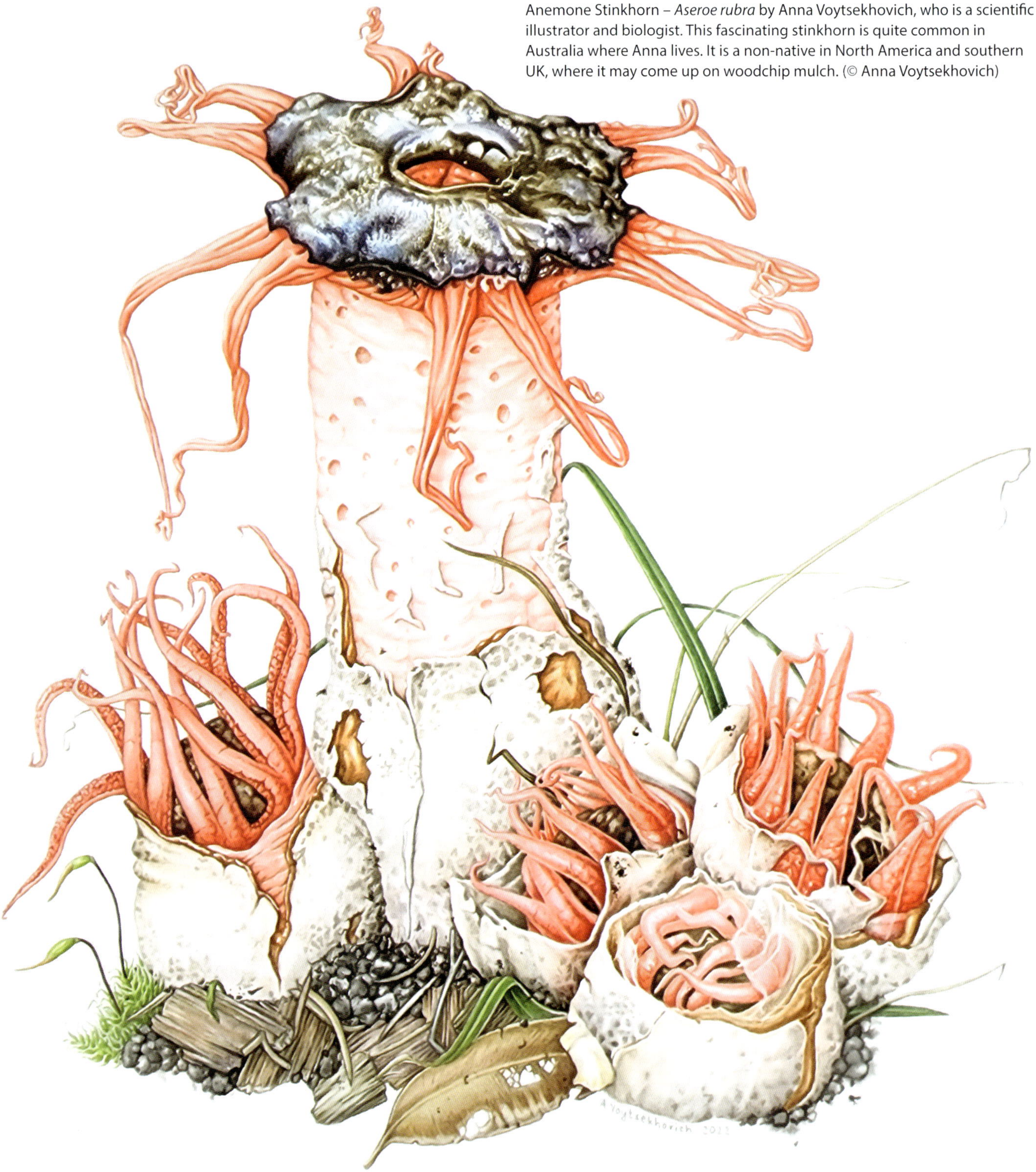

The stinkhorn – *Phallus impudicus*. The stinkhorn is very common in woodlands and is usually smelt before it is seen. It produces a foul-smelling dark-coloured slime at the tip that contains the spores. It has the extremely pungent odour of supposedly rotting meat, which attracts flies that then go on to spread the spores. Not a subject to take back to the studio! The appearance of this phallic subject can cause much sniggering and snorting and as such it was once used as an aphrodisiac and for erectile dysfunction. Their look is a reminder that all fungal fruiting bodies can

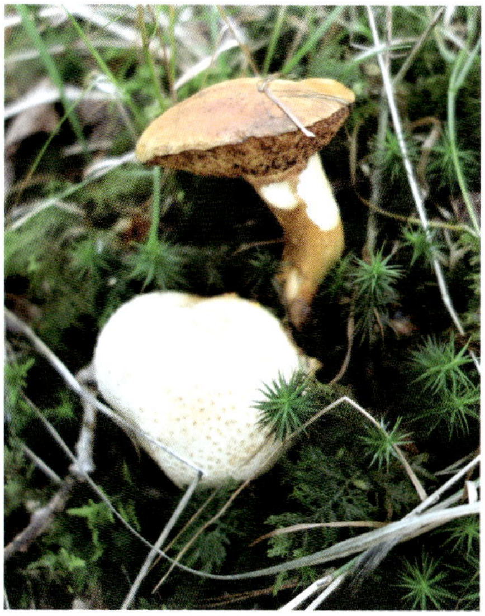

Here is a common earthball – *Scleroderma citrinum* with a parasitic boletus partner called *Pseudoboletus parasiticus* sprouting from it. Experts are not 100 per cent sure as to whether they are completely parasitic on the earthballs or just partners.

be seen as just the sexual organs of the actual mushroom organism itself underneath the ground. They do also have the strange look and texture of polystyrene, with a honeycomb structure, which could be good depicted in graphite or pen.

There is another similar fungus called the dog stinkhorn – *Mutinus caninus*. It is not as common or as smelly and also has a smaller and thinner shape.

In the previous mushroom season, I found a very strange stinkhorn called the devil's fingers – *Clathrus archeri* – for the first time in a very good waxcap site, but unfortunately before I could draw or photograph it, it had sadly been crushed and destroyed. It has around six red and black arched fingers that protrude from an egg and an unpleasant smell.

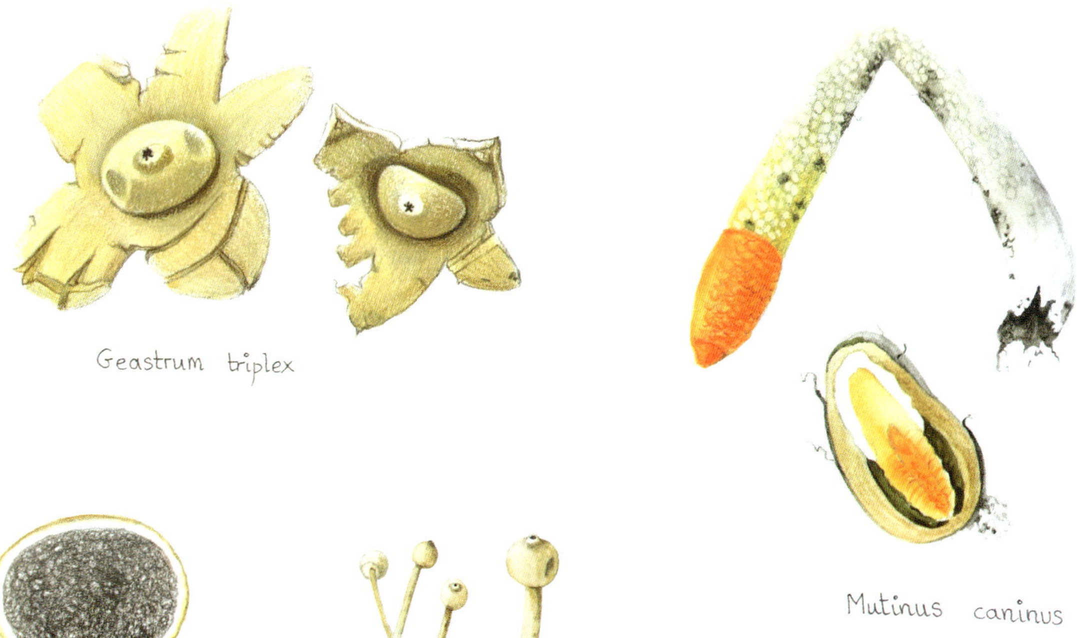

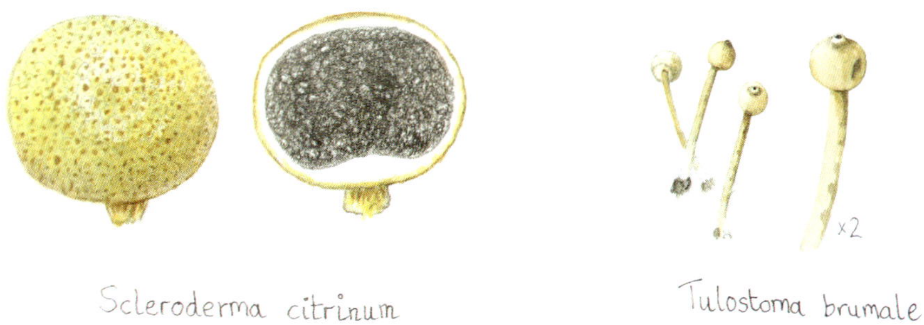

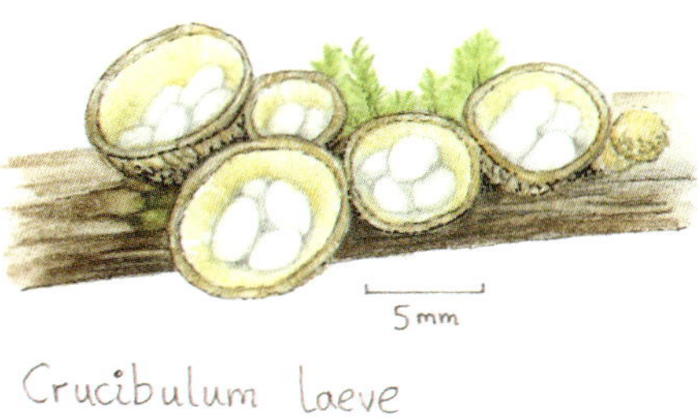

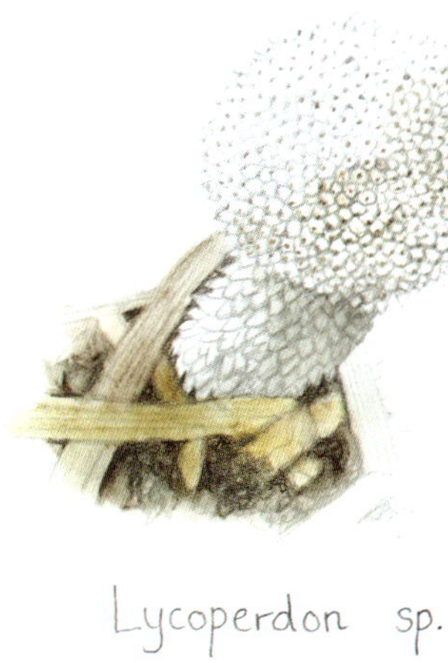

Study of mixed gasteroid fungi in mixed media – dog stinkhorn and egg cross section – *Mutinus caninus*, common bird's nest fungus – *Crucibulum laeve*, collared earthstar – *Geastrum triplex*, common puffball – *Lycoperdon perlatum*, common earthball – *Scleroderma citrinum* and winter stalkball – *Tulostoma brumale.*

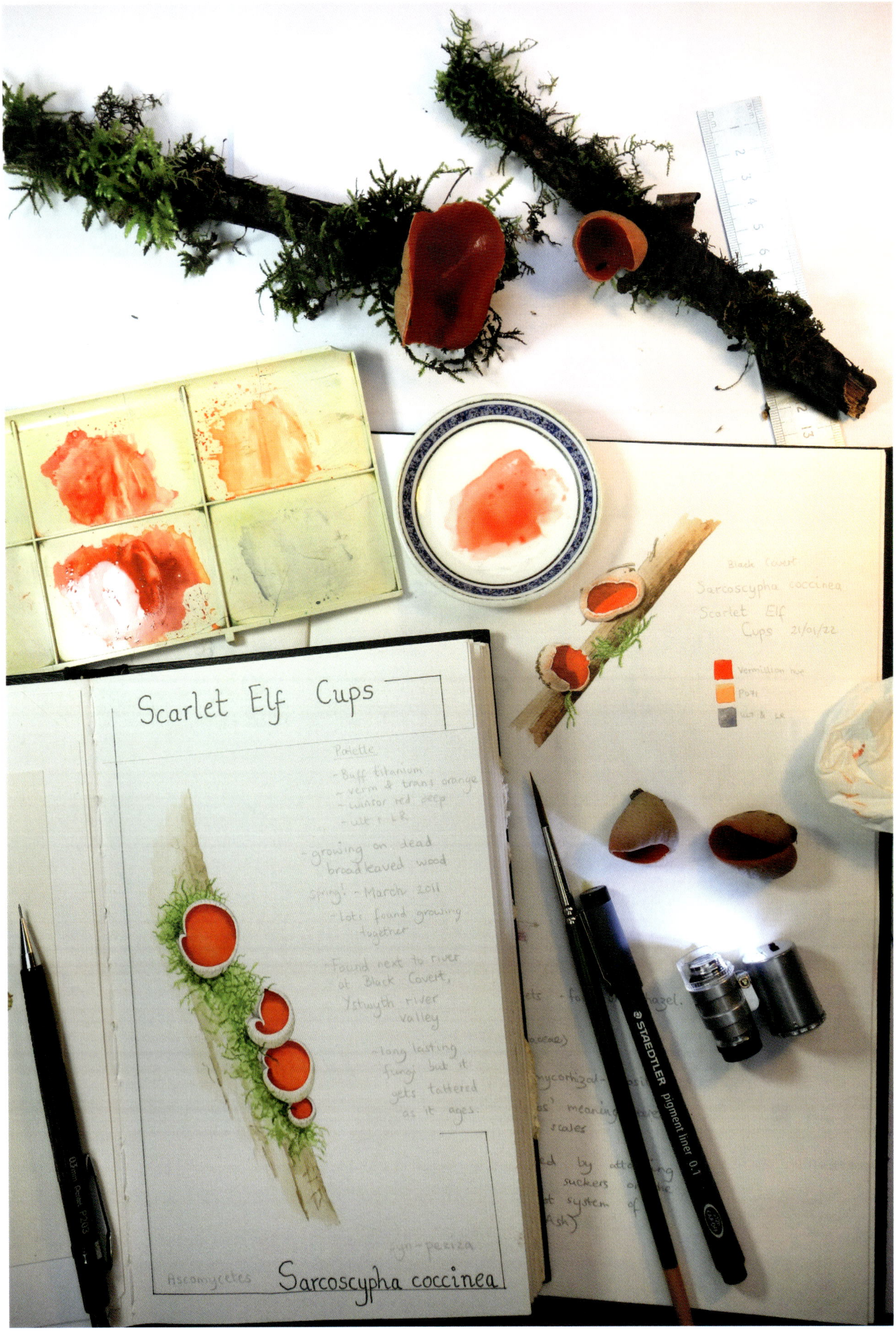
Scarlet Elf Cups
Palette
- Buff titanium
- verm & trans orange
- winsor red deep
- ult + LR
- growing on dead broadleaved wood
spring! - March 2011
- lots found growing together
- Found next to river at Black Covert, Ystwyth river valley
- long lasting fungi but it gets tattered as it ages.
syn - peziza
Ascomycetes
Sarcoscypha coccinea
Black Covert
Sarcoscypha coccinea
Scarlet Elf Cups 21/01/22
Vermillion hue
STAEDTLER pigment liner 0.1

CHAPTER 9

ASCOMYCETES – THE 'CUP' AND 'SAC' FUNGI

The Ascomycota group of fungi is the largest division in the Kingdom with over 60,000 species. Many fungi in this group are known as the 'sac' and 'cup' fungi as one of their main characteristics is that their spores called *ascospores*, are formed within a sac-like structure or *ascus*. This word comes from the Greek and means wineskin or sac. Many ascomycetes increase their reproductive chances by having an asexual stage where they produce *conidia*, which are asexual spores, as well as the sexual stage that produces the ascospores. Some are purely asexual and do not produce ascospores at all. Many of the cup fungi, such as *Peziza* spp. and *Scutellinia* spp. produce ballistospores, which are fired out of the *ascus* into the air to be spread by the wind. They are the 'spore-shooters' and if studied closely, spores can often be seen in a cloud above the fruit body.

Most ascomycetes are miniscule and so very easily overlooked, often only noticed as little black dots, moulds or teeny tiny cups on decaying stems, leaves and other organic matter. Many are pathogens of plants and animals such as mildews, Dutch elm disease, ash dieback, ergot and *Aspergillus* spp. but they are also the fungi associated with foods, fermenting and brewing, such as baker's yeasts, those expensive truffles, the strange forms of morels and the antibiotic penicillin. Also, the fungal partners in most lichen species belong to this group of fungi. Many ascomycetes have curious lifecycles that make fascinating journal study pages.

ASCOMYCETES

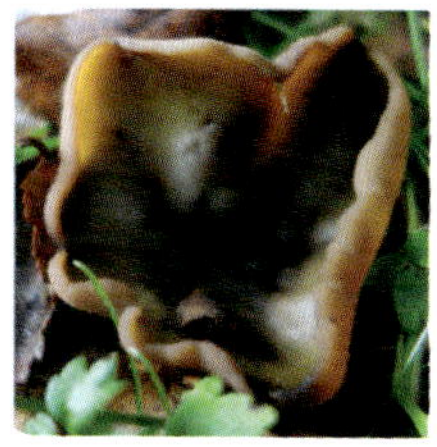

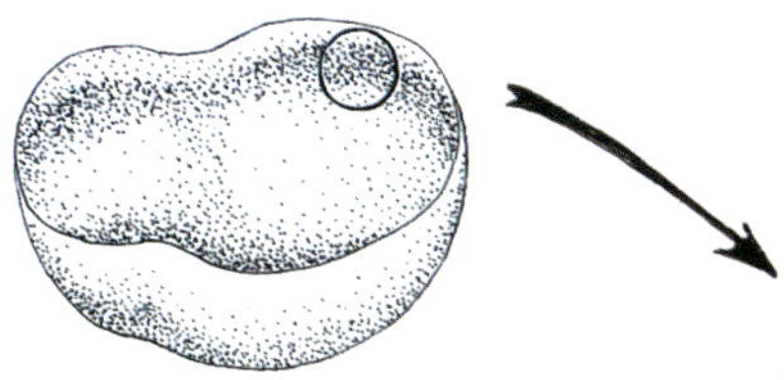

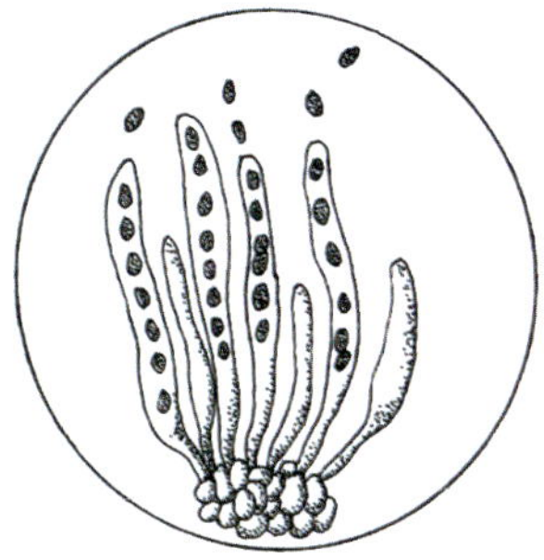

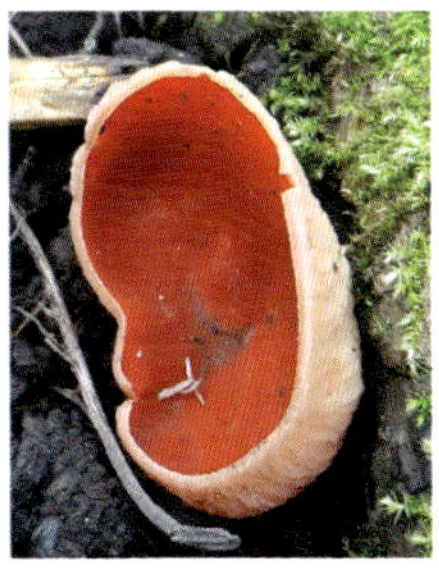

ASCI - Spore sac

Diagram showing the characteristics of a cup fungi, one of the higher ascomycetes within this group of fungi. The spores are formed within the *ascus* in groups of eight and are ejected forcibly up and out into the air.

Studying scarlet elf cups – *Sarcoscypha* sp, colourful little ascomycete cup fungi that are found in late winter and early spring.

STEP-BY-STEP: MOREL IN WATER-SOLUBLE GRAPHITE

The morel – *Morchella* spp. – Morels are renowned as a delicacy of the mushroom world; I've never actually tried one, but people tell me that they taste good. They are poisonous when raw so do have to be cooked well. In the UK, morels are not found very often, fruiting erratically in the springtime and preferring a more calcareous soil such as chalk or limestone. They have been known to pop up in peoples' gardens happily growing on woodchip and apparently, they can also be found growing near burnt areas such as old bonfires. They have a strange pitted, honeycomb-like appearance, an interesting subject for illustrating if you can find one. For the step by step here I took inspiration from (but not copying) photographs from Pixabay, the copyright free photo website, as I have never found them growing; my last mission in spring to find them was unfruitful. I would prefer to use my own photographs but sometimes needs must!

I was originally going to try drawing this species in charcoal but felt that I wouldn't be able to get the fine detail that I wanted unless I supersized it so, I decided on water-soluble graphite for the morel itself. I used an Inktense block from Derwent for the background as it is permanent and so you can achieve a flat and even effect after a few layers. You could just as easily use a black gouache, or acrylic gouache which is permanent or watercolour paint in layers instead.

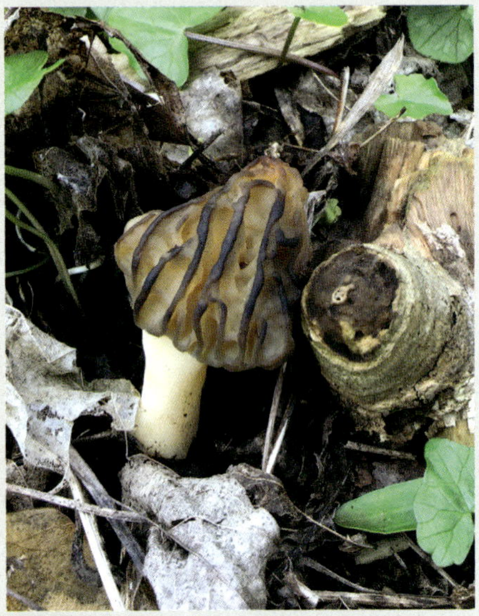

I did actually find a species of small morel in England the following spring, the semi free morel – *Morchella/Mitrophora semilibera*. You can see the pitted, honeycomb structure and if you cut it open it would be half attached to the cap, whereas other morels have larger caps that are hollow inside. False morels – *Gyromitra esculenta*, have more of a brain-like, lobed structure and are not hollow.

MATERIALS USED:

- Arches 140lb hot press watercolour paper
- Frisk masking film on a roll
- Low-tack artist's masking tape
- Sheet of glassine paper
- Plexiglass sheet
- Large mop brush
- Small size 1 brush
- Masquepen masking fluid
- Warm black Derwent Inktense block
- Faber-Castell water-soluble graphite – HB, 2B, 4B, 6B and 8B

1

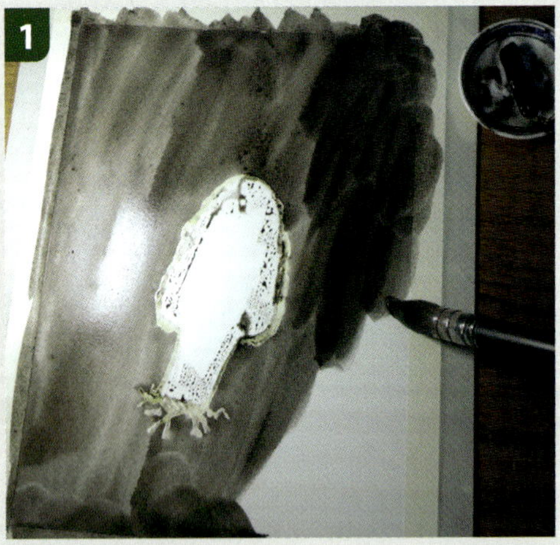

The paper was taped down to the plexiglass, the subject's outline was drawn out and then masked out with some Frisk film that was cut out to just under the size of the subject and stuck down – the film uses a low-tack adhesive. Then I outlined the actual outlines with masking fluid as the paint will find its way underneath the Frisk film without it.

2

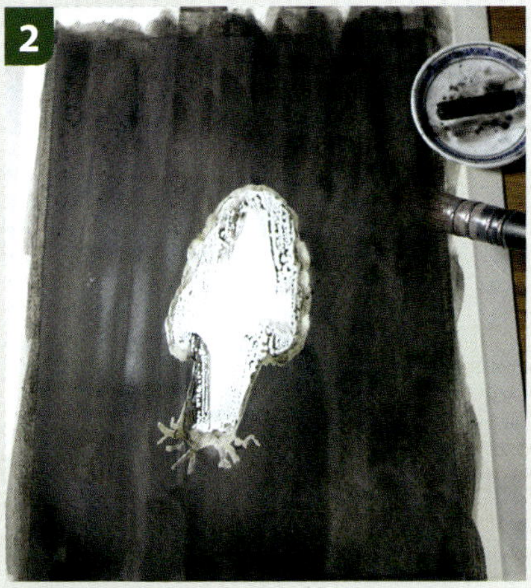

The background was added using the black Inktense block as if it was a pan of watercolour and washed on quickly with a large mop brush and allowed to dry. It's important to lay it down as quickly as possible to avoid any hard lines forming and to keep it blended. Normal watercolour or gouache paint could just as easily be used instead. I did not use graphite for the background as it gives quite a distracting shiny look.

3

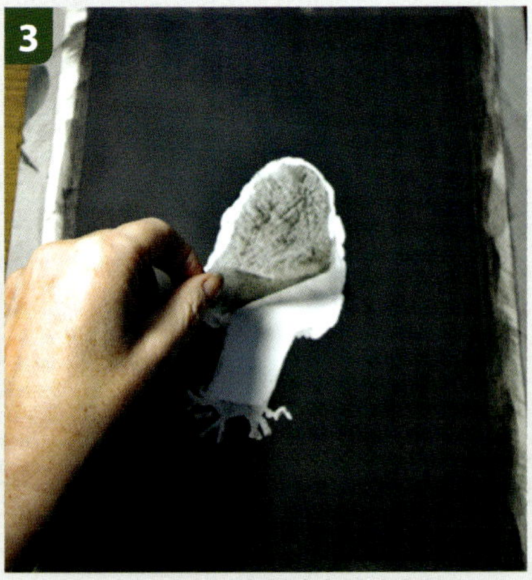

After three layers, I was happy with the finish so I carefully peeled the mask off. I could've added further layers if I'd wanted but felt it was smooth and strong enough.

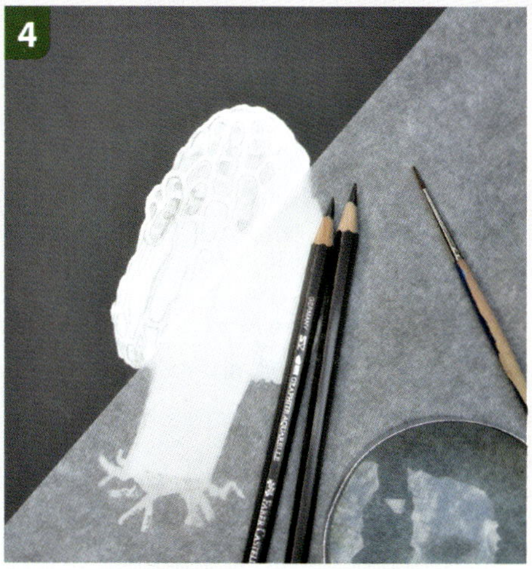

I put a sheet of glassine paper under my hand to protect the paper and started drawing in the details of the morel with the HB graphite. It has an amazing honeycomb-like structure with recesses that I carved out using the palest tones.

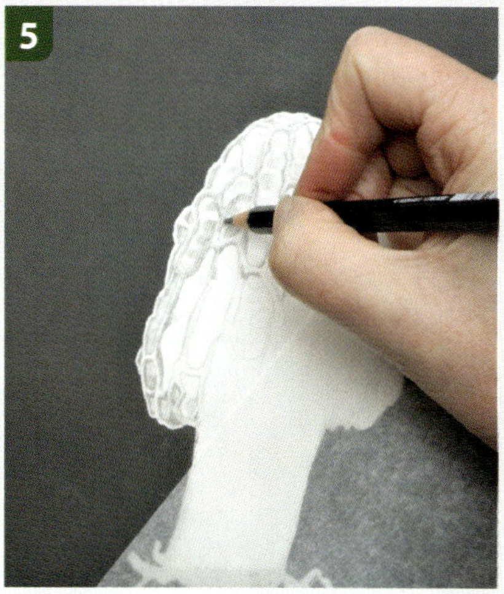

Here I am adding the more textured edges to the recesses and saving some highlights along their edges.

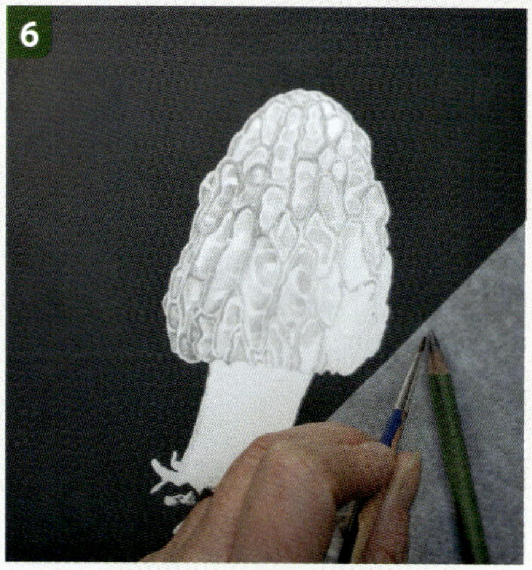

I added tone from the tip of the pencil using a damp paintbrush rather than drawing on with the pencil in some of the paler areas. When adding the graphite with a brush you can gain a smoother wash. If you want more of a textured look then draw on with the pencil and don't blend out with water and brush. Adding the graphite with water also makes the graphite look more matt but harder to erase as it has absorbed into the core of the paper.

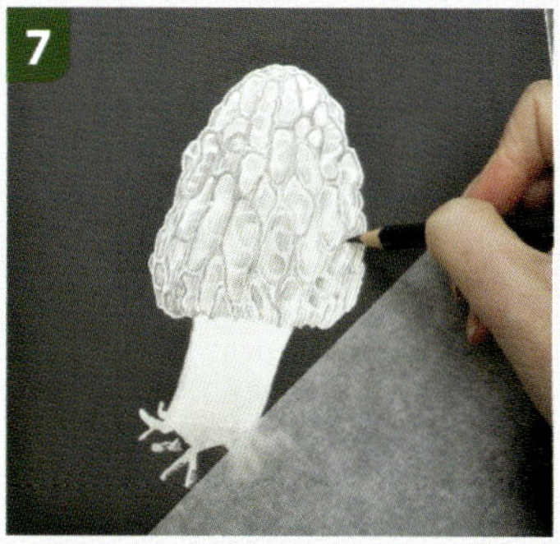

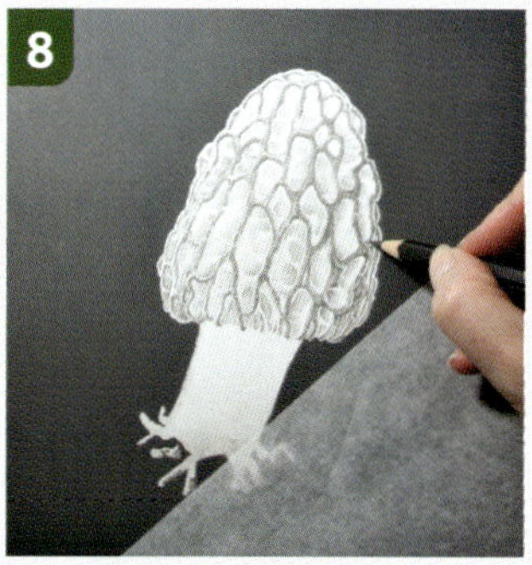

The tones are increased gradually using the 2B, 4B and 6B pencils. It's important to keep the pencils sharp and I used a small piece of fine grade sandpaper to do this.

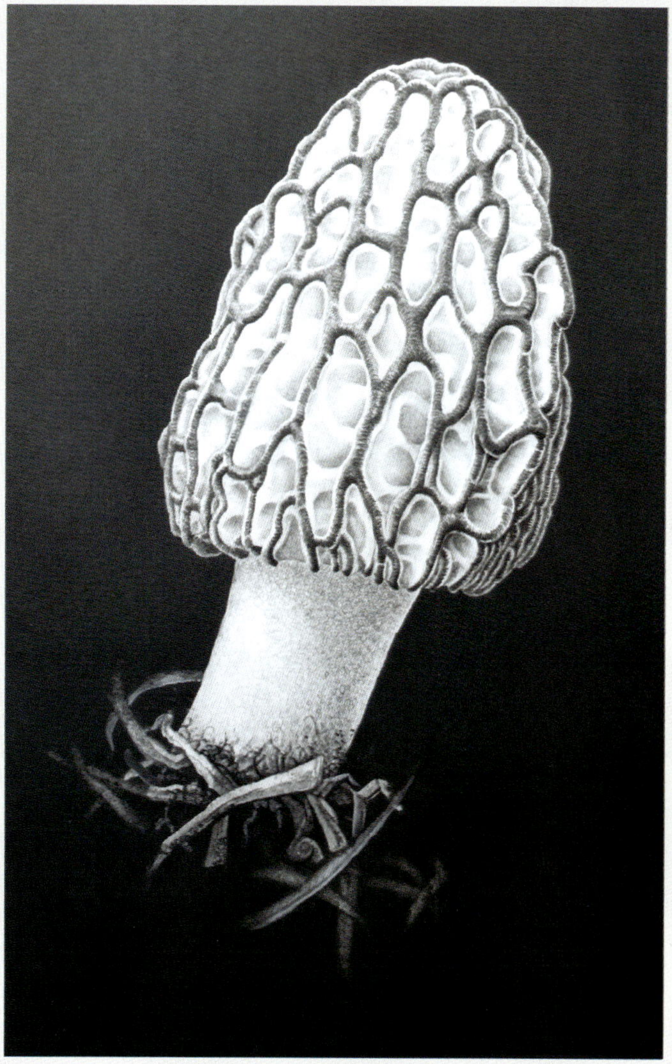

Last stage. The final tones are added last with the darkest 8B pencil and touches of the black Inktense block painted on. Then, the stipe is added with shading textures and at the base some grasses and woody debris are hinted at. Some pale tones there were erased out gently with a tough ink eraser and also a little added white gouache.

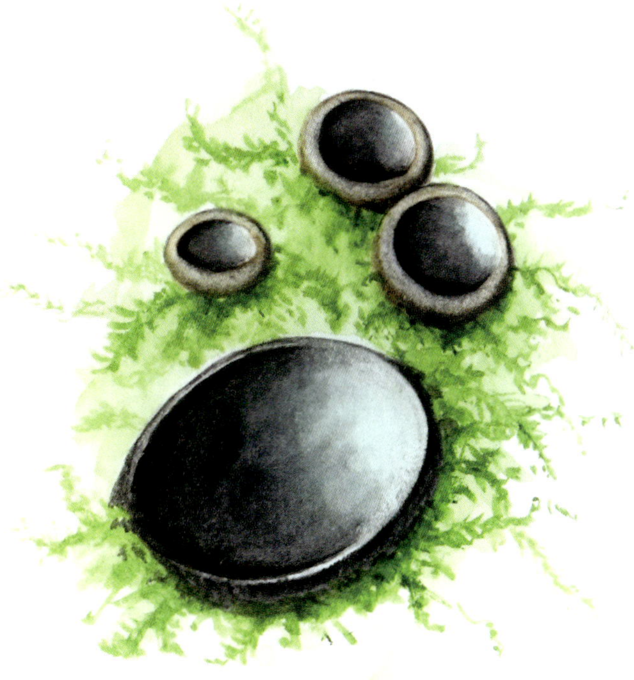

There are many cup fungi species of assorted colours. One is Black Bulgar – *Bulgaria inquinans*, also known as Black Jelly Drops and they really do look like gummy sweets or even liquorice. It can be found growing on fallen hardwood trees such as beech. The sheen is painted in blue, a reflection of the sky.

Earthtongues – *Geoglossum/Microglossum/Trichoglossum* spp. are equally strange little fungi, some looking like small spoons or tiny black lollipops. They are often seen in grasslands, meadows, graveyards and along verges and in the UK their presence is a good sign of grassland with a rich mycoflora; they are one of the CHEG species used to assess the biodiversity of grasslands. Their colours can be black, brown or green, and they can be long, thin and grow to around 4–6cm (1–3in).

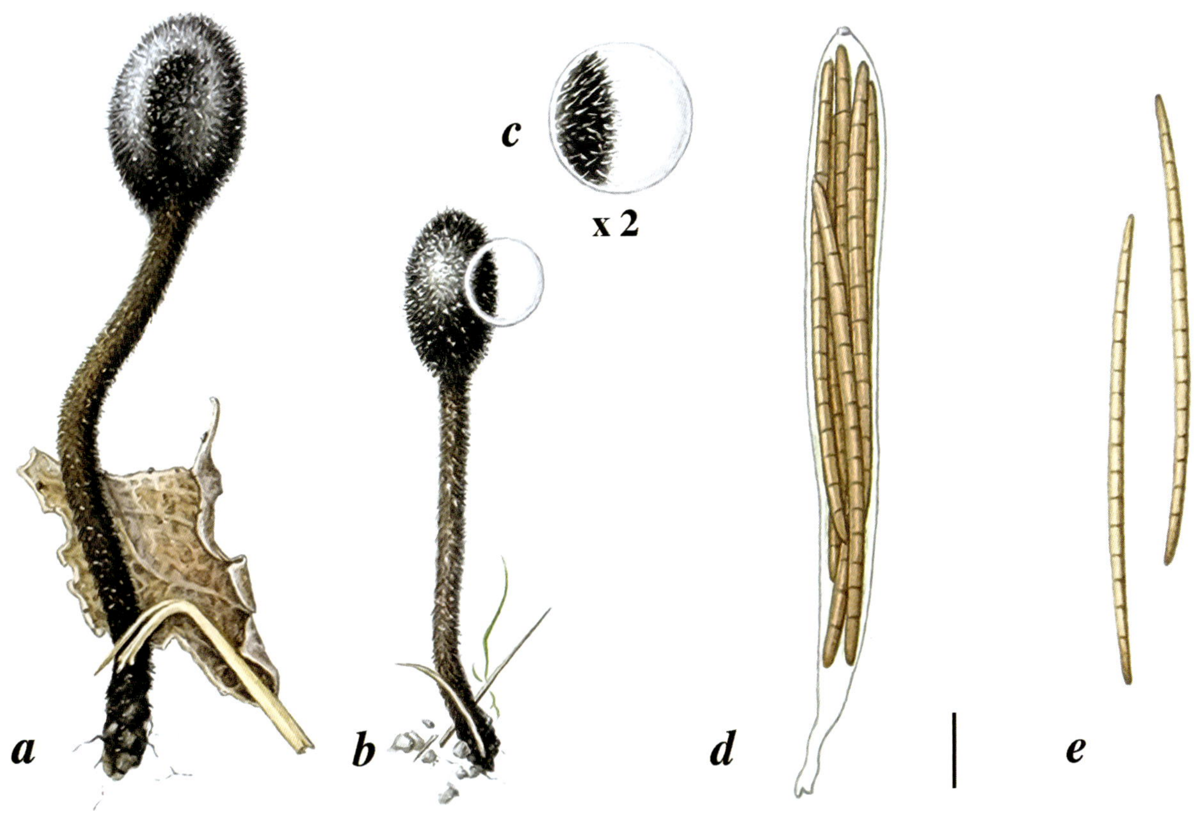

Hairy Earthtongue – *Trichoglossum hirsutum* by Anna Voytsekhovich. a – mature fruit body (ascocarp), b – young fruit body, c – magnified detail of densely setose surface (bristled), d – ascus (spore sac with eight spores), e – released ascospores (brown, 15-septate). Scale bar: a,b -20mm, d,e -20μm. (© Anna Voytsekhovich)

FOCUS STUDY: EXPERIMENTS WITH SHADING

Shading is one area that can often be difficult for beginners; a lot of students have told me that they struggle with this aspect of natural history illustration. But it all comes with experience and experimentation. So, I wanted to experiment with different shading techniques on the vibrant scarlet elf cup fungi – *Sarcoscypha* sp. in my sketchbook.

In the UK, scarlet elf cup – *Sarcoscypha austriaca* – and ruby elf cup – *Sarcoscypha coccinea* – are the commoner species but there are other very similar ones and possibly as many as twenty-eight species in the genus worldwide. These bright little cups can only confidently be told apart using a microscope to study the spores. They are found in late winter to early spring on deciduous hardwood twigs and wood like hazel, willow and sycamore often amongst lots of damp-loving moss. I always find them quite commonly in local woodlands every spring.

MATERIALS USED:

- Seawhite's of Brighton A4 sketchbook
- 2H Faber-Castell 9000 graphite pencil
- Small tortillion
- Ultramarine Finest and Transparent Orange (PO71 – Schmincke), Winsor Red (PR254) and Light Red (PR102 by Winsor & Newton), Vermillion Hue (PR255 by Daler Rowney)

Row 1. I drew out the four elf cup images into four squares in my sketchbook; if you try this, you may want to use actual watercolour paper, but the washes are so small that I didn't find any issues. Then in each square I tried different shading methods to see how they compared. The first row in the image used an underlayer shading technique called *Grisaille*, from the French word for grey. It is a good way of mapping out tonal areas and shadows using grey and neutral mixes before you begin to add colour. I have found it a valuable technique for yellow subjects using a pale violet underlay and for brown, a darker violet can be used (seen in Chapter 7 on the Pepper Bolete).

The grey shadow colour that I used was a mix of Ultramarine Finest and Light Red. When it was dry, I painted on a scarlet red mix of Vermillion Hue and Transparent Orange, very carefully so as not to lift the underlayer, so vital for a clean look.

Row 2. Here I painted on the scarlet mix first and allowed it to dry, then added the same shadow colour in Row 1 over the top. In the image you can see that both these methods have given a very strong shadow, but this can be paler with a less concentrated mix if wanted – so many variables!

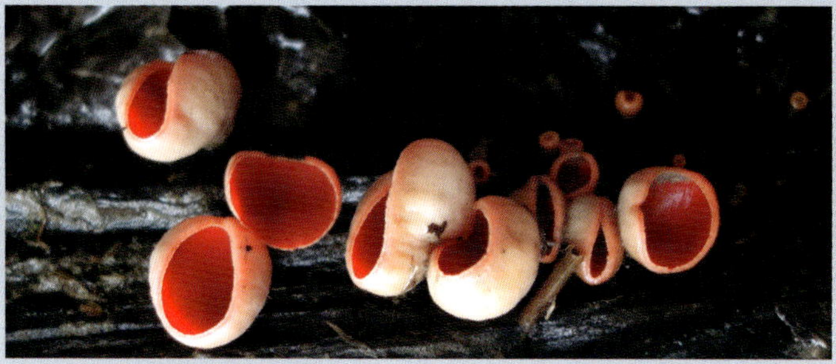

Spring Elf-cups by a stream.

Row 3. In this row I used analogous shading with the darker, cooler hue of Winsor Red to shade the cup. This has given a more delicate shadow effect, but it can be more defined using a wet on dry technique and a deeper red, perhaps with a touch of Ultramarine added or give a softer effect when added wet into wet and blended out.

Row 4. Here I used *Grisaille* again, this time with a 2H graphite pencil that has been blended smooth with a tortillion before the scarlet mix is painted on. It can be a subtle way to shade for a less confident painter. Another method of shading would be with pen and wash, adding the shadow tones on with pen stippling and then adding the red wash on top.

So, to sum up, there are various techniques for shading, each one with a similar look, give or take the concentrations of pigment; it just proves that there is never just one way of working and no way is wrong or right, just personal preference.

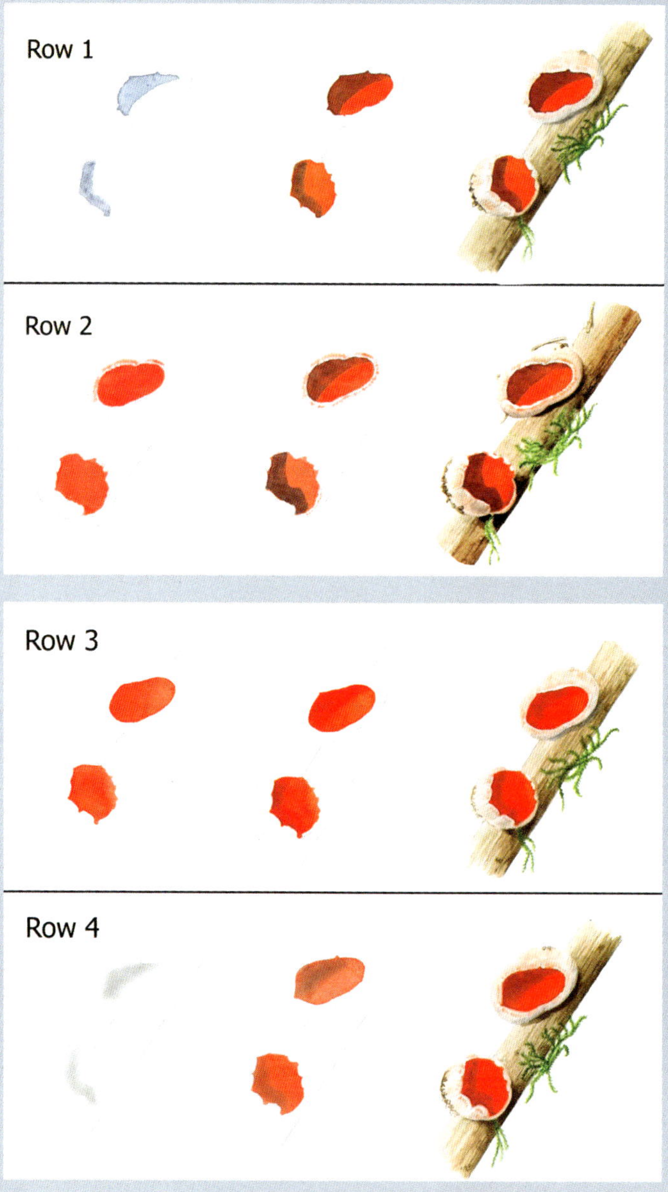

Eyelash fungus – *Scutellinia* spp. These tiny but beautiful and brightly coloured fungi contain many very similar looking species, around thirty, but you'd need a microscope to identify them to species level confidently. They are called eyelash fungi due to the hairs that surround the disc-shaped fruitbody. They are very common around the world but being so small they're easy to miss. You can find them on any type of rotting wood and also the dung of animals such as cows and horses.

Scarlet caterpillar club – *Cordyceps militaris*, a strange, bright orange fungus that parasitises insects buried in the soil, usually in grasslands. It forms a small fruit body about 3–4 cm (1in) long. This species looks good with a hand lens as there is an interesting texture to its surface. Another similar species found in tropical forests that most people will be familiar with now, is *Ophiocordyceps*, a parasitic fungus that dominates its insect hosts body and turns it 'zombie', making it climb up high before bursting alien-like from its head to release its spores.

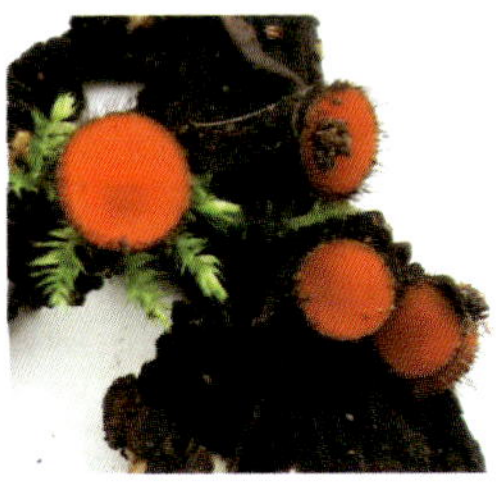

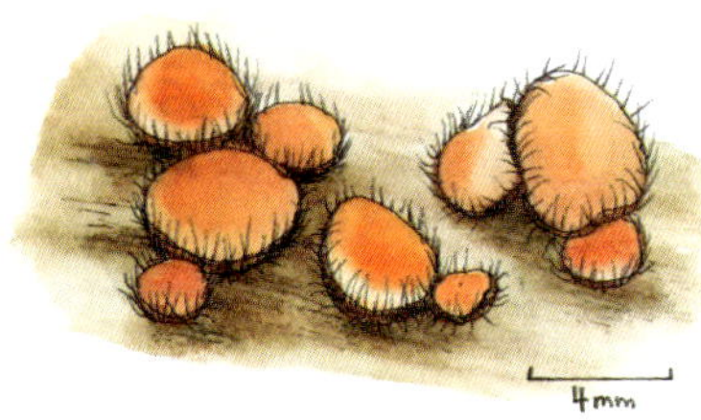

Eyelash fungus *Scutellinia* sp. is tiny but perfectly formed, the fruitbodies are usually at the most 4mm across and illustrating these species certainly needs magnification and a scale bar to give information on their actual size. In this illustration they are magnified by five times.

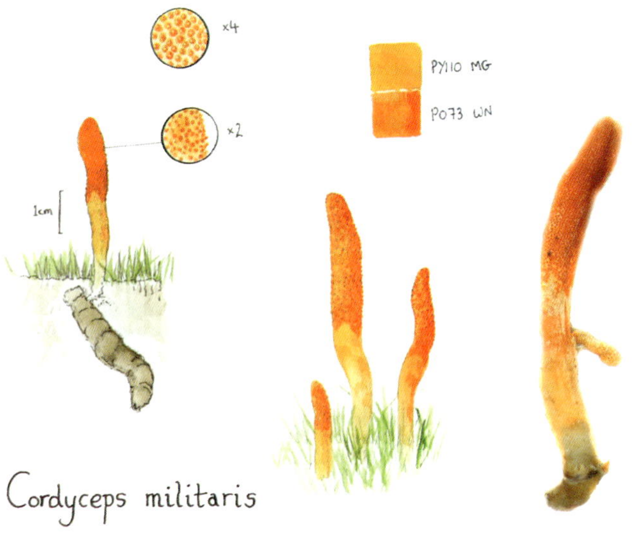

Scarlet Caterpillar Club quick sketchbook study – with magnification. The top of the fruit body, called the stroma is covered with tiny pimples or cones called perithecia that release the spores. In the picture you can see the underground insect, which is usually a caterpillar or other insect larva or pupa. To the right is an actual specimen enlarged.

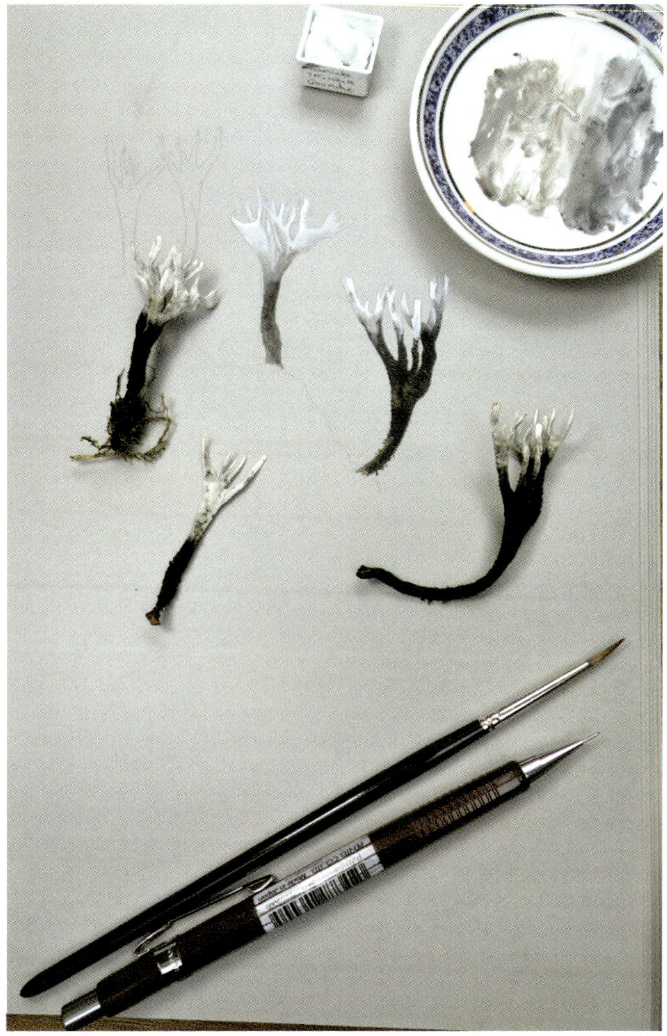

This *Xylaria* sketch is in the Stilman and Birn Nova grey paper sketchbook using white gouache, Neutral Tint and Sepia watercolours by Winsor & Newton. White gouache can give a cool, blue tone so a little underlayer of Sepia warms it up a little.

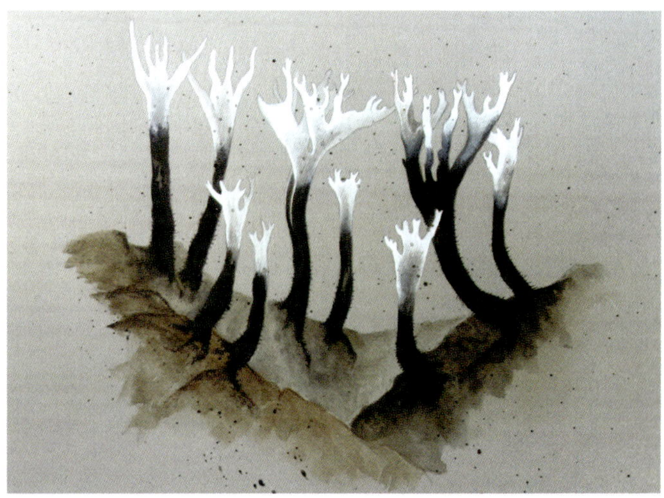

Xylaria hypoxylon study finished with a little splatter of paint. The white gouache is perfect for giving that powdery look to their tops, and some black pen details are added to give the lower fruit body its fuzzy look. Several coats of gouache are needed for the whitest parts as gouache always fades and darkens annoyingly when dry.

Species within the *Cordyceps* genus have also been used as medicine by the Chinese for centuries, claiming that they have different health benefits and research is currently being done on this.

Candle snuff fungus – *Xylaria hypoxylon* is a tough little fungus that grows on well-rotted dead wood, looking very much like little black and white antlers. The black lower body has a sooty look and a fuzzy texture and the white coating produces conidia – the asexual spores. All black fruit bodies are the fungus in the sexual stage, not seen very often with this species. The name comes from the Greek word for wood – *xylem* – and this is very much what you'll find this tiny ascomycete growing on.

Other *Xylaria* species include *Xylaria polymorpha* or the aptly named dead man's fingers, which do look remarkably like black and swollen fingers. Not quite so appealing! Throughout the year, it can change colour as it matures, hence the species name of *polymorpha*.

The sycamore tarspot – *Rhytisma acerinum*, is one of the most common and widespread of ascomycete fungi seen in Britain and Ireland and is also seen in Europe and the US. It occurs wherever there are sycamores and maples and where the air is fairly clean – this fungus is particularly sensitive to sulphur dioxide air pollution, so you won't find it close to industrial centres. It is a parasitic fungus, but different in that it doesn't damage its host as it only grows on the leaves.

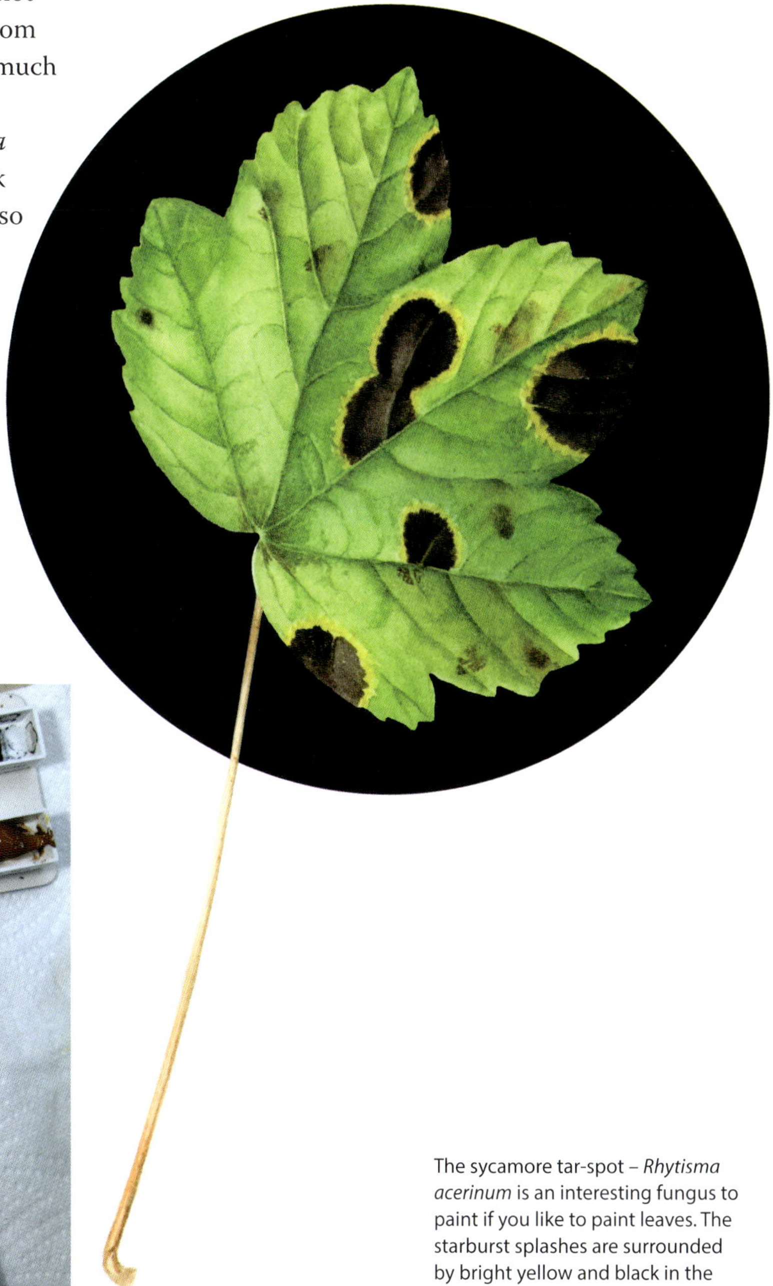

The sycamore tar-spot – *Rhytisma acerinum* is an interesting fungus to paint if you like to paint leaves. The starburst splashes are surrounded by bright yellow and black in the centre – hence the common name. The black is mixed from Indanthrene, Perylene Maroon and Winsor Yellow for a colourful black rather than using a black pigment.

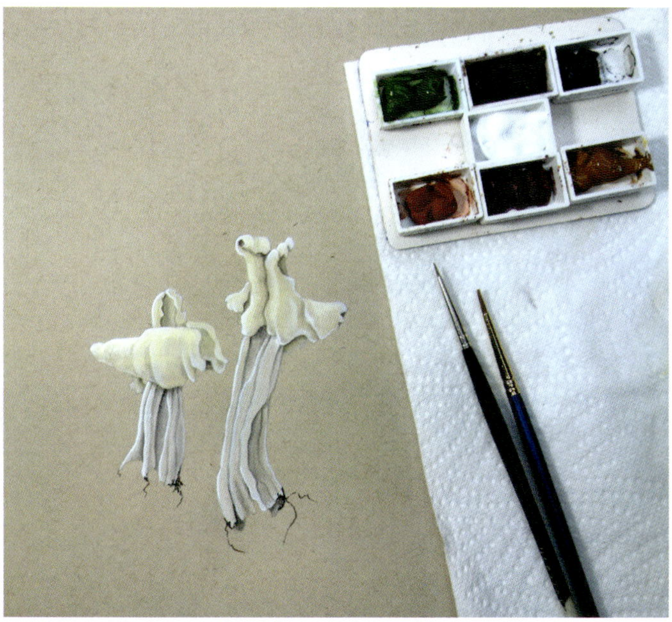

White Saddle – *Helvella crispa*. The elfin saddle fungi are interesting ascocarps that take on a variety of curiously, contorted shapes, some looking a bit like saddles. Here they've been painted on Strathmore toned tan paper using gouache paint.

King Alfred's cakes or cramp balls are the common names of *Daldinia concentrica,* an inconspicuous black fungus that grows on broad-leaved trees, especially ash and beech. It has no stipe and has spores as black as soot that turn the fruiting body black and rather like something burnt (such as King Alfred's reputedly burnt cakes!).

The species name of *concentrica* refers to the silvery growth rings inside its body that grow over several seasons. The rings don't show yearly growth cycles like trees, just seasons of growth, as they may not sporulate if conditions are not right. They were called cramp balls as it was once thought that they could stop any attacks of cramp from happening if you kept them with you! Also once used as a firestarter, and for burning like charcoal, and they do look like lumps of charcoal.

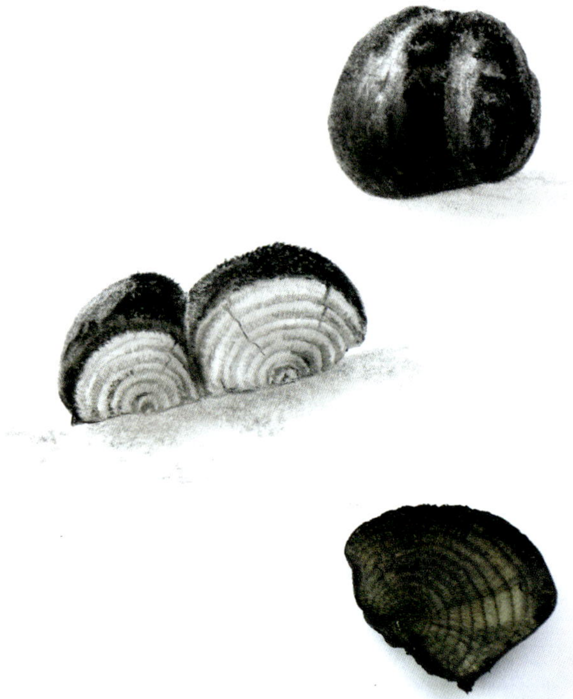

Cramp balls – *Daldinia concentrica,* one whole and one cut in half to show the concentric rings. The inside had a pale sheen to it so was executed in graphite but the exteriors were coated with a layer of very sooty looking, black spores, perfect to be described using charcoal. To the lower right is an actual specimen.

Ergot – *Claviceps purpurea,* the infamous fungus that grows on the inflorescences of different grasses and cereals such as rye. If ergot-contaminated grains are consumed it can cause ergotism which can display some alarming symptoms, including hallucinations, mania, paralysis, and even gangrene and abortion in livestock. In medieval times, it had the common name of 'St. Anthony's Fire', which was named after an order of monks who treated victims of ergotism. Ergot may have possible links with the Salem witch trials and also the Eleusinian Mysteries of Ancient Greece. The active ingredient is lysergic acid and ergotamine, which are precursors of the hallucinogen LSD. There were outbreaks all over Europe and the US mainly in the cooler, wetter summers, which are the funguses' favoured growing conditions. The last outbreak was in 1928 in the UK, in Manchester.

It was also once used to staunch bleeding wounds as it is a powerful vasoconstrictor. Today ergot extract is used to treat some conditions including migraines and to control bleeding after childbirth.

BIGGING UP THE SMALL STUFF – THE MIGHT OF THE MICRO

There are many tiny and so overlooked ascomycete fungi, too small to really be able to study effectively by eye, but through a hand lens or via macro-photography they can come into their own.

Discos – *Lachnum* spp. – grow on woody debris and stems, but you can only capture their miniscule forms through the lens. Take a look at old, decaying plant stems such as rush or bracken stalks with a 10x hand lens to hunt for tiny cup fungi.

The haw goblet – *Monilinia johnsonii* – is a tiny goblet shaped fungi that grows on old hawthorn berries in the undergrowth and soils. It is the sexual stage (*teleomorph* stage) in the lifecycle of a mould that grows on hawthorn leaves in spring when the flowers open. The mould releases a sweet, sharp scent similar to the hawthorn flowers, which attracts insects to disperse the conidia in that asexual stage (*anamorph* stage) of the mould. If you come across any blighted leaves on a hawthorn in May (in the UK), have a sniff of one to smell the scent. So, it isn't just flowers that attract insects with a sweet scent. This is similarly seen in the Ergot fungus described in the section above that uses a sticky honeydew that attracts insects.

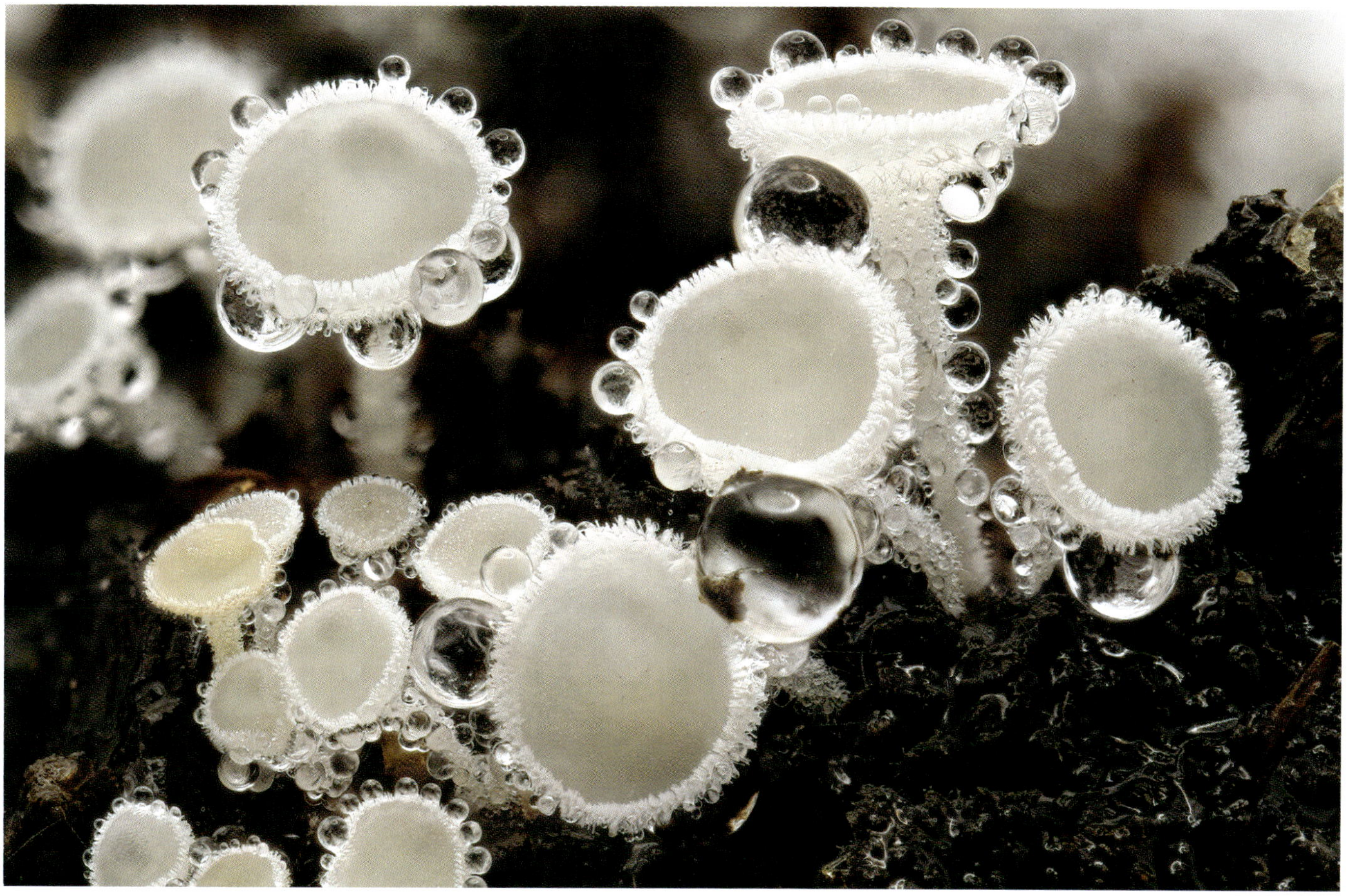

The tiny *Lachnum* sp. on a beech nut seen here in this perfect photo by Steven Murray was taken by a Canon camera with a macro lens and focus tubes. The droplets are liquid given out by the fungus, called *guttation*.

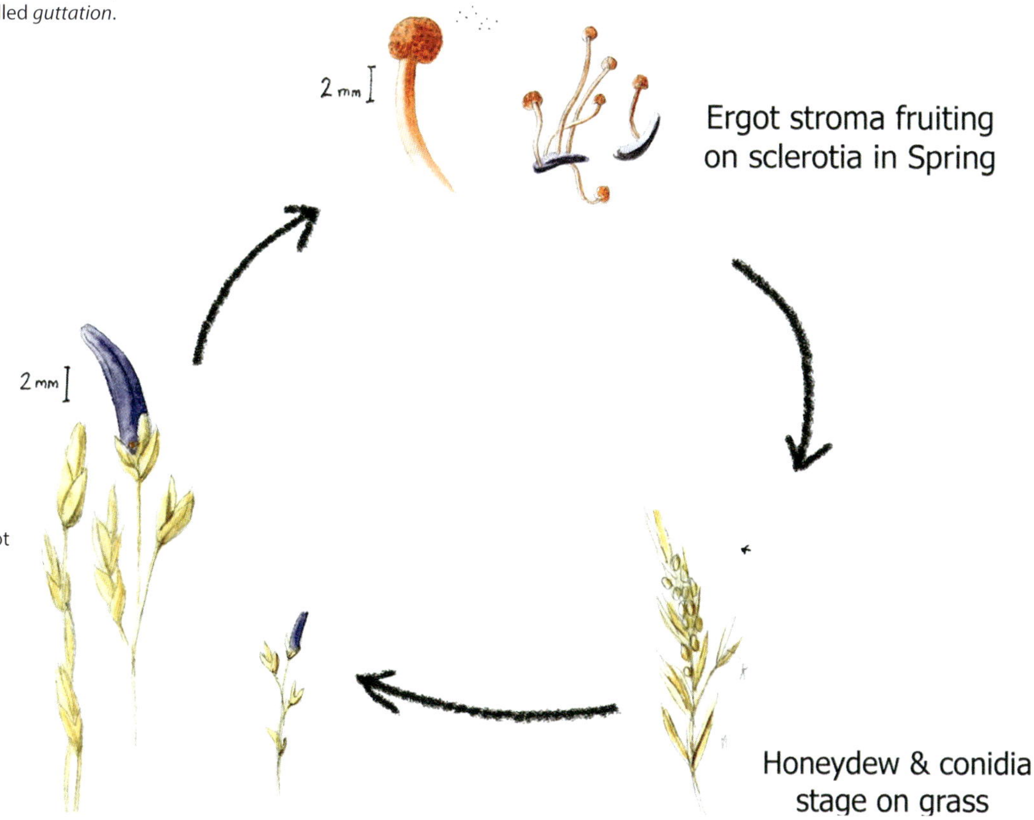

Ergot – *Claviceps purpurea* lifecycle; the elongated, claw-like forms of Ergot sclerotium grow on an infected grass seedhead in autumn, the fruiting bodies appear from sclerotium in spring releasing ascospores to infect grass inflorescences that then produce honeydew and conidia in an asexual stage. Insects transmit the conidia to more flowerheads and the sclerotium form in autumn to repeat the cycle over.

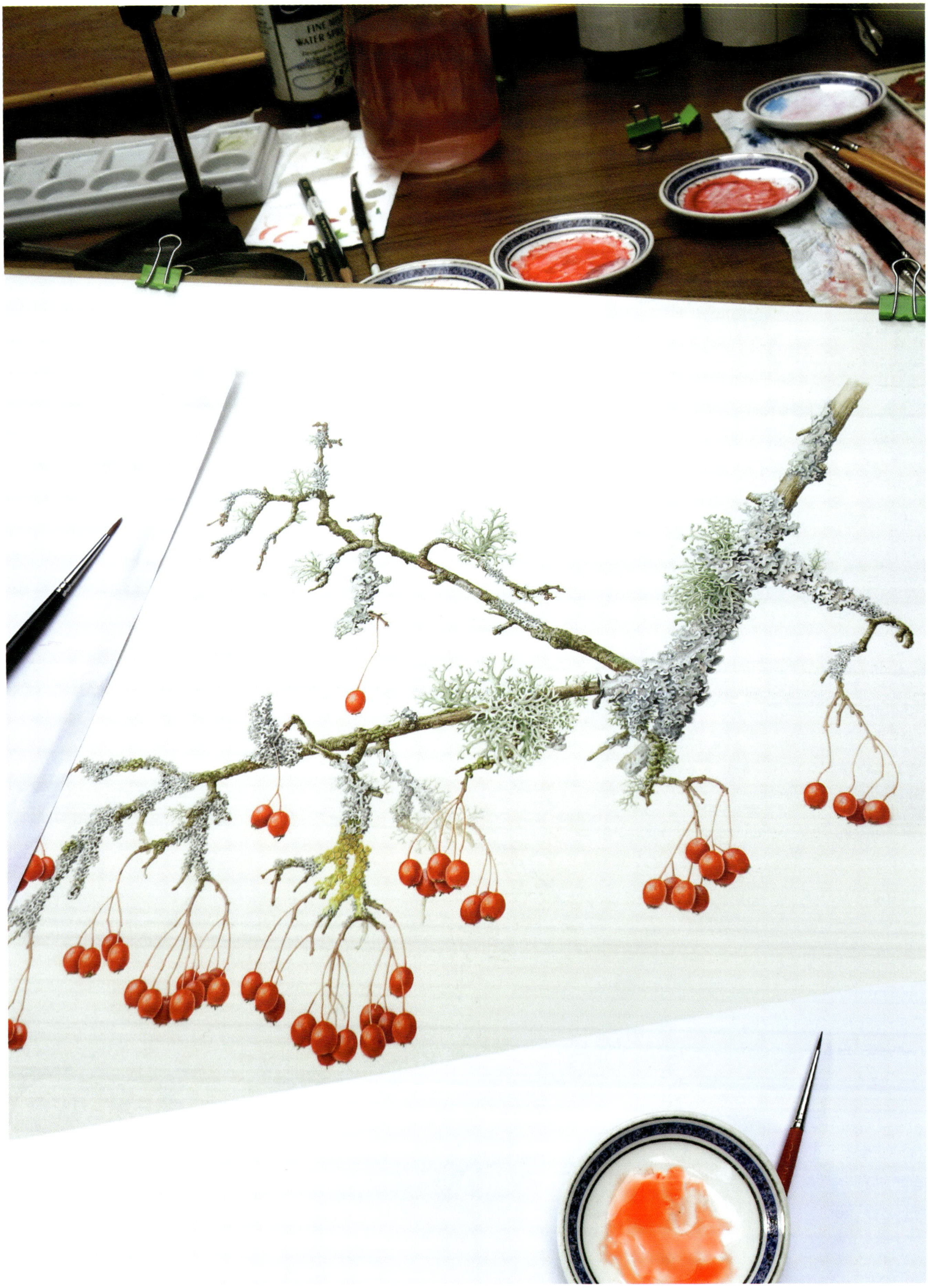

CHAPTER 10

LICHEN

> 'Lichens are fungi that have discovered agriculture.'
> LICHENOLOGIST AND NATURALIST
> TREVOR GOWARD

Lichens are strange and fascinating organisms. They are an example of more than one species living together in a symbiotic relationship, usually between an algae or cyanobacteria, sometimes both, and a fungus (and some species actually contain more than one fungus). The algae or cyanobacteria (the photobionts) in the relationship are photosynthetic, deriving their energy from the sun and they provide sugars to the fungal partner (the mycobiont) and in return the fungus provides water and minerals as well as providing a home that can give protection against desiccation and sun damage. This gives them the capacity to live in some of the harshest of environments on the planet, including polar regions and semi-desert. They are known as colonisers as they can grow on bare rock and other similar substrates where other species would struggle to survive. And they are also key to essential processes within the environment including the formation of soil, that then allows other species to take hold.

In the UK there are approximately 1,700 species, in the USA around 3,600 with 20,000 + worldwide; and as with fungi, there must be many more that are unrecorded. The oldest fossil of a lichen dates from the Devonian period, 400 million years ago and was found in the fascinating, volcanic fossil beds of the Rhynie Chert rock in Scotland. This place holds many fossil records of the first land plants and fungal hyphae as well as insects and has given us numerous clues to the evolution of species on Earth. At the time that the fossils were preserved there, Scotland was situated close to the equator in the large landmass that was called Laurussia, grouped together with North America, northern Europe and Greenland.

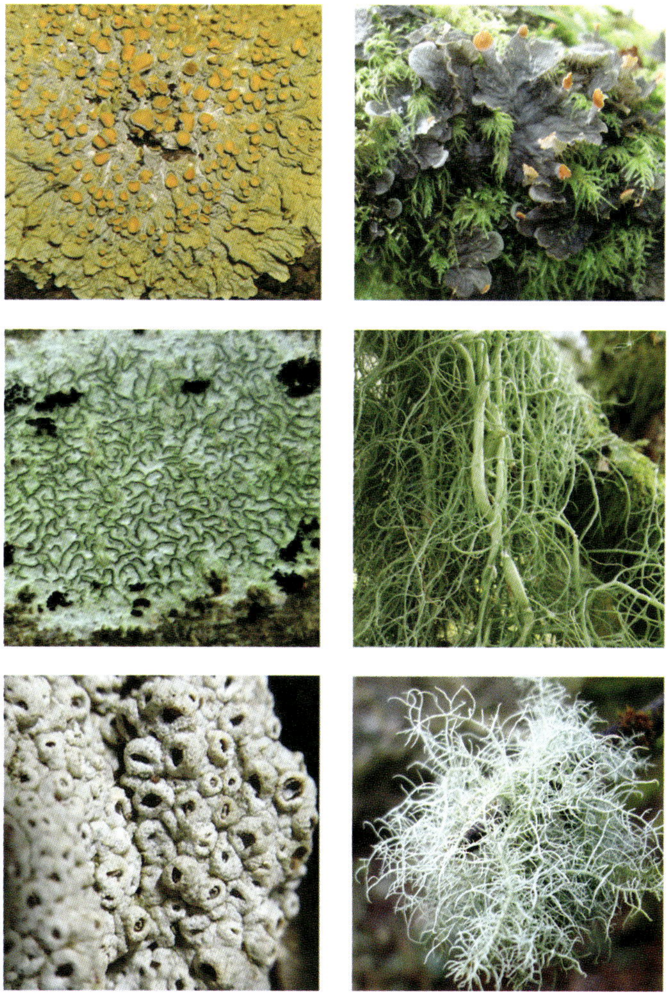

The wonderful diversity of lichen form. Clockwise top left: *Xanthoria* sp, *Peltigera* sp, *Usnea articulata, Usnea subfloridana, Thelotrema lepadinum and Graphis* sp.

Work in progress of a branch of hawthorn covered in different lichens, including *Evernia prunastri, Parmelia sulcata, Physcia tenella and Xanthoria* sp.

Lichens are also important pollution indicators as many species either die out or thrive in polluted areas and so their absence or existence can be used to monitor this. Sulphur dioxide pollution, increased levels of atmospheric nitrogen oxides and ammonia produced by agriculture and diesel vehicles have reduced many species of lichen that cannot tolerate them, such as species from the *Usnea* genus and *Evernia prunastri*. But there are winners; the bright yellow lichen *Xanthoria parietina* that grows on twigs and rocks flourishes in nitrogen rich environments, so not all lichens are so sensitive to nitrate pollution. Lichens are affected by pH and the nature of the bark or rocky surface upon which they live just as plants are; so calcareous species will colonise base rich bark and rocks such as limestone and cement too. I have heard people, mainly gardeners comment that lichens may damage trees, but this is not the case; they are not parasitic in any way, just purely living upon the bark or twigs as a support.

The fungal partner is usually an ascomycete, and you will see their fruiting bodies on the thallus or body of the lichen or growing from it; each fungal species will have a different fruiting body or apothecia that contains the *asci* where the spores are expelled. Some look like little jam tarts, others like black dots or specks and there are some that look like writing, the so called *lirellate* or script lichens within the *Graphis* genus (among others). Barnacle lichens look like little volcano craters with a central hole. There are a few that fruit with tiny mushroomoid basidiomycete apothecia, but on the whole lichens are mainly comprised of the cup, ascomycete fungi.

Lichens procreate asexually as well by means of tiny pieces of their thallus called *soredia* or *isidia* that break off to form new colonies. *Soredia* are granular in appearance and give lichens their textured forms. *Isidia* are tiny projections that break off from the surface. These fragments contain both the photobionts and the mycobionts that provide greater chances of propagation than by sexual means.

Many lichens grow very slowly, some as slow as a millimetre a year, and therefore take many years to grow to any size. Some are so small within their niches that we pass by without noticing them at all. But it's worth taking

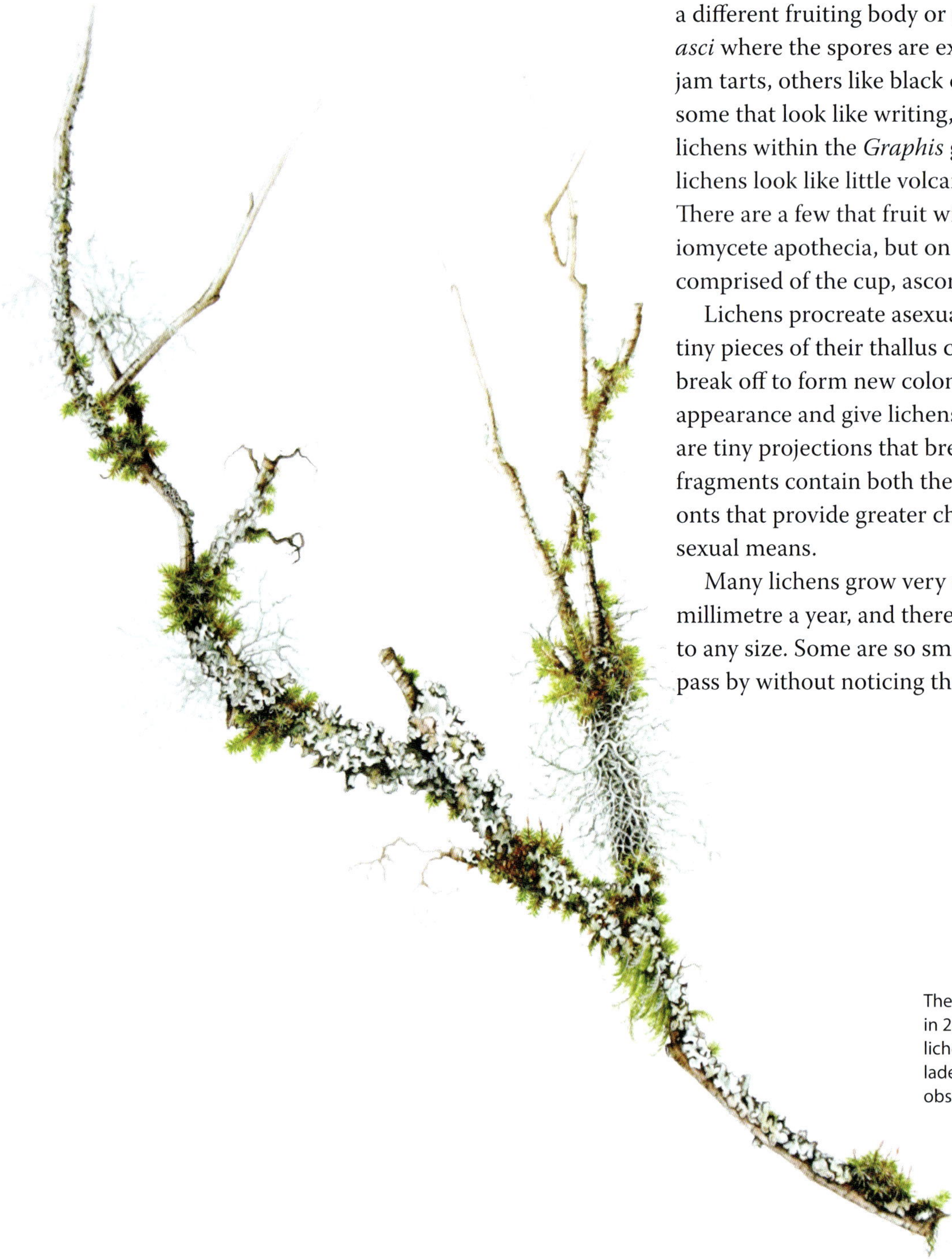

The Apple Tree Twig painted in watercolour in 2012. It was packed with many species of lichen, moss and even a tiny liverwort. These laden twigs make superb studies of intricate observation.

the time to stop with a 10x hand lens by an old veteran tree and look for the myriad of different species there are, all with different forms, textures and sometimes bright colours. Indeed, a lichen foray can centre around a few old trees without covering much ground at all compared to a meandering fungi foray.

Some of the damp, cool woodlands of west Wales near where I live are classed as Atlantic temperate rainforest and are well known for all the lower plants – lichens, ferns, mosses and liverworts. There is not much ancient woodland left in the UK, but these havens do feature a few rarer species and so will hopefully be protected for this reason.

LICHEN FORMS

There are different forms of lichen to be familiarised with:

- Leprose: powdery and flaky
- Crustose: flat, scaly and adhering to the substrate
- Foliose: with leafy lobes
- Fruticose: shrubby, pendant or club-like and usually found hanging from the branches of trees or on rocks attached by a holdfast
- Squamulose: scaly but with edges curled up from the substrate
- Gelatinous: jelly-like
- Filamentous: hairy or threadlike

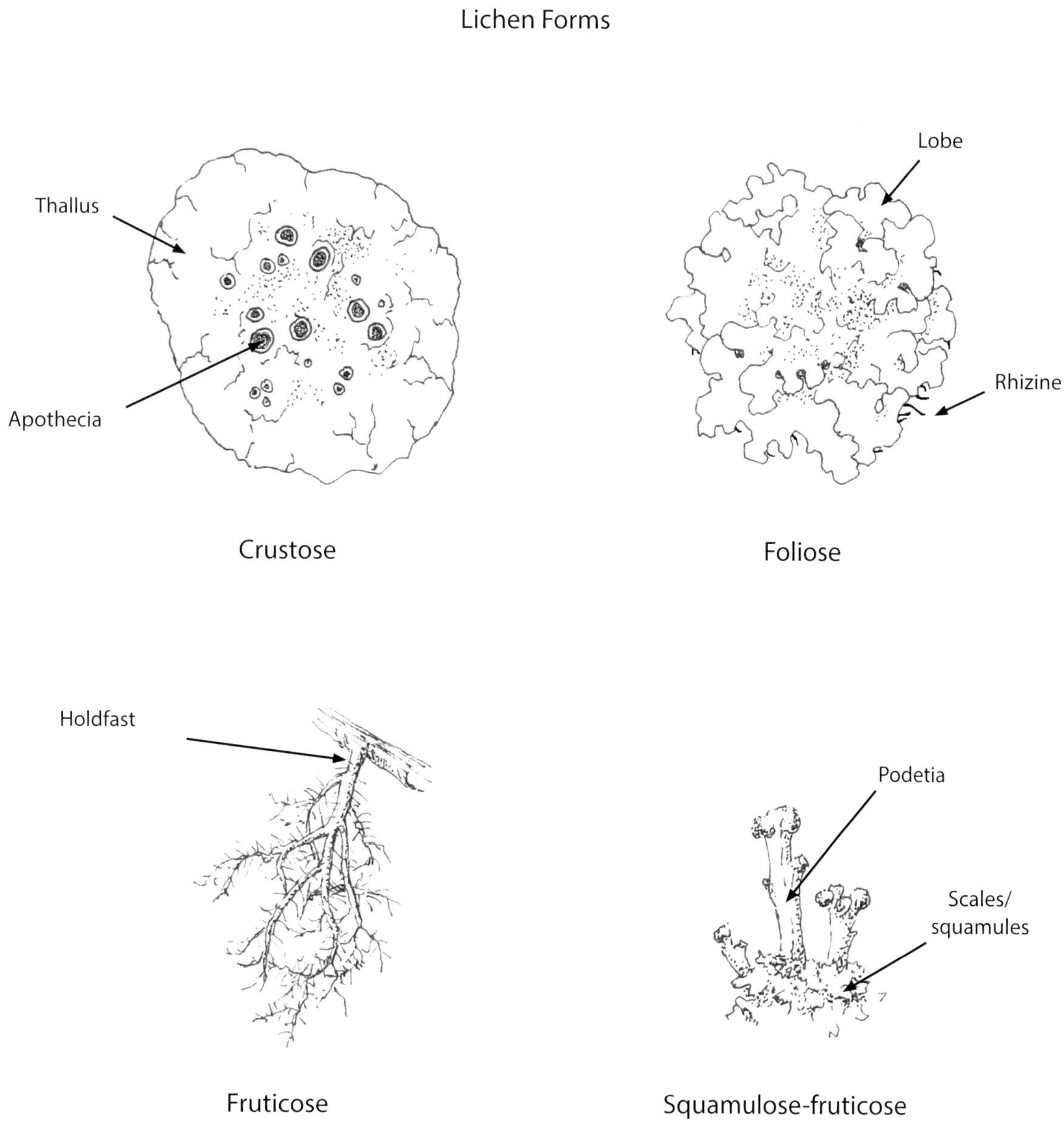

Diagram of main lichen forms; Crustose – flat against the substrate, Foliose – quite flat against the substrate but with leafy lobes, Fruticose – bushier types usually hanging from substrates and Squamulose – with scales like in the *Cladonia* genus.

Crustose Types

e.g. *Lecanora* spp.

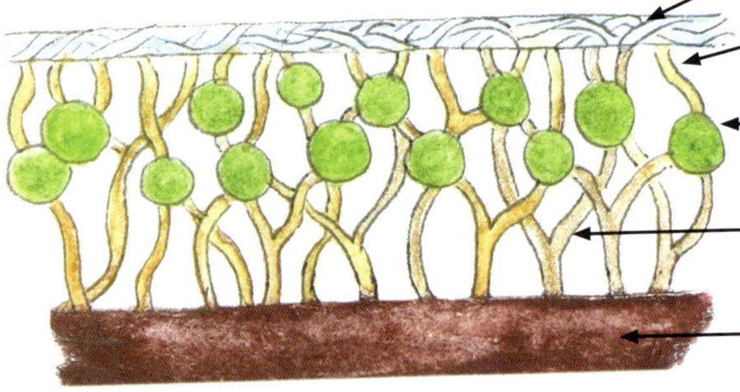

Fruticose Types

e.g. *Usnea* & *Ramalina* spp.

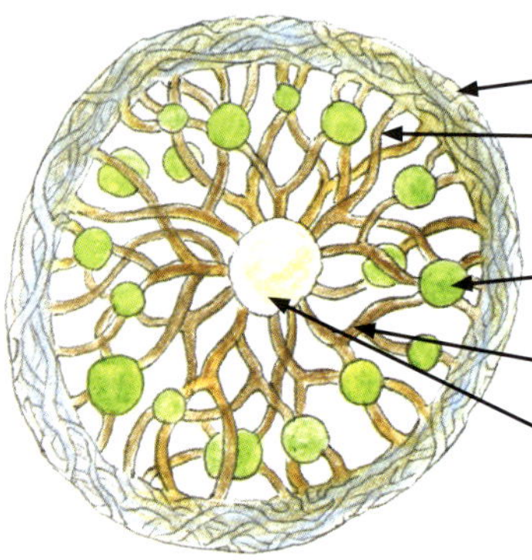

The structure of lichens. You can see the weaving threads of fungal hyphae with a layer of green algae or cyanobacteria (or both) embedded in it. Not pictured are the leprose types that are without a cortex layer and the foliose types that have the addition of a lower cortex that attaches to the substrate.

LICHEN FACTS

- Dyes were extracted from lichens for many years before the discovery of synthetic dyes and were called 'cudbear dyes' after their discoverer, Cuthbert Gordon. The lichen *Ochrolechia tartarea* among others was used to create many purples, reds and brown colours. Other lichens, mainly from species in the *Parmelia* family were called 'Crottle' and were used to dye yarn to make the famous Harris Tweed.
- The dyes used in litmus paper come from species of lichen, especially *Roccella tinctoria*; they work by causing a colour reaction according to the pH of the test subject.
- Some lichen dyes are produced as a defence against UV radiation to protect them from sun damage.
- Reindeer feed and rely upon lichen species such as *Cladonia* spp. in the harsh winters of the arctic lands and are commonly called reindeer moss.
- Lichens along with fungi produce antibiotic compounds such as Usnic acid in the *Usnea* spp. among other genera. They would have been used in the past for making poultices for healing wounds.

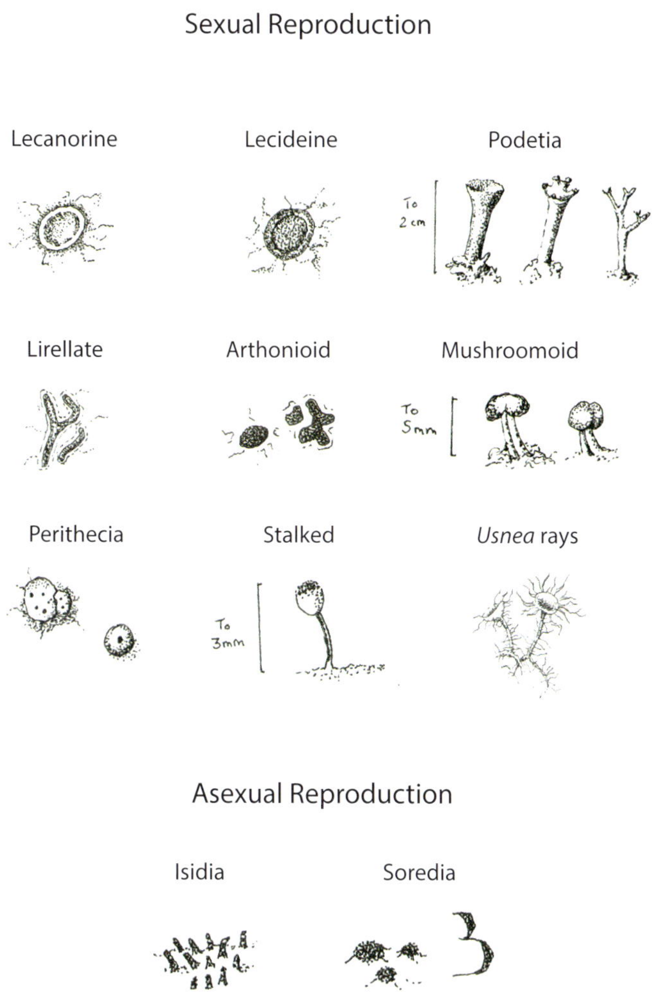

Sexual and asexual reproduction in lichens. Here you can see the diversity of lichen fruiting bodies or apothecia. Different types of crustose lichens that often grow in communities include script, comma, barnacle and the unfortunately named wart and pox lichens.

LICHENS AND ART FROM THE PAST

John Ruskin (1819–1900) a writer, poet and also a great drawing advocate. He would often get students to study and draw the close-up intricacies of lichens, claiming that in order to draw the larger scenes, one must first study the smallest. In *The Elements of Drawing* from 1857 he states: 'Be resolved, in the first place, to draw a piece of rounded rock, with its variegated lichens, quite rightly, getting its complete roundings, and all the patterns of lichen in true local colour.'

Another wonderful quote from Ruskin says to 'look at a green lane with a sketcher's eyes: where the old and gnarled wood is covered with the brightness,—the jewel brightness of the emerald moss, or the variegated and fantastic lichens, white and blue, purple and red, all mellowed and mingled into a garment of beauty for the old withered branch.'

Ernst Haeckel (1834–1919), was a German naturalist and artist among many other things. His work *Kunstformen der Natur* (Art Forms in Nature) from 1904 depicts many highly detailed illustrations of a plethora of organisms from every ecosystem. Haeckel had a strong impact on the combining of art and nature at the time, including some influence on the Art Nouveau movement as his work was so strong in design and repetitive pattern.

Illustrations from *Svenska lafvarnas färghistoria* (Sweden's Colour History) depict lichens for dyeing textiles and other household applications. It was written from 1805 to 1809 by Johan Peter Westring who was a doctor and lichenologist and was also tutored by Carl Linnaeus at the University of Uppsala in Sweden.

Ernst Haeckel. This is a lithography print depicting various intricately detailed lichens from *Art Forms in Nature* (1904), plate 83: Lichens. The black and white gives such a strong contrast.

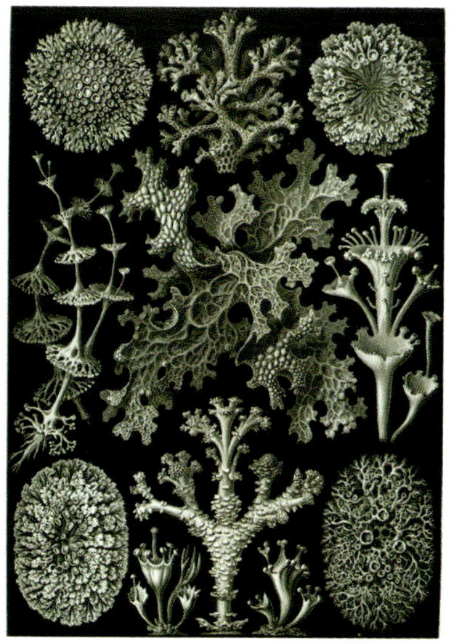

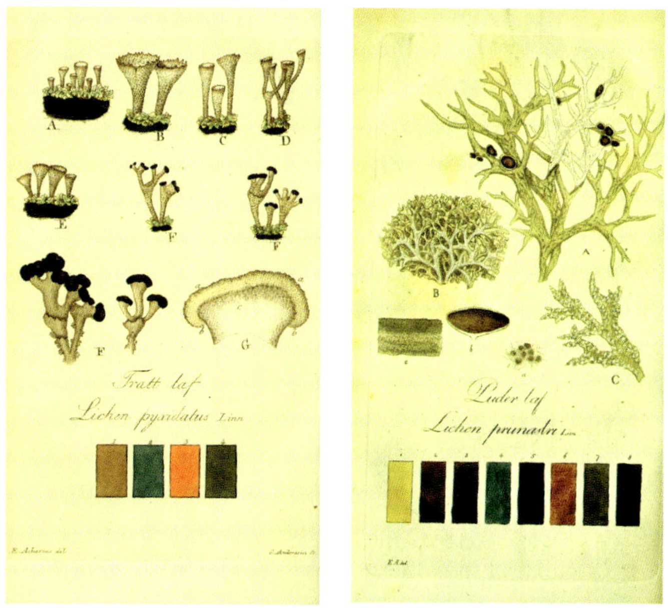

Illustrations from *Sweden's Colour History*. Johan Westring hand coloured the plates and the swatches show the dye colours that could be produced from each species.

CONTEMPORARY LICHEN ART

Christina Hart Davies is a botanical and nature artist who paints with intricate detail. She now has six RHS gold medals, five of which are for her lichen artworks. Her latest medal was awarded in 2018 – she is a great inspiration.

Claire Dalby is a Scottish artist mainly working in watercolour and gouache, with an accomplished career having been awarded an RHS gold medal and the Jill Smythies award for outstanding botanical art by the Linnean Society. She has also illustrated many books and created two fantastic wallcharts of lichens, one for rock species and one for tree species.

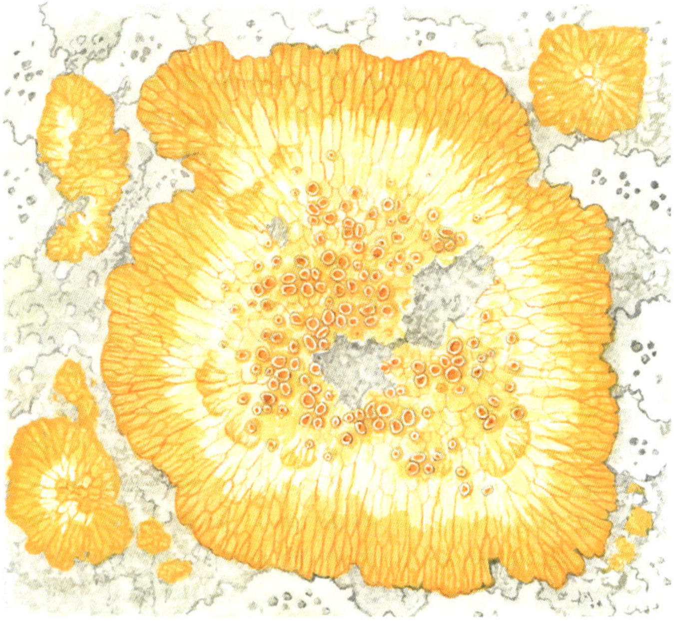

Caloplaca flavescens by Christina Hart Davies. This is an example of a saxicolous lichen that is found on calcareous rocks, walls and cement often on gravestones. (© Christina Hart Davies)

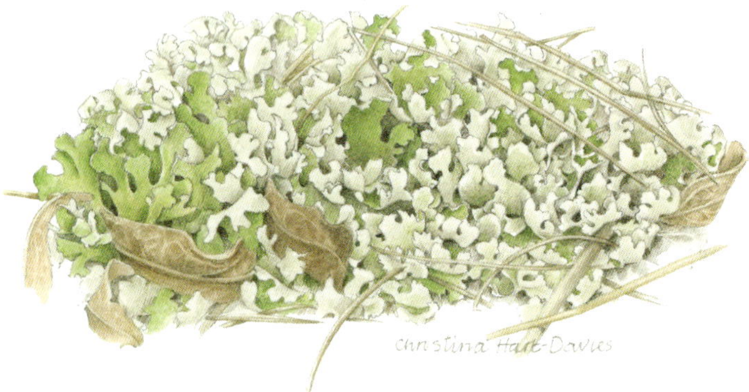

Cladonia convoluta by Christina Hart Davies. This is an example of a terricolous lichen. It has the wonderful attribute of uncurling and turning bright green when you pour water on it. Lichens can have quite marked differences between their wet and dry states. (© Christina Hart Davies)

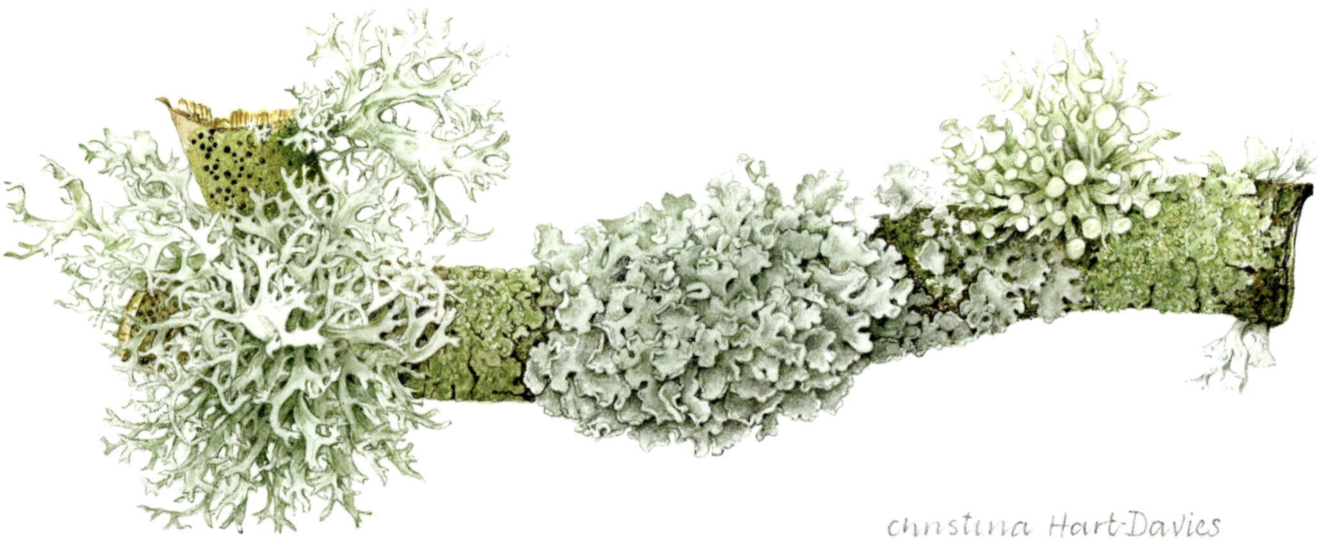

Hampshire lichens by Christina Hart Davies. *Evernia prunastri* (at left), *Parmotrema perlata* (centre), *Ramalina fastigiata* (at right), plus others. Christina says, 'Good teaching point: I always thought *Evernia* was a fruticose lichen, but in fact it's a foliose one with exceptionally long lobes. You can tell it from a true fruticose as it has white undersides, while fruticose lichens (*Ramalina* to right) are the same colour both sides.' (© Christina Hart Davies)

ILLUSTRATING LICHENS

Lichens make fantastic subjects in any media, with the opportunity to depict their strange yet often beautiful forms. They make for interesting, textural drawings in graphite only studies, in pen and ink, coloured pencil, in watercolour or other painting mediums or in mixed media. They can be the inspiration for abstract patterns and designs or an exercise in textural mark making, detailed or otherwise.

A lot of lichens can be very small so you'll need to focus in on their world with magnification and macro photography. For those tiny and awkward to study species, it will be useful to take photos in the field to be able to enlarge them up and see their intricate details close up. Sketching in the field will obviously be more difficult, apart from perhaps quick and loose habitat sketches. The bushier specimens such as those belonging to the *Usnea, Evernia* or *Ramalina* families, will clearly be easier to observe, being much larger and so able to take back to the studio for further study. They are also very obliging as drawing subjects as they last for a long time, perhaps just a gentle spray with a water-mister (rainwater is best) will bring them back to life. For this reason, photographs are not really needed and working from life should be relatively easy. However, photographic reference will be very useful if you do intend to enlarge your subjects, or if they are a rarer species and also if they are crustose and cannot be removed from their substrates. It can be tricky to take quality close up photographs; the depth of field could be very narrow and parts of the subject may be blurred, so it's best to take a variety of shots using a macro lens if possible.

A walk in the woods after a storm will see many windblown twigs and branches littering the ground with potential drawing subjects. Interesting twigs could also be discovered after tree pruning, perhaps in an apple orchard. You will often find a variety of different species of lichens all growing together in communities, sometimes with mosses and liverworts also. Hosts of frilly, fruticose species along with the most minuscule of crusts all decorating the twigs of trees, sometimes in such profusion. Fascinating crustose lichens can also be found on boulders, loose rocks and gravestones may host interesting species too.

For realistic drawing, it's good practice to identify your subjects first as then you can look out for characteristics of that particular species and any points of reference such as the fruiting bodies or textural patches of *soredia*. I recommend obtaining a good identification book for your region. I use *Lichens: An Illustrated Guide to the British and Irish Species* by the late Frank Dobson which is very thorough if you want a comprehensive guide. There are helpful websites too with ID tips, some I have listed in the resources section at the back of this book. As with fungi identification, it will help to go out on a foray with experts. A lichenologist may use chemicals such as K – potassium hydroxide, C – bleach and I – iodine to confirm the identity of a species. When applied to the thallus they will usually react with a colour change. Some species, such as *Cladonia portentosa* are fluorescent and UV lamps can be used to identify them.

It can help to note down what substrate the lichen is growing on as it may help with identification; some lichens prefer base rich substrates, others acidic. Some species such as the *Cladonias* have really interesting structures called *podetias*, sometimes brightly coloured, like red matchsticks. The crustose types with apothecia like tiny 'jam-tarts', many within the *Lecanora* genus, make interesting enlargements. Their mosaic patterns on the trunks of trees are often beautiful observations of intricate pattern and can be abstract like an alien landscape. Look out for any dark outline around these crustose types – the *prothallus*, and if you have a leafier species, check the thallus for textures from *soredia* and *isidia* and maybe you see the pore-like markings *of Pseudocyphellae*. Check the undersides too for colour, and hair or root-like projections of *cilia* and *rhizines*.

The subject will also move and change as it dries out, not only in shape but in colour too so the subject will need to be studied in one state, either wet or dry. It is inevitable as with some LBM's that you will not be able to identify some species of lichens but as with fungi, if you can get it to the genus level and add sp. it can be enough.

The crustose lichens make the simplest subjects to illustrate as they lie flat against their substrates. I like to draw them with a mechanical pencil with size 0.3 mm lead that I find can sometimes be better for precision work when drawing these very small and intricate subjects. I tend to make quite a detailed line drawing initially and then add small washes of paint to build up the painting in layers using a small brush (No. 1 and 0 or 00) and making sure to reserve any highlights by painting around them. The bushier subjects are obviously a little more complicated. I always like to study these from life and draw them life-size, starting off with a clear line drawing of the main branches and any apothecia, then lightly adding in a few background branches that will indicate depth, nothing too dark or definite. To illustrate in pen, you can use a variety of line work and techniques such as stippling, scumbling or squiggle marks to depict the variety of textural effects seen in the subject matter.

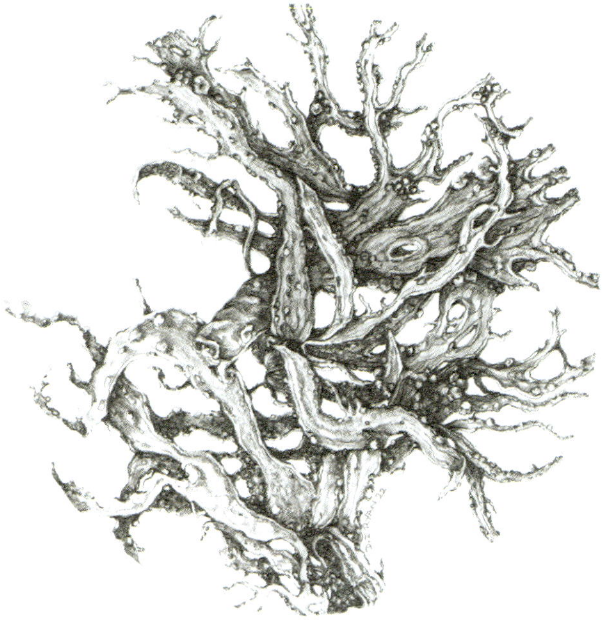

Strap Lichen II by Denise Ryan. Both studies are drawn in graphite pencil on Hahnemuhle HP paper. She says, 'At art school we were encouraged to observe closely (always from life) and draw in a free, spatially aware way – accuracy and intuitive mark making combined. The essence of this training has stayed with me over the years.' (© Denise I. Ryan)

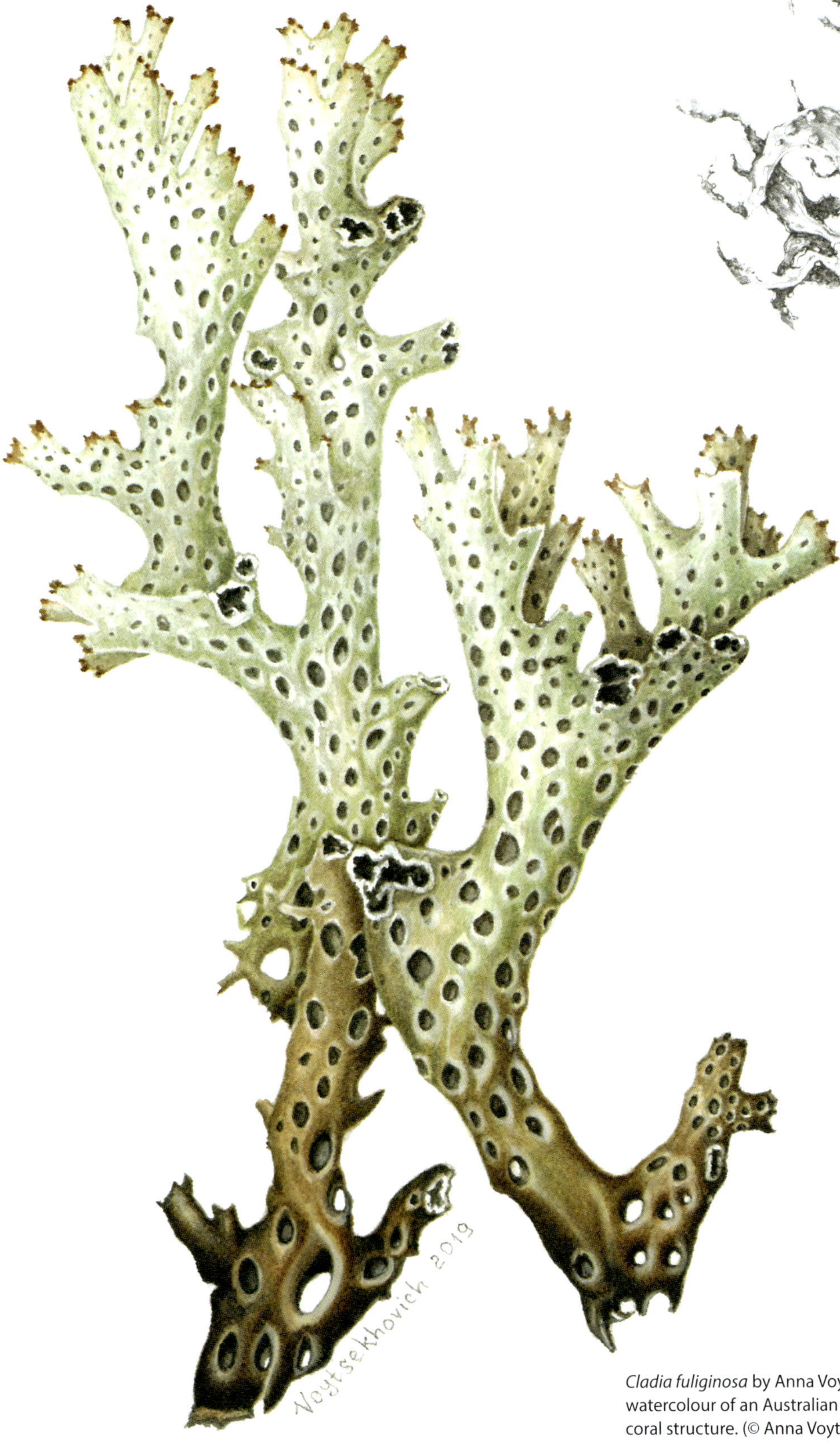

Cladia fuliginosa by Anna Voytsekhovich. This stunning illustration in watercolour of an Australian native lichen has the look of an underwater coral structure. (© Anna Voytsekhovich)

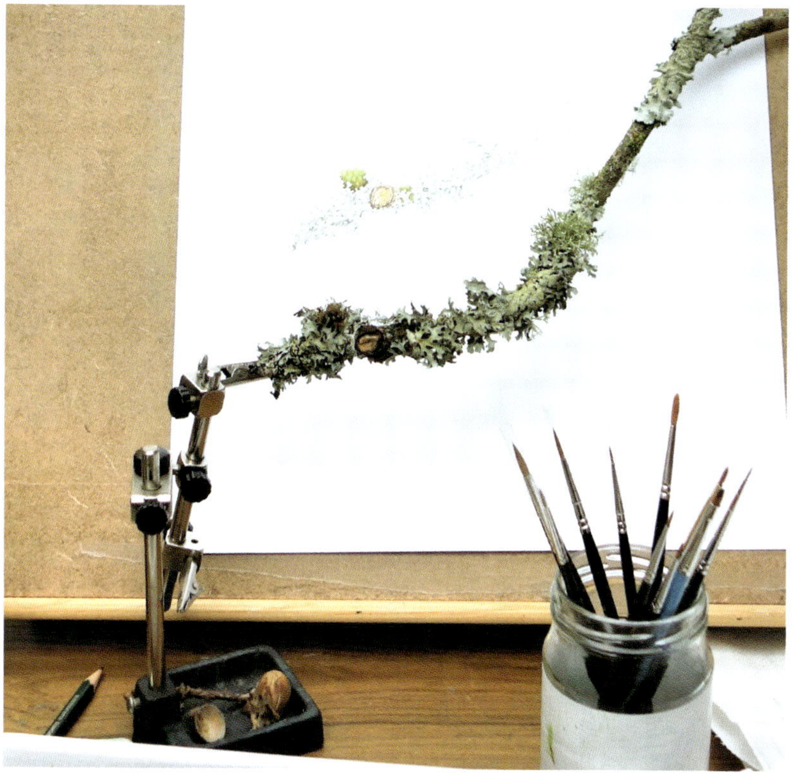

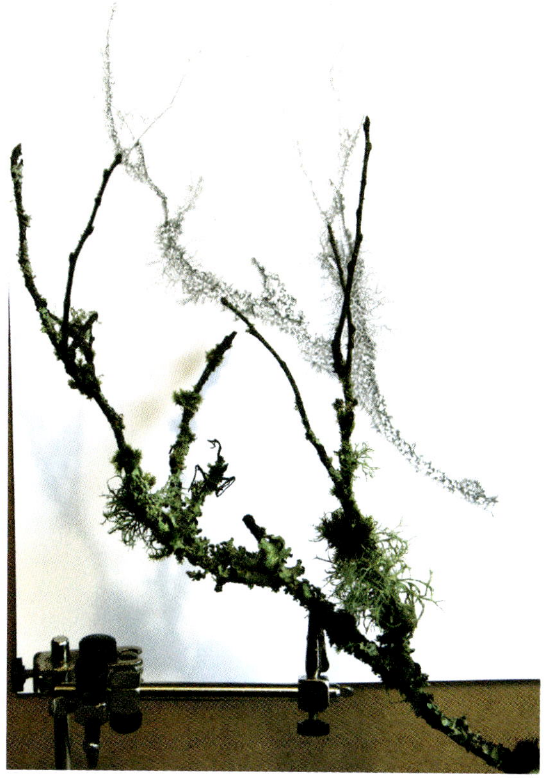

The helping hands holder seen here is very useful for supporting lichen twigs while drawing them. This one did have a magnifying glass attached but I have removed it to use separately.

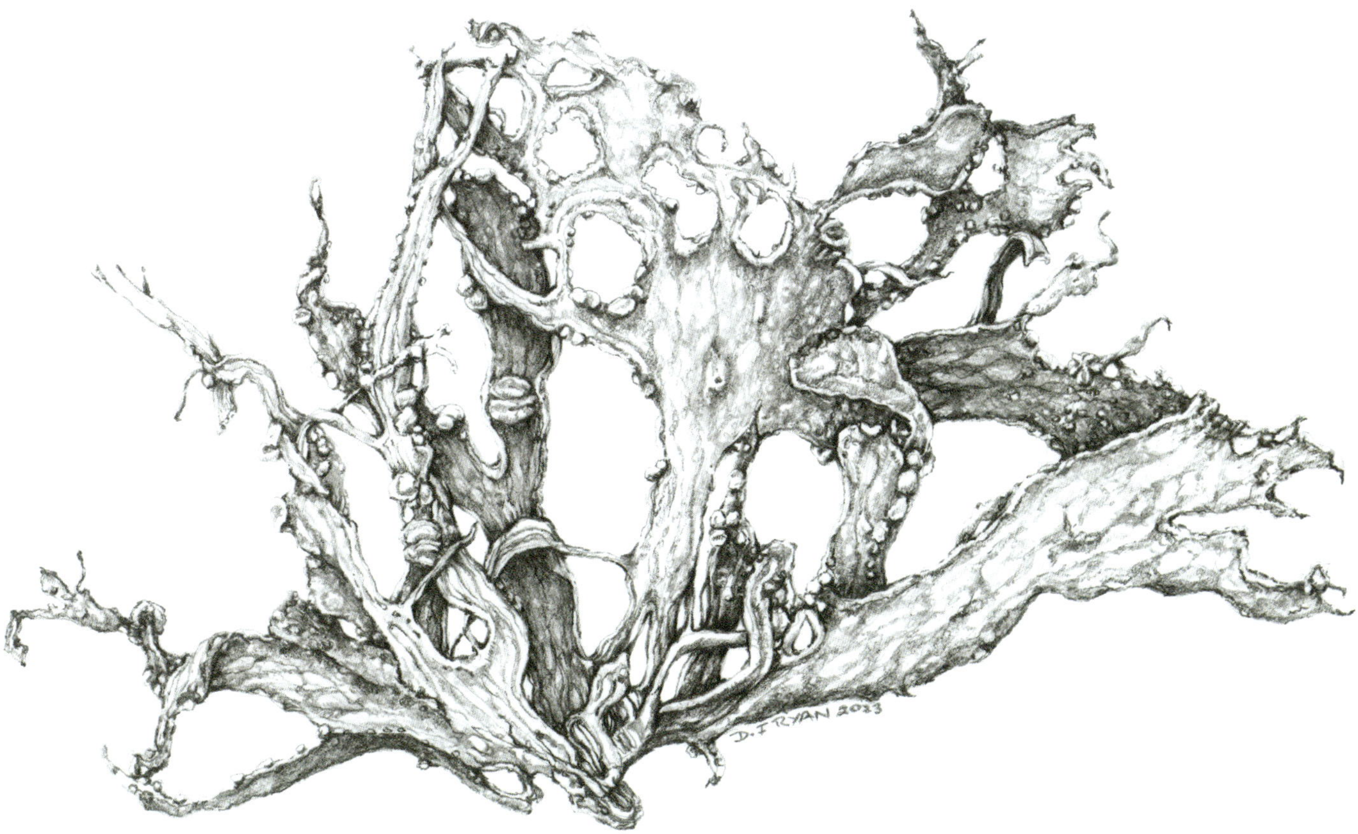

Strap Lichen I – *Ramalina* sp. by Denise Ryan, who is an artist based in New Zealand. Denise has been working on a series of lichen studies in graphite on paper, rendering texture, form and detail through close observation. Along with this intense study she allows each drawing to develop intuitively. She says, 'I'm endlessly fascinated by the subtle transformations which seem to occur during these periods of deep concentration.' (© Denise I. Ryan)

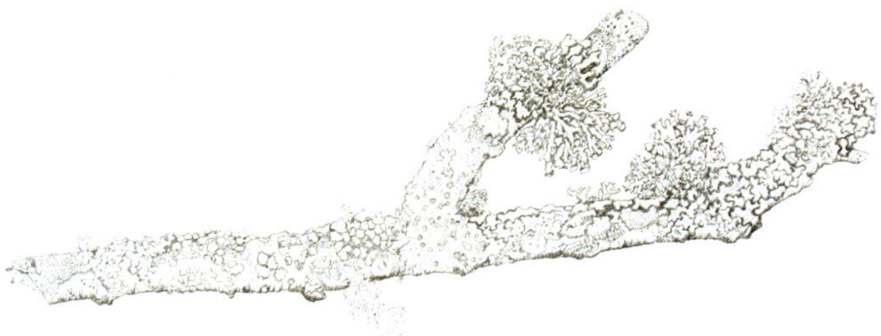

An old 2005 Lichen twig study in pen using a variety of marks such as stippling, scumbling and scribbling. A very absorbing and meditational activity to get into.

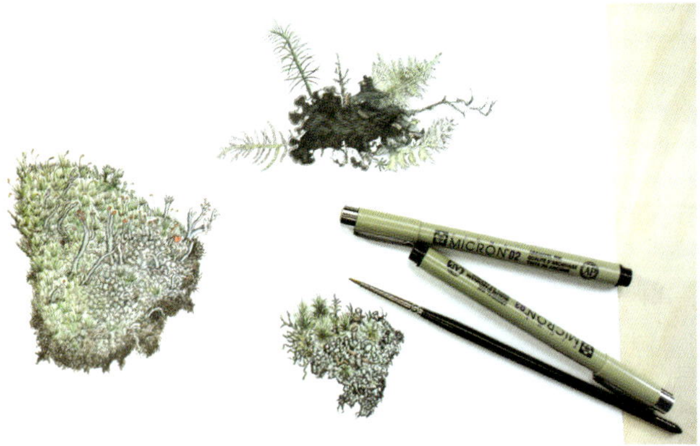

Lichen and moss turf studies from 2005 in the sketchbook using pen and wash. The top right lichen with the mosses is a Dog Lichen – *Peltigera* sp. – that has white root-like *rhizines* underneath looking a little like whiskers. In the past it was thought to be a cure for rabies.

LICHEN COLOURS

Lichens tend to have more muted and subtle colours than fungi; with hues of tinted creams, pale earthy greens, duck egg blues, dull greys and milky tans but a few like to splash the rocks, twigs or trunks of trees with bright egg yolk yellows or vibrant orange hues such as *Xanthoria* spp. often called the Sunburst lichens for obvious reasons. Although they may be greener in the shade as they produce the vibrant yellows with exposure to the sun. Other bright yellow lichens are the crustose family of *Candelariella* spp. often found on rocks where birds perch along with *Xanthoria* spp. thriving on nitrates and ammonia deposits. Another rock coloniser is the map lichen – *Rhizocarpon geographicum* so called as its apple green thallus is surrounded by a black border and it can resemble little islands on a map. The goldeneye lichen – *Teloschistes chrysophthalmus* is a rare lichen in the UK that adorns twigs with tiny splashes of bright orange. Devil's Matchsticks – *Cladonia floerkeana* and *C. macilenta* bear bright red podetia tips for little additions of vibrant colour. Other *Cladonias* have plain brown ones and some bear milky green pixie cups while others have only their pale bluey-green scales. Some lichens do show off with colourful apothecia, in reds, pinks, yellows and tans. A few leafy lichens are distinctly green such as the pale minty colours of *Flavoparmelia caperata* often seen decorating the trunks of trees, while others are more of a light cool blue to grey, such as the common, foliose lichen *Physcia tenella*. The strap lichens – *Ramalina* spp. and frilly beard lichens – *Usnea* spp. also appear in dull blue greys and glaucous green hues clinging to tree branches in areas with cleaner air lacking in nitrogenous pollution.

I like to add a little Titanium White watercolour or gouache to get the colour I need to match that pale, milky and opaque look that I see in some of the subjects, especially the bushier types. Colours for lichens could include mixes of blues and warm yellows with a dash of white. You can experiment with different mixes such as Prussian Blue and Raw Sienna or Ultramarine and Yellow Ochre, with the addition of white. Lichen greys can be made with Ultramarine and Light Red, Davy's Grey or blends of the three cool primaries. A good lichen colour, again with a bit of white added is Oxide of Chromium (PG17). It is a green pigment that is very lightfast and opaque. It is associated with camouflage and used by the military for this purpose.

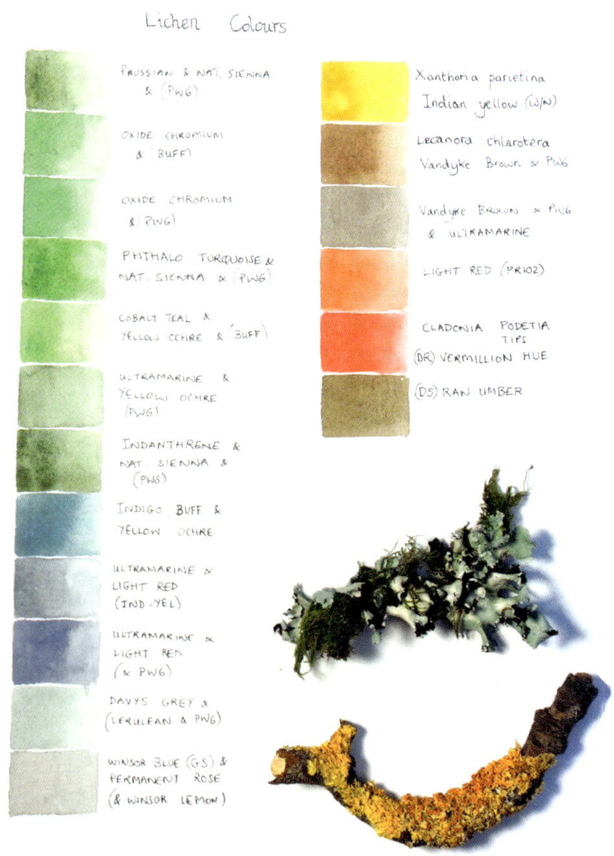

A lichen colour chart with various different lichen hues mixed from a range of blue pigments and earth yellows and Oxide of Chromium (all Winsor & Newton) with a dash of Titanium White or Buff Titanium by Daniel Smith.

Using Masking Fluid

For subjects such as the bushy, fruticose beard lichens – the *Usnea* species, you can use masking fluid to mask out the main branches when using watercolour. Then when dry, paint in the background branches; the masking fluid will reserve the white paper for your main branches, which can then be painted in when the further back ones are completed. The main details, with careful attention to shadows and highlights, will go on to these main foreground branches, less so on the background ones. This will create the illusion of depth in the picture and a three-dimensional look. Any lost highlights can be added with a touch of opaque white gouache. But you don't have to use masking fluid; in that case you just work methodically around the main branches to reserve them. It is worth remembering that there is always more than one approach to illustrating a subject.

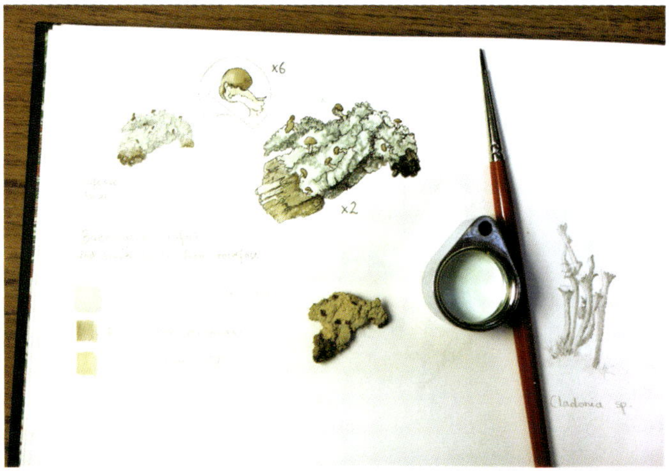

Baeomyces rufus sketchbook study. Adding enlargements can enhance a composition and can highlight important features of the subject. I use a magnifying glass and a 10x hand-lens. There are also magnifying glasses with inbuilt lighting that you can clamp onto your desk for hands-free ease of use.

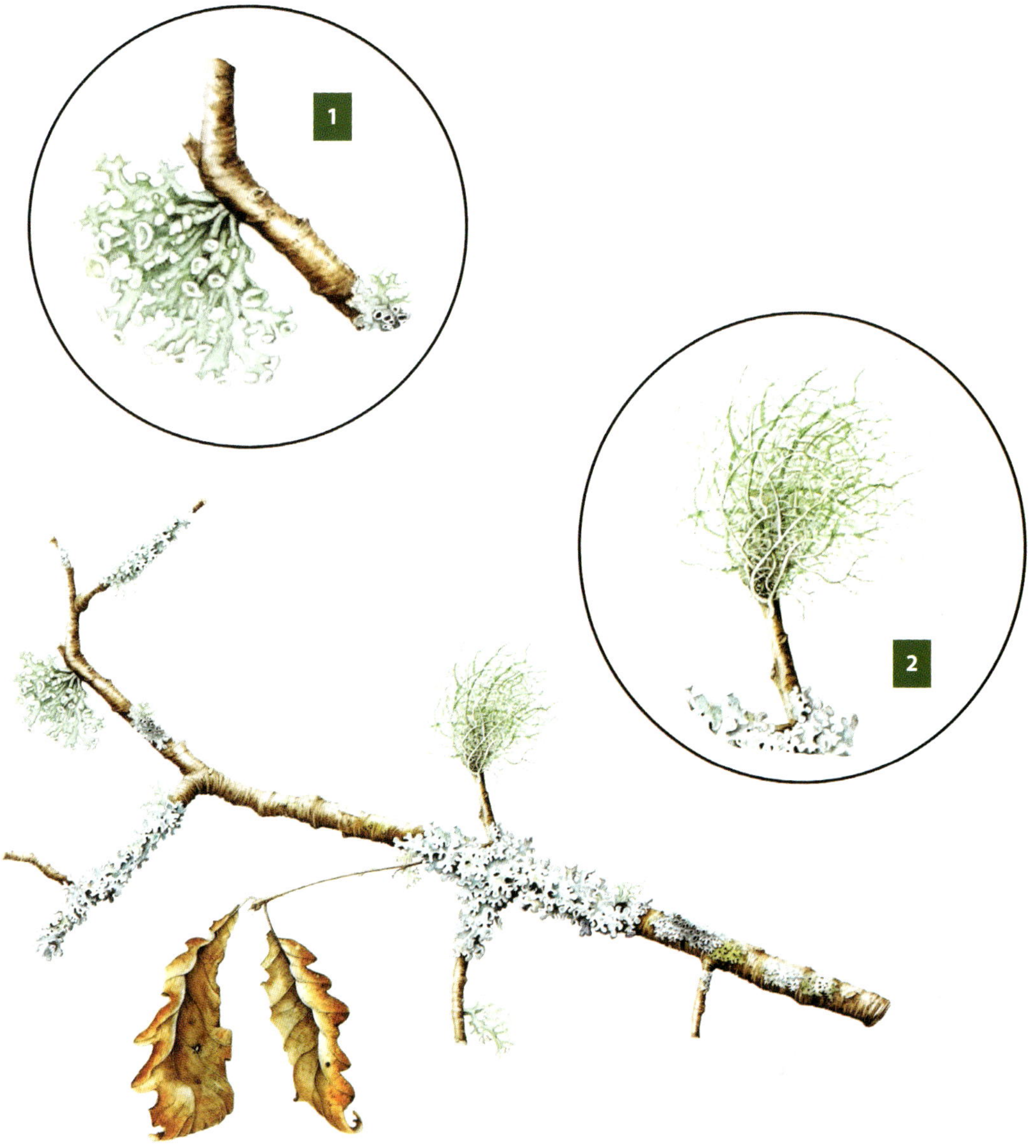

Oak Twig 2012. On this branch is one of my favourite lichens *Ramalina fastigiata* (1). Commonly found sprouting from twigs, it has flat, strap-like branches that end with flattened apothecias almost looking like nail heads. I just painted around these, no masking fluid. For the fruticose *Usnea* species (2) I used masking fluid on some of the primary branches while painting in the smaller back ones.

Cladonia spp. studies in coloured pencil and watercolour showing their squamulose-fruticose forms. They bear their apothecia on the clublike *podetia* structures some with bright colours and a few have common names such as devil's matchsticks, British soldiers and pixie cups.

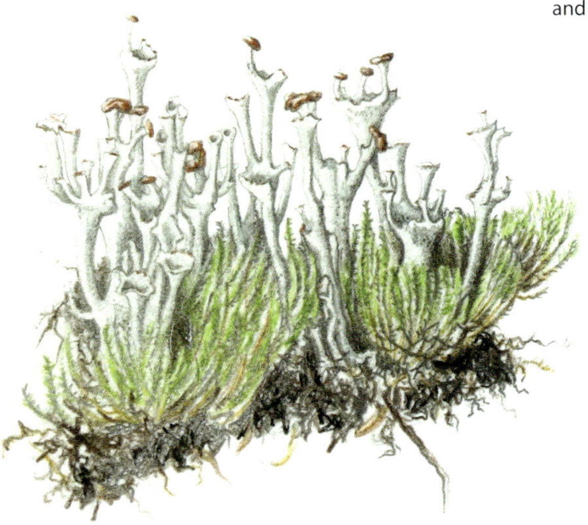

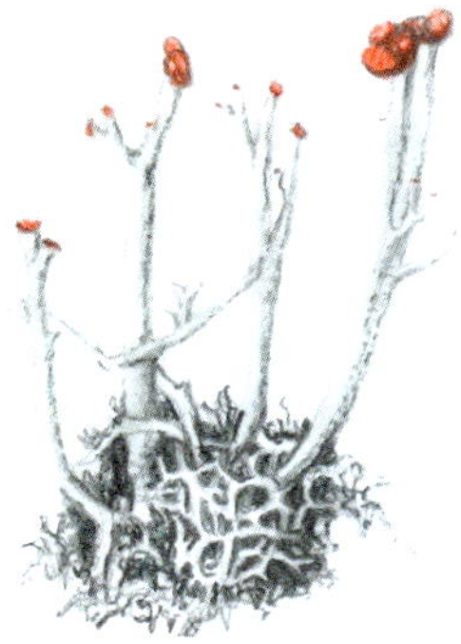

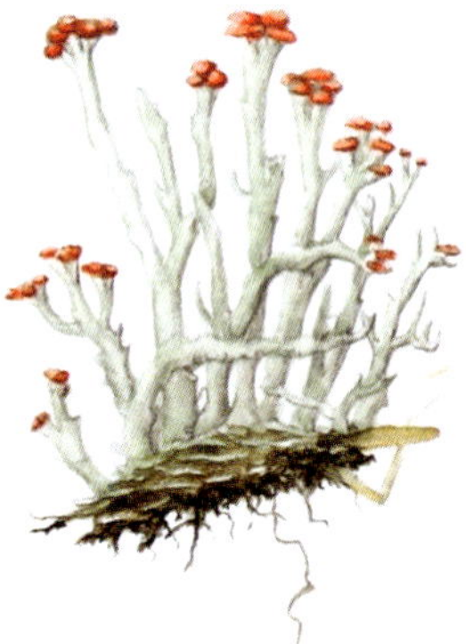

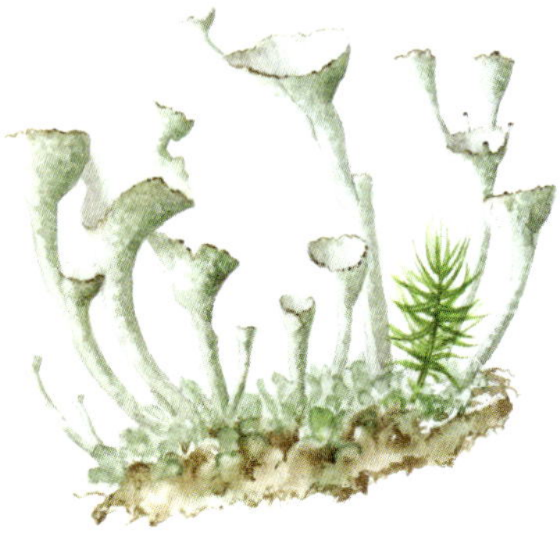

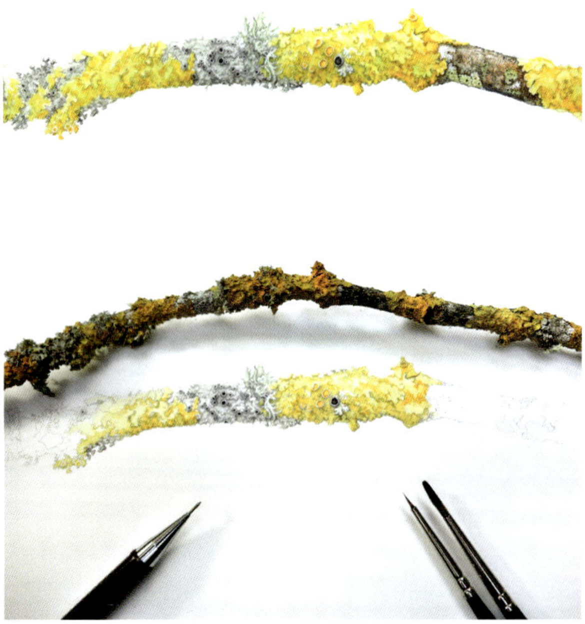

Lichen twig study with *Xanthoria* sp. and *Physcia* sp. Realistic painting of lichens can often be described as drawing with the brush and if grey tones are a struggle, then watercolour over graphite tone can always be tried.

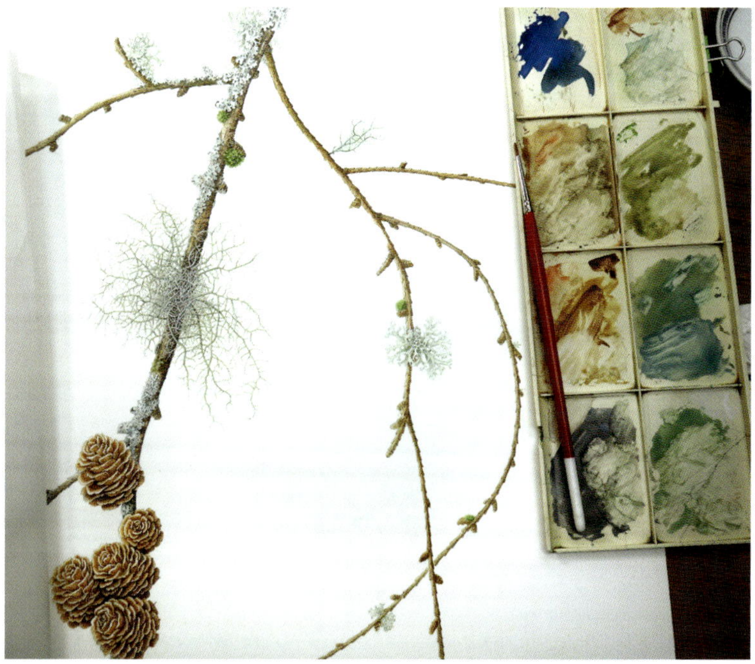

Working on a larch twig with lots of lichens in watercolour, all worked from life studies, with fresh specimens when needed. You can see that here it is mainly detailed dry brush work with small brushes. Using the dried colour on the palette like this is the easiest way to work for the dry brush technique.

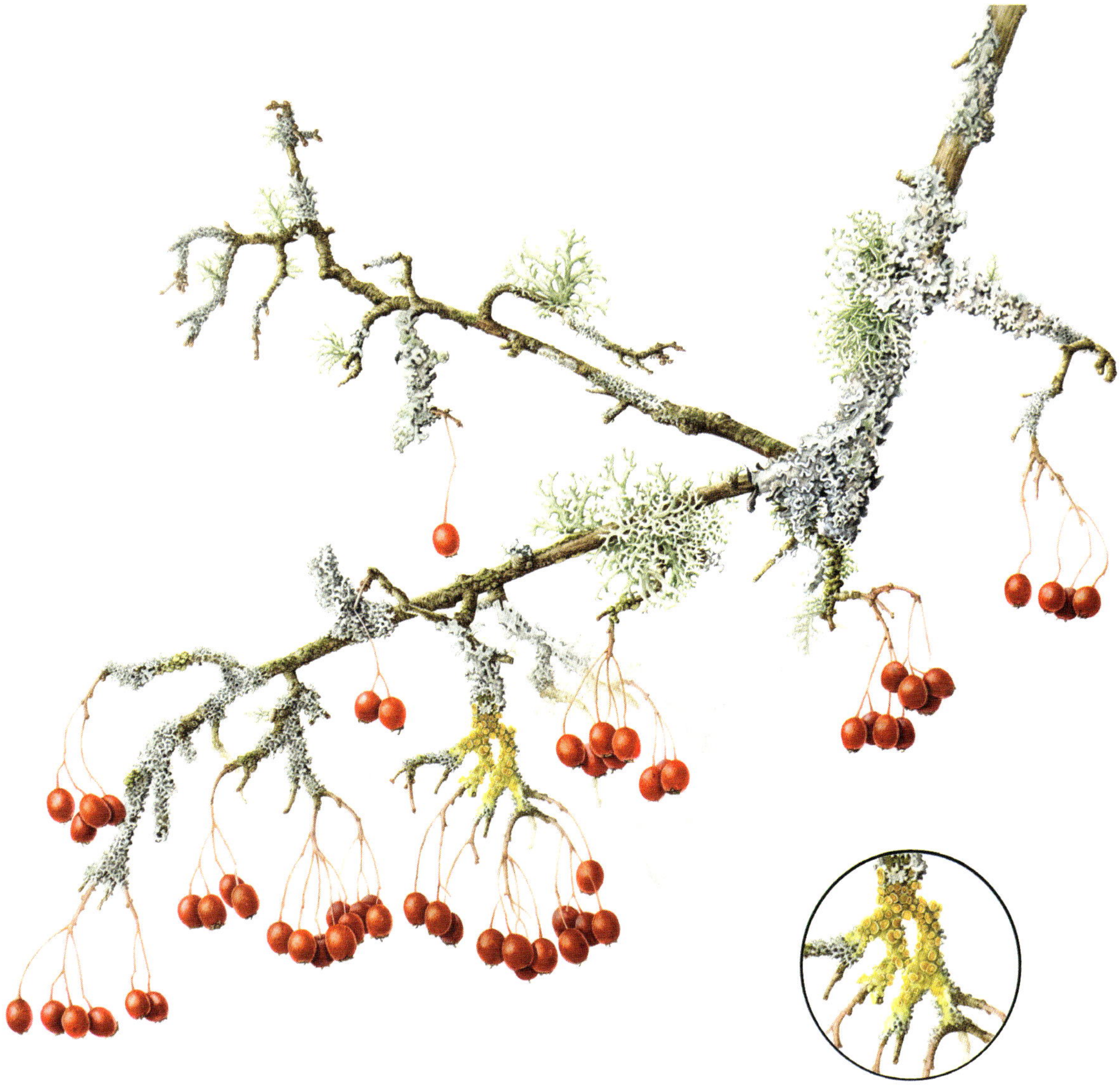

Hawthorn from Gilfach, 2019. This heavily laden twig features around nine different species of lichen and was drawn and painted from life. The *Xanthoria* species has been enlarged showing its darker yellow apothecia.

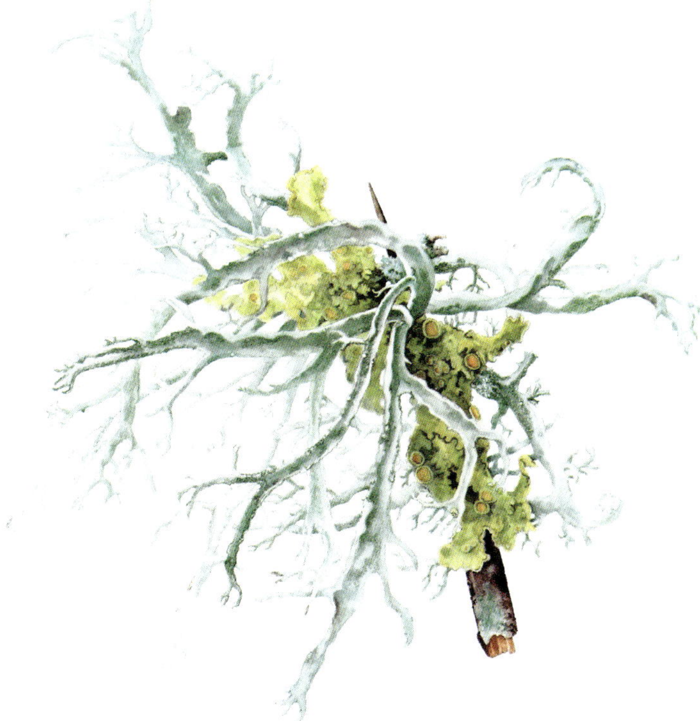

Two's Company – *Ramalina* and *Xanthoria*. This little hawthorn sprig clad in its lichens is in watercolour and enlarged three times. It was drawn out initially from life at life-size and then, in nearly the same way as in Chapter 3 with the Velvet Shanks, the squares were sized up by three times to enlarge it.

Lichens on Vellum Golden Eye Lichen – *Telochistes chrysophthalmus*

Shevaun Doherty, my friend and fellow President of the Society of Botanical Artists has painted many lichen subjects from the Irish woodlands near her home. She has won many awards for her work and paints her subjects intricately and often on vellum. For the past couple of years Shevaun has been involved with the Ellen Hutchins Festival in Bantry, Ireland. Ellen was Ireland's first female botanist and botanical artist (1785–1815). She died at an early age but managed to make a name for herself in the scientific community for her beautiful illustrations and her ability to discover rare lichens and seaweeds, six of which have been named after her. Shevaun was given access to her illustrations and her dried specimens in Trinity College Herbarium, and inspired by her attention to detail, decided to create a series of paintings depicting lichens on vellum for the RHS. She wanted to take a contemporary approach to lichens, so rather than paint them as scientific illustrations, she would do them as 'portraits' on mounted calfskin vellum.

She says, 'As the paint sits on the surface rather than sinking into the tooth this brings a unique luminosity to the watercolour paint and the artist is able to get very crisp edges. I like the historic connection of painting on vellum – this is a very old tradition that is slowly being lost. There are only two makers of vellum in the world, William Cowley (UK) and Pergamena (US). What really appeals to me is the way that the organic markings on the vellum can be incorporated into the painting. Each piece of vellum tells you about the life of the animal and how it lived. Animals are not killed to make vellum, it is a by-product of the meat/dairy industry.'

The Painting Process

To prepare the vellum for painting, the surface was rubbed down with pounce (fine grade pumice powder with chalk). This removed the surface oils that may adversely affect the application of watercolour paint. The scaled-up drawing was transferred onto the vellum using tracing paper. The pigments used were Winsor & Newton, Schmincke and Daniel Smith Artist grade watercolours. W&N white gouache (tinted with watercolour) was used in the areas where the speckles were not desired like in the golden apothecia and then transparent watercolour was floated over the surface.

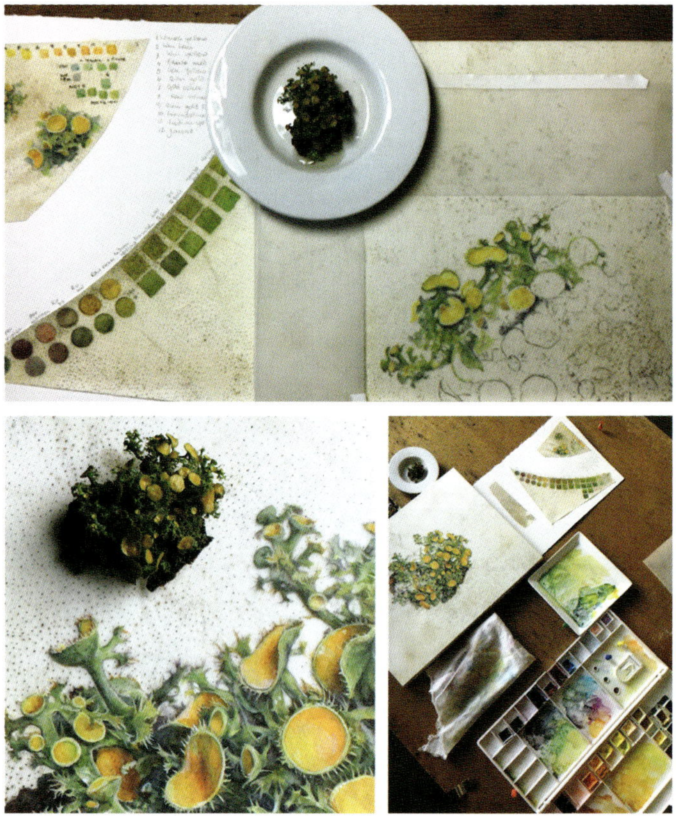

The Golden Eye work in progress. The lichen was drawn out at four times life-size and transferred to the vellum using graphite. Colour testing was done on the vellum offcuts to understand how the pigments looked on the vellum. There is a notable colour shift between working on paper and the darker colour of vellum.

Lichens on Oak Twigs

The study painting *Lichens on Oak Twigs* by Italian artist Giovanni Cera was completed in 2012. Giovanni says, 'On one occasion while working as an architect, I had to do a survey in a wooded area by the Tuscan Apennine. My attention was caught with some dried branches of oaks, which showed interesting shapes and colours due to the growth of lichens and mosses. I picked up and brought home some twigs and decided to paint them, as a test, on a piece of vellum that I'd got some time before in Florence. The vellum was not of a high quality (and a while after I could have tested the excellent calfskin and goatskin bought in London). So, I painted the twigs with almost dry watercolours on this thick, fat, yellowish support that smelt of sheep and I actually got better results than I'd have expected.'

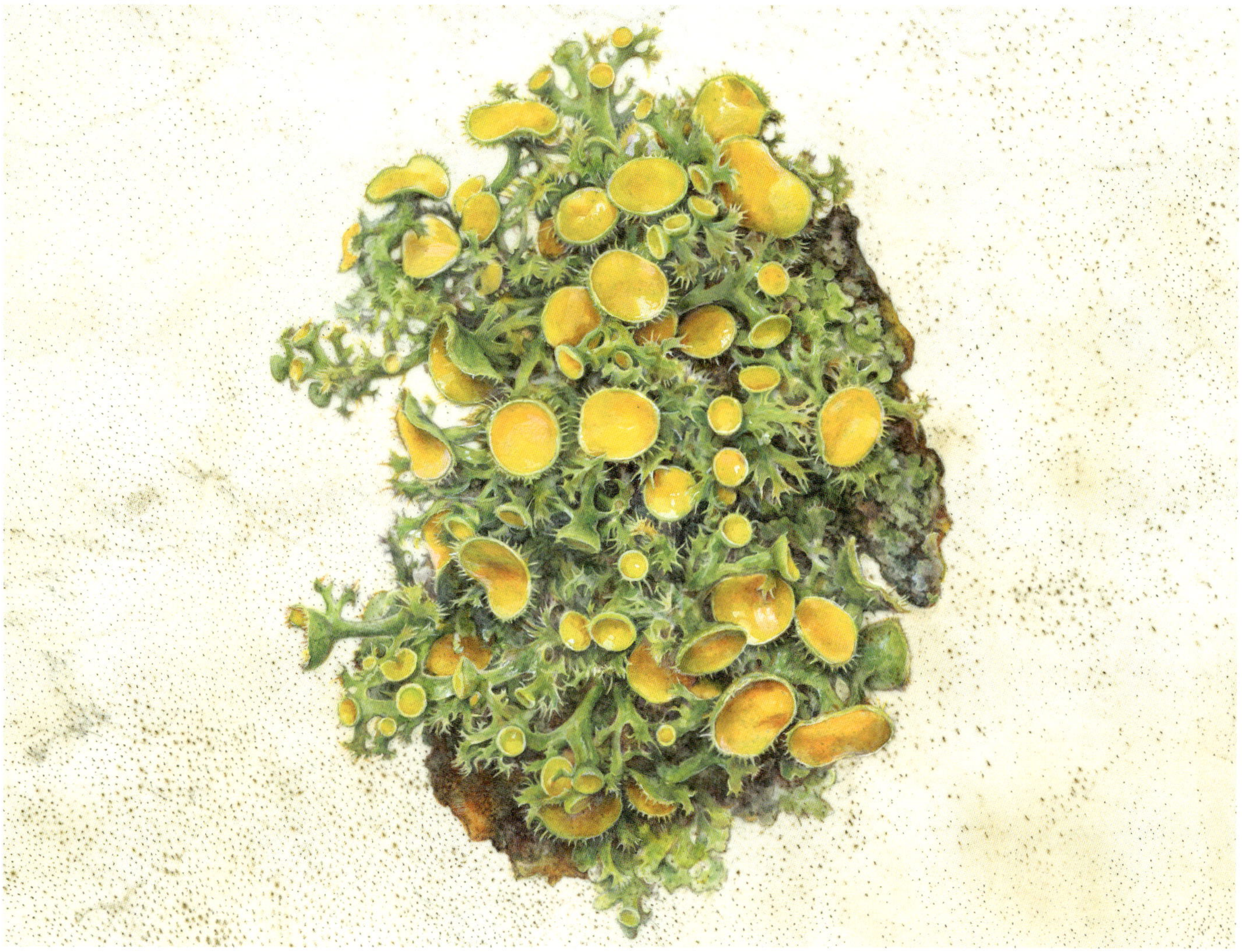

Golden Eye lichen – *Telochistes chrysophthalmus* – the finished painting on natural vellum by Shevaun Doherty. You can see the pores and textures of the vellum surface giving such character to the artwork. (© Shevaun Doherty)

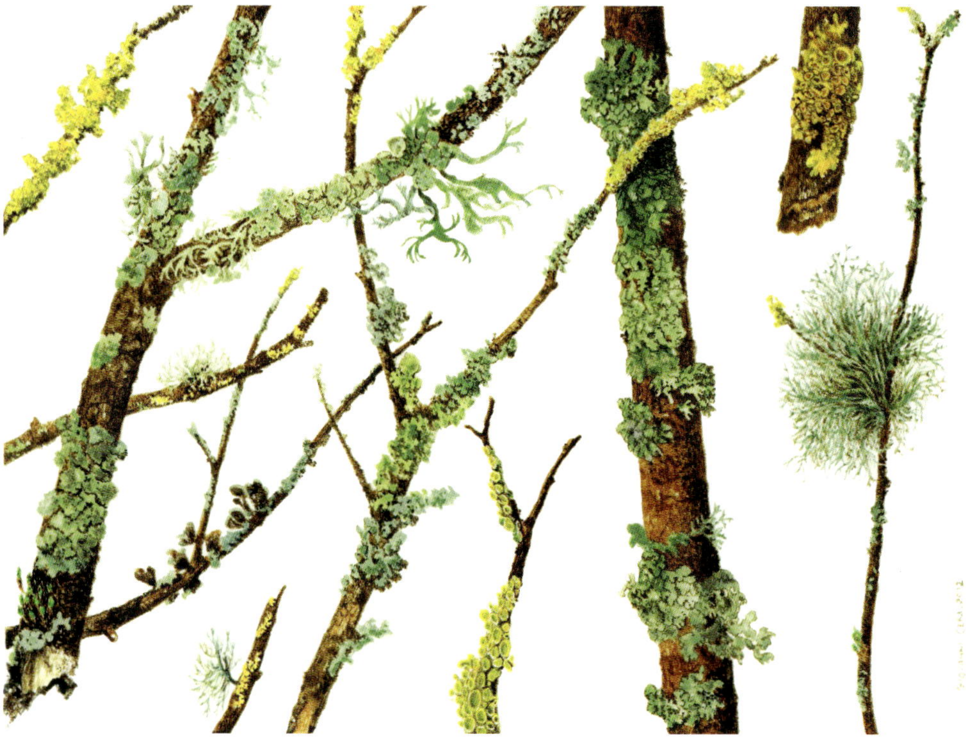

Lichens on Oak Twigs, a study by Giovanni Cera using watercolour on vellum. The lichen species are the yellow *Xanthoria parietina*, and the common blue/green lichens Oak moss – *Evernia prunastri* and *Physcia tenella*. (© Giovanni Cera)

STEP-BY-STEP: LICHEN MOSAICS ON STONES

A fun and experimental study for capturing the intricate patterns of lichen mosaics is looking out for them on small stones and rocks and using mixed media for different effects. Some beautiful and interesting subjects can be found out on heathland. Some of these crustose lichens will have a noticeably dark border to their edges, especially where they meet with other species. This is called a *prothallus* and is an area of the lichen that doesn't have any algal cells.

MATERIALS USED:

- Bockingford HP watercolour paper
- French Ultramarine, Light Red (PR102) and Winsor Violet (all by Winsor & Newton), Quinacridone Deep Gold and Raw Umber (by Daniel Smith)
- 70 per cent rubbing alcohol
- White gouache (Winsor & Newton)
- Pigma Micron 01

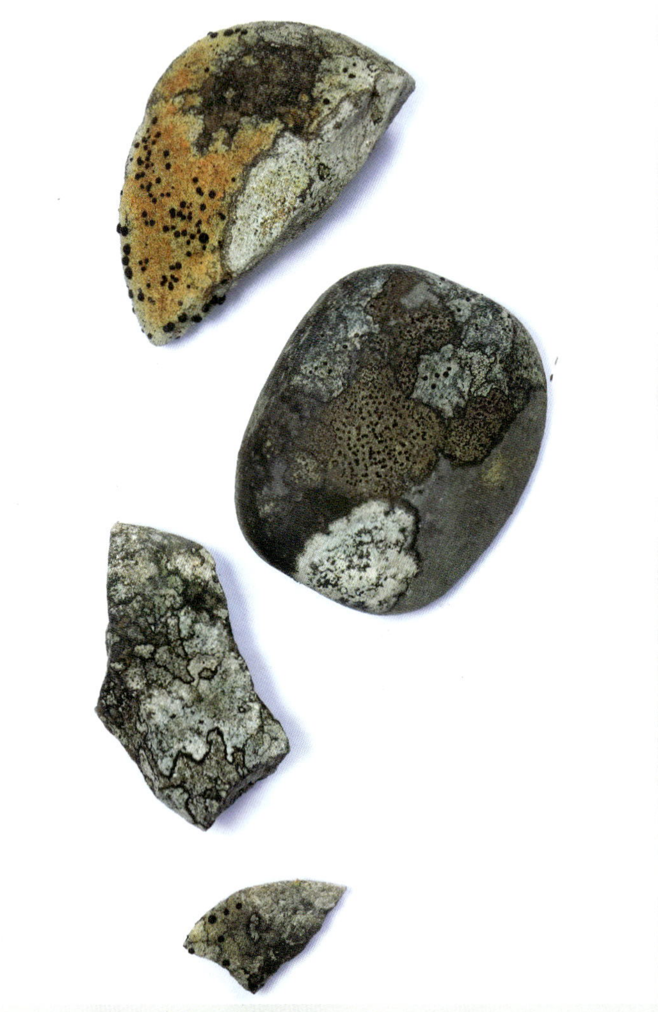

Lichen mosaics are not only found on tree trunks, twigs and huge rocks but on small stones too. I found these colourful and intricately patterned stones at a local heathland. After painting I put the stones back where I found them on the heathland.

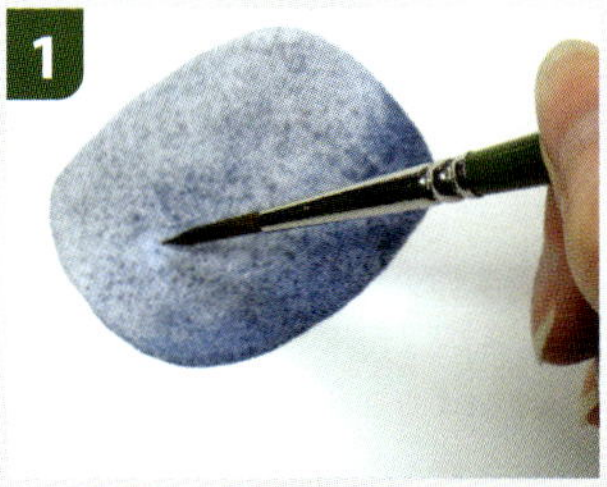

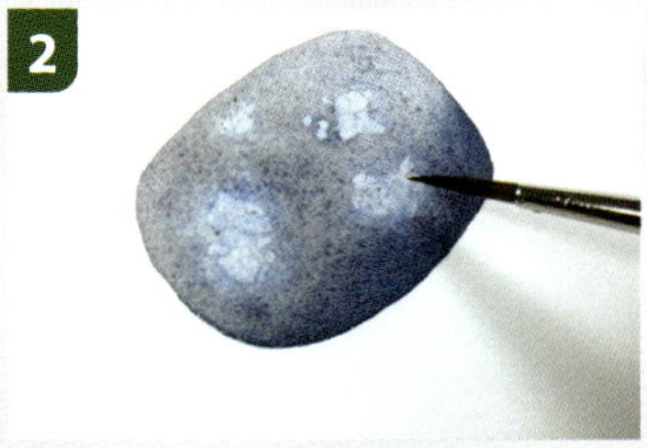

To start with I painted a grey mix of French Ultramarine and Light Red in the shape of a stone, charging more concentrated paint in on the shadow side wet into wet. The French Ultramarine created some nice granulation textures which is what I wanted. When starting to dry a little, I added a drop of water with the brush, and also little drops of rubbing alcohol to the wash to create the paler lichen discs. Both these methods are effective at pushing back the pigment to give this effect. The alcohol drops give a much more defined look than the water drops so there are differences. If you don't have rubbing alcohol, not to worry; a few drops of strong white gouache paint could form the white areas quite well but it may give a feathery, fuzzy edged look and may fade, as gouache tends to do. Experimentation is a must to find the right look that you are after for depicting your subject.

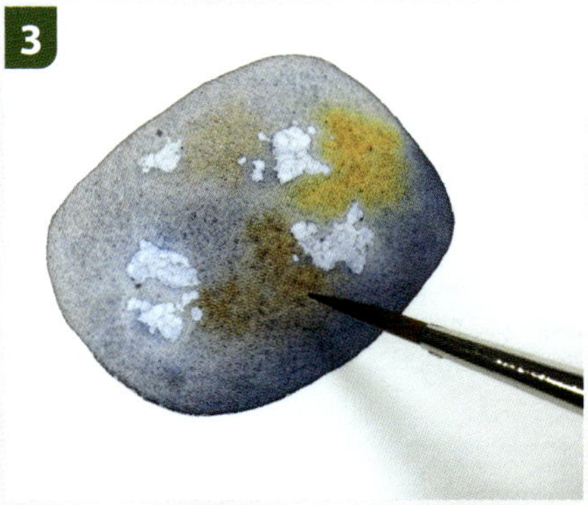

I dropped in the Quinacridone Deep Gold and Raw Umber when the initial glaze was still wet to add the different lichen colours. It's important to have quite strong mixes of colour and not too runny or it could ruin the wash.

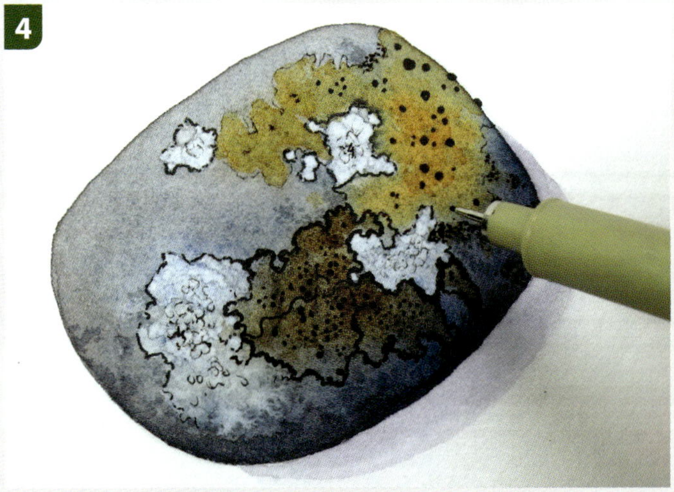

With the Pigma Micron, pen work detail of the prothallus and apothecia is added on when the paint was completely dry. If the colours need strengthening, they can be added on top, wet on dry but I didn't need to as I'd added a strong enough dilution in the first layer. I did add a cast shadow of the stone, wet on dry with pale Winsor Violet mixed into a bit of the grey mix to tone it down.

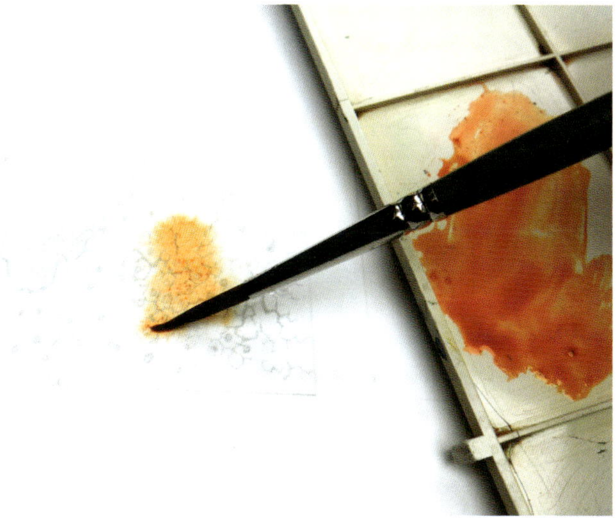

Crustose lichens make interesting abstract patterns and textures. These were drawn in 2H graphite pencil with watercolour washes painted in on top wet into wet. They could also be drawn in fine-tipped pens like Pigma Microns for a pen-and-wash technique.

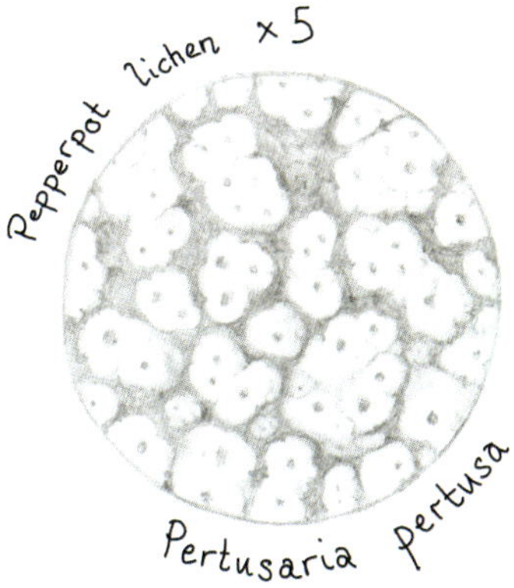

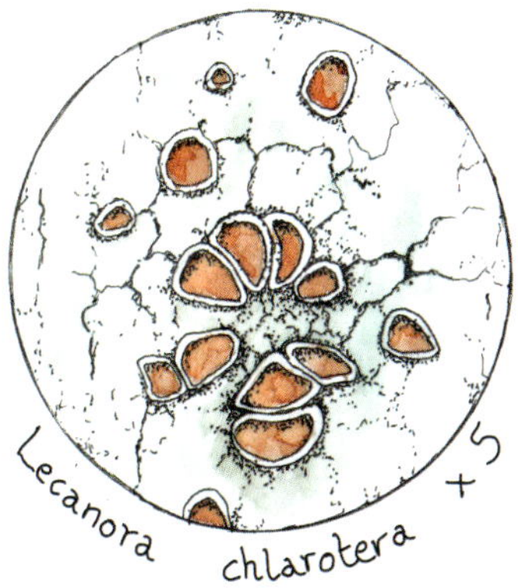

Crustose lichen form studies, enlarged by five times. I like drawing these enlargements in circles to mimic the magnifying glass. The top study is a wonderful species called the Pepperpot Lichen – *Pertusaria pertusa* and is drawn in graphite. The lower study is *Lecanora chlarotera* painted in watercolour. Both were growing on tree trunks.

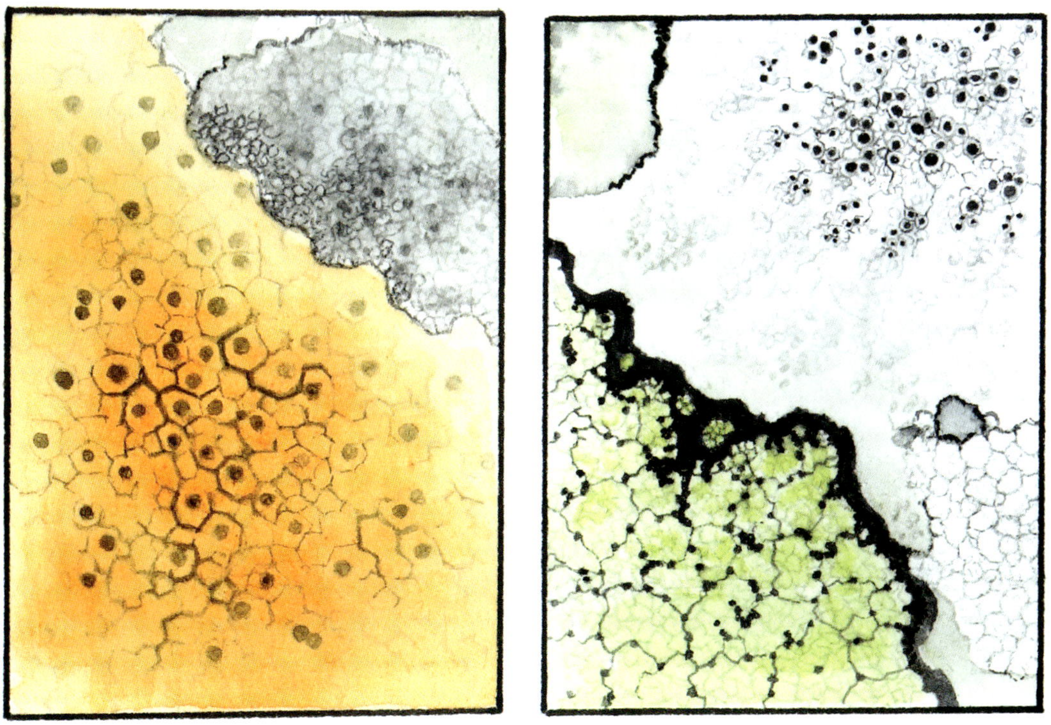

Mosaics within mosaics. Interesting large rock crustose lichens found at Gilfach NNR. On the left is the rusty orange *Tremolecia atrata* with its areolate structure, so coloured due to it taking in iron compounds. On the right you can see the green Map Lichen edged with its black *prothallus*.

INSPIRATIONAL LICHENS

The artist Sharon Field describes her inspirations for painting lichens: 'Lichens, fungi and mosses are so fundamental to our existence, yet we know so little about them. Some we see regularly, others we see only rarely, if at all. Each has a job to do. Even though we barely acknowledge their existence, without them, we would not exist.

'As the sun sets on the horizon and the sky darkens, the night sky and the earth become one. While we (people) set ourselves apart from so much in the natural world, when the evening falls, we too become one with the earth. So, let's look after our natural heritage. We need it.

'The title of this work has been drawn from the writings of the wonderful Australian poet, Judith Wright who was known as 'the conscience of the nation' for her commitment to the environment and Aboriginal land rights. Her aesthetic centres on the relationship between people and the environment, which she viewed as the catalyst for the creation of her poetry. I wonder what she would say to us today.'

There is something so wonderful about fungi and lichens, their symbioses, the interconnectedness of their existences with all the other organisms on this planet. They are simple yet complex, living often quite hidden and secretive lives, overlooked and misunderstood. Perhaps we can learn from them about coexistence to make a better world where we live sustainably and in tune with all the inhabitants of Earth.

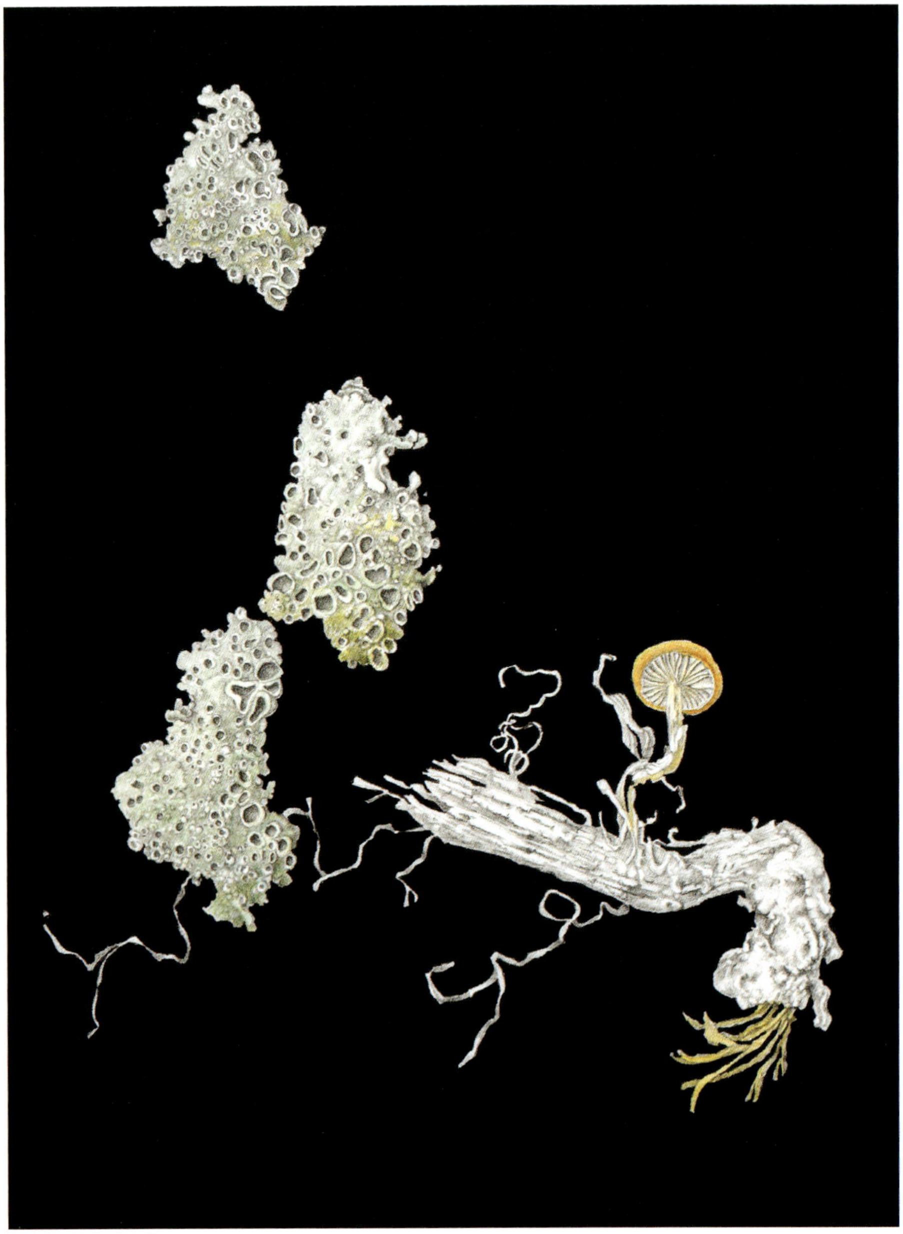

Blotched with a Green Lichen by Sharon Field. Sharon first drew in graphite on watercolour paper and added some watercolour to about 80 per cent completion. She then put in the black background in gouache, around eight layers were needed for a velvety darkness. Then more graphite and watercolour to completion, strengthening the colour and tones so that they would not be lost in the background. (© Sharon Field)

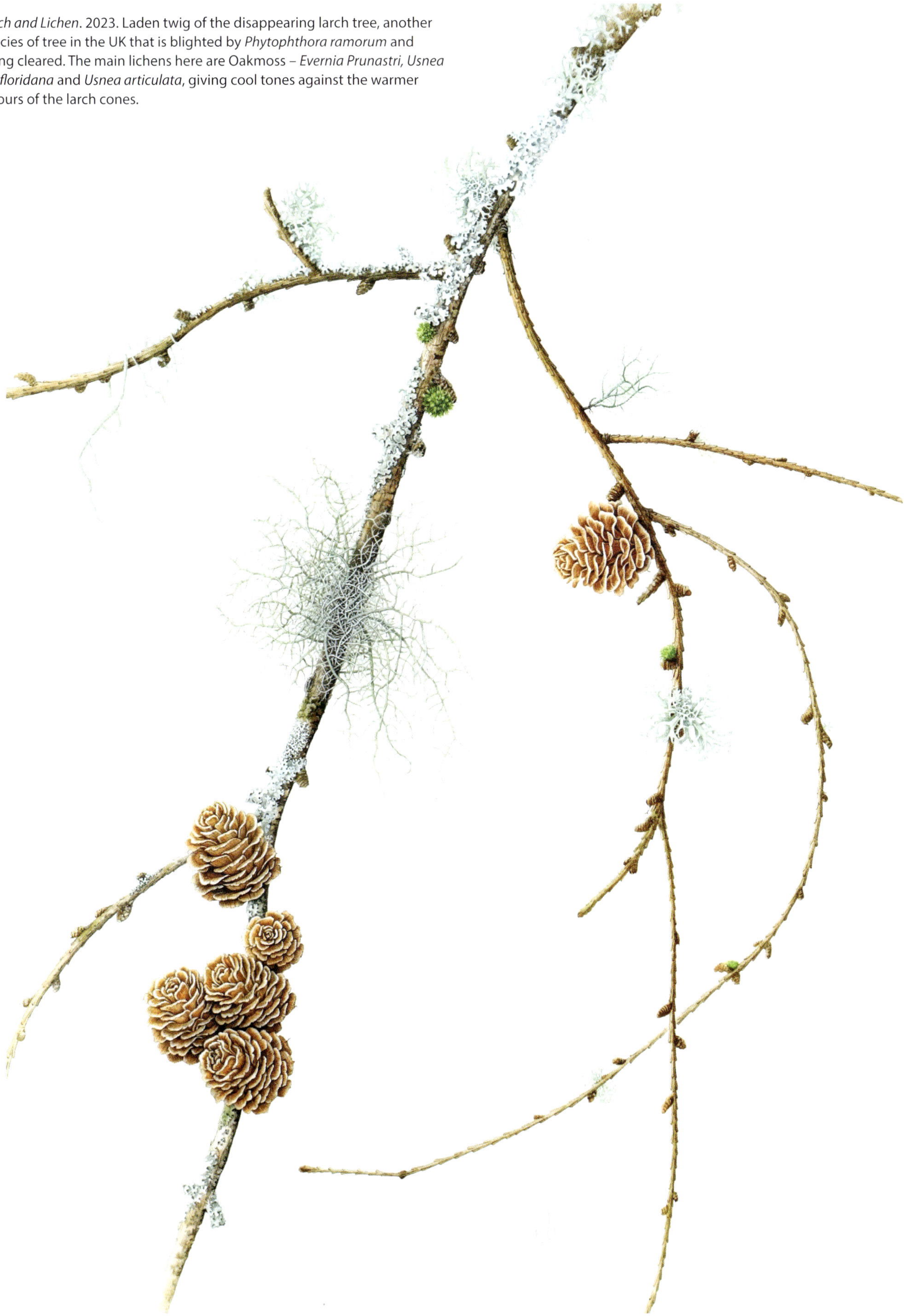

Larch and Lichen. 2023. Laden twig of the disappearing larch tree, another species of tree in the UK that is blighted by *Phytophthora ramorum* and being cleared. The main lichens here are Oakmoss – *Evernia Prunastri, Usnea subfloridana* and *Usnea articulata*, giving cool tones against the warmer colours of the larch cones.

INDEX

First published in 2024 by
The Crowood Press Ltd
Ramsbury, Marlborough
Wiltshire SN8 2HR

enquiries@crowood.com
www.crowood.com

This impression 2025

British Library Cataloguing-in-Publication Data

A catalogue record for this book is available from the British Library.

ISBN 978 0 7198 4332 7
Cover design by Sergey Tsvetkov

All work in this book is the author's own unless otherwise stated.

Typeset by SJmagic DESIGN SERVICES, India.
Printed and bound in India by Nutech Print Services

Contributing Artists

Kathleen Baker – ronbaker777@hotmail.co.uk
Margaret Best – bestbotanical.com
Giovanni Cera – www.flickr.com/photos/ciuccio51
Christina Hart Davies – www.christinahartdavies.co.uk
Shevaun Doherty – shevaundoherty.com
Jean Emmons – jeanemmons.com
Sheila Etchingham – Instagram: @etchinghamsheila
Sharon Field – sharonfieldartist.com.au
Jackie Isard – www.jibotanicals.co.uk
Jean Mackay – jeanmackayart.com
Sarah Morrish – www.natures-details.com
Sally Pond – www.sallypond.co.uk
Polly O'Leary – www.pollyoleary.co.uk
Denise I Ryan – www.facebook.com/worksonpaperartist
Dianne Sutherland – www.diannesutherland.com
Claire Kathleen Ward – www.claireward.net
Anna Voytsekhovich – Instagram: @trebouxia
Alexander Sasha Viazmensky – www.alexandermushrooms.com

Resources

British Mycological Society – https://www.britmycolsoc.org.uk/
North American Mycological Association – https://namyco.org/
Mycological Society of America – https://msafungi.org/
European Mycological Association – www.euromould.org
First nature website – www.first-nature.com/fungi/
A fantastic resource for identifying specimens.
British Lichen Society – https://britishlichensociety.org.uk/
American Bryological and Lichenological Society – https://www.abls.org/

Acknowledgements

Many thanks to my family for putting up with my mushroom madness and torturously slow walks!

Special thanks to all the contributing artists who have shared their work that has so enriched this book. Emma Williams, who is an inspirational mycologist, for her collage of spores under the microscope in Chapter 2 and for passing on her enthusiasm and knowledge to me. Ray Woods, for dispensing his zeal, knowledge and expertise on many lichen and fungi workshops.